EDUCATION
AND
SCHOOLING
IN AMERICA

EDUCATION AND SCHOOLING IN AMERICA

GERALD L. GUTEK
Loyola University of Chicago

PRENTICE-HALL, INC.   *Englewood Cliffs, N.J. 07632*

Library of Congress Cataloging in Publication Data

GUTEK, GERALD L.
  Education and schooling in America.

  Includes bibliographies and index.
  1. Education—United States—History. I. Title.
LA209.2.G87 1982   370'.973   82-12257
ISBN 0-13-240523-7

Editorial/production supervision by Marion Osterberg
Cover photos courtesy of Ken Karp and New York Public Library Picture Collection
Cover design by Jeannette Jacobs
Manufacturing buyer: Ron Chapman

L A 209.2
G 87
1983

Printed in the United States of America

10 9 8 7 6 5 4 3 2 1

ISBN 0-13-240523-7

Prentice-Hall International, Inc., *London*
Prentice-Hall of Australia Pty. Limited, *Sydney*
Editora Prentice-Hall do Brasil, Ltda., *Rio de Janeiro*
Prentice-Hall Canada Inc., *Toronto*
Prentice-Hall of India Private Limited, *New Delhi*
Prentice-Hall of Japan, Inc., *Tokyo*
Prentice-Hall of Southeast Asia Pte. Ltd., *Singapore*
Whitehall Books Limited, *Wellington, New Zealand*

For my wife, Patricia,
and my daughters, Jennifer and Laura

Contents

7 The State Role in Education   103

8 The Local Role in Education   114

9 Financing Public Education   127

PART THREE THE INSTITUTIONALIZATION OF AMERICAN EDUCATION

10 Early Childhood Education   143

11 Elementary Education   170

12 The Junior High School 191

13 American Secondary Education 203

14 Patterns of American Higher Education 223

PART FOUR   THE SCHOOL SYSTEM AND CURRICULUM

15 The School System and Staff 248

Preface

My intention in writing *Education and Schooling in America* is to provide instructors and students with a balanced and comprehensive introduction to public education in the United States. The book's plan and organization follow the premise that prospective teachers need a perspective into the origins and development of their discipline and that the general understanding of education should precede specific career decisions. In order to provide the reader with an educational perspective, the majority of the chapters begin with an historical overview into the topic being examined. From the historical treatment, contemporary developments and issues are then examined. It is hoped that this approach will help future teachers to avoid the tendency that has caused many individuals working in professional education to ignore the past and to repeat old errors. Further, I believe that an historical perspective can provide a sense of time that helps us from being overwhelmed by events.

The chapters are arranged to treat the more general matters that relate to education before dealing with the specific matters of schooling and teaching. The choice of examining the general historical, philosophical, cultural, political, and economic issues first was a deliberate one. After the general foundations have been examined, then the specifics of school organization, curriculum, staffing, teacher preparation, certification, and employment are discussed. The book concludes with an examination of the issues relating to the teaching profession.

The book's title, *Education and Schooling in America,* recognizes that there are distinctions between education and schooling. The book is written with the view that education and schooling can be, indeed ought to be, related and mutually supporting of each other.

It is my wish that *Education and Schooling in America* will be useful in helping prospective teachers and general readers to understand the origins, development, and contemporary condition of education and schools in our country.

Gerald L. Gutek

EDUCATION AND SCHOOLING IN AMERICA

1

Education and Schooling in American Society

Chapter 1 is designed to provide a perspective on the book and its contents. The book's title, *Education and Schooling in America,* reflects the book's focus; it suggests that education and schooling are different entities, with different meanings and purposes. However, in American life and society, as in other societies, education and schooling exist in relationship and ideally are mutually supportive of each other. The book takes the position that, while teachers are engaged primarily in schooling, it is necessary and useful for them to relate schooling to education. Since Americans have often regarded education and schooling as synonymous, this chapter examines their relationships and differences.

EDUCATION

Since the concept education is broader in scope and more comprehensive than is that of schooling, education is discussed first. Education is a total lifelong process that begins with one's birth and ends only with one's death. Before entering a school, children know many things, have a stock of experiences and ideas, and have a generalized system of values and ethics. They know and use language and can communicate with others. Children are already social beings who relate to and interact with their peers. All these important human developments took place as the child interacted with his or her environment, parents, family members, and playmates. The kind of learning that takes place in early childhood is generalized; it is not structured deliberately or organized. Educators often refer to this generalized kind of learning as informal education, enculturation, or socialization.

Enculturation

Although informal education has various names, the term "enculturation" is useful in describing the process. It means literally that at only the moment of our birth are we "culture-free" and immediately thereafter are enveloped by the culture into which we are born in much the same way that an infant is wrapped in a blanket. Our learning of the culture, its requirements, knowledge, values, behaviors, and expectations begins immediately and is ongoing. We acquire our culture by living and participating in it. We have no choice about the matter. We simply are born into a culture. However, a culture is a heritage and a way of life that is complex. While our entry into the culture may be simple, our living and learning or our taking on of the culture is complex.

The Informal Education

While much of the process of enculturation is more or less automatic, much of it is done deliberately by a large number of informal educational agents. These persons or agencies are not trained teachers or schools, but they have a large and pervasive educational impact. Informal educators include the following.

(1) *Parents or guardians* with whom children have their initial contact and with whom they live during their formative years are primary or direct educators who impart language, knowledge, and values to their children. The values that parents convey to children are important to later school and life success. If parental values are supportive of schooling, the teacher can build on these predispositions. If parental attitudes are negative to schooling, then children's attitudes are also likely to be negative.

(2) *Brothers, sisters, playmates, and the peer group* also exert important influences on child development. The child's patterns of socialization such as assertiveness, competitiveness, and cooperativeness are generally based on peer group experience. The peer group grows in significance as the person passes from childhood to adolescence and to early adulthood. In the United States, in particular, the adolescent subculture is of special importance. With its own styles of speech, music, dress, and behavior, the adolescent subculture is an important force in a person's total education. Many persons have reflected on the joys, challenges, and traumas of their adolescence. Teachers recognize the importance of the peer group as a formative educational force.

(3) *The neighborhood,* the child's immediate residential area, is an early and crucial agent in enculturation. It is from the neighborhood that the child learns the styles of behavior that are accepted or rejected when a person leaves the home. Neighborhoods have their own speech styles, communication patterns,

and socialization networks. They also have informal criteria that govern a person's acceptance into the neighborhood community.

Many American educators such as John Dewey and William H. Kilpatrick portrayed American society as a community of neighborhoods in which a social consensus arose that united and integrated American life, institutions, and values. Throughout the modern era, but especially in the twentieth century, a great transformation has been taking place as the United States changed from being a small-town rural society into an urban, industrial, technological society. While the modernization process has brought us many innovations and inventions that have improved our lives in a material sense, it also has generated rapid change, mobility, and social dislocation that has eroded the feeling of community and neighborliness. Teachers need to recognize that social change has also altered American family and community life.

The neighborhood's, or the community's, attitude to schooling is an important factor in the school's success. If the community regards the school and teacher as aliens, then the school tends to be isolated from the community and draws little financial or moral support from it. On the other hand, when the school is viewed as a vital institution, it enjoys community support, protection, and affection.

(4) *The church* is also an important educational force for many Americans and their children. Religious outlooks on the meaning and purpose of life and on human values are powerful determinants affecting a person's informal education or enculturation. The religious practices in the home and family and the instruction given to children by the various denominations help to form a person's world view. In the United States, separation of church and state also has meant the separation of the church and the public school. Nevertheless, teachers need to recognize the powerful role of religious institutions in shaping attitudes and values.

(5) *Radio, television, movies, the popular press, or mass media* are pervasive educational forces in modern society. Combining entertainment with information delivery, the media have shaped American attitudes and values. Teachers need to listen to the radio programs and view the television programs that their students are listening to or watching to identify some of the factors that are shaping students' attitudes and values.

Through the medium of television, students are aware of events taking place in space, internationally, and in their own nation. Television also presents images conveying life-style and values. As a transmitter of public affairs information, the television commentator acts as an informal teacher. Consider the impact of such events on the political education of children and youth: the Cuban missile crisis; the election of a president; the war in Vietnam; the assassinations of President Kennedy, Senator Robert Kennedy, and Reverend Martin Luther King; the Watergate hearings. All these events, amply covered by television, represent only a few of the momentous occasions that have shaped our perceptions.

While television represents a dramatic and moving information explosion, it is also confusing. Despite the sophistication of the modern television portrayal of events, the structure and explanations of these events are often unclear. Their very immediacy and drama lack perspective. These events occur quickly, their suddenness is direct, but their impact in the totality of learning is unclear. While their drama is usually greater than that of the classroom, their structure and perspective are often undeveloped.

In *Crisis in the Classroom,* Charles Silberman examined the role of the media in transmitting information. While the media may be competent in reporting the immediate and urgent issues of the day, Silberman contends that it might miss or fail to recognize truly important problems. The dramatic event may be captured vividly by the television camera, but its meaning may be lost in the confusion of immediate reaction. The transmission of knowledge in schools, on the other hand, is seasoned by time and has a distance from the event or situation that is helpful in creating a sense of perspective. However, classroom instruction pales before the quickness of the rapid-fire televised portrayal of an event.

Silberman finds the basic weakness of television to be that of reinforcing the status quo in a world where people need to understand and know how to deal with change. Media persons, Silberman argues, rarely view themselves as educators. They rarely ask the educational questions that they should. For example, what really constitutes the significant information? How does the television portrayal of a situation shape public conceptions of events? What values or lessons are being conveyed in the televised portrayal of commentary?[1]

In this chapter, we can identify only a few of the many informal educators. There are many more, however, such as the library, social organizations, ethnic groups, museums, art galleries, parks, recreation centers, athletic teams, and so on. These informal agencies of education seek to enculturate us and to shape our outlook and values. What we have learned outside either advances or retards what takes place inside the school.

SCHOOLING

Education is the process that brings children into their culture. Education takes place inside the schools and outside them. Although many agencies, such as the home, church, community, and media, are informal educators, advanced cultures use schooling as the process designed specifically to facilitate cultural transmission and enculturation. As a special learning environment, staffed by specialists in education, the school is designed to educate by providing the young with a structured and organized access to culture's tools, skills, knowledge, and values.

As a specialized cultural agency, the school cannot be isolated from the culture it serves. It must be related intimately to that particular society and cultural heritage. American education draws its content and values from its heritage and society.[2]

In addition to conserving and transmitting the cultural heritage, the

[1]Charles E. Silberman, *Crisis in the Classroom: The Remaking of American Education* (New York: Random House, 1970), pp. 30–41.

[2]George S. Counts, *Education and American Civilization* (New York: Teachers College Press, Columbia University, 1952), p. 34.

school is also an agency of social renewal and change. The heritage that the school transmits is vast and complex. To the school falls the immense problem of selecting some parts of the heritage for transmission and rejecting others. As a selective agency, the school serves moral purposes. Educators charged with introducing the young to participation in their culture must make their selection according to a criteria acceptable to the society. American educators have generally followed a democratic social philosophy.

American teachers have the twofold responsibility of introducing each generation to its heritage and of providing the knowledge and skills needed to continue to reformulate the democratic ethic in the face of contemporary challenges.

As part of its task, the school tries to identify cultural elements most likely to produce integrated individuals within an integrated society. An integrated society is not necessarily a monolith characterized by common conformity but, rather, is a harmonious blend of divergent elements in a unified social fabric. For example, the United States is a nation of immigrants of various ethnic, racial, and religious persuasions. Although commonly committed to the democratic process, Americans enjoy a wide range of political, social, and religious beliefs. A democratic society may encourage many forms of cultural pluralism and adhere simultaneously to underlying ethical, social, and political precepts that unite it. The school communicates these values in a graduated environment by selecting cultural elements, skills, and knowledge according to the maturity level of the learner.

Schooling does not occur in social isolation. As a dynamic and ongoing experience rooted in the past, it also actively affects the present situation and influences the future as each new generation is educated. Since our schools have a history, prospective teachers need to understand their origins or roots as educators. The past can be used to interpret the present and to help shape the future. Since schooling deals with current problems, prospective teachers need to examine educational philosophies, theories, methods, curricula, organization, psychology, and administration that are the working tools of the professional educator. Prospective teachers also need to think in terms of the future to prepare students to live in the twenty-first century.

Although most of the book is intended to introduce prospective teachers to schooling, it will do so with the rationale that schooling is related to and a part of the large cultural process of education.

DISCUSSION QUESTIONS

1. Distinguish between education and schooling.
2. Write a short biographical sketch in which you identify the agents of enculturation that have shaped your attitudes and values.
3. Discuss the influence of your current peer group on your education.
4. How did your neighborhood community influence your educational decisions?
5. Examine the educational role of radio, television, and motion pictures.
6. List the informal educators that have an impact on schooling in order of priority.

FIELD EXERCISES

1. Visit a museum or art gallery and identify the ways in which that agency acts as an informal educator.
2. Watch the television programs that children or adolescents are likely to view. Identify the life-styles and values conveyed in these programs.
3. Read a newspaper and identify the ways in which it acts as an educational agency.
4. Interview members of your family and try to ascertain their views on education and schooling.

SUGGESTED READINGS

COUNTS, GEORGE S. *Education and American Civilization.* New York: Teachers College Press, Columbia University, 1952.

CREMIN, LAWRENCE A. *Public Education.* New York: Basic Books, 1976.

ILLICH, IVAN. *Deschooling Society.* New York: Harper & Row, 1970.

MILLER, STEVEN. *An Introduction to the Sociology of Education.* Cambridge, Mass.: Schenkman, 1977.

ORNSTEIN, ALLAN C., AND HEDLEY, EUGENE W. *Analysis of Contemporary Education.* New York: Thomas Y. Crowell, 1973.

SILBERMAN, CHARLES E. *Crisis in the Classroom: The Remaking of American Education.* New York: Random House, 1970.

2

The Historical Foundations of American Education

The early history of American education began as Europeans discovered and then settled in the New World. While the English, who established a chain of colonies along the Atlantic coast, had the greatest impact on American education, the French, Spanish, and Dutch also founded colonies and schools. The French established a far-flung but sparsely populated empire that reached from Canada down the Mississippi River Valley to Louisiana. French priests, in particular the Jesuits, journeyed with the explorers and fur traders to convert and educate the Indians in Christian ways. Jesuits and religious communities of nuns, such as the Ursulines, taught the children of the French settlers in such towns as Quebec and New Orleans. When French dreams of an American empire ended with the English victory in the French and Indian Wars in 1763, their educational efforts also waned.

The Spanish in the southwestern region and in California, too, established an empire known as New Spain. With the *conquistadores* also came priests, especially Franciscans, who worked to convert the Indians to Catholicism. The missions of the Franciscan friars usually included schools for the Indians to learn agricultural and vocational skills. The priests often had to protect the Indians living near their missions from the cruelty and exploitation of the conquerors. The Spanish influence had a long-lasting impact, especially in language.

The Dutch, too, made an attempt to establish a North American empire, but it was short-lived, as they fell victim to British power. The Dutch colony of New Amsterdam became New York when it fell into British hands, but the remnants of the Dutch heritage survived, in the Dutch Reformed Church and its schools. In addition to the Dutch, various communities of German Pietists, particularly Moravians, located in the North American colonies in the late seventeenth and eighteenth centuries. The Moravians worked to convert the Indians to their version of Christianity and were skilled in translating the Bible and other religious books into the Indian languages. While these various groups contributed to the foundations of American education by transplanting European ideas into the New World setting, the English colonists had the most significant impact.

EDUCATION IN THE ENGLISH COLONIES

To a large extent, the English colonists in North America sought to relive their European educational experience in the New World. The schools and colleges that they founded expressed their commitment that they were in America to stay and that their religion, culture, and language would be transmitted to their children through organized education. The educational ideas that they brought with them as a common heritage were diversified by the varying conditions of the regions in which they settled. Puritan New England, the culturally pluralistic Middle Atlantic colonies, and the plantation-owning South shared a common heritage that was reshaped by the American environment. First, we examine the common educational heritage brought by the English to North America; then, we examine its regional variations.

The English colonists shared what was essentially a similar educational heritage. Although of differing religious persuasions, they inherited from the Renaissance the belief that the well-educated gentleman knew the classical languages of Latin and Greek. From the Reformation, they inherited a belief that schooling should be steeped in religious doctrine so that the young would be nurtured in their faith and be ready to defend it.

The colonists' conception of institutionalized education was decidedly centered on social class. The children of workers and peasants should have a minimum primary education, in vernacular schools, to learn reading, writing, arithmetic, and religion. While the lower-class children were to have only a few years of primary schooling, the male offspring of the middle and upper classes would attend the Latin Grammar school, a college preparatory institution, and then go on to college. Thus, the colonists believed in a two-track system of schools—one for the poor and another for the wealthy.

Then, as now, much of a person's education went on in informal situations such as the family, church, farm, and shop. Lawrence Cremin, in his definitive work on colonial education, holds that throughout the North American colonies the family was the basic social and economic agency.[1] In particular, the

---

[1]Lawrence A. Cremin, *American Education: The Colonial Experience, 1607–1783* (New York: Harper & Row, 1970), pp. 135–136.

New England Puritans regarded the family as fundamental to a healthy religious and civil society.

The family household was the place of sustained religious, literary, and vocational instruction. Parents taught their children to read the Bible and other religious books. Children's chores introduced them to the world of work. Children were expected to embrace the cherished values of piety and respect for parents, elders, and civil and religious authorities.[2] The informal education of the family was the foundation upon which the formal education—the school— was built.

It was upon this common educational tradition that the English established their schools in America. Although they shared a common European intellectual tradition, the colonists of the New England, Middle Atlantic, and southern colonies had to readapt and reshape this heritage when faced with America's wilderness to meet the unique needs of their region of settlement.

New England

The New England Puritans, who followed the theology of John Calvin, were intensely religious. Subscribing completely to Calvin's doctrine of predestination, they believed that only the righteous would be saved and that the unrighteous would be damned. The righteous Puritans, an elect set apart, were to be literate, hardworking, diligent, frugal, and law-abiding men, women, and children. The Puritan ethic stressed that schooling was to be a means of cultivating these values. Formal education, or schooling, reinforced by the informal educational agencies of home and church, was an instrument that would bring up children properly in Calvinist doctrine and laws of the Commonwealth. The Puritans saw schooling as a means of preserving their religious, social, and political beliefs by transmitting them to their children.

While the concept of separation of church and state is an important principle in American education today, just the opposite was true in the colonial era. In Puritan New England, particularly in Massachusetts, church, state, and school were closely related. Schools were often governed by the same trustees that were the governing bodies of the church.

PURITAN VIEW OF CHILDHOOD.   Elsewhere in this book, particularly in Chapter 10, on early childhood education, you will encounter the ideas of such educators as Rousseau, Pestalozzi, Froebel, and Montessori, who emphasized the dignity and importance of childhood as a time of human growth and development. The New England Puritan would have rejected such theories as permissive poison that would spoil the child by sparing the rod. For the Puritans, the infant was conceived in sin and born in corruption.[3] Savage and primitive creatures, children needed training, discipline, and indoctrination so that they could control their weak human natures. Not childish, the good child behaved like an adult. To break children's willful behavior, schoolmasters were to use corporal pun-

---

[2]Bernard Bailyn, *Education in the Forming of American Society* (New York: W. W. Norton, 1972), p. 16.

[3]Stanford Fleming, *Children and Puritanism: The Place of Children in the Life and Thought of the New England Churches, 1620–1847* (New Haven, Conn.: Yale University Press, 1933).

ishment when necessary. Puritan ministers, such as the famous clergyman Jonathan Edwards, admonished parents:

> let children obey their parents, and yield to their instructions, and submit to their orders, as they would inherit a blessing and not a curse. For we have reason to think, from many things in the word of God, that nothing had a greater tendency to bring a curse on persons in this world, and on all their temporal concerns, than undutiful, unsubmissive, disorderly behavior in children towards their parents.[4]

PURITAN STRESS ON SCHOOLING.   The Puritans stressed schooling as a means of establishing and maintaining a proper society peopled by righteous men and women. Literate people, they believed, would be good citizens whereas ignorant people would soon corrupt society. As early as 1642, the Massachusetts General Court required parents and guardians to see that their children could read and understand religious principles and the civil laws. The Law of 1642 was one of the first educational ordinances in the New World. In 1647, the Massachusetts General Court enacted the "Old Deluder Satan Law," requiring towns of fifty or more families to appoint a teacher of reading and writing. Towns of one hundred or more families were to employ a Latin teacher as well, to prepare students for college entry. The Old Deluder Satan Law stated that

> It being one Chiefe project of ye ould deluder, Satan, to keepe men from the knowledge of ye Scriptures, as in former times by keeping ym in an unknowne tongue, so in these lattr times by perswading from ye use of tongues, yt so at least ye true sence & meaning of ye originall might be clouded by false glosses of saint seeming deceivers, yt learning may not be buried in ye grave of our fathers in ye church and commonwealth, the Lord assisting our endeavors,—
>
>   It is therefore ordred, yt evry towneship in this jurisdiction, aftr ye Lord hath increased ym number of 50 housholdrs, shall then forthwth appoint one within their towne to teach all such children as shall resort to him to write & reade, whose wages shall be paid eithr by ye parents or mastrs of such children, or by ye inhabitants in genrall, by way of supply, as ye major part of those yt ordr ye prudentials of ye towne shall appoint; provided, those yt send their children be not oppressed by paying much more yn they can have ym taught for in othr townes; & it is furthr ordered, yt where any towne shall increase to ye numbr of 100 families or housholdrs, they shall set up a grammar schoole, ye mr thereof being able to instruct youth so farr as they shall be fited for ye university, provided, yt if any towne neglect ye performance hereof above one yeare, yt every such towne shall pay 5 £ to ye next schoole till they shall performe this order.[5]

[4]H. Norman Gardiner, ed., *Selected Sermons of Jonathan Edwards* (New York: Macmillan, 1904), p. 148.

[5]Nathaniel Shurtleff, ed., *Records of the Governor and Company of the Massachusetts Bay in New England* (Boston: n.p., 1853), II, p. 203.

These early Massachusetts laws of 1642 and 1647 were significant in American educational history in that they (1) illustrated the concern of civil government over schooling, (2) established a tone or atmosphere that gave civil authorities some control of schools, and (3) pointed to taxation for school support. The enactment of these laws demonstrated Puritan stress on schooling.

SCHOOLING IN NEW ENGLAND. The New England town schools, such as those required by the Massachusetts laws of 1642 and 1647, were vernacular schools that offered a basic curriculum of reading, writing, arithmetic, and religion. Reading, the primary subject, was taught according to the ABC method in which children learned the letters of the alphabet, then syllables and words, and finally sentences. The first reader was a Hornbook, a single sheet of parchment covered by a transparent material, that contained the alphabet, vowels, and syllables; the doctrine of the Trinity; and the Lord's Prayer. The *New England Primer,* a popular and widely used colonial schoolbook, which first appeared in 1690, was called New England's "Little Bible." The *Primer* contained twenty-four rhymes, one for each letter of the alphabet, illustrated by a woodcut drawing. The first rhyme, "In Adam's Fall, We Sinned All," was evidence of the close relationship between reading and religion that was so dear to the Puritans. The *New England Primer* also contained vowels, syllables, "An Alphabet of Lessons

The Hornbook, an instructional material used in colonial schooling, was printed on parchment, and included the alphabet, vowels, and Lord's Prayer. *(New York Public Library Picture Collection)*

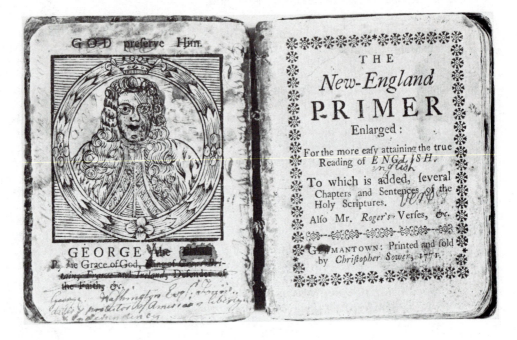

The *New-England Primer* was a widely used colonial textbook. *(New York Public Library Picture Collection)*

for Youth," "The Dutiful Child's Promises," the Lord's Prayer, the Apostle's Creed, the Ten Commandments, "The Duty of Children Towards Their Parents," "Names and Order of the Books of the Old and New Testaments," and an abbreviated version of the Westminster Catechism.[6]

The teacher in the New England town school was a person whose preparation varied considerably. For him teaching might be a temporary situation as he prepared for a higher-status career as a minister or lawyer. Teachers were occasionally indentured servants who were "paying off" their passage to the New World.

The town school was typically a one-room building that enrolled children—both boys and girls—of various ages. The typical method was the recitation in which children individually repeated before the teacher lessons they had memorized earlier. The catechetical method in which children repeated memorized responses to questions was popular. As indicated earlier, a failure to produce the required response or a breach of discipline was often dealt with harshly by the teacher. With the exception of the women who taught in Dame Schools, the colonial teachers were men. The educational preparation and social status of the town school teacher was generally less than that of the master who taught in the Latin Grammar school.

[6]Paul Leicester Ford, ed., *The New England Primer* (New York: Dodd, Mead, 1899).

The New England town school was often a single room in which children learned by reciting lessons before the school teacher. *(New York Public Library Picture Collection)*

Schooling in the Southern Colonies

The southern colonies of Maryland, Virginia, Georgia, and the Carolinas had a different social, economic, religious, and educational situation than prevailed in New England.

Because the subtropical climate favored crops such as tobacco, rice, sugar, indigo, and cotton, the chief unit of agriculture was the plantation, supported by a work force of black slaves. The plantation economy and society produced rigid class distinctions among both whites and blacks. The owners of large plantations associated with each other but not with the small farmers, known as "poor whites" who had been pushed to the infertile scrub lands of the "back country." The black slaves were organized in a hierarchical fashion according to their job assignment on the plantation.

The plantation owners, as a class, considered themselves descendants of the Cavaliers, the English aristocrats who had supported the Stuart kings against Cromwell's "Roundheads." According to the "Cavalier myth," these displaced aristocrats emigrated to the American South, where they re-established the old aristocratic way of life in the plantation society. Historically, the "Cavalier myth" is more legend than fact.

Social class distinctions and the often long distances between plantations retarded the development of a formal school system in the southern colonies. Although schools existed in the Tidewater cities, the plantation owners often employed tutors who lived with the family and taught their children. Frequently, the sons of leading families were sent to England for their preparation and higher education.

For the poor whites, education was largely informal. The boys learned to hunt, fish, and farm from their fathers; girls learned to sew, weave, and cook from their mothers. Formal schooling in the backwoods areas was minimal. Occasionally, the Anglican Missionary Society, the society for the Propagation of the Gospel in Foreign Parts, conducted a few schools. Benevolent plantation owners sometimes would build a school on a piece of land that had been worn out by successive plantings of tobacco. In many respects, however, the prevalent attitude was that parents were responsible for educating their children. The poor white population included many illiterates due to the limited number of schools that were available, a condition that inhibited progress in the South in later years.

The black slaves, who worked on the plantations, had been uprooted from their societies in Africa. Seized by slave traders or sold into slavery, they were torn away from their families and tribal societies. When they arrived in the southern colonies, they were trained to perform specific functions of the plantation economy. Some slaves were trained to be field workers, others tended livestock, and others were trained as blacksmiths, wheelwrights, and mill hands. At the top of the slave society were the household servants such as butlers, maids, valets, and coachmen. On most plantations, the slaves were not taught to read or write. In fact, the formal education of slaves was forbidden in most of the South. There were exceptions, however, as some masters taught slaves, particularly household servants, to read. Some slaves also taught themselves to read. Fearful of slave insurrections, the majority of southern plantation owners made no attempt to provide formal education to their slaves.

Although much of the education in the South was informal, there were some instances of formal education. Virginia and North Carolina made the apprenticeship of orphans and pauper children compulsory. When so apprenticed, orphans were indentured to masters of specific trades to learn a particular skill. The master was also required to provide instruction in reading and writing.

More formal education in the South was also provided by various private denominational schools, supported by private endowments or gifts. But this kind of schooling was sporadic and lacked the support given by the New England Puritans.

Schooling in the Middle Atlantic Colonies

Because of their location between New England and the southern colonies, New York, New Jersey, Pennsylvania, and Delaware were called the Middle Atlantic colonies. These colonies were ethnically, linguistically, and religiously diverse. Unlike Puritan New England, which was religiously homogeneous, the middle colonies were settled by Dutch Calvinists, Anglicans, Lutherans, Quakers, Presbyterians, Roman Catholics, and Jews. The presence of English, Dutch, Swedes, French, Danes, Jews, Irish, Scottish, and Germans resulted in cultural and language pluralisms. While the New England colonists shared common religious and cultural traditions, such was not the case in the Middle Atlantic colonies. Different ethnic, language, and religious groups sought to preserve their unique heritage by establishing their own parochial schools. If the precedents for the American public school system were established in New England, the roots of the private and parochial schools of America were planted in the middle colonies.

Representative examples of schooling in the Middle Atlantic colonies are provided by New York and Pennsylvania.

Until 1664, New Amsterdam, later New York, was a Dutch colony. The most powerful religious denomination there was the Dutch Reformed Church, a Calvinistic church that believed in an educated ministry and laity. While the Dutch West India Company financed schools, the Reformed Church controlled and maintained vernacular reading and writing schools. After the English occupation, these Dutch schools continued as the Dutch community sought to preserve its cultural identity as a minority group in the English colony. The English established several charity schools, supported by the Church of England, which provided instruction in reading, writing, arithmetic, catechism, and religion. Since New York was a commercial colony, a number of informal commercial training situations developed in which young people learned various skills such as navigation, surveying, printing, and accounting. These "training situations" occurred in apprenticeship arrangements or in private venture schools, operated by teachers for a profit. The "private venture schools" were an educational response to the demand for practical skills and knowledge.

Schooling in Pennsylvania was similar to that in New York. The Quakers, who originally settled in William Penn's colony, had fairly liberal ideas about education. Quaker elementary schools stressed religion, reading, writing, and arithmetic. The Quakers rejected corporal punishment as inhuman and were attentive to childrens' individual needs. In addition to the Quaker schools, German Pietists also established parochial schools to transmit the Germanic culture and language. As in New York, private venture schools prepared individuals for certain commercial trades.

EDUCATION IN THE EARLY NATIONAL PERIOD

After the thirteen colonies had won their political independence from Great Britain, they had to learn to become Americans rather than transplanted Englishmen. In the early national period from 1776 to the 1830s, a cultural transformation took place in which educational ideas and institutions were repatterned to fit the needs of the United States. Major trends that occurred in the early national period that influenced education included the following:

1. Education became a state rather than a federal responsibility.
2. Concepts of civic or citizenship education emerged that eclipsed religious domination of educational theory.
3. American cultural nationalism became a major theme in American educational thought.
4. Experimentation occurred with various philanthropic approaches to schooling.

Education Becomes a State Prerogative

Under the Articles of Confederation, Congress enacted the Northwest Ordinance of 1785, by which the territory was divided into townships of six square miles each, which were further subdivided into thirty-six sections. The income from the sixteenth section was reserved to support schools. Two years later, the Ordinance of 1787 encouraged education as "necessary to good government and the happiness of mankind." Although the Ordinances of 1785 and 1787 predated the federal Constitution, they anticipated a federal concern for education that would grow in the late nineteenth and twentieth centuries. These ordinances also showed that the federal government was prepared to use land—a readily available asset in the new republic—to advance the cause of education.

The U.S. Constitution, ratified in 1788, did not mention education. Under the "reserved powers clause" of the Tenth Amendment, ratified in 1791, educational prerogatives remained with the individual states of the Union. Following the New England tradition, many states delegated substantial educational responsibility to local school districts. Although education remained a state function, local school districts and boards were delegated an important role in matters of educational support and control.

Planning for Civic Education

After the American Revolution ended the colonial period, the citizens of the republic became conscious of their new cultural and political identities. Various leaders of the new nation such as Benjamin Franklin, Thomas Jefferson, Benjamin Rush, and Noah Webster sought to devise new educational strategies and institutions to educate Americans in the processes of republicanism. These leaders wanted to replace Old World values and commitments with new loyalties. For them, organized education was a potent instrument to foster Americanism in the nation's citizens and children. The proponents of a new philosophy of civic education stressed the concepts of republicanism, science, and nationalism as key elements in American education.[7] These concepts were to have an impact on the common school movement of the midnineteenth century.

Republicanism, based on the political theory of John Locke, asserted that government arises from the consent of the governed. When a government violates the inalienable rights of "life, liberty, or property," its citizens have a right to replace it with a new government. Unlike a monarchy with power vested in a king, authority in a republic arises with the citizens—those who constitute the government. Education for republican citizenship was designed to cultivate the skills, knowledge, and attitudes needed for participation in a democratic government and society.

The concept of "nationalism" stressed a sense of American identity and a common commitment and loyalty to the United States as an independent and sovereign nation. The concept of a "science" was based on the Enlightenment belief that asserted that individuals could discover the laws of the universe. Calling for a willingness to experiment, a scientific attitude claimed that old

---

[7]Allen O. Hansen, *Liberalism and American Education in the Eighteenth Century* (New York: Macmillan, 1926).

commitments had to be re-examined and changed if need be for progress. For the theorists of the early national period, a philosophy of education suited for the republic would prepare patriotic Americans who would be eager to experiment and now create a scientific and progressive society.[8]

Benjamin Franklin and an English Language Academy

Benjamin Franklin (1706–1789), an early advocate for American independence, was esteemed as the young republic's elder statesman. Although his own formal schooling was minimal, Franklin was recognized as a scientist and political philosopher in both Europe and America. A prominent Philadelphian, he helped to found the American Philosophical Society. The admonitions of *Poor Richard's Almanack* were read by Americans who eagerly accepted his emphasis on the values of frugality, diligence, thrift, hard work, and inventiveness. Franklin's philosophy was that of the common sense of the self-made and largely self-educated man.

Franklin, a practical man, distrusted the classical emphasis that dominated education. An advocate of utilitarian and scientific education, he proposed the establishment of an English grammar school in Philadelphia in 1749.[9] Franklin's proposal is of significance in that it (1) presented an alternative to the Latin Grammar school and (2) anticipated the academy and high school. In contrast to the classical language curriculum of the Latin Grammar school, Franklin's plan incorporated humanistic and utilitarian studies.

Grammar, composition, rhetoric, and public speaking were a part of English language studies; instruction was to be in English, the language of commerce and politics, rather than in Latin. Vocational training included carpentry, shipbuilding, engraving, printing, painting, cabinetmaking, carving, and gardening.

Mathematics, including arithmetic, geometry, astronomy, and accounting, was to be an applied subject. History was to provide students with a sense of time and with biographical models that illustrated the lives of famous historical persons. Greek, Roman, English, and colonial history were offered.

Although English was the language of instruction, students could study a second language related to their vocational needs. Prospective clergymen would study Latin and Greek; physicians would study Latin, Greek, and French; and merchants would study French, German, and Spanish. Other subjects in the curriculum were science, agriculture, technology, physical education, and character education.

Franklin's proposed school was a significant innovation because it introduced many practical skills into the formal school that had been ignored or left to private venture teachers. With prophetic insight into America's future, Franklin gave special attention to science, invention, and technology.

Although Franklin's proposed academy was established in Philadelphia,

---

[8]Frederick Rudolph, *Essays on Education in the Early Republic* (Cambridge, Mass.: Harvard University Press, 1965).

[9]John H. Best, ed., *Benjamin Franklin on Education* (New York: Teachers College Press, Columbia University, 1962).

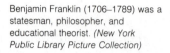

Benjamin Franklin (1706–1789) was a statesman, philosopher, and educational theorist. *(New York Public Library Picture Collection)*

Thomas Jefferson (1743–1826) was the third president of the United States and the founder of the University of Virginia. *(New York Public Library Picture Collection)*

Noah Webster (1758–1843) was schoolmaster of the Republic and the author of the *American Dictionary*. *(Library of Congress).*

Franklin, Jefferson, and Webster—Proponents of Civic Education for the New Republic.

it was located in the same building with the Latin Grammar school whose head-master favored Latin rather than English.

Nevertheless, the school's enriched curriculum, responsive to the needs of the rising commercial class, was an improvement over the narrowly prescribed Latin Grammar curriculum.

Thomas Jefferson and State-Supported Schooling

Thomas Jefferson (1743–1826), son of a wealthy and socially prominent plantation owner, was born in Virginia. He attended the local vernacular and Latin Grammar schools and later graduated from William and Mary College. Because of his study of politics, philosophy, architecture, and science, Jefferson was elected to the American Academy of Arts and Sciences and served as president of the American Philosophical Society from 1797 to 1815. As a leading statesman during the formative republican period, Jefferson held the positions of member of the Virginia legislature, delegate to the Continental Congress, governor of Virginia, minister to France, secretary of state, vice-president, and president.

Jefferson stated that his epitaph should refer to only three of his accomplishments: writing the Declaration of Independence, writing the Virginia Bill of Rights, and founding the University of Virginia. As the author of the Declaration of Independence, Jefferson stated his political beliefs that every man was endowed with inalienable rights of "life, liberty, and pursuit of happiness."[10]

In 1779, Jefferson introduced a "Bill for the More General Diffusion of Knowledge" into the Virginia legislature. Jefferson's proposal was based on the following beliefs: (1) schools in the new republic had the political function of educating a literate citizenry, (2) the state was responsible for providing schools, (3) state schools should be secular rather than religious, and (4) schools should also exercise the selective function of identifying intellectually able persons.[11]

In Jefferson's plan, Virginia's counties were subdivided into wards, each of which had an elementary school to provide instruction in reading, writing, arithmetic, and history. All white children in Virginia were to attend ward schools for three years of publicly supported elementary education. After completing three years of elementary school, parents could continue to enroll their children by paying tuition. Although it would appear to be minimal by today's standards, Jefferson's proposal involved a state commitment to support education that was significant for its time.

The second stage of Jefferson's plan called for establishing twenty grammar (secondary) schools in Virginia. It was at this stage that the selective function became operative. Jefferson believed that state schools had the function of identifying the most academically able persons and of preparing them for positions of civic leadership. To this end, the most able student who was unable to pay tuition, would be given a scholarship.

These scholarship students were to continue in the grammar school for two or three years, where they would study Latin, Greek, English, geography, and higher mathematics. The most promising student from among this group would then receive an additional six years of education, and the rest of the class unable to pay tuition would be dismissed. The highest-ranking twenty students, selected annually, were to complete grammar school. At the end of this period, ten would become elementary teachers in the ward schools and the remaining ten would go on to higher studies at William and Mary College.

Although not enacted, Jefferson's bill is noteworthy for the perspective that it provides on education in a republican society. To encourage citizenship education among the general population, he wanted every white child to have at least three years of publicly supported schooling. At the same time, he wanted secondary and higher schools to identify and prepare a selected number of academically promising students for leadership positions.

[10]Roy J. Honeywell, *The Educational Work of Thomas Jefferson* (Cambridge, Mass.: Harvard University Press, 1931).

[11]Jefferson's educational ideas are analyzed in Gordon C. Lee, "Learning and Liberty: The Jeffersonian Tradition in Education," in *Crusade Against Ignorance: Thomas Jefferson on Education* (New York: Teachers College Press, Columbia University, 1962).

Noah Webster

Noah Webster (1758–1843) is often called the "Schoolmaster of the Republic" because of his influence on the development of language and language teaching in the United States.[12] A cultural nationalist, Webster believed that although the United States had won its political independence from England, it had yet to secure sovereignty over its language. A unique American language, Webster believed, was the means by which Americans would achieve their cultural identity and unity. To create a distinctive American language, Webster wrote his widely used *American Spelling Book* and his definitive *American Dictionary*.

When the Constitution became the law of the land in 1789, Webster argued that the United States needed its own system of "language as well as government." The language of Great Britain, he claimed, "should no longer be our standard; for the taste of her writers is already completed, and her language on the decline."[13] Arguing that a sense of national identity could be conveyed through a distinctive national language and literature, Webster wanted to reshape the English language used in the United States into a uniquely American language. A distinctively American language would (1) eliminate the residues of European usage, (2) create a uniform American speech free of local usage, and (3) promote conscious American cultural nationalism and pride.

Webster believed that a unique American language could be transmitted to the future citizens through schooling. Such an American language would be taught deliberately and systematically in the nation's schools. As they learned the American language, children also would learn to think and act as Americans. Since the values prized in these American schools would be shaped by the students' reading, Webster devoted himself to writing spelling and reading books. The first part of his *Grammatical Institute of the English Language,* published in 1783, was later printed as *The American Spelling Book,* which was popular throughout the United States in the early nineteenth century. It has been estimated that fifteen million copies had been sold by 1837. Webster's great work, *The American Dictionary,* was completed in 1825, after twenty-five years of painstaking research.[14]

The educational plans of Franklin, Jefferson, and Webster demonstrated that these early leaders of the republic were searching for an educational system for the new nation. They especially wanted to create an education that would foster a civic sense of effective citizenship.

Recognizing the importance of education as a means of preparing citizens for the civic responsibilities of self-government, these leaders realized that the individual's education was directly related to the national well-being.

[12]Harry R. Warfel, *Noah Webster: Schoolmaster to America* (New York: Octagon, 1936); Ervin C. Shoemaker, *Noah Webster, Pioneer of Learning* (New York: Columbia University Press, 1936).

[13]Noah Webster, *Dissertations on the English Language* (Boston: Isaiah Thomas, 1789), p. 20.

[14]Henry Steele Commager, ed., *Noah Webster's American Spelling Book* (New York: Teachers College Press, Columbia University, 1962).

SOCIAL AND EDUCATIONAL CHANGE
IN NINETEENTH-CENTURY AMERICA

The foundations of the American public school system were established during the social transformation of the nineteenth century. The common or public school system was developed and implemented in the years before the Civil War in the northern states. After the war ended, it was extended to the South. The second half of the nineteenth century saw the rise of the American public high school. Land grant colleges and universities were funded by the Morrill Act of 1862. These educational changes need to be considered in the context of important socioeconomic and political changes that transformed the United States from a rural-agricultural society into an industrial and urban nation. Throughout much of the nineteenth century, the United States was a developing nation. By the beginning of the twentieth century, it was a leading world power.

When it began in New England, the common school movement was one of many reforms such as the abolition of black slavery, women's rights, temperance, and penal reform. The Abolitionist movement marked the beginning of the end of slavery; the common school movement marked the beginning of the American public school system. Before the common school won the commitment of large numbers of people, some states experimented with various nonpublic philanthropic alternatives.

Philanthropic Education

During the phenomenal industrial and urban growth of the early nineteenth century, some business and political leaders recognized that a mass education system was needed to train immigrant and working class children. Large cities, such as New York and Philadelphia, inaugurated voluntary or philanthropic schools, usually Lancasterian, as an educational response. Often, wealthy benefactors funded these schools.

Support of voluntary and philanthropic schools rested on the premise that education was a private rather than a state function. Philanthropists who supported voluntary schools wanted to provide minimal, basic literacy and character training to children from the lower social and economic classes.

In contrast to those who used education for social control, others wanted popular education to stimulate social change. For example, many workers' associations wanted schools to provide knowledge to working classes. Eventually, working class leaders hoped to gain political power by educational rather than revolutionary means.

William Maclure (1763–1840), a scientist, geologist, and philanthropist, in *Opinions on Various Subjects,* argued that industrial schools should be established for the working classes.[15] In such schools, working class children would learn to recognize the real political and economic interests of their class. Maclure, who anticipated vocational education, designed a curriculum that stressed basic science and its agricultural and industrial application. He also introduced the Pes-

---

[15]William Maclure, *Opinions on Various Subjects, I.* (New Harmony, Ind.: School Press, 1821), pp. 65–70.

talozzian method of education (see Chapter 10) to the United States. Maclure believed in using education for social change rather than for social control.

The Sunday school was a philanthropic endeavor that reflected the impact of the industrial revolution on working class families. In both England and the United States, children toiled as cheap laborers in the factories and mines. Because they worked a six-day week, Sunday was the only day available for them to attend school. Sunday school instruction was limited to the basics of reading, writing, religion, and character formation. With the inauguration of the common school, the Sunday school declined as an agency of basic education. Today, it is used exclusively for religious education.

The infant school was also a response to early industrialization. Since women worked in factories, the infant school was a place where children could stay while their mothers were absent. The infant school concept, a prototype of the modern day care center, was developed by Robert Owen (1771–1858), a British industrialist and communitarian socialist, at New Lanark in Scotland.[16] Basically, the infant school was a nursery school where young children, ranging from ages two to six years, received moral, physical, and intellectual training.

The monitorial school was one of the most popular alternatives to public or common schools. Monitorial education was devised by Joseph Lancaster (1778–1838), who claimed that it was possible to educate large numbers of children effectively, efficiently, and cheaply.[17]

According to Lancasterian monitorial education, a master teacher was to train advanced students to teach basic skills to beginning students. Since students did most of the teaching, costs were low. To accommodate large enrollments, Lancaster developed large factorylike schools. Using a semimilitary system, lessons were reduced to small elements, and each instructional phase was assigned to a particular monitor. Children of relatively similar ability were grouped together so that instruction could proceed uniformly. Each phase of instruction had its appropriate lesson plan. Instruction in writing and arithmetic was also arranged into groups based on ability levels. To keep expenses down, inexpensive materials were used. Large wall charts were used instead of books to teach reading. Students traced letters with their fingers on sand tables instead of using pen, ink, and paper.

The Lancasterian monitorial system was confined to basic skill learning. After enjoying popularity in the early nineteenth century, the monitorial method was discarded and replaced by common public schools.

The Common School

The common school movement of the nineteenth century was one of the major events in American cultural, social, educational history. Although defined in various ways, common schools were publically supported and controlled institutions that offered a curriculum of reading, writing, arithmetic,

[16]Harold Silver, *Robert Owen on Education* (Cambridge: Cambridge University Press, 1969), pp. 109–110.

[17]Carl F. Kaestle, *Joseph Lancaster and the Monitorial School Movement* (New York: Teacher's College Press, Columbia University, 1973), pp. 176–180.

In midnineteenth-century common schools, children used Dean's *Moveable ABC* to learn the alphabet. *(New York Public Library Picture Collection)*

penmanship, grammar, history, geography, and health. They also instilled the values of punctuality, hard work, and industry. The common school grew out of New England's tradition of local control. As the frontier moved westward, common schools were built in the new towns and settlements. Common schools were also used to assimilate or Americanize the children of immigrants.

An important argument for common schooling came from political and educational reformers such as James Carter, Horace Mann, and Thaddeus Stevens, who were concerned with the extension of civic education. Democratic processes and procedures required literate voters who were capable of electing public officials. American nationalism was also a motive behind the common school movement. Common schools could encourage shared values and loyalties and cultivate a sense of "Americanness" among people of ethnically, racially, and linguistically diverse backgrounds. In addition, the middle classes wanted a more utilitarian education that would prepare skilled workers.

In 1827 Massachusetts instituted the support of common schools via compulsory taxation. Other states in New England and in the Midwest followed Massachusetts. The movement to publicly supported education took a slower course in the Middle Atlantic states where Lancasterianism held on. Public schools did not develop in the South until the post–Civil War Reconstruction era.

While the common school movement varied from state to state, some general observations can be made. First, the state enacted legislation that permitted the voters of a given district to tax themselves to support common schools. This permissive legislation recognized school districts as units with administrative and taxing powers. Second, the state encouraged districts to organize by providing funds from the general school fund to those districts that had voted to support public schools. Third, the state required the formation of school districts and the levying of local taxes to provide elementary education for the children resident in the district.

HENRY BARNARD: A COMMON SCHOOL LEADER. Henry Barnard (1811–1900), a leader in the common school movement, was secretary of the Connecticut Board of Education from 1838 to 1842. He also served as state commissioner of the public schools in Rhode Island, 1845–1849, chancellor of the University of Wisconsin, 1858–1860, and U.S. commissioner of education, 1867–1870. Barnard was recognized, along with Horace Mann, as a "Founding Father" of the common school. As a journalist, he popularized public education through the *Connecticut Common School Journal* and the *American Journal of Education*. He introduced teachers to the ideas of European educational reformers such as Pestalozzi, Froebel, and Herbart.[18]

Barnard traveled throughout Connecticut and reported on the condition of public schools to the members of the state board. While he believed that common schooling should establish a solid foundation in basic skills, he also wanted teachers to emphasize civic values, the principles of health and diet, and the methods of accurate observation and clear reflection. Barnard's *First Annual Report,* in 1838, advised Connecticut teachers on subjects ranging from writing to religion.[19] Reading, writing, and arithmetic, the primary branches of learning, he wrote, were the foundations of later education and of work. The most important subject was the English language, which included spelling, reading, speaking, grammar, and composition. Practical arithmetic also should be stressed.

Barnard also urged more adequate teacher education, the establishment of normal schools, and increased financial compensation for teachers.

WILLIAM TORREY HARRIS: PUBLIC SCHOOL CONSOLIDATOR. After the Civil War, a great transformation occurred in American life as industrialism created an increasingly urban and technological society. The rapid growth of big cities and the massive influx of central and eastern Europe immigrants required educational leaders capable of administering efficiently the growing urban school systems. William Torrey Harris (1835–1909) was such an administrator of a large urban public school system. As the major statesman of American education after the Civil War era, Harris sought to consolidate the work of the earlier common school leaders and to relate American public education to the needs of an industrial society.[20]

From 1868 until 1880, Harris was superintendent of schools in St. Louis,

---

[18]Merle Curti, *The Social Ideas of American Educators* (New York: Littlefield, Adams, 1959), pp. 139–168.

[19]John S. Brubacher, *Henry Barnard on Education* (New York: McGraw-Hill, 1931).

[20]Selwyn K. Troen, *The Public and the Schools: Shaping the St. Louis System, 1838–1920* (Columbia: University of Missouri Press, 1975), pp. 1–4.

Henry Barnard (1811–1900) was a common school leader and U.S. commissioner of education. *(New York Public Library Picture Collection)*

William T. Harris (1835–1909) was a leader in school administration, St. Louis superintendent of schools, and U.S. commissioner of education. *(New York Public Library Picture Collection)*

Henry Barnard and William T. Harris—Public School Leaders of the Nineteenth Century.

a growing commercial and industrial city. An interesting national crossroads, its location between North and South gave St. Louis a population harboring both southern and northern sentiments. Racially and ethnically diverse, it had a large black community as well as a large immigrant population, especially German Americans. In this urban diversity, Harris established the basic administrative and organizational patterns for schools in an industrial society. As he dealt with the quantitative problems of organizing, classifying, and structuring a modern school system, Harris earned a reputation as being an efficient, effective, but conservative administrator.

Harris believed that a society had reached a high level of civilization when its social institutions such as the family, state, church, and school were well developed. To promote civilized life, the school was to emphasize the values of self-discipline, civic commitment, obedience to law and order, and respect for private property in the young. Harris saw the school's role to be that of efficiently transmitting the cultural heritage to the young through a curriculum that was a graded, structured, and cumulative sequence of studies.

In the United States, schools were to prepare individuals for life in a technological society of growing complexity and specialization. By stressing work, diligence, punctuality, and perseverance, schools prepared people to contribute to an emergent technological society. Under Harris's command, the schools were to prepare a trained labor force and managerial class for the nation's new industrial economy.

Believing strongly in the importance of early childhood education, Harris established the first successful public school kindergarten in St. Louis in 1873. After the kindergarten, children would then be prepared for the elementary school curriculum of mathematics, geography, literature and art, history, and grammar. When the elementary curriculum was completed, secondary students would then study classics, mathematics, and language.

As an administrator, Harris believed that efficient teachers were needed to transmit the curricular subjects effectively. He urged teachers to emphasize silence, industriousness, regularity, and discipline in their classrooms and to impress upon students the need of incorporating these values into their daily lives.[21] Harris's style of school management and classroom discipline rewarded children who conformed to adult standards and existing social values.

Harris and other urban school superintendents of the late nineteenth century faced the problems of overcrowded classrooms, poorly prepared teachers, and wide divergence in students' backgrounds. Harris's superintendency in St. Louis was marked by careful planning, the ordering of educational priorities, and efficient administrative procedures. His attention to planned administration led him to classify and group students meticulously. He developed the graded school where the work of each year was organized into a specific grade. To make compulsory attendance effective, school administrators had to compile and maintain statistics and attendance reports. Further, the school administrator was concerned with noninstructional matters such as the school's physical facilities, lighting, heating, architecture, and ventilation.

---

[21]William T. Harris, *Compulsory Education in Relation to Crime and Social Morals* (Washington, D.C.: printed privately, 1885), pp. 4–9.

Although Harris wanted schools to preserve existing social institutions and values rather than to change them, he also was prepared to deal with social issues. While he believed that public schools should assimilate immigrants into American society, he also felt that Americanization should be gradual, evolutionary, and noncoerced. To this end, he encouraged bilingual and bicultural education for St. Louis's large German community that was designed to bring German-speaking children into the larger English-speaking American society.

Because of his work in St. Louis, Harris gained a national reputation and was recognized as the elder statesman of American education. As the U.S. commissioner of education from 1889 to 1906, he became the authority on American public education. He was a member of the most important educational associations and commissions and was particularly influential in the National Education Association.

The establishment of common schools was an important stage in the development of the American public school system, as the various state legislatures enacted laws to tax for public support. Educational leaders such as Mann, Barnard, and Harris developed the pioneering models of effective school administration in the United States. With common schools as its basic foundation, it was possible to extend public education through the secondary level and to create a complete system of public supported and controlled educational institutions.

The High School

While the common school created the base for public education in the United States, it was the public high school that linked public elementary schools with state colleges and universities. In the early nineteenth century, the colonial Latin Grammar school declined and was replaced by the academy, a secondary school serving the educational needs of the middle-class youth by offering a wide range of curricula and subjects for both college preparatory and terminal students. Generally private institutions, a few academies were semipublic and received some funds from cities or states. Characterized by loosely organized instructional programs, educational quality varied considerably from academy to academy, with variations in the competency of instructors and aptitude of the students.[22]

After the 1870s, the academies declined and were replaced by the public high school. However, a small number of private academies continued to educate a small percentage of the secondary-school-aged population.

The high school became the major institution of American secondary education in the second half of the nineteenth century. In the 1870s, a series of court cases such as Michigan's *Kalamazoo* case in 1874 ruled that school districts could establish and support public high schools with tax funds. By the years 1889–1890, the 2,526 public high schools in the United States were enrolling 202,063 students in comparison with the 1,632 private academies that enrolled 94,391 students.[23]

[22]Theodore R. Sizer, *The Age of Academies* (New York: Teachers College Press, Columbia University, 1964).

[23]Edward Krug, *The Shaping of the American High School, 1880–1920* (New York: Harper & Row, 1964).

The rise of the high school can be explained by the impact of convergent socioeconomic forces. The United States experienced a great transformation from an agricultural and rural to an industrial and urban society. By 1930, more than 25 percent of the U.S. population was located in seven great urban areas of New York, Chicago, Philadelphia, Boston, Detroit, Los Angeles, and Cleveland. Urbanization stimulated a growing need for specialization of occupations, professions, and careers.

The high school represented an institutional response to the educational needs of modern society. It educated the growing number of students who were continuing their formal education beyond the eight years of elementary schooling. It served terminal students who were completing their formal schooling in the high school and continued to provide college preparatory schooling for those who would enter institutions of higher education.

As a school for adolescents of varying social, economic, racial, religious, and ethnic backgrounds, the comprehensive high school was a new kind of secondary institution. In contrast to European secondary schools that separated the academic from terminal students, the American high school was a comprehensive institution that sought social integration in an environment of curricular differentiation.

When the high school became the dominant institution of American secondary education, it became possible for a student to attend a sequence of publicly supported and controlled institutions, beginning with the kindergarten, extending to the elementary school and through high school, and reaching the college and university. The high school linked elementary and higher educational institutions and completed the American educational ladder.

TWENTIETH-CENTURY TRENDS IN EDUCATION

After the consolidation of public education in the early twentieth century, the public schools tended to become formalized and routine. The Progressive Movement was an effort to reform and liberalize education as well as politics and society. John Dewey (1859–1952) exercised a great influence on twentieth-century American education. Dewey's *The School and Society* (1898) described his laboratory school at the University of Chicago. His *How We Think* (1910) stressed problem solving as a method of science and education. *Individualism Old and New* (1929) examined social change in relation to American civilization. *Democracy and Education* (1916) remains his classic statement of educational philosophy.

Dewey's Laboratory School

Dewey's work at the Laboratory School of the University of Chicago, which he directed from 1896 to 1904, operationalized his Experimentalist philosophy of education. Dewey's books, *The School and Society* (1898) and *The Child and the Curriculum* (1902) describe his work at the Laboratory School. By solving personal, social, and intellectual problems, children exercised their intelligence and used the knowledge and science accumulated by the human race. Dewey detailed three levels of learning activity used at the Laboratory School: (1) children exercised their senses and developed physical coordination, (2) children used materials and tools present in the environment, and (3) children used their intelligence to discover, examine, and use ideas.[24]

After Dewey concluded his work at the Chicago Laboratory School, he returned to writing in formal philosophy and the philosophy of education at Columbia University. Dewey's educational philosophy exerted a profound influence on the "new education" of the twentieth century.

Progressivism in Education

The origins of progressive education began with the Naturalistic educators of the late eighteenth and nineteenth centuries. Rousseau, Pestalozzi, and Froebel developed educational theories that challenged traditional practices. The eighteenth-century Enlightenment and nineteenth-century social reform produced the notion of "progress" by which people could shape their environment by using reason and science.

In the United States, the early twentieth century was the era of the progressive movement in politics. Robert LaFollette, Theodore Roosevelt, and Woodrow Wilson campaigned against graft, corruption, and monopoly. LaFollette's Wisconsin Idea encouraged a working relationship between education and political reform. The social work of Jane Addams, the journalism of Lincoln Steffens, and the legal opinions of Oliver W. Holmes, Jr., expressed progressivism in society, literature, and law. Progressivism in education and politics challenged traditionalism and sought to reform society.[25]

Progressive educators believed that schooling could exercise a reforming influence. However, schools first had to be reformed. A number of educators formed the Progressive Education Association in 1919 under the leadership of Stanwood Cobb.[26]

In the 1920s, progressive education was characterized by educators who worked to liberate the child's creative impulses as educators such as Marietta Johnson and Caroline Pratt sought to develop instructional methods to release the child's creativity. Johnson, as director of the School of Organic Education at Fairhope in Alabama, stressed the child's interests and needs and emphasized music, singing, dancing, stories, and creative artwork to awaken the child's creativity. Caroline Pratt, founder of the Greenwich Village Play School, developed the principle that children would learn the truths of the universe through their play activities.

While the more child-centered educators neglected social issues, other progressive educators worked for the cause of social reform. Several of this socially oriented wing of progressive education were members of Columbia University's Teachers College faculty in the late 1920s and during the 1930s. Such Teachers College professors as Harold Rugg, William H. Kilpatrick, and George

---

[24]Arthur G. Wirth, *John Dewey as Educator: His Design and Work in Education, 1894–1904* (New York: John Wiley, 1966), pp. 96–99.

[25]Lawrence A. Cremin, *The Transformation of the School* (New York: Knopf, 1962).

[26]Patricia Albjerg Graham, *Progressive Education: From Arcady to Academe, A History of the Progressive Education Association, 1919–1955* (New York: Teachers College Press, Columbia University, 1967).

S. Counts are of major significance in the history of progressive education. Rugg sought to integrate both creativity and social reform into his theory of education. Kilpatrick worked to provide progressivism with a coherent methodology of instruction. Counts popularized the view that schools should be transformed into agencies of active social reform.

Critics of Progressivism

Progressive education had a number of critics such as the Essentialist educators William Chandler Bagley and Isaac Kandel, who argued that the purpose of education was to cultivate intellectual skills and knowledge. The Essentialists believed that schools should train children systematically in the basic subjects of reading, writing, arithmetic, history, English, and foreign languages. They believed that schools should stress hard work and discipline and should transmit the cultural heritage rather than seek to inaugurate social, economic, or political change.

In the post-Sputnik era of the 1950s, Arthur Bestor, in *Educational Wastelands* and *The Restoration of Learning,* attacked the "educationist establishment" and urged a return to basic education grounded on intellectual disciplines. Max Rafferty, in his *Suffer, Little Children,* charged that progressive reformers had weakened educational standards.

Racial Integration and School Desegregation

In *Brown* v. *Board of Education of Topeka,* in 1954, the Supreme Court ruled racial segregation in public schools unconstitutional. The *Brown* case marked the beginning of a concerted movement for civil rights and racial integration. In September 1957, Congress passed a Civil Rights Act that established a commission to investigate charges of the denial of voting rights and equal protection of the laws due to color, race, religion, or national origin. In 1960, the passage of another Civil Rights Act empowered federal courts to appoint referees to examine state voting qualifications that denied the right to vote because of race or color. The Civil Rights Act of 1964, the most far-reaching law of its kind, protected voting rights and guaranteed civil rights in employment and education. It guaranteed equal access to public accommodations and strengthened the machinery for preventing employment discrimination. In education, the act empowered the federal government to file school desegregation suits and to withhold federal funds from districts that practiced discrimination in federal programs. The Civil Rights Act of 1968 protected the civil rights of workers and provided severe penalties for interfering with the rights of attending school or working.

Along with the Civil Rights Acts, several Supreme Court decisions advanced racial integration in the schools such as *Griffin* v. *School Board of Prince Edward County* in 1964.[27] In Prince Edward County in Virginia, the board of supervisors had refused to levy taxes for the 1959–1960 school year with the result that the public schools were closed. A private association, the Prince Edward School Foundation, formed to operate private schools for white children, drew its major financial support from state and county tuition grants. The Su-

---

[27]*Griffin* v. *School Board of Prince Edward County,* 377 U.S. 218 (1964).

preme Court ruled that the closing of the Prince Edward County public schools had denied black students the equal protection of the laws guaranteed by the Fourteenth Amendment since the county supervisors' action had forced children to attend racially segregated schools that received county and state support.

In 1969, the Supreme Court in *Alexander* v. *Holmes County Board of Education* discarded the "all deliberate speed" criterion for school desegregation when it reversed lower court decisions that granted an extension of time to some Mississippi school districts for desegregation.[28] The Court ruled that every school district in the land was to terminate dual school systems "at once" and operate only unitary schools.

In 1971, in *Swann* v. *Charlotte-Mecklenburg Board of Education*, the Supreme Court ruled that busing was an acceptable means of achieving school desegregation.[29] It also stated that future school construction must not be used to perpetuate or re-establish segregated schools. Following the *Swann* decision, district courts began attacking de facto segregation in northern and western urban areas such as San Francisco, Philadelphia, Pittsburgh, Detroit, Los Angeles, Denver, and Boston. The first phase of the legal thrust against racial inequality was directed against de jure segregation in the South. The second phase of the movement toward racial equality was the attack launched against de facto segregation in the large northern cities.

CONCLUSION

Chapter 2 has presented a general historical overview of major educational developments in the United States. More detailed and specific background will be presented in relation to the topics treated in subsequent chapters. From the era of the common school movement to the present, the general trend in American education has been to shape conditions that increased the educational opportunities of larger numbers of persons. This trend to provide greater educational opportunities was marked particularly by the emergence of the tax-supported public elementary and secondary school.

DISCUSSION QUESTIONS

1. Trace the major institutional developments in colonial education.
2. Examine the Puritan impact on schooling.
3. Examine the concept of civic education as exemplified in the theories of education of the early national era.
4. Define the common school and trace the common school movement.
5. Examine the impact of William T. Harris on educational administration in an urban era.
6. Examine the major trends in twentieth-century education.

[28]*Alexander* v. *Holmes County Board of Education*, 396 U.S. 19 (1969).
[29]*Swann* v. *Charlotte-Mecklenburg Board of Education*, 402 U.S. 554 (1971).

FIELD EXERCISES

1. Write a short biographical sketch of your own education.
2. Interview several experienced teachers and ask them to identify the major changes that have occurred in the public schools.
3. Set up a round table discussion in which members of the class act out the roles of Franklin, Jefferson, Rush, and Webster and carry on a dialogue on educational theory.
4. Invite an historian of education to visit your class and present his or her interpretation of American educational history.
5. Examine several textbooks from different periods of history.

SELECTED READINGS

BAILYN, BERNARD. *Education in the Forming of American Society: Needs and Opportunities for Study.* New York: W. W. Norton, 1972.

BEST, JOHN H., ED. *Benjamin Franklin on Education.* New York: Teachers College Press, Columbia University, 1962.

BLINDERMAN, ABRAHAM. *Three Early Champions of Education: Benjamin Franklin, Benjamin Rush, and Noah Webster.* Bloomington, Ind.: Phi Delta Kappa Educational Foundation, 1976.

COHEN, SHELDON S. *A History of Colonial Education: 1607–1776.* New York: John Wiley, 1974.

COMMAGER, HENRY STEELE, ED. *Noah Webster's American Spelling Book.* New York: Teachers College Press, Columbia University, 1962.

CREMIN, LAWRENCE A. *American Education: The Colonial Experience, 1607–1783.* New York: Harper & Row, 1970.

CURTI, MERLE. *The Social Ideas of American Educators.* New York: Littlefield, Adams, 1959.

FLEMING, STANFORD. *Children and Puritanism: The Place of Children in the Life and Thought of the New England Churches, 1620–1847.* New Haven, Conn.: Yale University Press, 1933.

FORD, PAUL L., ED. *The New England Primer.* New York: Dodd, Mead, 1899.

GREVEN, PHILIP J. *Child-Rearing Concepts, 1628–1881: Historical Sources.* Itasca, Ill.: F. E. Peacock, 1973.

HESLEP, ROBERT D. *Thomas Jefferson and Education.* New York: Random House, 1969.

JOHNSON, CLIFTON. *Old-Time Schools and School Books.* New York: Macmillan, 1904.

KNIGHT, EDGAR W. *A Documentary History of Education in the South Before 1860.* Chapel Hill: University of North Carolina Press, 1949.

LEE, GORDON, C., ED. *Crusade Against Ignorance: Thomas Jefferson on Education.* New York: Teachers College Press, Columbia University, 1962.

MADSEN, DAVID L. *Early National Education: 1776–1830.* New York: John Wiley, 1974.

MIDDLEKAUFF, ROBERT. *Ancients and Axioms: Secondary Education in Eighteenth-Century New England.* New Haven, Conn.: Yale University Press, 1963.

MORGAN, EDMUND S. *The Puritan Family: Religion and Domestic Relations in Seventeenth-Century New England.* New York: Harper & Row, 1966.

WAGONER, JENNINGS L., JR. *Thomas Jefferson and the Education of a New Nation.* Bloomington, Ind.: Phi Delta Kappa Educational Foundation, 1976.

3

Philosophy and Education

Chapter 3 explores the relationships between philosophy and education. To aid in analyzing the chapter, you might focus your attention on the following questions:

1. Why should teachers be aware of issues in philosophy of education?
2. What are the major divisions in philosophy and how do they relate to educational issues and problems?
3. What are the major educational philosophies?
4. What general guidelines to educational policy can be derived from the various systematic philosophies of education?
5. How can prospective teachers formulate their own educational philosophies?

EDUCATION AND PHILOSOPHY

Philosophy of education is one of the most important subjects that prospective teachers study. At times, teachers become immersed so immediately in the urgent tasks of teaching that they do not consciously examine the philosophical consequences of their activities. Preparing lessons and attendance reports, leading field trips, or participating in parent conferences are only a few of the many immediate activities that occupy a teacher's day. However, when teachers look beyond the immediate daily demands on their time, they often find themselves reflecting on the general and long-term issues of significance for themselves, their students, and the society in which they live.

Perhaps the most direct but also the most significant question that arises upon reflection is, What difference does it make? Another way of stating this question is to ask, What is true? What is good? and What is beautiful? What does it mean to lead a life that is true, good, and beautiful? Certainly, a genuine education should focus on these questions.

Philosophy as Speculation

Since the earliest recorded history, individuals have speculated about the nature of reality and of the meaning of life itself. In doing so, these persons have dealt with one of the most basic but also most pervasive concerns of human existence. The history of philosophy records the efforts of Plato, Aristotle, Plotinus, Zeno, Epicurus, Augustine, Aquinas, Locke, Rousseau, Kant, Hegel, Marx, Bertrand Russell, William James, John Dewey, and others to answer these basic questions. These philosophers and many others have speculated about the nature of reality. When they recounted or recorded their speculations, they attempted to describe the nature of reality. Based upon their insights into reality, philosophers also have sought to prescribe values and ideals.

If you reflect on education—either as enculturation in the informal sense or as formal schooling—it becomes clear that the educative process involves both descriptive and prescriptive components. Much of what goes on in school involves descriptions that identify and explain certain features of reality. The kindergarten child who has brought a favorite toy to school for "show and tell" is describing an aspect of his or her reality to the other children. The books that students read and discuss in history, chemistry, and other subjects account for or describe specific dimensions of reality. The statement "John Kennedy was elected president of the United States in 1960" describes an historical event. The statement "The chemical formula for water is H_2O" seeks to describe a different sort of reality.

While schooling is descriptive, much of it is also prescriptive in that it seeks to inculcate desired or approved ethical and aesthetic behavioral standards. Whenever our language is conveyed with the words "ought" or "should" or "ought not" or "should not," we are prescribing behavior. When we say "you should wash your hands before eating," "you should not cheat on examinations," "you should be a good citizen," or "you should not litter parks and playgrounds," we are prescribing or recommending behavior.

The descriptive and the prescriptive phases of education are ultimately philosophical. While the descriptive phase seeks to describe reality, the prescriptive seeks to guide behavior by recommending some actions over other actions.

RELATIONSHIPS OF PHILOSOPHY
AND EDUCATION

As is true for other bodies of knowledge, philosophy is subdivided into areas of specialization. In this section, we define and describe such areas as metaphysics, epistemology, axiology, and logic and relate them to education.

Metaphysics

Metaphysics, the most abstract and speculative subdivision of philosophy, seeks to answer questions about the nature of ultimate reality. What is it about life and the universe that is really real? The branch of metaphysics that examines the nature of reality is known as *ontology* and that which seeks to explain the origin and structure of the universe is known as *cosmology.*

Based upon their speculations about the nature of reality, philosophers have constructed metaphysical descriptions about the nature of the universe and the life and place of human beings in that universe. In the most general sense, much of the school's curriculum is also descriptive of the various aspects of reality. For example, history and the social sciences seek to describe aspects of mankind's social life on this planet. The natural and physical sciences are descriptive of the structures, patterns, and relationships of physical and natural phenomena. It should be pointed out that each area of knowledge or science describes in a detailed way one phase of reality. Metaphysics, in contrast, seeks to describe all of reality in general rather than in specific terms.

The curriculum is comprised, in part, of knowledge derived from the various social, natural, and physical sciences. Regardless of the particular mode of curricular organization, the total curriculum provides the learner with a sense of reality. It represents a particular society's conception of reality. Although educators may not carry their curricular conceptions to the most general level of discussion, metaphysical concerns are always present—either consciously or unconsciously—in the curriculum. As students learn what "was" or "is," they gain a world view.

Epistemology

While metaphysics examines reality, *epistemology* probes questions such as What is knowledge? and How do we know? Metaphysics is concerned with the content of our knowledge; epistemology deals with the process of knowing. In terms of education, epistemology relates closely to how we think, know, and learn. The use of various instructional methods such as the lecture, the experiment, and the project rests on the assumption that there is an effective and efficient method of teaching and learning. The various philosophies of education examined in this chapter argue that a particular epistemological strategy is to be preferred over other strategies. To develop this theme further, we look at several of these strategies.

One of the oldest and most widely accepted theories of knowing is that of *revelation,* which means that God has revealed Himself or has disclosed truth to certain specially inspired men and women. God has given a message to these persons who have recorded it in a sacred or holy book or document. For the Christian, the sacred book is the Bible; for the Moslem, the Koran; and for the Hindu, the Bhagavad-Gita. A basic requirement in revelation is that the knowledge seeker must believe on faith that the truths of the sacred book are divinely inspired. When this condition is met, the sacred book becomes the authoritative source for knowing. Educationally, students study the sacred book by reading and often memorizing its passages. Learned men, often priests, seek to explain and to apply the unchanging message to the present. Religious schools place great emphasis on studying and interpreting the sacred literature.

Another approach to truth is *rationalism*. The Western intellectual tradition from the Greek classical period, through the eighteenth century Enlightenment, to the present has emphasized human reason as the most valid authority for recognizing and establishing knowledge. As an epistemological doctrine, rationalism asserts that reason is the source from which we derive universally valid judgments. The rationalist strategy of knowing propounds first principles as a priori statements that are held to be universally true and then derives subsidiary principles from them. For example, if we accept as universally true the general statement that human beings are mortal, we can then reason that all men and women will die. Or, if we accept as true that "man is endowed with inalienable rights of life, liberty, and property," it is possible to establish governmental systems to protect these rights. The rationalist tradition, which is pervasive in Western thought, has influenced our ideas of government, law, and society.

Empiricism, still another epistemological theory, bases the quest for knowledge on observation and experience. Those who subscribe to empiricism hold that knowledge originates in sensory experience of the environment and that ideas are formed on the basis of observed phenomena. Modern science is empirically based, and Pragmatic philosophers, such as John Dewey, have constructed a theory of knowledge based on the scientific method. Educational methods such as the scientific, project, and activity methods rest on the assumption that human experience is the best guide to truth. For Pragmatists, truth is neither eternal as it is for those who hold to revelation nor universal as it is for Rationalists; rather, it is tentative and subject to further research and investigation.

Axiology

As philosophy is a quest for truth, so is it also a search for the good and the beautiful. This search for goodness and beauty leads both philosophers and educators in the axiological dimension of education. *Axiology,* the study of values, is subdivided into ethics, which examines morality and conduct, and aesthetics, which is concerned with beauty. In education, axiology leads to a consideration of many value-laden questions, such as

What is the good and beautiful life?
What does it mean to be a good human being or a good citizen?
What are appropriate standards of behavior?
What is right and wrong?

Are values permanent or are they changing?

Are values universal or are they particular to a given time, place, and culture?

What standards should a person use to judge a book, a musical composition, a play, or other works of art?

Should schools reflect prevailing cultural values or should they seek to change them?

All education and all forms of schooling are immersed in the value dimension of life. There is no education that is value-free. Either consciously or unconsciously, teachers are value agents. They, themselves, represent models of value; they either reinforce or challenge the values of students.

The school is an agency that is prescriptive as well as descriptive. It prescribes certain approved ways of behaving for students. Prescriptive language is conveyed by the words "should or shouldn't," "ought or ought not." In performing its prescriptive function, the school is a corrective agency. In a very obvious way, teachers correct spelling, addition, subtraction, and many other behaviors on the basis that they are either right or wrong. In a less obvious way, teachers also prescribe more complex and subtle forms of personal, social, political, aesthetic, and intellectual behavior. In these more complex areas of life, the answers are not those of simple spelling or addition but often are not clearly defined or commonly accepted. In a racially, ethnically, religiously, economically, and socially pluralistic society, as that of the United States, competing and often conflicting standards of behavior make it difficult to arrive at a generally acceptable common core of values.

Logic

Logic, referring to the study of correct reasoning, examines the rules of valid inference, which enables us to move correctly from one argument to another. As there is a logical way of thinking, there is also a logic that can be used to order instruction. Logical patterns are either deductive or inductive. Deduction, as a form of reasoning, moves from a known principle to an unknown, from the general to the specific, or from a premise to a logical conclusion. Deductive reasoning is particularly appropriate to a rationalist position. In contrast, induction is the process of developing generalized explanations, hypotheses, or laws from collections of facts. It is the kind of reasoning that moves from a particular instance to a general conclusion.

PHILOSOPHIES OF EDUCATION

Now that we have identified the subdivisions in philosophy, we can explore the major educational philosophies. In this chapter, we examine such traditional philosophical positions as Idealism, Realism, Thomism, Perennialism, and Essentialism. In the following chapter, we examine the more pragmatic or recently developed philosophies of Experimentalism, Progressivism, Reconstructionism, Existentialism, and Philosophical Analysis. In our investigation of philosophies of education, we use a "systems approach" that looks at the particular philosophic position as a complete system of thought. That is, each philosophy presents a developed perspective on metaphysics, epistemology, axiology, and logic. From this perspective, implications can be drawn to such educational areas as the aims of education, the nature of the school, the organization of the curriculum, the appropriate methodology to be used in instruction, and the nature of the teaching-learning relationship. Of the educational philosophies that will be treated, it is possible to classify them on the basis to which they represent complete systems.

Idealism, Realism, Thomism, and Experimentalism represent complete philosophical systems that can be applied to educational issues. Education is only one of many dimensions to which the philosophy applies. In the case of Perennialism, Essentialism, Progressivism, and Reconstructionism, these educational theories do not present fully developed metaphysical, epistemological, and axiological perspectives.

In this chapter, we begin with a discussion of a particular philosophical and theoretical position and then apply that position to specific educational issues. We examine each philosophical or theoretical position and then state what the particular position holds for education.

Idealism

Idealist metaphysics asserts that ultimate reality is spiritual or mental. The existence of matter and of the body, itself, depends upon the spiritual force that gives its energy and life. Reality can be understood to be ideas in relationship to each other. Although the Idealist metaphysical orientation is difficult to understand, it might be perceived as a relationship between the mind of God or the Absolute and the mind of man.[1]

For Idealists, there is one source, a single point of origin, from which all reality flows. This supreme and all-encompassing source is given various names, but they all refer to the same World Mind or originator. For Jews and Christians, God is a spiritual and a personal Creator. For Hindus, Brahma is the all-encompassing World Being. While the religious conception of God may be compatible with Idealism, not all Idealists perceive of the World Mind in religious terms. Nor, for that matter, are all religious people Idealists.

The all-pervasive World Mind is also referred to as the Absolute, the Over Soul, and the Macrocosm. Whether defined in the theological sense or in a strictly philosophical sense, the World Mind is the source of all ideas and is the force that keeps these ideas in existence. Everything that exists, including human beings, originates as a concept or an idea in the World Mind, which is eternal, perfect, unchanging, and orderly. The ideas of the World Mind are in a perfect time and space relationship.

Human reality is also spiritual, mental, and intellectual. What is most real about a human being is the person's mind or intelligence, which, depending upon the particular Idealist, may or may not have a religious dimension. The

---

[1]Idealism as an educational philosophy is treated in J. Donald Butler, *Idealism in Education* (New York: Harper & Row, 1966).

human mind contains concepts or ideas, as does the World Mind. While the ideas in World Mind are limitless and complete, the ideas in the human mind are limited. What is important is that the reality in the World Mind and the human mind is of the same substance—ideas.

Idealist epistemology, or theory of knowledge, is closely related to the philosophy's metaphysical position. While the Mind of the Absolute, or God, or the World Mind is perfect, the human being's mind is imperfect and limited. Human beings are prisoners of their bodies. At birth, the human mind is encased in a body and is subject to the world of appearance, to hunger, cold, noise, to the senses and the appetites. The shock of birth itself pushes the ideas of the mind far back into the recesses of the unconscious. All that is to be known is latently present in the mind but it is repressed. The process of knowing, for Idealists, involves bringing these ideas forward into consciousness.

If knowing means bringing latent ideas to consciousness, then instruction, or teaching and learning, is designed to facilitate this process. The process of instruction can be illustrated by the Socratic dialogues, written by Plato.[2] In

This medieval drawing depicts the ancient Greek philosophers, Socrates and Plato. The Socratic dialogue is a teaching method which asks basic philosophical questions about life, truth, and beauty. *(New York Public Library Picture Collection)*

[2]For a discussion of the Socratic-Platonic method, see Jerome Eckstein, *The Platonic Method: An Interpretation of the Dramatic-Philosophical Aspects of the Meno* (New York: Greenwood, 1968).

these dialogues, Socrates is typically questioning a group of students about the meaning of life, truth, beauty, virtue, or courage. At first, the students reply by stating opinions that refer to particular instances of truth or beauty. However, Socrates' skillful and unrelenting questioning forces the students to recognize their ignorance and abandon their diverse and often erroneous opinions. Eventually, they are led by Socrates to conclude that particular instances of courage, beauty, or truth are based on a general and more abstract concept of these virtues.

The teacher who follows the Idealist strategy of instruction, as did Socrates, is a midwife of ideas. The instructional task is twofold: first, the learner must realize that the senses can deceive and that opinions can be erroneous; then, once the learner is ready to abandon the world of appearances, he or she can turn within and find the truth that is present in the mind. Although the teacher can stimulate learning, only the learner can bring to consciousness and illuminate the ideas in the mind. Since learning is a recalling or remembering of ideas already present, the process is referred to as "re-cognition" or rethinking.

Since each particular idea leads back to one great idea that encompasses all existence, Idealists emphasize the interrelatedness of ideas. The metaphysics, epistemology, axiology, and logic of Idealism are all interrelated. This connectedness or interrelatedness can be illustrated by considering the relationship of the school to civilization. Idealists argue that the school, as an institution, is a civilizing agency. Its primary function is to civilize the young by imposing and transmitting the cultural heritage upon them.

Idealists regard civilization as the slow process of accumulating knowledge and of developing values over the centuries of human life on this planet. Each generation of human beings has inherited knowledge from its predecessors and has added to that cultural legacy. Each generation has likewise inherited and has further refined the values to be transmitted to the young.

Civilization, then, is the continually accumulating growth of knowledge and the advancement of morality to higher stages of development. In the continuing evolution of civilization, certain enduring trends have persisted into the present while others enjoyed but a fleeting existence. To preserve its intellectual and moral legacy, mankind has created social, religious, political, and educational institutions. Each of these institutions has a particular role to perform in protecting and preserving civilization. For example, the family is designed to rear children; the government to maintain law and order; the church to provide a comprehensive view of truth and morality in a religious context; and the school to transmit the intellectual, cultural, and moral heritage to the young so that they can share in and add to it.[3]

The Idealist's conception of the school as a civilizing institution can be seen by examining their views of curriculum and behavior. Seen as the repository of the cultural inheritance, the curriculum is a carefully organized, sequential, subject matter arrangement. Those subjects that contain the greatest intellectual and value possibilities are given priority over those that are more technical and vocational. In deciding what should be included and what should be excluded

[3]John Paul Strain, "Idealism: A Clarification of an Educational Philosophy," *Educational Theory*, 25 (Summer 1975), pp. 263–271.

from the curriculum, Idealists have been guided by the wisdom of the past. Those books and works of art that are classics are given priority, since they embody a universal meaning that transcends the special interests of a particular generation. Children are prepared for the future by learning about the cultural accomplishments of the past.

In terms of subject matter, Idealists emphasize reading and writing as necessary tools in comprehending the cultural legacy. Arithmetic is a tool for sharpening reasoning. History and geography provide a perspective into temporal and spatial relationships. History also portrays the record of mankind's past accomplishments. The biographies of great men and women can be used as models for imitation by the young. Language and literature, both one's own vernacular and that of foreign origins as well, are useful in understanding and expressing the cultural inheritance. The preferred works of literature are selected carefully as both literary and moral exemplars that can be imitated by students. While science has a place in the Idealist curriculum, it should be treated conceptually and related deliberately to the humanistic dimension of education. For the Idealist, the subjects of the curriculum should be organized separately and carefully and presented through systematically written books that stand as compendiums of mankind's recorded knowledge.

In Idealism, the axiological or value dimension of education is closely related to the cognitive or knowledge domain. In fact, the books selected for instructional purposes should convey ethical and aesthetic as well as intellectual models. Certain values, such as discipline, order, and self-control stand out as important for both life and school success.

For the Idealists, children possess immense spiritual and intellectual potential. It is the responsibility of the school and the teacher to help children to actualize their potential. The primary habit to be stressed is that of self-control. As they acquire self-control, they learn to use their minds to repress immediate impulses and instincts. By moving beyond immediate satisfaction and gratification, they learn to defer action and to place decision making in a temporal perspective. Through schooling, children are introduced to the routines and standards of civilization.

Idealists also assert that truly disciplined persons have a sense of order. In a child's education, discipline is a mutual responsibility of the home and the school. Together, parents and teachers are to cultivate habits of cleanliness, neatness, orderliness, punctuality, courtesy, obedience, and accuracy. The educated person, according to the Idealist value criterion, would (1) be polite and courteous in social behavior, (2) respect society's moral codes and (3) realize that civilized progress requires discipline and perseverance.

In the area of aesthetics, Idealists seek and use models that portray the persistent ideals of civilization. They encourage students to know and to read the great classics of literature, to attend and to re-enact the great dramas, to view and to appreciate the great paintings, and to hear and to perform the great musical compositions. The crucial standard in measuring a classic is conveyed by the word "great," which means that a given work of art or a book possesses qualities that enable it to endure and to appeal to persons across the span of time.

Idealist teachers are to be models of knowledge and values that students can imitate. They should be able to integrate their lives harmoniously. As students imitate their teachers, they, too, are expected to develop a sense of order and perspective.

The Idealist conception of education and of schooling is conservative and traditional. It seeks to preserve the cultural heritage of the past by transmitting it to children, the immature members of society, so that they continue and extend human civilization into the future. A great priority is placed on studying and learning systematically organized bodies of knowledge and on cultivating socially acceptable standards of behavior.

The critics of Idealism contend that it is too abstract and vague to be of real use in schools. They argue that its objectives can be neither specified nor verified empirically. Many of its claims while inspirational cannot be used to guide practice. Further, the critics allege that Idealism is too oriented to the past and does not relate effectively to contemporary problems or to future directions in education.

Realism

As with Idealism, Realism is a traditional educational philosophy that is oriented to a subject matter curriculum and to teacher-centered instruction. The metaphysical and epistemological bases of Realism, however, are quite different from that of Idealism. Metaphysically, Realist philosophers assert that (1) an objective order of reality exists that is independent of human knowing or willing, (2) patterns and relationships exist between the objects found in reality, (3) human beings are capable of knowing about these objects and their relationships, and (4) human action and behavior is most intelligent when based on knowledge of the objective order of reality.[4]

Stated most directly, the Realist metaphysical position means that you or I exist and that we live in a world of objects. We inhabit a world of many beings such as other people, the planets, animals, plants, trees, houses, schools, rocks, oceans, and so on. Everything that exists is related to other objects but is also independent of them. These objects possess two essential characteristics: matter and form. They are made of something. They are material. This matter has a structure that gives it a shape, form, or design.

Epistemologically, Realists assert that human beings can know the objects that they encounter. We can know about objects because we possess such sensory powers as sight, hearing, touching, tasting, feeling, and smelling that enable us to acquire information—sensory data—about objects. This information is then conveyed to our minds where we sort it out in a manner that is similar to the operation of a computer. Our mind determines what there is about an object that is always found in that class of objects (i.e., essential to that object) or that is sometimes found in the object. We abstract "necessary" or essential qualities of the object into a concept that signifies the general class or category of objects. For example, we see many kinds or types of dogs. They are large dogs, small dogs, pedigreeds, and mixed breeds. There are poodles, pomeranians, pekinese, and pugs. From this varied experience with different types of dogs, we can arrive

---

[4]An excellent statement of Realist philosophy is provided by John Wild, *Introduction to Realist Philosophy* (New York: Harper and Brothers, 1948), p. 6.

at a general concept of dog, that which is necessary for a particular object to be in one category and not in another. Our ability to conceptualize rests on our twofold and related powers of sensation and abstraction.

Realist metaphysics and epistemology have direct implications for the purposes of the school and for curriculum organization. As with Idealism, Realism asserts that each social institution has a primary or specialized function to perform. In a rationally organized society, each institution—such as the family, government, church, or school—performs its function and does not encroach on the domain of other institutions. The school's primary function, in Realist terms, is to educate students about the world, the reality, in which they live. The school's task, then, is to transmit knowledge, or information, to students so that they can act rationally.

The Realist curricular pattern is a subject matter organization. If we return to the Realist conception of reality, we can see that objects are either like or unlike each other. The simple game of animal, vegetable, or mineral indicates how we classify objects according to similarities or differences. We can extend these three broad classifications to all the objects that we encounter and can derive more complicated and sophisticated kinds of classifications. For example, concepts that deal with the composition and properties of substances can be classified under the discipline, or subject matter, of chemistry. Concepts dealing with plants and their life, structure, and growth can be classified with botany. Concepts that relate to government, diplomacy, political organization, and management can be classified as political science. A visit to the card catalogue of a library illustrates the divisions of knowledge and the subdivisions that exist within these areas. Based on these divisions of knowledge, the curriculum at each level of schooling represents a more complex arrangement of these categories of knowledge or subjects.

Realist epistemology suggests how our concepts about reality should be organized, taught, and studied. Essentially, research is designed to tell us about the objects we encounter so that we can know, appreciate, and use them. In their research, scientists and scholars seek to know objects more precisely. The more accurate our knowledge of objects, the more accurately do our concepts conform to the object in reality. Scientists and scholars in the various disciplines, often university professors, publish their research in books and articles and disseminate their findings and interpretations in lectures. College students, including prospective elementary and secondary school students, attend courses taught by these scholars or read books and articles written by them. Knowledge acquired is then reorganized into the elementary and secondary school curriculum. Within the subjects of the curriculum, teachers organize instructional units and lessons that adapt the subject matter to the learners' readiness, ability, and needs.

The actual Realist curriculum resembles that of the Idealists in that it follows a subject matter mode of organization. The elementary school curriculum emphasizes reading, writing, arithmetic, and research as necessary skills and language arts, science, mathematics, history and social science as significant content areas. The secondary school curriculum refines these subjects further into more complex and substantial bodies of knowledge such as English and foreign languages, literature, natural and physical sciences, history, and social sciences. The college curriculum is still more refined, subdivided, and sophisticated.

Realist instructional methodology involves three necessary elements: (1) a teacher who possesses and knows how to teach some skill or knowledge, (2) the actual skill or body of knowledge and (3) a student who lacks that skill or knowledge and who wants to learn it. This methodological strategy implies that a skill or body of knowledge must always be present in the teaching-learning relationship. In its absence, teaching degenerates into indoctrination or becomes an interpersonal relationship that lacks conscious instruction. Essentially, the teacher must know both the subject matter and how to teach it effectively.[5]

In terms of axiology, or ethical and aesthetic values, Realists tend to follow the ancient dictum of Aristotle that "man is a rational being." This means that human beings have the power to think, to frame alternatives, and to choose from among them. It is this power of choice that liberates human beings and gives them the possibility of being free men and women. When we make our choices, we should be guided by knowledge rather than by our appetites, emotions, or unfounded opinions. As choice makers, our best guide is knowledge such as that contained in the liberal arts and sciences. The word "liberal" here means that which liberates or frees.

Thomism

As a philosophy, Thomism closely resembles Realism. Indeed, it is a form of religious or theistic Realism that is associated largely with Roman Catholic theology and education. Its name is derived from that of Thomas Aquinas (1225–1274), a Dominican expert on theology and philosophy, who taught at the University of Paris in the thirteenth century. Aquinas effected a synthesis of Christian theology and Aristotelian philosophy.[6]

Similarly to Realists, Thomists assert the existence of an objective order of reality that we can come to know. For them, this reality has been created by God, a perfect spiritual being who is the cause and source of all existence. Human beings are endowed with a soul, a spirit, that gives them the power of reason and free will. The soul is immortal and has the possibility of having the direct vision of God that unites the faithful person to God after the death of the body.

Epistemologically, the Thomist, as does other Realists, asserts that we come to know the physical world through a twofold process of sensation and abstraction. Our knowledge of reality moves to a greater completion by revelation of God's word in the Scriptures, traditions, and teaching authority of the Church. Thomists contend that there is no conflict between faith and reason or between theology and science. Faith and reason are held to be complementary to each other and contribute to a more complete knowledge of reality.

The axiology of Thomism incorporates the values of Christianity and of reason. Since God is a Universal Creator, truth, goodness, and beauty are also universal, eternal, and unchanging. Although the circumstances of modern life may change, the principles that should guide action are found in the truths of faith and reason.

The aims of education, the function of the school, the curriculum, and

---

[5]William O. Martin, *Realism in Education* (New York: Harper & Row, 1969), pp. 3–18.

[6]John W. Donohue, S.J., *St. Thomas Aquinas and Education* (New York: Random House, 1968), pp. 23–57.

Thomism was a philosophy developed by Thomas Aquinas (1225–1274), a theologian at the medieval university of Paris. *(New York Public Library Picture Collection)*

the teacher-learner relationship are best viewed in Thomism by examining human nature. Human beings have twofold but complementary aspects to their nature. We have, they assert, a spiritual soul and a physical body. It is the soul that relates us most closely to God and that gives us the power of intellect. The body, living at a given time and place, has physical, economic, social, and political needs. The basic aim of education is to help men and women to experience divine truth and love so that they will live the kind of earthly life that will lead them to eternal life. Subsidiary educational aims are directed to meeting economic, social, political, intellectual, and aesthetic needs. While the school provides for its students' physical, social, and religious development, its essential function is intellectual.

The Thomistic curriculum reflects the dualistic character of human nature in that certain subjects are religious, based on or derived from theology, and others are social, political, cultural, and economic. The elementary school curriculum would include reading and language arts, arithmetic, history and geography, and religion. The secondary curriculum would include theology and religious education, language and literature, art and music, physical and natural sciences, history and social sciences, and in some instances logic. The milieu of the school is also very important in the students' education in that it should provide opportunities for religious liturgies, ceremonies, and observances that reinforce and exemplify the formal curriculum. In higher education, the Thomists prefer a traditional liberal arts and science curriculum that is arranged hierarchically. Theology and philosophy are given priority in the curriculum and are regarded as the disciplines that serve to integrate the total educational experience.

As is true of Idealism and Realism, the Thomist curriculum follows a subject matter arrangement. Thomists define a subject as *scientia,* a body of knowledge consisting of established principles and interpretations and conclusions based on these principles. The teacher is a mature person who possesses knowledge of these principles, their derivations, and applications and can transmit them to the student. The learner is regarded as possessing a capacity for actively acquiring and using these bodies of knowledge. Further, Thomists hold that teaching is highly integrative in that it incorporates both the contemplative and active modes of life. It is contemplative in that the teacher must be a researcher who quietly plans for instruction. Teaching, itself, is an activity by which the teacher motivates students and presents carefully organized bodies of knowledge to them.

Perennialism

Perennialism is an educational theory that is derived from the general philosophical orientation provided by Realism and Thomism. The word "perennial" as used here means that true educational principles are lasting, continuing, and reoccurring. Perennialist educators claim that truth, goodness, and beauty are eternal and unchanging. Although human beings have adapted themselves to varying geographical, historical, social, political, and economic circumstances, Perennialists claim that human nature has remained the same throughout the ages. The enduring quality and defining characteristic of human beings have been their rationality and their quest for truth. Education is designed to prepare human beings to use their rationality and to seek, find, and use the truth.

One of America's leading Perennialist advocates was Robert Maynard Hutchins (1899–1977), who argued that the real purpose of education was to draw out the elements of our common human nature, which were the same in any time or place. He argued further that (1) education implies teaching, (2) teaching implies knowledge, (3) knowledge is truth, and (4) since the truth is everywhere the same, education should also be everywhere the same.[7] Hutchins advocated an intellectual education based upon the arts and sciences and the enduring classics of Western civilization.

In curricular matters, the Perennialists stress permanent studies. In the elementary school, these are the tool skills of reading, writing, arithmetic, and reasoning. In secondary and higher education, they are language, grammar, rhetoric, history, logic, mathematics, ethics, politics, economics, and the physical and natural sciences. The curriculum is integrated by the great themes that have appeared in the enduring works of Western civilization.

Essentialism and Basic Education

With persistent regularity, there have been several movements in American education that have urged a return to the teaching of the essential or basic skills or subjects in the schools. Although there have been advocates of fundamental learning throughout the history of education, contemporary American education has witnessed three important movements: (1) the Essentialist movement of the 1930s, (2) the academic critics of the 1950s, and (3) the "Back to Basics" movement of the 1970s. Since these movements have many similar elements, we will treat them from the common theoretical perspective of Essentialism, or basic education, and will use the terms interchangeably.

In terms of philosophical orientation, Essentialism bears a strong resemblance to the traditional philosophies of Idealism, Realism, Thomism, and Perennialism. The proponents of Essentialism argue that (1) schools should be academic rather than social agencies, (2) curricular organization should be based on carefully selected and well-defined skills and subjects, (3) the teacher should be an authority figure, and (4) learning should be teacher directed.

The term "Essentialist" was used to identify a group of educators who organized the Essentialist Committee for the Advancement of American Education in 1938. The leading spokesperson for the committee was William C. Bagley, who wrote the "Essentialist's Platform."[8] The Essentialists developed both a critique and a program for American education. The Essentialist critique attacked several tendencies in American education that were regarded as weakening the academic standards of the schools. Among the Essentialist criticisms were the following: (1) the standards of achievement of American students in

---

[7]Robert M. Hutchins, *The Higher Learning in America* (New Haven, Conn.: Yale University Press, 1936), pp. 65–68.

[8]William C. Bagley, "An Essentialist Platform for the Advancement of American Education," *Educational Administration and Supervision*, 24 (April 1938), pp. 241–256.

fundamental skills and subjects were deficient in comparison to other countries, (2) increasing numbers of students in junior and senior high schools were functionally illiterate because of reading deficiencies, (3) many school systems had abandoned rigorous standards of scholastic achievement for promotion and merely passed students to higher grades on schedule, (4) progressive educators had weakened instruction by replacing exacting subjects with ill-defined projects and activities, and (5) an erroneous theory of child freedom had been used to eliminate discipline, order, and sequence from American schools.

To remedy the weaknesses that they perceived in American education, the Essentialists developed an educational theory that defined the role of the school, the nature of the curriculum, and the function of the teacher in terms of the learning of basic skills and subjects.

The school, according to the Essentialists, had the special function of transmitting the intellectual and social skills and knowledge that were a product of the long course of human civilization. This body of social and intellectual skills and knowledge constituted the "essentials" that were indispensable to the maintenance of a civilized society. Bagley's "Essentialist Platform" defined the essentials as (1) the basic civilized skills of reading, recording, computing, and measuring; (2) a perspective in time that acquainted the student with the past; (3) a widening of the space horizon through the study of geography; (4) health instruction and the inculcating of health practices; (5) the elements of natural science; (6) the fine arts; and (7) the industrial arts.[9]

In addition to a curriculum based on fundamental skills and subjects, the Essentialists argued that it was the responsibility of the teacher to organize and direct the school's instructional program. As a mature adult, the teacher was to guide, control, and direct the instruction of the immature. Instruction should be logical, structured, ordered, and sequential. Further, students should be impressed with the fact that learning required hard work and sustained effort.[10]

In the mid-1950s and early 1960s, a demand for more academic rigor in the schools occurred that was similar to the earlier Essentialist movement. Leading critics, such as Arthur Bestor, Max Rafferty, and Hyman Rickover, attacked declining academic standards, permissiveness, and "life adjustment" education and argued for a return to standards of academic excellence. In particular, Arthur Bestor, a professor of history and a founder of the Council for Basic Education, presented the arguments of the critics of the 1950s in his books, *Educational Wastelands* and *The Restoration of Learning*. Bestor charged that (1) academic standards in American schools had deteriorated because of an anti-intellectual philosophy that had divorced education from the scientific and scholarly disciplines and (2) a narrowly educated coalition of professional educators and bureaucrats had gained control of the teaching profession by manipulating certification requirements.[11] Bestor asserted that the trend to anti-intellectualism

[9]Ibid., 251–254.

[10]William C. Bagley, "Just What Is the Crux of the Conflict Between the Progressives and the Essentialists?" *Educational Administration and Supervision,* 26 (1940), pp. 508–511.

[11]Arthur E. Bestor, *Educational Wastelands* (Urbana: University of Illinois Press, 1953); *The Restoration of Learning* (New York: Knopf, 1955).

could be reversed if the schools returned to an academic program based on the rigorous study of intellectual disciplines. For Bestor, it was imperative that the secondary school curriculum should stress the systematic study of the intellectual disciplines of English, foreign languages, history, mathematics, and science.

In the 1970s, the general Essentialist point of view was revitalized by the "Back to Basics" movement. Although this contemporary Essentialism exhibits a variety of rather diverse tendencies that range from patriotism to drill, its most articulate forum has been the Council for Basic Education. A. Graham Down has stated that the council perceives of basic education as more than "three R's." It means that students "should receive competent instruction in all the fundamental disciplines, especially English, mathematics, history, geography, government, science, foreign languages, and the arts."[12]

In summary, the Essentialist position is a subject matter, teacher-centered theory of education. It assigns to schools a strictly academic function that views instruction as essentially an art of transmitting literary and mathematical skills in the elementary school and subjects, based on learned disciplines, in the secondary school. It is generally cautious of educational innovations of a methodological nature, preferring to rely on a curricular emphasis.

CONCLUSION

In this chapter, we have examined the general relationships that exist between philosophy and education. In particular, we have identified the areas of philosophy, such as metaphysics, epistemology, axiology, and logic, and have indicated the implications that they have for education. The more traditional educational philosophies of Idealism, Realism, Thomism, Perennialism, and Essentialism were examined. In the next chapter, we describe and analyze such recently developed philosophies as Experimentalism, Progressivism, Reconstructionism, Existentialism, and Philosophical Analysis. Areas of agreement among the traditional, pragmatic, and emerging philosophies are summarized in the listing that follows.

PHILOSOPHIES OF EDUCATION

Traditional Philosophies	*Areas of Agreement*
Idealism	Subject matter curriculum
Realism	Knowledge arranged in a hierarchy
Thomism	
Perennialism	Authority of the teacher
Essentialism	The school as an intellectual agency
	Content over method

[12]A. Graham Down, "Why Basic Education?" *The National Elementary Principal*, 57 (October 1977), pp. 28–32.

Pragmatic Philosophies	*Areas of Agreement*
Experimentalism	Emphasis on change
Progressivism	An activity or problem-solving curriculum
Reconstructionism	Focus on learner-centered instruction
	Use of experience and scientific method
	Relative "truth" and value

Emerging Philosophies	*Areas of Agreement*
Existentialism	Distrust of philosophical systems and categories
Philosophical Analysis	

DISCUSSION QUESTIONS

1. Analyze a particular class in the course in which this book is being used. To what degree is the language used in this class descriptive or prescriptive?
2. In class discussion in this course, try to determine the students' metaphysical, epistemological, and axiological views.
3. Analyze a chapter in a textbook in professional education. Try to arrive at the author's underlying philosophy.
4. Read and review a book in philosophy of education.
5. Compare and contrast the philosophies of education treated in this chapter.
6. What is the philosophical rationale for basic education?

FIELD EXERCISES

1. Visit a class in an elementary or secondary school. Observe the degree to which the language used in instruction in that class is descriptive or prescriptive.
2. Examine the curriculum guide that is being used in a particular school. Identify the general philosophical statements and try to determine how consistent the curriculum is with that statement.
3. Interview the instructor in this course and attempt to identify his or her philosophical assumptions.
4. Interview teachers at the kindergarten, primary, intermediate, and upper grade levels and try to identify their philosophical assumptions. Is there a relationship between their philosophy of education and the particular grade that they teach?
5. Interview an older friend, neighbor, or relative. Through questioning, attempt to identify his or her philosophy of education.

SUGGESTED READINGS

BESTOR, ARTHUR E. *Educational Wastelands*. Urbana: University of Illinois Press, 1953.
———. *The Restoration of Learning*. New York: Knopf, 1955.

BUTLER, J. DONALD. *Idealism in Education.* New York: Harper & Row, 1966.

DONOHUE, JOHN W., S.J. *St. Thomas Aquinas and Education.* New York: Random House, 1968.

GRUBER, FREDERICK C. *Historical and Contemporary Philosophies of Education.* New York: Thomas Y. Crowell, 1973.

GUTEK, GERALD L. *Philosophical Alternatives in Education.* Columbus, Ohio: Charles E. Merrill, 1974.

HOWICK, WILLIAM H. *Philosophies of Western Education.* Danville, Ill.: Interstate Printers and Publishers, 1971.

HUTCHINS, ROBERT M. *The Higher Learning in America.* New Haven, Conn.: Yale University Press, 1936.

LUCAS, CHRISTOPHER J. *What Is Philosophy of Education?* New York: Macmillan, 1969.

MARTIN, WILLIAM O. *Realism in Education.* New York: Harper & Row, 1969.

MORRIS, VAN CLEVE, AND PAI, YOUNG. *Philosophy and the School.* Boston: Houghton Mifflin, 1976.

OZMON, HOWARD. *Dialogue in the Philosophy of Education.* Columbus, Ohio: Charles E. Merrill, 1972.

SHERMIS, S. SAMUEL. *Philosophic Foundations of Education.* New York: American Book, 1967.

STOOPS, JOHN A. *Philosophy and Education in Western Civilization.* Danville, Ill.: Interstate Printers and Publishers, 1971.

TROXELL, EUGENE A., AND SNYDER, WILLIAM S. *Making Sense of Things: An Invitation to Philosophy.* New York: St. Martin's Press, 1976.

WILD, JOHN. *Introduction to Realist Philosophy.* New York: Harper and Brothers, 1948.

WINGO, G. MAX. *Philosophies of Education: An Introduction.* Lexington, Mass.: D. C. Heath, 1974.

WIRSING, MARIE E. *Teaching and Philosophy: A Synthesis.* Boston: Houghton Mifflin, 1972.

4

Modern Educational Philosophies

Chapter 3 examined traditional philosophies of education such as Idealism, Realism, Thomism, Perennialism, and Essentialism. In Chapter 4, more recently developed educational philosophies such as Experimentalism, Progressivism, Reconstructionism, Existentialism, and Philosophical Analysis are described and analyzed. The more traditional philosophies have existed throughout the centuries. For example, Idealism and Realism originated in ancient Greece; Thomism emerged in the medieval era. The philosophies treated in Chapter 4 are more recent developments of the late-nineteenth and twentieth centuries.

EXPERIMENTALISM

The Experimentalist philosophy of education was developed by John Dewey (1859–1952), one of America's leading advocates of Pragmatism. To establish the context of Experimentalism, it is first necessary to describe Pragmatism.

    The Pragmatic mood or temperament is typically associated with the American predilection on the practical, on practice, on usefulness. Benjamin Franklin, an early exponent of the merger of science and utility, wanted education to achieve practical results. In the American historical experience, the westward movement of the population into new frontiers required an elastic and flexible attitude that enabled the pioneers to adapt to different and initially inhospitable environments and to transform them into congenial and productive living places. The westward-moving frontier created a willingness to change and to experiment. It fostered an attitude in which people were close to and interacted with their environment.

Near the end of the nineteenth century, several thinkers placed the pragmatic American orientation into a philosophical context. In addition to the American pragmatic temperament, the Darwinian scientific revolution also had an impact on the development of Pragmatism. Charles Darwin's theory of evolution postulated that living organisms had evolved over the centuries as a result of successful adaptation to their environments. Rather than being created in final and fixed form, the various species of living creatures survived because of their ability to adapt to changing circumstances. It was in this context of the American attitude to change and the Darwinian scientific revolution that Charles Saunders Peirce, a mathematician, William James, a psychologist, and John Dewey, a philosopher, each in his own way, contributed to what became Pragmatism. Essentially, the Pragmatist viewpoint emphasized that

1. Human beings are intelligent, flesh-and-blood organisms who live in, interact with, and are capable of transforming their environment in ways that enhance life.
2. The world in which we live is an open, ever-changing universe in which human beings create their own purposes.
3. The most intelligent human behavior is to use the scientific method to solve problems.
4. To be valuable and valid, ideas must be tested in human experiences: ideas must work and have consequences that can be measured by their impact on our lives.

John Dewey

While Peirce and James contributed to Pragmatism, it was John Dewey who had the greatest impact on educational philosophy. Dewey, a native of Vermont, grew up in Burlington, a small New England city, where he experienced the democratic ethic and process. After attending local elementary and high schools, Dewey went on to college and to the recently established Johns Hopkins University, a graduate-level institution that was at the forefront of scholarly research. At Johns Hopkins, Dewey specialized in philosophy. From 1894 to 1904, Dewey was a professor at the University of Chicago where he founded the well-known Laboratory School, which enrolled children of elementary school age in an experimental educational setting. Many of Dewey's philosophical ideas either originated or were tested at the Laboratory School.[1]

[1]For accounts of Dewey's University of Chicago Laboratory School, see Katherine C. Mayhew and Anna C. Edwards, *The Dewey School* (New York: Appleton-Century, 1936); also, see Arthur G. Wirth, *John Dewey as Educator: His Design for Work in Education, 1894–1904* (New York: John Wiley, 1966).

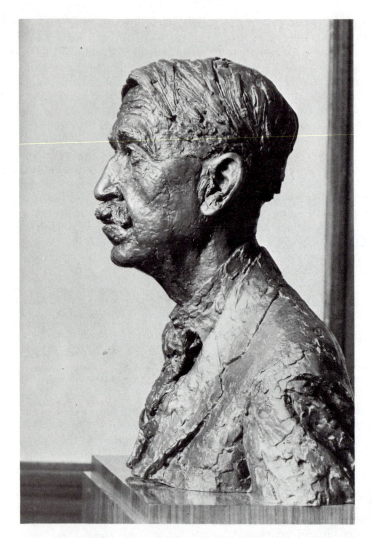

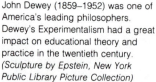

John Dewey (1859–1952) was one of America's leading philosophers. Dewey's Experimentalism had a great impact on educational theory and practice in the twentieth century. *(Sculpture by Epstein, New York Public Library Picture Collection)*

This experimental and progressive school emphasized that learning is an active process in which children act on their ideas to solve problems. After leaving the University of Chicago, Dewey joined the philosophy department of Columbia University. He was a prolific author whose articles and books dominated American philosophy of education during the first half of the twentieth century. In particular, Dewey's *Democracy and Education* put forth his general stance on educational philosophy; his *Experience and Education* summed up his impressions of progressive education.[2]

Dewey's brand of Pragmatism is referred to as Experimentalism or In-

[2]John Dewey, *Democracy and Education* (New York: Macmillan, 1906); *Experience and Education* (New York: Macmillan, 1938).

strumentalism. The following brief definitions of these terms illustrate his general philosophical orientation:

> *Experimentalism* is a philosophy that emphasizes that we learn by using the scientific method to solve our problems; life is like a laboratory in which we experiment to solve our problems.
>
> *Instrumentalism,* another name for Experimentalism, emphasizes that objects in the environment are instruments that become our tools to accomplish tasks and to solve problems. More important, ideas are also instruments or tools that can be used to accomplish our purposes.

With this general orientation, we can examine the Experimentalist conception of metaphysics, epistemology, axiology, and logic—the basic subdivisions of philosophy.

Metaphysics

Unlike the traditional philosophies of Idealism, Realism, and Thomism, Experimentalism is not concerned with metaphysical issues. The traditional philosophies build their whole philosophical structure on a metaphysical base. For example, Idealism builds its structure on the Absolute Idea, and Realism builds its structure on the matter-form hypothesis. Experimentalists view such metaphysical bases as empirically nonverifiable since they cannot be tested in human experience. Rather than searching for metaphysical absolutes, Dewey identified the human being or human organism and the environment as the base of human experience. Human beings live within and interact with an environment. They can alter the environment but are also changed by that environment. In educational terms, the learner lives within an environment, often a school situation. That learning environment has problems within it that are occasions for learning to occur.

Epistemology

Experimentalists are heavily involved with the issue of epistemology, or the process of how we know and learn. In fact, experimentalism is often referred to as a process-oriented philosophy. Dewey and other Pragmatists assert that we know most accurately when we use the scientific method to solve our problems. In educational terms, learning is problem solving.

Dewey developed a five-step method of problem solving called the "Complete Act of Thought." The five steps are

1. The person encounters a problem that is a condition or factor that is new and different from previous experience. This new situation means that the learner is involved in a *problematic situation.*
2. To begin to resolve the problematic situation, it is necessary to identify and define exactly what it is that is causing the problem. In other words, the person needs to *define the problem.*
3. Once the problem has been defined, the person can investigate the various factors or characteristics of the situation. Such an investigation in-

volves *reflecting on past experience* with similar situations, *doing research,* and *gathering information* that may be useful in solving the problem.

4. After the problem has been researched sufficiently, the person constructs some possible ways of solving the problem. These possible solutions, called *tentative hypotheses,* can be stated as "if then" statements. If I choose to do such and such, then this is likely to happen.

5. The last step in problem solving is to choose the tentative hypothesis that is most likely to solve the problem and to test it by acting upon it. In Dewey's method of problem solving, it is necessary to act; merely conjecturing consequences is incomplete.

For Dewey and the Experimentalists, the "Complete Act of Thought" or problem solving according to the scientific method is not only the way in which we think correctly but it is also the most effective method of teaching and learning. Problem solving can be used by primary-aged children who may be experimenting with establishing a balanced aquarium or with gardening. It can be used by more advanced students to define and deal with a wide range of problems. Each time that students solve a problem successfully, they add the solution to their repertoire of experience. Each problem-solving episode will lead to other problems and to an increase in the student's network of experience.

Axiology

Dewey placed great emphasis on publicly shared experience, which to him was a foundation of a democratic society. In a democracy, the people shared much in common; they held commonly shared values and aspirations; they were free to and indeed expected to participate in enjoying the benefits and in solving the problems of the society. A democratic society, Dewey reasoned, was an open and experimental community.

Dewey and the Experimentalists placed great emphasis on the educational possibilities of the human group. Children were to work together in defining and solving problems. Each participant contributed his or her unique skills and resources to solving the group's common problems. This mutual sharing was a socially enriching form of human experience.

Ethics and aesthetics in Experimentalism were arrived at socially, publicly, and experimentally. As society changed, ethical norms and aesthetic standards were also subject to change. Unlike the more traditional philosophies that asserted that ethics and aesthetics were based on unchanging universals, Experimentalists claimed them to be variable with time and relative to culture.

Logic

For Experimentalists like Dewey, logic followed the inductive route of going from the particular instance or case to the general principle. Correct reasoning followed the scientific method. It was empirical and publicly verifiable.

School and Society

When he founded his Laboratory School in Chicago at the turn of the century, Dewey saw his new experimental school as a "miniature society" and an "embryonic community." Throughout his career, Dewey continued to stress the close and intimate relationship of the school to the society that it served. Unlike the strictly academic institution of the Idealists and Realists, Dewey's school was part of society and involved in its problems. Learning was not to be isolated within the four walls of the school; rather, schooling was to be part of the ongoing life of the society.

PROGRESSIVISM

Progressive education has had its zealous proponents and its vociferous detractors. Advocates of Basic Education trace many social ills and educational weaknesses to the influence of progressive educators. Progressives see themselves as agents of an education that liberates human beings. It is difficult to define or describe Progressive Education, since many different educators—often with conflicting viewpoints—gathered under the umbrellalike standard of Progressivism.[3] An historical perspective is useful in understanding progressive education.

Progressive Education in Historical Perspective: Antitraditionalism

The major outlooks of Progressive Education can be examined in two dimensions: (1) the long-standing attack on the traditionalism of formal schooling and (2) the Progressive Movement in American society, politics, and education. As these two dimensions of Progressivism are examined, it should be noted that Progressive Education is more a mood, a temperament, a posture, and an ideology than a fully developed philosophy.

Throughout history, the school has been a formal institution, governed by routine and regulation, in which learning is defined as the study and mastery of literary materials, especially books. In such a setting, teachers tend to lecture and students tend to recite prescribed lessons. Throughout history, there have been educators who challenged and sought to change schooling into an active rather than a passive center of learning.

Many of the individuals who have been identified as educational reformers such as Comenius, Rousseau, Pestalozzi, Froebel, Francis Parker, and John Dewey contributed to the idea and practices associated with Progressive Education. Although they differed in particulars, these educational reformers generally asserted that

1. Children should be viewed as active rather than as passive agents in the learning process. Education should begin with the child's interests, needs, and problems rather than with a curriculum prescribed and organized by adults.
2. Learning is an active process in which learners investigate and explore their own environment, thoughts, and emotions.

[3]The definitive history of progressivism in education is Lawrence A. Cremin, *The Transformation of the School* (New York: Random House, 1961); the Progressive Education Association has been examined in Patricia A. Graham's, *Progressive Education: From Arcady to Academe* (New York: Teachers College Press, Columbia University, 1967).

3. Teachers should be flexible persons who facilitate learning by stimulating the interests of children or arranging the environment in ways that excite curiosity and interests.

4. The school environment should be designed to encourage learning; it should be capable of flexible arrangements that can be varied to accommodate the different projects that arise in child and student life.

5. The atmosphere or milieu of the school and the personality of the teacher should be open and permissive. There should be no psychological or physical coercion or punishment.

Progressivism in American Life and Education

While Progressive Education in the United States shared a broad anti-traditionalist orientation, it also was part of the Progressive Movement in American society, politics, and education. Historians have identified the period from 1900 to 1920 as the "Progressive Era" in American history. In these two decades, leaders such as Theodore Roosevelt, Woodrow Wilson, and Robert LaFollette dominated American politics and inaugurated a series of regulatory reforms to control trusts and monopolies and to open political processes to more direct, popular participation. Social reformers such as Jane Addams worked in the settlement house movement to aid youths in the big cities and to assist in the assimilation of immigrants. John Dewey, Jane Addams, and others associated with Progressive Education saw it as an instrument of broad social reform.

In the years from the end of World War I to the beginning of the New Deal, from 1919 to 1932, political Progressivism was eclipsed by a conservative reaction. However, Progressive Education flourished in the 1920s and 1930s, especially in private schools and many teacher education institutions. In the 1920s, Progressive Education lost many of its broad social and political reform impulses and concentrated on the liberation of the child through the liberalizing of the school.

Progressive Education Orientation

In 1919, educators of a Progressive orientation met in Washington, D.C. to organize the Progressive Education Association. The new organization enlisted various types of progressive educators to its ranks, such as Deweyite Experimentalists and advocates of child freedom.

Progressives who followed Dewey's pragmatic Experimentalist philosophy included professors of education such as William H. Kilpatrick, Harold Rugg, George S. Counts, and John Childs who were to make their own contribution to Progressive Education.

Progressive educators often differed among themselves and lacked a unifying comprehensive educational philosophy. However, they agreed in their antagonism to the following traditional school practices:

1. the teacher who rules the classroom in an authoritarian manner;
2. the exclusive reliance on textbooks and bookish methods of instruction;
3. passive learning that stressed the memorization of facts as its own end;

4. the attempt to isolate schools from social change, conflicts, and issues; and

5. the use of psychological coercion and physical punishment as a means of maintaining order and discipline.

Progressives not only opposed traditional practices but they also developed their own educational principles. Among the principles adopted by the Progressive Education Association were that

1. children should be free to develop naturally;
2. interest, arising from direct experience, is the best stimulus for learning;
3. the teacher should be a researcher into educational processes and a guide to learning;
4. there should be close cooperation between the school and home; and
5. the progressive school should be a laboratory for educational reform and experimentation.[4]

Progressive educators devised alternative instructional models that stressed activities, field trips, problem solving, projects, and other nontraditional educational approaches. These alternatives centered on the child rather than on the subject matter; they emphasized activities rather than passive memorization and recitations; they encouraged cooperative and socially involved group learning rather than individualized lesson learning and personal competition among children. Progressives often viewed the use of democratic procedures in schools to be a prelude to community social reform. Progressives, who generally took a culturally relativistic approach to values, often challenged traditional customs and norms.

As was true of the Experimentalists, Progressives were generally not concerned with questions of abstract philosophical speculation, or metaphysics. While Perennialism and Essentialism were educational theories derived from Realism and Idealism, Progressivism was similarly an antitraditional educational theory rather than a systemic philosophy of education. In terms of epistemology, Progressives tended to see knowledge as tentative rather than absolute and unchanging. They preferred to concentrate on the process of learning rather than on the content of knowledge. Their axiological approach was equally tentative and relative. As with the Experimentalists, their tendency was to see values, ethics, and aesthetics in tentative and relativistic terms. By examining several of the major types of Progressive educators, it is possible to gain a better insight into the variety of educational positions that clustered together under the progressive orientation.

Progressive educators of a Deweyite persuasion saw education as a process by which learners used the scientific method to solve problems. Frequently, the project method was used in progressive schools. The project method was designed by William Heard Kilpatrick (1871–1965), a leader in Progressive Ed-

[4]Graham, *Progressive Education: From Arcady to Academe*, p. 51.

The project method, designed by William H. Kilpatrick, encourages learners to plan and implement their own learning experiences. *(Ken Karp)*

ucation and a professor at Columbia University's Teachers College.[5] Kilpatrick opposed traditional schooling as being authoritarian, too formal, and abstract from the learner's interests. In contrast, Kilpatrick claimed that his project method motivated children to take the initiative for their education by encouraging them to plan, direct, and execute their own learning.[6] Students would work in groups on a variety of projects. Some students might design stage properties and costumes for the school play. Others might investigate local politics by studying city govenment and taking field trips to various municipal agencies. Students might also work on construction projects in which they designed and built school museums, gardens, and play areas. Kilpatrick believed that the project method encouraged scientific attitude, cooperative democratic behavior, and practical skills.

In addition to Experimentalists, another important group of Progressive educators were child-centered persons who wanted to liberate childhood from repressive child-rearing practices and authoritarian schooling. Convinced that learning should come directly from children's interest and needs, Progressive champions of child freedom opposed having adults impose their objectives and values on children. Children should be free to learn according to their own impulses, needs, wants, and desires.

An early pioneer of child-centered Progressivism was Francis W. Parker (1837–1902). In his work at the Chicago Normal School, Parker distilled the educational concepts of Rousseau, Pestalozzi, and Froebel as a base for his own

[5]Samuel Tenenbaum, *William Heard Kilpatrick: Trail Blazer in Education* (New York: Harper and Brothers, 1951).

[6]William H. Kilpatrick, *The Project Method* (New York: Teachers College Press, Columbia University, 1921).

educational method that encouraged children to learn directly from nature and the objects present in their environment. Through his talks and lectures to teachers, Parker was an early disciple of child freedom.[7]

Marietta Pierce Johnson (1864–1938), founder of the School of Organic Education at Fairhope, Alabama, was also a well-known advocate of child-centered Progressivism. Her theory of organic education sought to educate the whole child—mentally, emotionally, and physically as well as cognitively. Seeking to prolong childhood as a time of crucial human growth and development, Johnson delayed introducing formal exercises in reading and writing until age ten. Organic education emphasized the development of creativity through field trips, handicrafts, and imaginative drama.[8] The concept of the "whole child" was emphasized by Progressive educators to bring about a broadened and enriched curriculum that included more than strictly academic subjects.

Child-centered Progressive educators such as Marietta Johnson opposed imposing adult standards and requirements upon children. In particular, they were especially opposed to using the school as an agency for indoctrinating children. In the 1930s, child-centered Progressives split off from their Social Reconstructionist colleagues in the movement.

Found among child-centered Progressives were neo-Freudian educators who were influenced by Sigmund Freud's psychoanalytical theory. Exalting the principle that children should have freedom of self-expression, they wanted to purge child rearing and educational practices from anything that repressed children's impulses. Neo-Freudian educators traced many emotional and psychological maladjustments to the repression of needs and drives in early childhood. They wanted teachers to undergo psychoanalysis so that they could be free to create nonrepressive classroom environments.

George Green, a leader in the application of psychoanalysis to schooling, found the classroom to be an emotionally charged environment for both children and teachers. He recommended that teachers use psychoanalytical methods to identify children's needs and to promote the cause of child freedom.[9]

In cultivating the "whole child" concept, some Progressive educators turned to art as both a way of learning and as a means of releasing children's creativity. Harold Rugg, Caroline Pratt, and other Progressives developed the concept of the artist-teacher, an educator whose teaching was a form of artistry. Caroline Pratt (1867–1954), who founded the Play School in New York's Greenwich Village, stressed creativity as the basis of learning. Emphasizing the creative use of direct experience, the children in Pratt's Play School took numerous field trips to parks, zoos, art galleries, fields, forests, and museums. When they returned to the Play School after their field trips, the children were encouraged to portray what they had seen and experienced. They were encouraged to act as artists and to use a variety of artistic media, such as clay, paints, paper, cardboard, and crayons to externalize their concepts. Progressives, like Caroline

---

[7]Francis Parker, *Talks on Pedagogics* (New York: John Day, 1937). For a biography of Parker, see Jack Campbell, *The Children's Crusader* (New York: Teachers College Press, Columbia University, 1967).

[8]Marietta P. Johnson, *Youth in a World of Men* (New York: John Day, 1929).

[9]George H. Green, *Psychoanalysis in the Classroom* (New York: Putnam, 1922).

Pratt, viewed children as artists who had an intense desire to express their own reality as they had experienced it.

SOCIAL RECONSTRUCTIONISM

As indicated earlier in this chapter, the early stage of the Progressive Education movement closely related educational reform to social reform. By the 1920s, however, the social reform impulse in Progressive Education subsided and was eclipsed by the child-centered orientation. During the Great Depression of the 1930s, some Progressives such as George S. Counts believed that Progressive Education should seek to create a cooperative society in which wealth would be shared more equitably. Counts later broadened his call to all educators in his *Dare the School Build a New Social Order?*[10]

Counts's challenge to the educational profession was the genesis of the Social Reconstructionist philosophy of education. Basically, Counts's argument was the following:

1. Western civilization, including that in the United States, had experienced a great transformation from an agricultural and rural society into one that was industrial and technological.
2. Although material change had occurred, Western civilization's values had lagged behind the course of technological change.
3. Human beings were still following archaic individualistic and selfish patterns of behavior.
4. World War I and the Great Depression were symptoms of a lack of cooperative planning.
5. Education needed to reduce the cultural lag between mankind's material knowledge and values; it needed to prepare people to plan and to implement a design for a cooperative society.

Counts's call to "build a new social order" attracted adherents from the ranks of progressive educators. Eventually, Social Reconstructionism developed into a distinctive educational ideology that contained both an analysis of society and a plan for social reform.

Social Reconstructionists argue that civilization is in a state of profound cultural crisis. If schools continue to mirror the social status quo, then Reconstructionists claim that schooling will merely transmit societal ills and injustices. Schools will really be training children to play the roles required in an archaic and self-destructive society. Rather than relying on metaphysics as a theoretical rationale, Reconstructionist educators use the findings and methods of such social sciences as economics, anthropology, sociology, and psychology to provide the basis for their plans of social reform.

Social Reconstructionists want to use education as a means of designing policies that will bring about a new society. Such an education, they argue, cannot

[10]George S. Counts, *Dare the School Build a New Social Order?* (New York: John Day, 1932).

be neutral but must be committed to bringing about deliberate social change. It must prepare future generations to be social engineers who can use science and technology to create a new and better world society.

According to Reconstructionists, educators, teachers, students, and schools should

1. identify major social problems by critically examining the present condition of society;
2. analyze social problems, issues, and controversies with the aim of resolving them in ways that enhance human growth and development;
3. be committed to bringing about constructive social change and reform;
4. cultivate a planning attitude among students that will be carried into adult citizenship activities; and
5. join in promoting definite programs of social, educational, political, and economic reform.

Social Reconstructionists believe that a new society can be created only as educators challenge obsolete conceptions of education and schooling and initiate carefully planned change that will lead to social reform. Since social sciences such as anthropology, economics, sociology, political science, and psychology are useful in providing the background and methods for planned social change, they should be emphasized in the curriculum. Education should awaken the students' consciousness about social problems by encouraging them to question the status quo and to examine controversial issues in religion, society, economics, politics, and education. By examining rather than ignoring controversial issues, the Reconstructionists believe that students will develop alternatives to the status quo.

The Reconstructionist teacher should encourage and respect divergent thinking by students. Divergent thinking should not be purely intellectual but should be used instrumentally to create alternative political, social, and economic institutions and processes.

Social Reconstructionists assert that a truly progressive education should create a world order in which people plan their own future. Future oriented rather than past oriented, Reconstructionists contend that traditional schooling is based on the past to the neglect of the future. If people are to control their own destinies, it is important that schools include futuristic studies in the curriculum.

Reconstructionists insist that teachers lead students to examine critically their culture. They should identify major areas of controversy, conflict, and inconsistency and seek to resolve them.[11] For example, the curriculum should include units on such problems as overpopulation, environmental pollution, world poverty, violence, and war. Education should examine these world problems and seek to resolve them so that people can improve the quality of life on the planet.

[11]Theodore Brameld, *Toward a Reconstructed Philosophy of Education* (New York: Dryden Press, 1965).

The Reconstructionists believe that technology has created an interdependent world. Events in one region of the earth will have an impact in other regions. In such an interdependent world, traditional schooling that stressed the past is obsolete. The new education must stress the reality of an interdependent and international world. Reconstructionists seek to internationalize the curriculum so that students learn that they are living in an interdependent world culture.

EXISTENTIALISM

Existentialism is a recent development in both philosophy and educational philosophy. Although its roots can be traced back into the beginnings of Western thought, Existentialism gained its greatest popularity after World War II. Some commentators observed that Existentialism was a reaction against the attempt of totalitarian regimes to destroy personal choice and freedom. In a contemporary sense, Existentialism presents a philosophical alternative to the standardization and mass conformity of the modern technological society. As with other recent developments in philosophy, Existentialism does not easily fit the metaphysical, epistemological, axiological, and logical divisions of the more traditional philosophical systems. Indeed, Existentialism is antithetical to attempts at systematization.

Existentialists view life in a very personal way.[12] Whereas Existentialism conveys a feeling of desperation with the human condition, it also brings forth a feeling of hope that human beings have the capacity to achieve true personal freedom. The word "feeling" is important for Existentialists, as it conveys the total human experience. Life is emotional and affective as well as intellectual. To achieve true personal freedom and authenticity, Existentialist educators emphasize personal reflection and commitment on life's significant choices.

Jean-Paul Sartre, the Existentialist thinker, once wrote that "Existence precedes essence." For Sartre, human beings are born into a world that is without an intrinsic purpose. They simply appear in the world at birth and as they become conscious are faced with a number of choices. While some choices are inconsequential, others reach to the very meaning of life and lead to personal self-definition. Human beings create their own definition or, as Sartre would have it, make their own essence. They are what they choose to be.

The more traditional philosophical systems of Idealism, Realism, and Thomism hold that we inhabit an orderly and purposeful universe. For them, human life draws its meaning from the very purpose that God or reality assigns to it. In contrast, most Existentialists assert that individuals live in a purposeless world and must create their own meaning in life. Christian Existentialists recognize that they live in a purposeful world, but they also assert that the individual person ultimately must make a decision to identify with God's purpose for humankind.

The Existentialist conception of a human being as an "essence creator" differs from the Idealists and Realists who see the person as a universal category.

[12]George F. Kneller, *Existentialism and Education* (New York: John Wiley, 1958).

Such a categorical definition is a precondition that circumscribes human free-dom. Since human freedom is total, the Existentialists, in contrast, claim that the individual has a total responsibility for choice.

Angst, or the feeling of pervasive dread, is an important Existentialist concept. Each person lives with the knowledge that his or her destiny is an inevitable one—death and disappearance. He or she knows that his or her presence in the world is but temporary. The individual bears this knowledge of ultimate demise and disappearance during every conscious moment. It is with this sense of dread that each person must make the choices that define him or her as a human being. In making the important decisions of life, only the choice maker knows how the choice affects the meaning of his or her life. As indicated, Existentialism believes that human life carries with it feelings of both desperation and hope. Human beings are desperate creatures who know that their life is temporary and their disappearance inevitable. They live in a world in which they are constantly encountering others—persons, institutions, and agencies—that are obstacles to choice and freedom. It is easy to pretend to abandon choice to other persons or institutions. Such abandonment is merely a pretense to escape from responsibility. Those who claim to be following orders have to choose to do so. Ultimately, the real question is, Do I choose to be self-determined or do I choose to let others define me? Every person can choose to be inner directed and authentic if he or she has the consciousness and courage to be such a person. An authentic person, who is free and aware of freedom, realizes that every choice is a personal decision. The authentic person is aware that self-definition is a personal responsibility.[13]

Existentialist Educational Implications

Existentialism has many implications for teachers and students. It seeks to create a certain consciousness and attitude about learning. The Existentialists know that physical reality exists; they also know that science is a necessary and useful part of the curriculum. However, many significant choices are personal and nonscientific. Existentialists contend that our most important knowledge is about the human condition and personal choice. Education is a way of developing consciousness about the human condition, the freedom to choose, and the personal responsibilities that authenticity brings to persons who seek to be free. An Existentialist education seeks to raise consciousness by examining choice making in its many human dimensions.

Existentialist educators encourage students to philosophize about the meaning of the human experiences of life, love, and death. An Existentialist teacher poses questions to stimulate self-consciousness. Such questioning, it is hoped, will grow into a dialogue among the students. The answers to these questions are personal and subjective. For questions of personal meaning, no single answer is correct for everyone.

An Existentialist curriculum would emphasize philosophizing, or dialogue, between students and between students and teacher. It would examine individual choice making. Since Existentialism is so personal and subjective, it

[13]Van Cleve Morris, *Existentialism in Education* (New York: Harper & Row, 1966).

vivifies life's emotional, aesthetic, and poetic dimensions. In an Existentialist curriculum, literature and biography are important means of examining personal choice.[14] Drama and film that portray the human condition and dilemma should be discussed by students. To create their own modes of self-expression, students should experiment with artistic media to dramatize their emotions, feelings, and insights. In the Existentialist school, teachers and students should be free to engage in dialogue and discussion about their own lives, choices, and identities. Subjects should be studied that illuminate choice making by examining the human condition as presented in literature, drama, biography, and history.

PHILOSOPHICAL ANALYSIS

Philosophical Analysis, a philosophical technique for analyzing language, was developed in the early twentieth century by philosophers who were dissatisfied with speculative philosophical systems.[15] G. E. Moore and Bertrand Russell were two pioneering theorists in developing the methods used by Analytical Philosophers. Russell, who sought to identify the logical structures underlying language usage, saw the task of philosophy as that of formulating the logical rules upon which language is based. The ideas of Russell and Moore were developed by other Philosophical Analysts, such as Ludwig Wittgenstein and his Vienna Circle.

Philosophical Analysis rejects the metaphysical bases of Idealism, Realism, Thomism, and other traditional philosophies that claim to be complete philosophical systems. For Analysts, metaphysical systems are pure speculation without verifiable meaning. They contend that metaphysics cannot be verified or tested in human experience. Analysts are also critical of some of the more recently developed contemporary philosophies. Existentialism, for example, is regarded as being too subjective, emotional, and poetical to be used as a basis for making educational policy decisions. Existentialist subjectivism obscures meaning rather than clarifies it. Social Reconstructionism, too, is regarded as another ideology that is merely contesting in political fashion against competing ideologies. Although Pragmatism is somewhat more acceptable because it relies on the scientific method, the language used by some Pragmatists in education is regarded as unclear. Such terms as "growth," "democracy," "consensus," and the "whole child," for example, commonly used by Experimentalist educators are regarded by Analysts as jargon ridden and in need of further clarification.

Philosophical Analysis is designed to analyze the language used in everyday as well as in technical discourse. In particular, it is used by educational theorists who believe that our communication about education has grown confused, polemical, and jargon ridden. To establish meaning, Analysts seek to render educational statements into empirical terms that are verifiable. Rather than being a systematic philosophy as is Realism or an ideology as is Social Reconstructionism, Philosophical Analysis provides a method for clarifying ed-

---

[14]Maxine Greene, *Existential Encounters for Teachers* (New York: Random House, 1967).

[15]D. J. O'Connor, *An Introduction to Philosophy of Education* (New York: Random House, 1957).

ucational issues. This clarifying process is regarded as a first step in resolving educational controversies and in explaining educational policies.

In clarifying the way in which we express ideas, the Analysts begin with the sentences used to express our propositions about reality. They regard only some of our sentences as candidates for meaningful expression. Meaningful sentences are valid either analytically or empirically.[16]

The following kinds of sentences may be examined as illustrations of the procedures used by Analysts to clarify language.

Analytical Propositions

Analytical propositions are statements in which the subject of the sentence is accepted as true and in which the predicate expresses the same thing or carries the identical value as the subject. Analytical propositions are often mathematical, for example,

$8 = 4 + 4$ (The number 8 is accepted as valid; $4 + 4$ means the same thing as 8. Note that $4 + 4$ tells us the same thing as is expressed by 8.)

Empirically Verifiable Statements

Empirically verifiable statements are candidates for presenting new information or knowledge to use. These statements are meaningful if they can be tested and verified. For example,

Paris is the capital city of France. (We can establish that Paris is a city, that France is a nation-state, and that Paris is its capital.)

John Brown weighs 185 lbs. (We can identify a person named John Brown, place him on an accurate scale, and determine his weight.)

While only analytical and empirically verifiable statements convey meaning from one person to another, there are other statements that, while they appear to carry meaning, are really subjective or emotional expressions. For example, the Idealist statement that "the world is spirit," and the Existentialist statement that "existence precedes essence" appear to be meaningful, but they are statements affirming their authors' commitment to believe that they are true. The Analysts would most likely assert that "the world is spirit" is not analytically valid nor is "existence precedes essence" empirically valid. The Analysts caution us to observe that many statements made in politics, philosophy, and education that purport to be factual are in reality merely preferences expressed by their author.

Philosophical Analysis is a response to the knowledge and communications explosions of the twentieth century. Human occupations, professions, and specializations have grown increasingly technical and complicated. Each specialty

---

[16]Albert J. Taylor, *An Introduction to the Philosophy of Education* (Dubuque, Iowa: Kendall/Hunt, 1978), pp. 142–148.

has developed its own language that is used by the experts in that field. The growing use of highly specialized terminologies has made it difficult to communicate across areas of specialization. By clarifying the language used in a complex technological society, the Philosophical Analysts seek to make our communication more meaningful.

Since education is simultaneously a public as well as a technical matter, it, too, is beset by the same problems of communication and meaning found in other areas of life. Public education in the United States involves national, state, and local politics; it is subject to the demands and particular programs of competing special-interest groups. Much that claims to be sound education upon examination can be found to mask special interests. The close examination of the language used in educational policy statements can serve to clarify and explain the true intent of the individuals and groups making these statements.

As a profession, education involves many areas of specialization. It involves social workers, psychologists, administrators, curriculum makers, sociologists, historians, philosophers, teachers, subject matter experts, and many other specialists. Each of these areas of specialization has brought its own specialized language into the field of education. It often becomes difficult for the various experts within education to communicate in a meaningful dialogue with each other. Language analysis can help those who work in education to understand and to communicate with each other.

CONCLUSION

Philosophy of education is one of the most basic and fundamental concerns of teachers. Although those beginning to teach will face many urgent problems in the early stages of their careers they will eventually come to consider the purpose of what they are doing with their life. Questions of basic purpose and meaning are never easy to deal with because they involve large and often seemingly overwhelming decisions and commitments. Philosophical thinking involves the difficult undertaking of trying to see your life and the lives of others in the most general terms. The abstract thought that philosophical thinking requires is reflective and eventually calls for judgments to be made. If you do not now have a philosophy of education, you will eventually develop one. As you philosophize about education and your role in it, consider the following questions:

1. What do I believe is ultimately real in life, in the world, and in my existence? How does my conception of reality influence what I teach children?

2. How do we know what we claim to know? What is the process by which we know? Is my conception of knowledge and knowing reflected in my teaching?

3. What is it that I hold to be valuable and beautiful? What are my values, ethics, and perceptions of beauty? How do values enter into my teaching and into the lives of those I encounter? What is the basis for my standards of conduct, behavior, and performance for myself and for others?

4. What are the principles by which I organize my life, my time, my modes of instruction?
5. Most important, what is the basis for my interaction with other human beings? What is my perception of human personality and human dignity?

DISCUSSION QUESTIONS

1. Prepare and present to the class short biographical sketches of Charles Peirce, William James, and John Dewey. Attempt to establish how their experiences contributed to the formulation of Pragmatism.
2. Read one of John Dewey's books and review it for class discussion.
3. Define the following terms: Pragmatism, Experimentalism, Instrumentalism, Scientific Method, Progressivism, Social Reconstructionism.
4. Describe the Progressive orientation to life and education.
5. Identify and examine the difference between a child-centered Progressive view of education and a Social Reconstructionist view.
6. Reflect on and discuss the possibilities of creating an Existentialist school.
7. Describe the functions of Philosophical Analysis.

FIELD EXERCISES

1. Invite a philosopher of education at your college or university to visit your class and to present his or her philosophy of education.
2. Visit a nontraditional school and report to the class on that school's underlying philosophy.
3. Design an activity for use in the classroom based on Dewey's "Complete Act of Thought."
4. Design an activity for classroom use based on Kilpatrick's project method.
5. Debate the proposition: Resolved, the school should build a new social order.
6. Identify a drama or book in which individuals face significant choice-making situations; then lead a class discussion that examines these choices.
7. Select a paragraph from a textbook used in an education course. Analyze the paragraph according to the procedures used by Philosophical Analysts.

SUGGESTED READINGS

BAYLES, ERNEST E. *Pragmatism in Education.* New York: Harper & Row, 1966.

BRAMELD, THEODORE. *Toward a Reconstructed Philosophy of Education.* New York: Holt, Rinehart and Winston, 1956.

CHILDS, JOHN. *American Pragmatism and Education.* New York: Holt, Rinehart and Winston, 1956.

COUNTS, GEORGE S. *Dare the School Build a New Social Order?* New York: John Day, 1932.

CREMIN, LAWRENCE. *The Transformation of the School: Progressivism in American Education, 1876–1957.* New York: Knopf, 1961.

DEWEY, JOHN. *The Child and the Curriculum.* Chicago: University of Chicago Press, 1902.

———. *Democracy and Education.* New York: Macmillan, 1916.

———. *Experience and Education.* New York: Macmillan, 1938.

———. *The School and Society.* Chicago: University of Chicago Press, 1923.

FITZGIBBONS, ROBERT E. *Making Educational Decisions: An Introduction to Philosophy of Education.* New York: Harcourt Brace Jovanovich, 1981.

GRAHAM, PATRICIA A. *Progressive Education: From Arcady to Academe.* New York: Teachers College Press, Columbia University, 1967.

GREENE, MAXINE. *Existential Encounters for Teachers.* New York: Random House, 1967.

GUTEK, GERALD L. *The Educational Theory of George S. Counts.* Columbus: Ohio State University Press, 1970.

KILPATRICK, WILLIAM H. *The Project Method.* New York: Teachers College Press, Columbia University, 1921.

KNELLER, GEORGE F. *Existentialism and Education.* New York: John Day, 1964.

MORRIS, VAN CLEVE. *Existentialism in Education: What It Means.* New York: Harper & Row, 1966.

O'CONNOR, D. J. *An Introduction to the Philosophy of Education.* London: Routledge and Kegan Paul, 1957.

POWER, EDWARD J. *Philosophy of Education: Studies in Philosophies, Schooling, and Educational Policies.* Englewood Cliffs, N.J.: Prentice-Hall, 1982.

RUGG, HAROLD O., AND SCHUMAKER, ANN. *The Child-Centered School.* New York: World Book, 1928.

SCHEFFLER, ISRAEL. *Conditions of Knowledge.* Glenview, Ill.: Scott, Foresman, 1965.

SOLTIS, JONAS F. *An Introduction to the Analysis of Educational Concepts.* Reading, Mass.: Addison-Wesley, 1968.

WASHBURNE, CARLETON. *What Is Progressive Education?* New York: John Day, 1952.

WIRTH, ARTHUR. *John Dewey and Education: His Design for Work in Education, 1894–1904.* New York: John Wiley, 1966.

5

Multicultural Education

In recent years, educators have given attention to the multicultural dimension of American society. This emphasis is based on the growing realization that the United States is composed of a variety of religious, ethnic, social, and linguistic groups and that each of these groups has a unique contribution to make to the still unfinished American social fabric. The respect for ethnic and social diversity, known as multiculturalism, reverses the patterns of earlier years when public schooling was conceived of as an agency for cultural assimilation or homogenization. Chapter 5 examines the rise of multicultural education and explores its impact on American education.

PUBLIC SCHOOLING AND ETHNICITY

As every child learns in social studies and history, the United States is a nation of immigrants. With the exception of American Indians, all others—Europeans, Africans, Hispanics, and Oriental Americans—were once newcomers to the United States. The patterns of immigration from the founding of the British colonies in North America until the midnineteenth century were basically from northern Europe, with English-speaking peoples predominating. Although there were

Dutch, French, Spanish, Swedes, and Germans, the population of the thirteen original colonies was dominated by English, Scots, and Scottish-Irish from the British Isles. The major religious creeds were Protestant.

In the nineteenth century, especially from the 1840s to the Civil War, two social and educational trends developed and converged almost simultaneously: (1) the origin and implementation of the common school system and (2) the beginning of a shift in immigration patterns from Protestant English-speaking groups to Catholic and non-English-speaking groups. Famine in Ireland caused thousands of Irish Catholics to immigrate to the United States and to locate in what was then Protestant New England. Political turmoil, particularly the Revolution of 1848, brought large numbers of Germans to the United States. In the years from 1870 to 1920, the pattern of immigration was to shift again as immigrants came from southern and eastern Europe. The historical convergence of the origin of the common school and the new immigration pattern worked to fix an assimilationist or Americanization policy upon American public education. The common school leaders saw that institution as an agency of assimilating immigrants by the Americanization process. In the midnineteenth century, Americanization meant that

1. The language of instruction in the public schools was English. Non-English-speaking children had to learn English to succeed in public schools.
2. Although the public school was not a religious institution, the generalized value attitude and formal exercises—such as Bible reading and opening prayers—followed a nondenominational Protestantism.

By the late 1840s and 1850s, the Americanization ideology dominated many common school systems. Restive Roman Catholics who feared that Americanization would mean the Protestantization of their children began to establish their own parochial schools. While Irish Catholics used English in their schools, Germans and other non-English-speaking groups established bilingual and bicultural schools.

During the long period from 1870 to 1920, millions of immigrants came to the United States from eastern and southern Europe. Italians, Poles, Czechs, Slovaks, Russians, Jews, Greeks, Hungarians, and Roumanians came to work in mines, factories, and farms. In many large northern and eastern cities such as New York, Chicago, and Pittsburgh, ethnic ghettos, known as "little Italy" or "little Warsaw" developed. The immigrant and "first-generation" children who attended public schools encountered and had to yield to an unbending assimilationist ideology that professed that a person became a "good American" by being ashamed of and forgetting his or her ethnic heritage.

According to the "melting pot" theory advanced in the early twentieth century, the various ethnic groups would lose their ethnicity through assimilation and eventually become one people, an American race. Although the term "melting pot" was used widely in the first half of the twentieth century as an accomplished fact, a new wave of sociologists in the 1960s called the "melting pot" a myth. They discovered that many ethnics had not melted into one homogeneous people and that ethnicity was alive and flourishing in the United States. A renaissance of ethnic consciousness contributed to multicultural education in the 1980s.

This family, part of the massive immigration from southern and eastern Europe in the late nineteenth century, contributed to making the United States into a multicultural nation. *(Library of Congress)*

Since the 1970s, the assimilationist ideology has been under attack and largely discarded by American public school educators. In place of cultural homogenization, the public schools have incorporated a multiethnic perspective into the curriculum based on the following principles:

1. Public schooling should emphasize the common, unifying, and integrative dimensions of American life in a manner that respects and encourages ethnic diversity and expression.
2. The American social and cultural experience is perceived as an "open" rather than "closed" society. Rather than being a monolithic social fabric, the American cultural experience is a mosaic in which each ethnic group has a contribution to make.
3. Educators should recognize that Americans live in an ethnically and culturally pluralistic society. The curriculum should include topics or units that provide insights into the contribution of the various ethnic groups to American culture and life.

PUBLIC SCHOOLING
AND THE AFRO-AMERICAN EXPERIENCE

As indicated, the American public school followed an assimilationist ideology toward ethnic groups throughout much of its history. Although some parallels exist between the ethnic and Afro-American experience in the public schools, black Americans encountered different attitudes because of different historical circumstances. The entry of Afro-Americans into the New World occurred in the early colonial years as blacks were transported to North America to work as slaves in the tobacco, rice, indigo, and cotton plantations of the South. Slavery, that peculiar and cruel American institution, had the effect of inducing a "cultural shock" on its victims. The Africans were literally torn out of their own culture and society by force, packed on slave ships, and sold as chattel to plantation owners. Often, members of a particular language or tribal group were isolated from each other to prevent communication and revolt.

The African slaves experienced a cultural shock in that they were uprooted from their homeland, their culture, their traditions and values, and their tribes and kinship groups. Such a complete "uprooting" often was disorienting and anxiety generating. In time, Africans established an Afro-American culture in the New World.

Although there were free blacks living in the United States throughout its history, the vast majority were slaves—primarily in the southern and border states—until the Civil War, the Emancipation Proclamation, and the Thirteenth Amendment ended slavery. Prior to their emancipation, the official policy and law in the slave states made it illegal to instruct slaves in reading and writing. Although some blacks learned to read and write, the majority were illiterate when the Civil War ended in 1865. The federal government, through the Freedmen's Bureau, inaugurated a literacy campaign among blacks by establishing schools and bringing northern teachers to the South as instructors. In addition to federal efforts, the legislatures of the southern states in the Reconstruction period, from 1865–1877, enacted laws that established common or public schools—supported by public taxation—in the South. It should be pointed out that many of these legislatures had substantial black representation in the Reconstruction decade and that the establishment of public schools in the South was a major achievement.

When Reconstruction ended, racial segregation was established in the South with the force of law. Although racially segregated schools were supposedly "separate but equal," the schools attended by black children were usually underfinanced and educationally inferior. Blacks generally suffered political, economic, social, and educational discrimination. The response of black leaders to racial segregation and discrimination has been illustrated frequently by the conflicting educational philosophies of Booker T. Washington and W. E. B. DuBois.

The Washington–DuBois Controversy

Booker T. Washington (1856–1915), a former slave who made his way to a position of national leadership, is today a controversial figure. As head of Tuskegee Institute in Alabama, Washington became the recognized leader and spokesman for black Americans. Following a conservative and often paternalistic educational ideology, Washington asserted that

1. Blacks should avoid political agitation for civil and legal rights and instead concentrate on making themselves economically indispensable as farmers, craftsmen, and artisans to the American, particularly southern, economy.

2. The appropriate education for blacks was not professional study of law, medicine, or higher education but vocational training for agriculture and occupational trades.

W. E. B. DuBois (1868–1963), a founder of the NAACP, was a sociologist and historian who fought for civil rights for black Americans and racial integration for American society. *(New York Public Library Picture Collection)*

Booker T. Washington (1856–1915) was president of Tuskeegee Institute and the proponent of the "Atlanta Compromise." *(New York Public Library Picture Collection)*

Washington and DuBois—Black Educational Leaders Who Debated the Purposes of Education for Black Americans. While Washington advocated basic skill training, DuBois urged higher and professional education.

In his "Atlanta Compromise" address, Washington advocated a symbiotic racial relationship between blacks and whites. Both races, he asserted, could live separate social lives but be mutually supporting in economic affairs. Today, Washington is frequently criticized as a compromiser who failed to advance the cause of his race and who said what the "White Power Structure" wanted to hear. Defenders of Washington claim that he was a survivor who was making the best of a "bad situation."

Washington's educational ideology was challenged by the historian and sociologist W. E. B. DuBois (1868–1963), who argued that the progress of black Americans required action in many areas: educational, political, economic, and social. DuBois, a founder of the National Association for the Advancement of Colored People, asserted that

1. Blacks should organize to gain the civil rights promised in the U.S. Constitution.
2. Blacks should not restrict themselves to vocational training but should pursue degrees in higher education and careers in law, medicine, politics, science, and research.

Whereas Washington believed that black progress would come slowly in short, gradual, and noncontroversial steps, DuBois did not fear controversy. Rather, DuBois believed that a black leadership elite, a "talented tenth" should be identified and lead the black people of America. This "talented tenth" would bring about progress for their race from the top downward.

AFRO-AMERICANS AND THE SCHOOL IDEOLOGY

In the century from Emancipation to the civil rights activism of the mid-1960s, the attitudes of the public school establishment toward black Americans experienced several changes. The common school leaders, many of whom were from the northeastern states, were generally sympathetic to the educational needs of the former slaves in the Reconstruction era after the Civil War. In some respects, the crusade for common schools and the Abolitionist movement to abolish slavery had originated in the northeastern states and then spread throughout the northern states. Political and educational leaders such as Horace Mann, Henry Barnard, Horace Greeley, Thaddeus Stevens, and others endorsed public education and also opposed slavery. In the post–Civil War Reconstruction decade, they aided efforts to educate the former slaves in the South.

From 1865 to 1900, the vast majority of Afro-Americans were located in the South. There was also a small but growing black population in the North. In the South, there was a dual school system, with students separated according to race. While black educators such as Washington and DuBois argued over educational policy, white educational leaders, too, had differing perspectives on black education.

William T. Harris, the U.S. commissioner of education and former superintendent in St. Louis, believed that black children needed the same basic literary and mathematical skills as whites. Harris also believed that all students needed to be introduced to the classics and to the sources of Western civilization. The general attitude to black education was that black children should learn the basics—reading, writing, arithmetic—and be introduced to white, Anglo-Saxon American culture. As was true of the schooling of immigrant children, black students were presented with a monolithic view of American culture. The Afro-American experience and contribution to American life was not incorporated into the curriculum. While the dominant ideology of American education predicted that the children of European ethnics would become part of a melting pot, such was not true of black children. Afro-Americans were to be inculcated with the ideas and values of white America. They were to read and study about white Americans and accept white heroes as value models, but they were also being prepared to accept a "second-class" role in American society.

In the early decades of the twentieth century, the black experience was portrayed narrowly in the literary and historical parts of the school curriculum as was the ethnic contribution to American culture. The treatment of slavery and the Reconstruction era found in school history textbooks illustrated the new official ideology. This historical version took the following lines:

1. Afro-American slaves were generally well treated and were content with their lot on the plantations of the South. Although slavery was a social evil, many white plantation owners were well-meaning persons who provided kindly care to their slaves.

2. After the Civil War, unscrupulous northern "carpetbaggers" and south-ern "scalawags" misled blacks by convincing them to take political power in the southern states. Once in power, black politicians and their white "radical allies" inflicted corrupt regimes on the former Confederate states.

3. After federal troops were withdrawn from the South, white political leadership was restored in the South and honest government was reas-serted.

4. The Afro-American path to progress would be slow and gradual. It would come from patience, hard work, and industriousness, not from political agitation. Booker T. Washington and scientist George Wash-ington Carver were cited frequently as examples of hardworking black leaders whose achievements were based on a willingness to help others.

This distorted and incomplete version of the Afro-American experience was challenged by John Hope Franklin, Rayford Logan, and other historians who condemned slavery as an evil institution that had personally and socially debilitating effects on both black slaves and white slave-owners. The Reconstruc-tion legislatures in the South—composed of a substantial number of black rep-resentatives—brought reforms and progressive policies to the southern states. For example, political participation was broadened and uniform systems of tax-ation were created. It was true that political corruption existed in the northern cities and states as well and often to a larger extent than in the South. When federal troops left the South, segregation was established by the new legislatures. "Jim Crow" laws, poll taxes, and disenfranchisement followed. It was not until midtwentieth century that more adequate and historically accurate interpreta-tions appeared.

Emergence of a New Black Consciousness

The period from World War I to the civil rights movement of the 1950s and 1960s marked the emergence of a new black consciousness. Although many black and white scholars and educators had rejected the standard textbook ver-sion of the Afro-American experience, it persisted until it was challenged aca-demically and publicly in midtwentieth century. Civil rights leaders such as Martin Luther King and historians such as John Hope Franklin called for a more complete and accurate examination and interpretation of the black ex-perience in America.

The Supreme Court decision in the *Brown* case in 1954 marked the beginning of the end of racially segregated schools in the United States. The incorporation of the Afro-American contribution in a multicultural society was not merely a matter of judicial decision making, however. It involved re-ex-amination of the cultural heritage, discovering hitherto neglected evidence, and creating a more adequate interpretation of the Afro-American past and contri-butions to the school curriculum. For black Americans, this often meant a pain-staking search to discover their roots, to celebrate the uniqueness of their her-itage, and eventually to create a synthesis with a multicultural context.

In educational institutions, especially at the college and secondary level, the first wave of the renascent black consciousness took the form of separate courses on black culture, literature, and history. Colleges often established Black Studies departments. The first wave of activity tended to emphasize the uniqueness and separateness of the black experience. Black heroes and heroines were identified as models for black children to imitate. Black pride, often expressed as "Black Is Beautiful," frequently was a dominant theme. Neglected sources were found and incorporated into older versions of the black experience. Importantly, the perspectives on black culture in America were broadened in this first wave. For example,

1. The African culture roots of the Afro-American experience were identified and examined for linkage and insight.
2. The emphasis on blacks in industry and politics was broadened to include the black contribution to art, literature, music, poetry, and science.

The first wave of black consciousness as it was felt in schools and in the curriculum had a positive effect of identifying a unique Afro-American experience for many black children. It had several negative consequences, however.

Where it concentrated on the separateness of the black experience, it lacked a multicultural dimension. The same phenomenon was true, however, of early ethnic studies programs that concentrated on a particular ethnic group in isolation from other groups. While a beneficial addition to American education, black or ethnic studies tended to suffer from cultural and educational isolation. Another defect was that, in the haste to prepare curriculum guides, textbooks, and other instructional materials, the treatment was sometimes superficial and uncritical.

The second wave of black consciousness, as well as ethnic consciousness, was to incorporate both Afro-American and European ethnic studies into the context of multicultural education. This new and broader context seeks to treat both the uniqueness of the particular group's experience and to examine its relationships and interactions with other social and ethnic groups and with the total society. Its purpose is to create a sense of racial or ethnic identity that recognizes uniqueness and also encourages transracial and transethnic understanding for all participants of American society.

PUBLIC SCHOOLING AND THE HISPANIC EXPERIENCE

In the same decades that European ethnics and Afro-Americans were experiencing a revived cultural identity and consciousness, a similar phenomenon was taking place among Spanish-speaking Hispanic Americans. Again, the Hispanic experience resembles but bears differences to the black and European ethnic experience. It shares the similarity of being generally neglected in American public education. It differs in that the Hispanic experience arises from unique historical circumstances. Further, the term "Hispanic" is a general category for Spanish-speaking that must be used carefully. While Mexican Americans, Cuban Americans, and Puerto Rican Americans share a common mother tongue, their cultural heritages are based on differing cultural contexts. The Hispanics share certain characteristics with the European ethics since they share a common European cultural origin. But, while most immigrants from southern and eastern Europe came directly to the United States from their native lands, the Spanish-speaking immigrants first settled and lived for centuries in other American countries such as Cuba, Mexico, or Puerto Rico before entering the United States. An exception to this generalization are many Hispanics who are descended from the Spanish colonists in the southwestern or western United States. A second very important difference is that the Hispanics are Spanish speaking; they share a common language, whereas the European immigrants lacked a common language to link them to other ethnic groups. While European ethnics have sometimes argued for bilingual instruction in public schools, they have not done so in a forceful or concerted fashion. Bilingual and bicultural education has been a generally successful demand of Hispanic Americans.

Examining the Hispanic Generalization

While the term "Hispanic American" is a convenient category, it is also overgeneralized. A genuine program of multicultural education needs to begin not only with the similarities but also with an explanation of the differences between Spanish-speaking groups.

Mexican Americans, or Chicanos, for example, present an historical and cultural experience that differs from the experience of other Hispanics. The Mexican-American experience can be examined from two perspectives: the older Mexican-American stock whose inclusion in the United States dates from the Mexican-American War (1846–1848) and the more recent immigrants from Mexico to the United States. The history of the older Mexican-American stock goes back to the Spanish colonial period when what is now the states of California, Texas, and New Mexico were part of New Spain. The descendants of the early Spanish settlers established *encomiendas,* agricultural estates, cities, and schools. Spanish Roman Catholic missionary orders met the religious and educational needs of the Spanish colonists and their descendants and worked to convert the Indians to Catholicism. A number of missions were established by the Franciscan friars to provide religious, craft, and agricultural education to the Indians and to protect them from exploitation.

As a result of the Mexican-American War, Mexico, which had earlier won its independence from Spain, was forced to cede large areas of land to the United States. The Spanish-speaking Mexican population of these lost areas became a "conquered people." With annexation, the English language became the official language of government and schooling. When public schools were established in the southwestern states, the standardized Anglo-centered curriculum was also imposed on Mexican-American children. Little was done to relate instruction to the language and culture of the Mexican American. Indeed, many school districts required that only English be used in instruction.

In the twentieth century, there has been considerable immigration from Mexico to the United States. These more recent immigrants have been employed as migrant agricultural workers or as unskilled laborers. Entering the United States as illegal aliens, the migrant workers have been frequently underpaid and exploited. Since midtwentieth century, the Mexican-American population of the large cities has increased.

As has been typical of other ethnic groups, Mexican Americans have experienced a rise in consciousness. The educational demands of the two groups of Mexican Americans are somewhat similar but also different. They are similar in wanting the Mexican-American heritage and contributions recognized in the school curriculum. Both groups also favor bilingual and bicultural education in Spanish and English. One major difference between the groups is that the more recent Mexican-American immigrants, particularly the children of migrant workers, often require compensatory educational programs.

Puerto Rican migrants to the continental United States are citizens, as Puerto Rico is an American commonwealth. Puerto Rico passed directly from Spanish to American control as a result of Spain's defeat in the Spanish-American War of 1898. The relationship between Puerto Rico and the United States has been mixed. Some Puerto Ricans seek independence; others prefer to continue some form of relationship with the United States. Puerto Ricans in the United States have tended to settle in large northern cities. As with other Hispanics, Puerto Ricans generally have endorsed bilingual and bicultural education. They also advocate the incorporation of appropriate units of Puerto Rican culture and contributions into the public school program.

A third major Hispanic ethnic group in the United States are Cuban Americans, many of whom are exiles from the Castro regime. The Cuban immigration to the United States has centered in Florida and from that state to other locations. The Cuban immigrants included many persons of middle-class origin such as physicians, lawyers, educators, and other professionals. As do other Hispanic Americans, they advocate bilingual, bicultural education and the recognition of the Cuban cultural contribution.

Bilingual, Bicultural Education

As indicated, Hispanic Americans generally are strong advocates of bilingual and bicultural education programs. Bilingual education means that instruction should be conducted in two languages: in Spanish and in English. Bicultural education is more comprehensive in that it includes not only instruction in two languages but learning about two cultures as well. Although the concept of bilingual education is well established in public schools in many areas of the country, there is controversy if such programs should be for transition or for maintenance. Transitional programs are designed to help Spanish-speaking children learn English by a series of gradual phases in which an initially large amount of instruction in Spanish is slowly replaced by English. Maintenance programs, in contrast, are designed to preserve and cultivate Spanish-speaking ability and to also make the students proficient in English as well. Bilingual and bicultural programs also require preparation of instructional materials and teachers in both languages.

PUBLIC SCHOOLING
AND THE ASIAN-AMERICAN EXPERIENCE

While much of the discussion about the European ethnic experience in the United States applies to Asian Americans, there are several obvious but noteworthy differences. The major Oriental-American ethnic groups are the Chinese, Japanese, Philippino, Indian, and Korean. More recent immigrants are groups from Southeast Asia such as the Cambodians, Laotians, Vietnamese, and Thais. The cultural and linguistic background of the Asian ethnics differs from the European ethnics. China, Japan, and India, in particular, represent ancient and complex civilizations. A genuine explanation of these highly developed civilizations is a major but necessary undertaking for a true multicultural educational program.

In the late-nineteenth and early-twentieth centuries, nativist sentiment was generally anti-Asiatic. Chinese workers who were brought to the United States to work in the mines and on the railroad construction in the West were feared as cheap laborers who were a threat to the more highly paid white workers. Federal legislation was passed that at first limited and then excluded the entry of Chinese immigrants to the United States. The general attitude to Chinese Americans has experienced several shifts in the twentieth century. During World War II, when China was an ally of the United States, Chinese were portrayed sympathetically in the press and in motion pictures. American missionaries and business interests that were active in China also encouraged American involvement and support for China. After mainland China adopted communism, relations with China cooled, particularly during the Korean conflict. Today, there is renewed interest by American political, business, and educational leaders in China. The Chinese government has also become more interested in improving relations with the United States in order to modernize the country. Despite the changing circumstances of international relations, the general public attitude in the United States often has been simplistic and stereotypic regarding China, the Chinese, and Chinese Americans.

The prevalent popular attitudes to Japanese Americans have been similar to those pertaining to Chinese Americans. However, while the Chinese enjoyed popularity during World War II, the reverse was true of Japanese Americans. After the bombing of Pearl Harbor in 1941, there was an almost hysterical suspicion toward the Japanese Americans. The Roosevelt administration, contrary to its general stance on behalf of civil liberties, reacted by confining Japanese Americans to resettlement or internment camps. Often without regard to their personal and property rights, the action by the U.S. government denied civil rights to Japanese Americans. During World War II, U.S. propaganda depicted the Japanese in stereotypic fashion.

Until the mid-1950s, the American public school curriculum generally ignored serious treatment of Asian cultures and civilizations. Courses in world history and world culture up to that time generally concentrated on Europe and North America. When Asia was discussed, the treatment was peripheral at best. The same was generally true of the textbook coverage of Africa and South America. When they were included, Asian civilizations were treated as outposts of Western nations. Generally, there was a passing reference to the "American open-door policy" toward Asia or to the European colonization of Asia. The mid-1950s marked a change in the place that Asia had in the public school curriculum. World history and world culture courses, particulary at the secondary level, were broadened to include a treatment of Asia in terms of its own civilizations. At the elementary level, the entry of anthropology and sociology units into the social studies contributed to an examination of stereotypic thinking and of the Asian contribution to world civilization.

PUBLIC SCHOOLING
AND THE AMERICAN-INDIAN EXPERIENCE

The American-Indian experience has often been neglected, distorted, or romanticized in both schools and in the public mind. Since the time of the Leatherstocking tales of James Fenimore Cooper, the American Indian has been portrayed as either a noble savage or a cruel adversary rather than as a person who is a member of a particular cultural group with its own traditions and lifestyles. From the Atlantic to the Pacific, the variety of American-Indian cultures is complex and varied; even to refer to the American Indian as a single group is to oversimplify. However, the dominant groups have frequently done so in their portrayal of the American Indian.

Much of the military history of the United States, particularly in the nineteenth century, was a detailed account of the Indian wars. The westward-moving waves of white settlers encountered, made treaties with the Indian tribes and then broke them when convenient to expropriate their lands. Nineteenth-century "pseudoscientific" studies often depicted the American Indian as a primitive who was an obstacle to the settlement and exploitation of the continent's natural resources. Official federal policy toward the education of the Indian varied. At times, federal policy sought to "Americanize" the Indians by teaching them white culture and English language. At other times, it permitted the native Indian culture to be the basis of education. This ambiguity has left its mark on many American Indians, particularly those who live off the reservation.

The richness and variety of the American-Indian experience is still a mystery to many Americans. Although efforts have been made to include realistic and accurate units of Indian life and culture into the curriculum, these have been minimal and peripheral even in multiethnic or multicultural education programs. A genuine multicultural program will explore and illustrate the uniqueness of the American-Indian contribution to American life. It should illustrate the commonalities of the American-Indian experience but also point out the cultural differences that exist between the various tribal and regional groupings.

WHITHER THE MULTICULTURAL DIMENSION
OF AMERICAN EDUCATION: A SUMMARY VIEW

Multiculturalism is a new but also an ill-defined phenomenon in American education. Today, many state departments of education, state legislatures, and accrediting agencies require units or courses on multiculturalism in the school curriculum and in teacher training programs. Ethnic and racial groups and organizations have argued for the recognition of their particular group's contribution to American culture. In many respects, this is as it should be. A portrayal of the American experience that omits or neglects the contributions of the racial and ethnic groups that are part of American life is distorted and incomplete. It is also time that racial and ethnic stereotyping ends in our schools. At the same time, it is important that multicultural education not just be another fad that will be discarded. The various books, articles, and materials that are being produced on multicultural education must be written accurately, organized carefully, and follow the best canons of scholarship.

The public school philosophy in regard to multicultural education also must be developed carefully. It was always a distortion of American life to portray the American experience as exclusively white, Anglo-Saxon, and Protestant. Multicultural education will serve to correct this narrow view of American life. On the other hand, public schooling also needs to emphasize the commonalities of American culture. The term "common school" means that there is something in common that all Americans share. The public school philosophy—as it develops its multicultural dimensions—will need to reflect the commonalities or consensus of American life and also the cultural differences that enrich that common life.

DISCUSSION QUESTIONS

1. Define and distinguish among "Americanization," "the melting pot theory," and "cultural pluralism."
2. Examine the various changes that occurred in the public school ideology toward black Americans.
3. Analyze the Hispanic-American cultural experience as it relates to education.
4. Analyze the educational experience of a particular Asian-American group.
5. Analyze the educational experience of a particular American-Indian group.
6. Define multicultural education.

FIELD EXERCISES

1. Invite the director of the black studies program at your college or university to describe the program to your class.
2. Invite representatives of Hispanic-American organizations to visit your class to present their educational objectives.
3. Invite representatives of Asian-American organizations to visit your class and present their educational objectives.
4. Prepare a directory of multicultural resources in your community, such as ethnic and racial museums, organizations, and cultural centers.
5. Examine several textbooks used in elementary and secondary schools. Identify examples of ethnic or racial stereotyping.

SUGGESTED READINGS

ALLOWAY, DAVID N., AND CORDASCO, FRANCESCO. *Minorities and the American City: A Sociological Primer for Educators.* New York: David McKay, 1970.

BANKS, JAMES A. *Multiethnic Education: Theory and Practice.* Boston: Allyn & Bacon, 1981.

BULLOCK, HENRY A. *A History of Negro Education in the South: From 1619 to the Present.* Cambridge, Mass.: Harvard University Press, 1967.

CORDASCO, FRANCESCO, AND BUCCHIONI, EUGENE. *Puerto Rican Children in Mainland Schools: A Source Book for Teachers.* New York: Scarecrow Press, 1968.

FUCHS, ESTELLE, AND HAVIGHURST, ROBERT J. *To Live on This Earth: American Indian Education.* Garden City, N.Y.: Doubleday, 1973.

GLAZER, NATHAN, AND MOYNIHAN, DANIEL P. *Beyond the Melting Pot: The Negroes, Puerto Ricans, Jews, Italians, and the Irish of New York City.* Cambridge, Mass.: M.I.T. Press and Harvard University Press, 1964.

HELM, JUNE, ED. *Spanish Speaking People in the United States.* Seattle: University of Washington Press, 1969.

HUNTER, WILLIAM A., ED. *Multicultural Education Through Competency-Based Teacher Education.* Washington, D.C.: American Association of Colleges for Teacher Education, 1974.

KENNEDY, JOHN F. *A Nation of Immigrants.* New York: Harper & Row, 1964.

KRUG, MARK M. *The Melting of the Ethnics—Education of the Immigrants, 1880–1914.* Bloomington, Ind.: Phi Delta Kappa Educational Foundation, 1976.

LEWIS, OSCAR. *La Vida: A Puerto Rican Family in the Culture of Poverty—San Juan and New York.* New York: Random House, 1966.

NAVE, JULIAN. *Mexican Americans: A Brief Look at Their History.* New York: Anti-Defamation League of B'nai B'rith, 1970.

ROSE, PETER I. *They and We: Racial and Ethnic Relations in the United States.* New York: Random House, 1974.

SENIOR, CLARENCE. *The Puerto Ricans: Strangers—Then Neighbors.* Chicago: Quandrangle, 1961.

6

The Federal Role in Education

As indicated in earlier chapters, after the American Revolution and during the early national period, organized education (or schooling) in the United States was regarded as an instrument related to the general civic welfare. In the American political system, each division of government plays an educational role. In the United States, educational authority was retained primarily by each of the states. Following the early New England precedents of local school control, the states, in turn, delegated important educational responsibilities to local school boards. Over the years, the once-limited federal role in education has grown. Chapter 6 examines the historical development and contemporary role of the federal government in American education.

AN HISTORICAL PERSPECTIVE OF THE FEDERAL ROLE IN EDUCATION

Earlier chapters examined the importance that the early American colonists gave to education and to establishing schools. A frequently cited historical example of this dedication to education is found in the Massachusetts Bay Colony Acts of 1642 and 1647 that required towns to provide instruction to children. Although differing educational patterns existed in the various states, the northern states generally imitated New England's decentralized pattern. The U.S. Constitution, ratified in 1789, did not refer specifically to education. According to the "reserved powers" clause of the Tenth Amendment, education was recognized as a state prerogative.

The federal government was responsible for administering the western territories before they were organized as states and admitted into the Union. The federal government encouraged and promoted education in the western territories with the greatest single resource available at the time—the land grant. Since land in the West was plentiful, the federal government used this resource to encourage internal improvements conducive to national development. Congress appropriated grants of federal land to stimulate road, canal, and later railroad construction. These internal improvements connected the various regions of the country, stimulated economic development, and promoted national unity. The establishment of schools in the western territories not only promoted the general welfare by facilitating popular education but also represented an internal improvement that spurred national development.

The precedents for the land grant system of aid to education occurred even before the Constitution's ratification. For example, the Land Ordinance of 1785, passed by Congress under the Articles of Confederation, provided that the Northwest Territories, the vast area of federal land bordered by the Ohio River and the Great Lakes, was to be divided into townships of thirty-six sections. The revenue earned from the sale of one of these sections was to be used to support education. The provision of the Northwest Ordinance of 1787 that stated, "Religion, morality and knowledge being necessary to good government and the happiness of mankind, schools and the means of education shall forever be encouraged," affirmed the federal government's early commitment to educational development.

Throughout much of the nineteenth century, the federal government used land grants to aid public education. From the time of the Ohio Enabling Act of 1802, the federal government granted land to each new state admitted to the Union. Throughout the history of the land grant mechanism, the federal government granted a total of 98.5 million acres to the states for public schools.[1]

Federal Aid after the Civil War

In 1862, Congress passed and President Lincoln signed the First Morrill Act, which provided the states with federal land grants to establish colleges for agricultural and industrial education. In the Reconstruction era, from 1865 to 1877, the federal government supported the education of the newly freed slaves.

During the war, federal aid supported schools for a small number of liberated blacks on Virginia's offshore islands. When the Civil War ended, severe educational as well as economic and political problems plagued the devastated former Confederate states. Because of restrictions imposed by their previous condition of servitude, the vast majority of the 2,700,000 freed blacks were

---

[1]Sidney Tiedt, *The Role of the Federal Government in Education* (New York: Oxford University Press, 1966), pp. 14–17.

illiterate. The federally funded Freedmen's Bureau, under the leadership of General O. O. Howard, established and staffed schools for blacks in the South.

In the great majority of nations, education is a national function that is subject to central control. In many countries, a minister of education or secretary of education serves as a member of the national cabinet. In contrast, the United States has followed a policy of decentralized rather than centralized educational control. Because of the tradition of decentralization, the United States did not have a secretary of education at cabinet level until the creation of the Department of Education by the Carter administration in 1979. There were, however, earlier departments of education and commissioners of education at the federal level.

For example, the first federal Department of Education was established in 1867 to (1) collect educational statistics in the states and territories and (2) promote the cause of education throughout the United States. The department, headed by Henry Barnard, existed at subcabinet level. It later became a bureau of the Interior Department, with a small staff and limited budget. Its function was not to frame national policies but to provide information on American education.

Nineteenth-Century Debates over Federal Aid

In the late nineteenth century, attempts to bring about greater federal involvement caused considerable controversy. In 1870, Congressman George Hoar of Maine introduced a bill to establish a national system of education by setting federal standards that the states would be required to meet. In states failing to meet these standards, the federal government was to intervene by appointing a federal superintendent of state schools who would correct the deficiencies.[2] Hoar's bill, designed to improve educational opportunities for blacks in the southern states, encountered strong opposition. States rights advocates saw it as an encroachment on the reserved rights of states. Some public school organizations opposed it as an attempt to undermine local control. Roman Catholics condemned it as an attempt to create a vast monolithic public school system designed to destroy private schools in the United States. While Hoar's proposal failed, it outlined the kind of opposition that federal aid to education would encounter until well into the twentieth century.

In the 1880s, Senator Henry Blair of New Hampshire introduced federal aid legislation on five occasions. The Blair bill passed the Senate in 1884, 1886, and 1888 but failed in the House of Representatives.[3] Among the provisions of the Blair bill were

1. Rather than using land grants, federal aid would be distributed as direct money grants based on the illiteracy rate.
2. States were to match the amount of federal funding in their own educational outlays.

[2]Gordon Lee, *The Struggle for Federal Aid: First Phase, 1870–1890* (New York: Teachers College Press, Columbia University, 1949), pp. 42–44.
[3]Ibid., pp. 88–98.

3. States were to distribute school revenues without distinction of race or color.

While the Blair bill was not enacted, its major provisions anticipated the direction of federal assistance in the twentieth century. The move from land to cash grants would mark a significant departure from earlier precedents for aid. While the Blair bill did not call for the ending of segregated schools, it did require an equitable distribution of funds to schools regardless of race. By requiring the states to match funds, the Blair bill was designed to encourage greater initiatives by state governments.

As the nineteenth century ended, the essential arguments of the opponents and proponents of federal aid to and involvement in education were clear. The opponents argued that

1. There was no need for the federal government to support education, as states and local funding was adequate.
2. Federal aid violated the long-standing principles of local educational control and initiative.
3. Federal aid would end the safeguard of educational decentralization and create a federally controlled monopoly over schools.

The proponents of federal aid used the following arguments:

1. Both the quantity and quality of education varies so greatly from state to state that children do not really enjoy equality of educational opportunity. Only the federal government can equalize state-to-state disparities.
2. Since education relates to the national interest, the federal government has an educational role to promote the general welfare.
3. Due to the mobility of the American population, the educational deficiencies of one state are likely to impact other states.
4. Some states have denied educational opportunity to certain of its citizens, particularly blacks in southern states, and the federal government should correct these inequalities.

Federally Assisted Vocational Education

In the twentieth century, the federal government encouraged vocational education. The movement for aid to vocational education illustrates the effect that special-interest groups can have on behalf of specific educational programs. When particular special-interest groups have educational objectives, they can be particularly effective in securing the passage of specific aid programs and often mandates at either the federal or state levels. General aid that requires a more integrated but less concentrated effort is more difficult to secure.

In the early twentieth century, the vocational education lobby was particularly strong. In 1917, the Smith–Hughes Act was passed to provide federal funding for agricultural, industrial, and home economics education in secondary schools. The Smith–Hughes Act provided for (1) grants to states, on a matching basis, for teachers' salaries, curriculum development, and administrative costs in the specified vocational subjects; and (2) establishment of the federal Board of Vocational Education to administer the program.

Throughout the twentieth century, vocational education received additional funding. In particular, the George–Barden Act of 1946 expanded vocational education programs and transferred their administration to the U.S. Office of Education.

RECENT FEDERAL AID PROGRAMS

From the 1930s to the 1950s, the history of the federal role in education was one of controversy and debate but also of inaction. During the depression of the 1930s, a number of Franklin Roosevelt's New Deal programs had an indirect rather than a direct educational impact.[4] For example, the Reconstruction Finance Act provided loans to school districts to aid in paying teachers' salaries; some school construction projects were financed by the Public Works Administration; the Civilian Conservation Corps provided instruction to its members; and the National Youth Administration also conducted some educational projects. During World War II, the Lanham Act (1941) aided school districts that were impacted by military mobilization with funds for school construction and provided auxiliary educational services such as nursery schools.

In the post–World War II era, from 1945 until the enactment of the National Defense Education Act in 1958, federal aid to education proposals were fraught with controversy. There was considerable public and congressional debate but little action. Shifting and often temporary coalitions came together to defeat federal aid proposals. During this period, southern conservative Democrats tended to oppose federal aid to education on the grounds that it violated states' rights and would be used to end segregated, dual school systems.

Roman Catholic opposition was strong to any provision that denied federal aid to private and parochial schools. Equally determined, a number of organizations condemned aid to religious schools as a violation of the doctrine of separation of church and state. Fiscal conservatives believed that federal aid to schools would open the federal coffers to an unending demand for more money once the initial grants were made.

The National Defense Education Act

As the 1950s neared their end, the continuing debate over federal aid to education was interrupted by fears that the United States was losing its scientific, technological, and educational superiority to the Soviet Union. The Soviet success in orbiting the Sputnik space satellite and well-publicized American space failures at that time engendered a feeling that "something was wrong with American schools." Although this mood was grossly exaggerated by Cold War fears,

---

[4]Frank J. Munger and Richard F. Fenno, *National Politics and Federal Aid to Education* (Syracuse, N.Y.: Syracuse University Press, 1962), pp. 4–7.

Table 6–1 Federal Programs for Elementary and Secondary Education and Related Activities, 1787–1979

YEAR	PROGRAM
1787	*Northwest Ordinance*—authorized land grants for the establishment of educational institutions.
1867	*Department of Education Act*—authorized the establishment of the Office of Education.
1917	*Smith–Hughes Act*—provided for grants to states for support of vocational education.
1933	School lunch programs—provided assistance in school lunch programs. The use of surplus farm commodities in school lunch programs began in 1936 and the *National School Lunch Act of 1946* continued and expanded this assistance.
1941	Amendment to *Lanham Act of 1940*—authorized federal aid for construction, maintenance, and operation of schools in federally impacted areas. Such assistance was continued under Public Laws 815 and 874, 81st Congress, in 1950.
1946	*George–Barden Act* (P.L. 79-586)—expanded federal support of vocational education.
1950	*Public Laws 815 and 874*—provided assistance for construction (PL 815) and operation (PL 874) of schools in federally affected areas.
1954	*School Milk Program* (PL 83-690)—provided funds for purchase of milk for school lunch programs. *Cooperative Research Act* (PL 83-531)—authorized cooperative arrangements with universities, colleges, and state education agencies for educational research.
1958	*National Defense Education Act* (PL 85-864)—provided assistance to state and local school systems for strengthening instruction in science, mathematics, modern foreign languages, and other critical subjects; improvement of state statistical services; guidance, counseling, and testing services and training institutes. *PL 85-926*—federal assistance for training teachers of the handicapped authorized. *PL 85-905*—authorized a loan service of captioned films for the deaf.
1963	*Vocational Education Act of 1963* (PL 88-210)—increased federal support of vocational education, including support of residential vocational schools, vocational work-study programs, and research, training, and demonstrations in vocational education.
1964	*Civil Rights Act of 1964* (PL 88-452).
1965	*Elementary and Secondary Education Act* (PL 89-10)—authorized grants for elementary and secondary school programs for children of low-income families; school library resources, textbooks, and other instructional materials for school children; supplementary educational centers and services; strengthening state education agencies; and educational research and research training.
1966	*Elementary and Secondary Education Amendments of 1966* (PL 89-750)—in addition to modifying existing programs, authorized grants to assist states in initiation, expansion, and improvement of programs and projects for the education of handicapped children at the preschool, elementary, and secondary school levels.
1968	*Elementary and Secondary Education Amendments of 1967* (PL 90-247)—in addition to modifying existing programs, authorized support of regional centers for education of handicapped children, model centers and services for deaf-blind children, recruitment of personnel and dissemination of information on education of the handicapped; technical assistance in education to rural areas; support of dropout prevention projects; and support of bilingual education programs. Also, authorized advance funding. *Vocational Education Amendments of 1968* (PL 90-576)—expansion of vocational education services to meet the needs of the disadvantaged.
1970	*Elementary and Secondary Education Assistance Programs, Extension* (PL 91-230)—authorized comprehensive planning and evaluation grants to state and local education agencies. *Environmental Education Act* (PL 91-516)—established an Office of Environmental Education for the purpose of curriculum development, initiation and maintenance of environmental education programs at the elementary-secondary education levels; distribution of material dealing with environment and ecology. *Appropriations for the Office of Education and for other purposes* (PL 91-380)—provided emergency school assistance for assistance to desegregating local education agencies.

Table 6–1 (cont.)

YEAR	PROGRAM
1972	*Education Amendments of 1972* (PL 92-318)—established a National Institute of Education, and a bureau-level Office of Indian Education. Amended current Office of Education programs. Prohibited sex bias.
1974	*Educational Amendments of 1974* (PL 93-380)—provided for the consolidation of certain education programs; established a National Center for Education Statistics.
1975	*Indian Self-determination and Education Assistance Act* (PL 93-638)—provided for increased participation of Indians in the establishment and conduct of their education programs.
1976	*Education Amendments of 1976* (PL 94-482)—extended and revised federal programs for education assistance for vocational education and a variety of other programs.
1978	*Education Amendments of 1978* (PL 95-561)—established a comprehensive basic skills program and a community schools program; authorized a study of school finance reform and equalization.
1979	*Department of Education Organization Act* (PL 96-88)—established the cabinet-level Department of Education.

From National Center for Education Statistics, *Digest of Education Statistics,* 1979 (Washington, D.C., G.P.O., 1979), pp. 157–162.

it served to bring contentious parties together in Congress to enact the National Defense Education Act (NDEA), in 1958. The NDEA was based upon congressional affirmation that

1. National security required the "fullest development of the mental resources and technical skills" of America's young men and women.
2. The national interest required that the federal government "give assistance to education for programs which are important to our national defense."[5]

The NDEA provided federal assistance to programs designed to improve instruction in mathematics, science, and foreign language—three curricular areas related to national defense. Mathematics and science were related to basic research and the development of technologies for the space age. Critics of foreign language instruction in the United States had charged that Americans were generally unprepared to cope with an international multilingual reality. The NDEA also provided grants, on a matching basis to the states, to improve guidance and counseling in secondary schools.

It should be noted that the NDEA provided specific assistance to defense-related areas rather than general aid to all educational areas. To avoid the controversies that had blocked passage of other proposals for federal aid, the NDEA provided categorical aid to specific programs.

The Elementary and Secondary Education Act

The enactment of the Elementary and Secondary Education Act (ESEA) in 1965, under the aegis of the Johnson administration, began a new era of federal aid to education. Unlike previous specific aid programs, ESEA provided

[5]Advisory Commission on Intergovernmental Relations, *The Federal Role in the Federal System: The Dynamics of Growth; Intergovernmentalizing the Classroom: Federal Involvement in Elementary and Secondary Education* (Washington, D.C.: G.P.O., 1981), p. 25.

general aid to elementary and secondary schools. By the mid-1960s, the national mood had changed. Civil rights activism, racial unrest in the large cities, and President Johnson's War on Poverty had identified new national priorities. As part of the War on Poverty, Johnson wanted to aid those who were disadvantaged economically, socially, racially, and educationally to enter the mainstream of what he termed the Great Society.

To avoid the religious controversies that had impeded federal aid programs in the past, the ESEA legislation followed the "child benefit" theory. Federal aid would be available to educationally disadvantaged children in both public and parochial schools; it would assist the child rather than the school. Among the major categories, or titles, of aid provided by ESEA were

1. grants to the states to improve school library resources and to purchase text books and other instructional materials;
2. funds to establish educational centers to provide educational services and encourage innovative programs;
3. educational research and training grants for universities to conduct and disseminate educational research; and
4. grants to state educational agencies to improve the planning, the collection of data, and the training of personnel.

The enactment of the ESEA set the basic directions in education that the federal government was to follow in the ensuing decade. Its major focus was educational reform and innovation, with a special concern for the education of the disadvantaged. The federal government was to encourage new programs to improve the education of the handicapped, those in poverty-impacted areas, bilingual education, and the education of Indian children. Table 6–1, on pages 92–93, summarizes federal programs for elementary and secondary education and related activities for the years 1787–1979; Table 6–2, on page 95, outlines estimated expenditures of public elementary and secondary schools by sources of funds for school years 1959–1979; Table 6–3, on page 96, lists federal funds spent for selected elementary and secondary education programs and related activities, 1960–1978.

THE FEDERAL COURTS AND EDUCATION

The federal government is divided into three major branches: the executive, legislative, and judicial. In the area of federal aid, the primary initiatives are with the executive branch, particularly with the president, and with the legislative branch, the Congress.

Since midtwentieth century, the federal judiciary has exerted an evergrowing impact on education. Some commentators on the federal role have called the U.S. Supreme Court "the national school board." While this may be an overstatement, decisions of the federal judiciary have changed substantially the course of American education. The following section examines the impact of the federal courts on American education.

Table 6–2 Estimated Expenditures of Public Elementary and Secondary Schools, by Source of Funds, 1959–60 to 1977–78[1]

SOURCE OF FUNDS BY LEVEL AND CONTROL	1959–60	1961–62	1963–64	1965–66	1967–68	1969–70	1971–72	1973–74	1975–76	1977–78
(Amounts in Billions of Current Dollars)										
Total public	$15.9	$18.7	$21.6	$26.5	$33.2	$41.0	$48.3	$57.2	$71.1	$82.7
Federal	0.7	0.9	1.1	2.1	3.0	3.4	4.6	5.1	6.5	7.8
State	5.6	6.7	8.0	9.6	12.1	15.8	18.0	23.5	31.1	36.1
Local	9.5	11.0	12.4	14.7	18.0	21.7	25.6	28.5	33.4	37.7
All other	0.2	0.1	0.1	0.1	0.1	0.1	0.1	0.1	0.1	0.1
(Percentage Distribution)										
Total public	100.0%	100.0%	100.0%	100.0%	100.0%	100.0%	100.0%	100.0%	100.0%	100.0%
Federal	4.6	5.1	5.0	8.0	9.0	8.2	9.5	8.9	9.2	9.4
State	35.4	35.9	37.2	36.3	36.5	38.6	37.2	41.1	43.7	44.9
Local	59.6	58.6	57.4	55.3	54.2	52.9	53.1	49.8	47.0	45.6
All other	0.4	0.4	0.4	0.4	0.3	0.3	0.2	0.2	0.1	0.1

[1]In addition to regular schools, these figures include "other" elementary and secondary schools such as residential schools for exceptional children, federal schools for Indians, and federally operated elementary and secondary schools on military posts.

From U.S. Department of Health, Education, and Welfare, National Center for Education Statistics, *The Condition of Education, 1977*, Vol. 3, Part 1 (Washington, D.C.: G.P.O., 1978), p. 170; *Digest of Education Statistics, 1977–78* (Washington, D.C.: G.P.O., 1978), p. 21.

Table 6–3 Federal Funds for Selected Elementary and Secondary Education Programs and Related Activities, 1960–1978 (in thousands of dollars)

PROGRAM	1960	1962	1964	1966	1968	1970	1972	1974	1976[1]	1978[2]
Elementary and secondary education[3]	63,529	54,821	71,489	915,174	1,436,732	1,467,792	1,869,081	1,766,412	2,166,322	2,586,118
Educationally deprived children[4]	63,529	54,821	71,489	746,904	1,049,116	1,170,355	1,570,388	1,460,058	1,760,814	2,129,400
Consolidated programs[5]				168,270	387,616	291,245	272,683	268,000	326,006	334,173
Bilingual education						6,192	26,010	38,354	79,502	122,545
School assistance in federally affected areas	258,198	282,909	334,289	409,593	506,372	656,372	648,608	558,526	598,884	810,300
Basic vocational education programs[6]	45,179	51,762	54,503	118,396	250,197	271,282	370,619	399,209	514,057	519,043
Education for the handicapped[7]	72	248	2,516	4,918	16,793	47,846	67,933	89,947	152,050	328,463
Emergency school aid[8]							92,214	196,045	204,027	265,860
Followthrough				5,291	7,437	10,608	2,024	46,595	39,825	57,300
Indian education								15,694	42,046	57,882
Office of Education salaries and expenditures[9]	11,608	12,664	14,251	25,901	40,906	47,714	84,694	77,411	117,618	132,450
School lunch and milk programs	305,512	366,900	411,700	421,900	543,845	676,196	1,213,075	1,266,673	1,890,276	2,810,082

[1]Does not include transition quarter amounts. / [2]Estimated. / [3]Includes amounts distributed under provision of the Elementary and Secondary Education Act of 1965 (ESEA) and the National Defense Education Act (NDEA). Funds authorized under Title VI of ESEA for education of the handicapped are not included here but under "Education for the handicapped." / [4]Title I of ESEA includes funds for students more than one year below grade level, Indian children, migratory children, handicapped children, and neglected and delinquent children. / [5]Includes amounts authorized under Titles II, III, and V of ESEA and NDEA Titles III, X, and a portion of V for guidance, counseling, and testing. / [6]Also includes program amounts for students with special needs. / [7]Amounts for teacher training not included. / [8]Also includes civil rights services and training. / [9]Includes higher education and amounts for technical service, planning and evaluation, and special studies, and projects not covered elsewhere.

From U.S. Department of Health, Education, and Welfare, National Center for Education Statistics, *Digest of Education Statistics, 1979*, (Washington, D.C.: G.P.O., 1979), pp. 166, 172.

Brown v. Board of Education

One of the most momentous events to bring the federal courts into education occurred in 1954 with the Supreme Court's decision in *Brown* v. *Board of Education of Topeka*. Overturning the "separate but equal" doctrine established in *Plessy* v. *Ferguson* in 1896, the Supreme Court in the *Brown* decision ruled segregated schools to be "inherently unequal" and in violation of the Fourteenth Amendment of the Constitution. Using sociological and psychological evidence, Chief Justice Earl Warren stated:

> Segregation of white and colored children in public schools has a detrimental effect upon the colored children. The impact is greater when it has the sanction of the law; for the policy of separating the races is usually interpreted as denoting the inferiority of the Negro group. A sense of inferiority affects the motivation of a child to learn. Segregation with the sanction of law, therefore, has a tendency to retard the education and mental development of Negro children and to deprive them of some of the benefits they would receive in a racially integrated school system.[6]

Although the NAACP and other organizations had taken initiatives to desegregate American schools, it was the *Brown* decision that gave official judicial sanction to desegregation efforts.

The desegregation ruling had its first impact on the dual school systems of southern and border states where segregation was de jure, with the force of state law as well as custom. In the 1960s and 1970s, desegregation efforts were to have an impact on the school systems of the large northern cities where racial segregation was de facto in that it was based on residential housing patterns and local attendance areas rather than by force of law.

The Civil Rights Act of 1964

In breaking the hold of segregation on American schools, judicial action went hand in hand with congressional legislation and civil rights enforcement by the executive branch, especially the Justice Department. A key element in the desegregation machinery and process was the enactment of the Civil Rights Act in 1964, which prohibited discrimination in public accommodations, employment practices, and education and provided for federal enforcement through the courts. Of particular importance in education was the provision that prohibited discrimination in programs that were federally funded. School districts and educational institutions that violated the nondiscriminatory provisions of the act could lose federal funds.

"With All Deliberate Speed"

Since the late 1960s, the Supreme Court and the federal judiciary sought to implement its decision that school desegregation should proceed "with all deliberate speed" in a series of court cases. In 1968, in the *Green* v. *County School*

---

[6]*Brown* v. *The Board of Education*, 347 U.S. 483 (1954).

97

Board and *Monroe* v. *Board of Commissioners* decisions, the Supreme Court ruled unconstitutional local plans that allowed students the option of transfer to avoid desegregation. In *Alexander* v. *Holmes City Board of Education,* the Court declared that districts were obligated "to terminate dual school systems at once." In its 1971 decision in *Swann* v. *Charlotte-Mecklenburg,* the Supreme Court upheld the use of citywide busing to achieve integration.[7]

The decisions of the Supreme and other federal courts in desegregation and civil rights matters has had a decided impact on American education and has resulted in a growing body of legal requirements with which school districts and other educational institutions must comply. Although this body of legal requirements is growing, it is also continually being reviewed. It is clear that racially segregated, dual school systems are unconstitutional and that, to achieve desegregation, the courts will redress grievances that come from racially motivated assignments of students, organization of attendance areas, construction of facilities, and teacher assignments that maintain segregated patterns of schooling.

The Federal Judiciary and the Handicapped

Following the precedents that aimed at ending racial discrimination, the courts began to hear cases in which parents challenged local school practices that excluded the handicapped. A federal district court in Pennsylvania heard a suit brought by the Pennsylvania Association for Retarded Children (PARC) against the Commonwealth of Pennsylvania in 1971. The court's decision was that handicapped children had a constitutional claim to free education as did nonhandicapped children. *Mills* v. *Board of Education of Columbia* in 1972 extended the right to an education to all handicapped children and guaranteed them the right to due process protection.[8]

The decisions of the federal district courts to guarantee the rights of handicapped children to an education anticipated the legislation that followed. Section 504 of the Rehabilitation Services Act of 1973 and the Education of All Handicapped Children Act of 1975 were far-reaching laws that are examined in Chapter 18.

In the 1970s, the Supreme Court also rendered a decision regarding bilingual education in *Lau* v. *Nichols.*[9] In the *Lau* decision, the Supreme Court ruled that the City of San Francisco violated the Civil Rights Act by failing to make appropriate educational provisions for non-English-speaking children of Chinese descent. The Court's decision in the *Lau* case has been interpreted to mean that schools receiving federal aid are to provide special instruction to non-English-speaking children.

[7]*Green* v. *County School Board* 391 U.S. 430 (1968); *Monroe* v. *Board of Commissioners,* 391 U.S. 377 (1968); *Alexander* v. *Holmes City Board of Education,* 396 U.S. 19 (1969); *Swann* v. *Charlotte-Mecklenburg,* 402 U.S. 1 (1961).

[8]*Pennsylvania Association for Retarded Children (PARC)* v. *Commonwealth of Pennsylvania,* 343 F. Supp. 279 (E.D. PA 1972); *Mills* v. *Board of Education of the District of Columbia,* 348 F. Supp. 866 (D.D.C. 1972).

[9]*Lau* v. *Nichols,* 414 U.S. 563 (1974).

Activity by the federal courts continues in the issue of separation of church and state. The First Amendment of the Constitution, stating that "Congress shall make no law respecting an establishment of religion, or prohibiting the free exercise thereof," led to a series of cases dealing with aid to parochial schools and religious observance and prayer in the public schools.

In the matter of federal aid to parochial schools, the Court has consistently ruled direct aid to parochial schools to be unconstitutional. However, in several specific cases, the Court has allowed indirect aid. In the *Everson* case in 1947, the Court upheld a New Jersey law that provided public transportation reimbursements to parents of both public and parochial school children. In *Walz v. Tax Commission* in 1970, the Court granted tax-exempt status to property used only for religious purposes. In the *Board of Education* v. *Allen* in 1971, the Court upheld the lending of state-approved textbooks to children attending parochial schools.[10]

In addition to cases related to public aid to religious schools, the federal judiciary also has heard cases relating to religion and the curriculum. In 1920, the Supreme Court, in *Pierce* v. *Society of Sisters,* upheld the right of parents to send their children to private schools—including religious schools—providing that these schools meet minimum state standards. In *Zorach* v. *Clauson* in 1952, the Court upheld "released-time" programs in which children attending public schools were allowed to attend religious instruction in facilities other than the public schools. In *Engel* v. *Vitale* in 1962, the Court ruled that state laws requiring prayer in the public schools violated separation of church and state.[11] In other decisions, the Supreme Court has ruled that it is permissible for public schools to teach about religion as an objective study but not to provide denominational religious education.

THE CONTEMPORARY FEDERAL ROLE
IN EDUCATION

By the 1970s, the principle of federal assistance to education appeared to have general acceptance. The administrations of President Ford and President Carter continued the assistance programs that had been enacted by previous administrations. A major tendency that occurred throughout the 1970s was the growing complexity of federal guidelines and regulations governing the application for and the receiving of federal aid. In 1978, for example, the Education Amendments of Congress showed a tendency to write very detailed legislation and to establish very specific administrative procedures in planning grant proposals and in expending and accounting for funds received and dispersed. Complaints were

---

[10]*Walz* v. *Tax Commission,* 397 U.S. 644 (1970); *Board of Education* v. *Allen,* 392 U.S. 371 (1971).

[11]*Pierce* v. *Society of Sisters,* 268 U.S. 310 (1920); *Zorach* v. *Clauson,* 343 U.S. 306 (1952); *Engel* v. *Vitale,* 370 U.S. 421 (1962).

frequently heard from the educational community and educational administrators about the time and energy required to deal with the federal bureaucracy.

Creating a Federal Department of Education

In his campaign for the presidency in 1976, Jimmy Carter urged creation of a separate Department of Education, at cabinet level, to focus national attention on educational issues and to identify a national agency to speak for education. The issue of the creation of a federal Department of Education provoked considerable controversy. Conservative political groups generally opposed the Department of Education as another example of federal expansion into areas that had been reserved previously to local and state governments. Although the majority of the nation's educational associations tended to favor the creation of a federal department, there was also opposition among some educational groups. The National Education Association led a strong campaign for the department. The American Federation of Teachers and the National Catholic Education Associations were opposed. After considerable debate, Congress created a federal Department of Education in 1979. Headed by Shirley M. Hufstedler, the new department administered programs that were scattered previously throughout several federal agencies. It assumed responsibilities for administering federal programs for overseas dependents, special education and rehabilitation services, elementary and secondary education, vocational and adult education, higher education, bilingual and minority language affairs, and educational research.

Figure 6–1   U.S. Department of Education

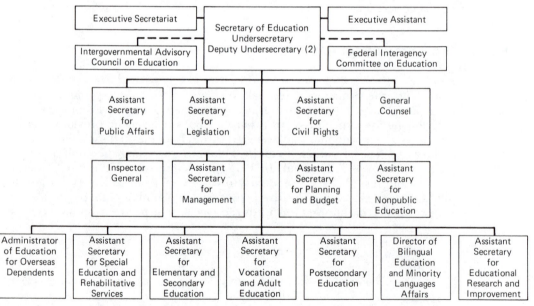

Published by the Office of Public Affairs, National Institute of Education, U.S. Department of Education

In the presidential election of 1980, the young Department of Education was again controversial. While Jimmy Carter, the Democratic candidate for re-election defended the new department, the Republican contender Ronald Reagan was opposed. With Reagan's election, the future of the federal Department of Education has been doubtful. President Reagan appointed Terrel Bell as secretary. Figure 6–1 illustrates the present organization of the U.S. Department of Education.

The Reagan administration has reduced federal aid to education substantially. President Reagan has proposed that federal funds be distributed in block grants to the states for redistribution to local school districts. Block grants are a major departure from categorical aid grants designed for specific purposes.

A much debated proposal favored by the Reagan administration is tuition tax credits. If approved by Congress, tuition tax credits would provide a tax credit for every full-time student enrolled in any eligible private or public educational institution at the elementary, secondary, or higher levels. Certain groups representing public education are opposed to federal tax credits as a threat to adequate financing of public institutions and as a violation of separation of church and state. Private school leaders generally are eager supporters of tuition tax credits as are those who argue for the creation of educational alternatives.

CONCLUSION

Since the establishment of the American republic, the federal government has very gradually increased its involvement in education, through programs of federal funding and assistance. The federal role in education has always been a controversial one, particularly in such areas as local initiative, states rights, and separation of church and state.

Since the 1950s, the federal role increased dramatically, especially as a result of the Supreme Court decision in the *Brown* case. The enactment of the National Defense Education Act and the Elementary and Secondary Education Act provided substantial assistance to schools. In the 1980s, it appears that the federal role will diminish as the amount of federal assistance is reduced. Federal involvement and assistance is unpredictable, however, because it depends on the public mood and the changing circumstances of American political life.

DISCUSSION QUESTIONS

1. Analyze the federal role in education until the Civil War.
2. Identify the organizations and groups that opposed federal aid to education in the century from the Civil War to the enactment of the NDEA. Analyze the motives of these groups in opposing federal aid.
3. Using the enactment of the Smith–Hughes Act for aid to vocational education as a case study, examine the role of special-interest groups in obtaining federal aid.
4. Describe the climate that led to the enactment of the NDEA.
5. Distinguish between categorical and block grants.

6. Describe the provisions of the Elementary and Secondary Education Act.
7. Analyze the reasoning of the Supreme Court in the *Brown* case of 1954.
8. Describe the role of the federal government in desegregation of American schools.
9. Comment on the role of the federal government in bilingual education and the education of the handicapped.
10. Comment on the decisions of the U.S. Supreme Court regarding separation of church and state that have a relevance to education.

FIELD EXERCISES

1. Identify a particular U.S. senator or member of the House of Representatives. Examine his or her record on federal aid to education.
2. Keep a log of the articles that appear in major newspapers or news magazines on the role of the federal government in education.
3. Invite a member of the administration of your college or university to visit your class and discuss the various areas of institutional involvement with the federal government.
4. Invite an elementary or secondary school administrator to visit your class and discuss his or her district's involvement with the federal government.
5. Debate the proposition: Resolved, federal aid to public schools should be increased.
6. Debate the proposition: Resolved, the federal government should provide tuition tax credits to the parents of private school children.

SELECTED READINGS

Advisory Commission on Intergovernmental Relations. *The Federal Role in the Federal System: The Dynamics of Growth; Intergovernmentalizing the Classroom: Federal Involvement in Elementary and Secondary Education.* Washington, D.C.: G.P.O., 1981.

BAILEY, STEPHEN K., AND MOSHER, EDITH K. *ESEA: The Office of Education Administers a Law.* Syracuse, N.Y.: Syracuse University Press, 1968.

BERMAN, DANIEL M. *It Is So Ordered: The Supreme Court Rules on School Segregation.* New York: W. W. Norton, 1966.

DUKER, SAM. *The Public Schools and Religion: The Legal Context.* New York: Harper & Row, 1966.

HOGAN, JOHN C. *The Schools, the Courts, and the Public Interest.* Lexington, Mass.: D. C. Heath, 1974.

MERANTO, PHILIP. *The Politics of Federal Aid to Education in 1965: A Study in Political Innovation.* Syracuse, N.Y.: Syracuse University Press, 1967.

MUNGER, FRANK J., AND FENNO, RICHARD F. *National Politics and Federal Aid to Education.* Syracuse, N.Y.: Syracuse University Press, 1962.

TIEDT, SIDNEY. *The Role of the Federal Government in Education.* New York: Oxford University Press, 1966.

WIRT, FREDERICK M., AND KIRST, MICHAEL W. *The Political Web of American Schools.* Boston: Little, Brown, 1972.

7

The State Role in Education

Unlike many of the nations of the world, the United States does not have a national school system. While many forces bring uniformity to American education, the United States has fifty state public school systems. Since the legal authority for education rests with each state, it is historically and legally accurate to speak of the Illinois, Texas, or Massachusetts systems of public schools rather than the American school system. The underlying reasons for the absence of a national school system and the existence of fifty state systems can be explained in part by the historical and social forces that have shaped American educational patterns.

HISTORICAL PERSPECTIVE ON STATE AUTHORITY

Although there was considerable discussion about a federal system of education in the early national period, the U.S. Constitution did not specifically address education. The Tenth Amendment, ratified in 1791, stated that "The powers not delegated to the United States by the Constitution, nor prohibited by it to the States, are reserved to the States, respectively, or to the people." Under the "reserved powers" clause, each of the states has the power to organize, administer, and support education.

In their own constitutions, the various states made some statement or provision concerning education. In each state, the legislature enacts laws, including those governing education and schools. Legally, then, the legislature of each state is the supreme policymaking body in that state. The state legislature enacts the laws that govern school organization, administration, and financing. From the initial statement of educational responsibility in the state constitution, each state evolved the historical patterns that shaped its schools. This chapter deals with the historical development and elaboration of state power and then turns to the contemporary role of the states.

Common Schools and the States

In the various states of the Union, it was the common school movement of the early nineteenth century that made the state constitutional provisions an institutional reality. It was the common school movement that culminated in the present-day public school. First, it is necessary to define what is meant by the term "common school." In its origins, a common school was an elementary school that was supported by public taxation, governed by elected officials, and served the educational needs of the children living in the area in which it was located. The common school, or school for all children, offered a curriculum that stressed the basic skills of reading, writing, and arithmetic and often history, geography, music, art, and health.

In each of the states in the early nineteenth century, there were those who wanted common schools and those who opposed them. Essentially, however, in the history of the state role in education, the crusade for common schools was a major episode in the emergence of state educational control. Although the actual historical events differed somewhat from state to state, a general pattern emerged.

First, the state legislature enacted permissive legislation that made it possible for the residents of the various sections of the state to organize school districts. Generally, the majority of voters who lived within the boundary lines of the proposed district would have to vote to establish a district. In most of the northern states, the district pattern of organization was based on that of New England, especially Massachusetts, which had established school districts as far back as the colonial period. The establishment of school districts was an important first step in that the state legislature was using the district as the basic unit for state control. The essential definition of a school district, framed in the early nineteenth century, has remained much the same.

A school district is an instrument or agency of the state, which operates under state laws and is intended to execute the state's policy for the administration of public education. The school district, internally, is governed by an elected board that is responsible for the establishment, maintenance, organization, administration, and support of the school or schools within its jurisdiction. The geographical jurisdiction of the school district is determined by boundary lines that designate the area whose population it serves and whose population will support it.

After the first step of permitting the organization of districts in the state, the state legislature then encouraged districts to organize and levy taxes for support of common or public schools. The state usually encouraged public education by giving funds, grants-in-aid, to districts that were taxing themselves for school support. The state was, at this stage, using such grants to encourage or to stimulate public education. It did not, however, mandate or make publicly supported common schooling compulsory. Several important characteristics of the emergent public school system appeared at this stage. The local district would raise most of the money needed to support schools through local taxes, usually a property tax. Local funds would then be supplemented by state aid.

The third stage in the development of the state system of schools came with a state mandate that made public or common schooling compulsory. In effect, the state now was requiring that school districts organize to provide public education to the children of the state. Also as a result of this historical experience, two kinds of state laws concerning education emerged: mandatory and permissive. While mandatory laws were to be followed uniformly throughout the state, permissive laws gave local school districts the option to use discretionary powers in certain limited situations.

In terms of chronology, the movement for common schools occurred first in New England, where Massachusetts was a leading state, then in the states of the old Northwest Territory, followed by the Middle Atlantic states. States in the South generally did not enact effective common school legislation until the Reconstruction.

In the various campaigns that were launched on behalf of common schools, certain major educational leaders emerged. Among them were Horace Mann in Massachusetts, Henry Barnard in Connecticut, and Calvin Wiley in New York. These individuals frequently popularized the idea of common schooling and led the campaign for it in the state legislatures. To examine the leadership role played by such leaders of the common school movement, the career of Horace Mann is examined.

Horace Mann as a Common School Leader

Horace Mann (1796–1859), often called the "Father of American Public Education," led the movement for common schools in Massachusetts. His public career shows him to be a leader who helped to define the concept of public education and who contributed to the state role in public education. A native of Massachusetts, Mann was educated in the town school of Franklin, graduated from Brown University in 1819, and entered the legal profession.[1] He was elected to the Massachusetts state legislature in 1827, where he served six years. From 1833 to 1837, he served in the Massachusetts state Senate. As a leading member of the Massachusetts legislature, Mann was concerned with education in his state. In this regard, he was not unlike other political leaders who recognized the need of improving public education in their states. As a result of the efforts of Mann

---

[1]For the definitive biography of Mann, see Jonathan Messerli, *Horace Mann: A Biography* (New York: Knopf, 1972).

Horace Mann (1796–1859), the "Father of the American Common School," was secretary of the Massachusetts Board of Education and a national leader of the public school movement. *(New York Public Library Picture Collection)*

and other like-minded legislators, Massachusetts passed An Act Relating to Common Schools in 1837.

When the Massachusetts Board of Education was established, Mann was appointed its secretary. Mann's function was to collect school statistics, make information available about the condition of schools, and encourage the improvement of schools and teaching. To accomplish these tasks, he visited schools throughout the state so that he could determine directly the condition of schools.

From 1837 to 1848, as secretary of the State Board of Education, Mann worked to increase support for common schools, to improve teacher preparation in normal schools, and to improve instruction. To publicize the cause of public education, Mann edited the *Common School Journal* and wrote his annual reports to the Board of Education, which are classic statements about the role and purposes of American public education. Mann's *Twelfth Annual Report,* in 1848, summed up his thoughts on public education: the "Common School . . . may become the most effective and benignant of all forces of civilization."[2]

As a result of the pioneering efforts of Mann, the state governments began to exercise a minimal supervisory function through a state board of education, state superintendent, or commissioner of education. The state superintendent became identified as the chief official for public education in the state. As the functions of the office developed in the nineteenth century, the state superintendent was responsible for (1) collecting educational statistics and data; (2) making recommendations for improving common schools; (3) preparing reports to inform the public, the board, and the legislature about educational conditions in the state; and (4) overseeing the distribution of school funds from

[2]Horace Mann, *Lectures and Annual Reports on Education* (Cambridge, Mass.: Cornhill Press, 1867), p. 80.

the state to the local districts. Near the end of the nineteenth century, state superintendents also assumed the responsibility of registering teachers' certificates and presenting minimal certification requirements.

EDUCATIONAL RESPONSIBILITIES WITHIN STATE GOVERNMENT

The authority of each of the states to provide and maintain schools is a broad area of responsibility that is subdivided between the various branches of the state government. Essentially, the state legislature enacts the laws governing education, and the executive branch of state government (the governor) enforces them. State courts often render decisions regarding litigation over school matters. It is important to note that the state government has delegated significant responsibilities to school boards (boards of education) in local school districts.

Responsibilities of the Legislature

In most states, the state constitution charges the state legislature with the responsibility of establishing and maintaining a system of free public or common schools. Within this general area of responsibility, local school boards are part of state government and serve as an agent of the state in performing their educational functions. Although local school boards have considerable powers, their authority is delegated to them and is exercised at the pleasure of the state legislature.

Legislation affecting schools enters into a range of complex areas, especially establishing the foundation formula that allocates state funds to local school districts. Although the state legislature must enact the laws governing schools, legislators are guided by recommendations from the state department of education and special committees and task forces on educational matters. In enacting school legislation, the members of the legislature have to deal with the conflicting arguments and demands of various educational lobbies, such as the school boards' association, teachers' unions and organizations, citizens groups, and other special-interest groups.

Much of the work preliminary to the enactment of legislation is done by committees of the senate and house of the state legislature, particularly those on finance and education. Committee recommendations are then brought to each house of the legislature for action. Bills that pass both houses are then sent to the governor for his or her signature or veto.

The School Code

The state legislature enacts the laws that govern the establishment, organization, administration, financing, minimum standards, minimum curriculum requirements, and other matters affecting public schools in that state. The state school laws are collected and published in a document called the state school code. The typical school code is a comprehensive and detailed compendium of the state's laws affecting education. Among the topics found in a school code are school board elections, child labor laws, transportation, conduct of school board meetings, school construction, education of handicapped children, budgets, tax rates, bonds, compulsory attendance, school holidays, and safety provisions. Teachers are affected directly by the provisions in school codes that relate to their employment, tenure and duties, and curriculum and instructional material. For example, the School Code of Illinois states that

> History of the United States shall be taught in all public schools and in all other educational institutions in this State, supported or maintained, in whole or in part, by public funds. The teaching of history shall have as one of its objectives the imparting to pupils of a comprehensive idea of our democratic form of government and the principles for which our government stands as regards other nations including the studying of the place of our government in world-wide movements and the leaders thereof, with particular stress upon the basic principles and ideals of our representative form of government. The teaching of history shall include a study of the role and contributions of American Negroes and other ethnic groups including, but not restricted to, Polish, Lithuanian, German, Hungarian, Irish, Bohemian, Russian, Albanian, Italian, Czechoslovakian, French, Scots, etc., in the history of this country and this state. No pupil shall be graduated from the eighth grade of any public school unless he has received such instruction in the history of the United States and gives evidence of having a comprehensive knowledge thereof.[3]

Although the school codes are technical and detailed, they set forth the statutes governing education in each state. Final legal authority in each state over the constitutionality of a state law is held by that states' court of highest appeal, usually the state supreme court. In many instances decisions have been appealed to the U.S. Supreme Court.

Executive Responsibilities

At the executive level of state government, responsibility for education is lodged with the governor, the chief state school officer (usually the state superintendent of public instruction or school commissioner), and the state board of education and its staff. The governor is charged with enforcing school laws. As a political leader in the state, the governor influences party members in the legislature to support or to oppose particular bills affecting education. The governor's budget recommendations are crucial for school support in that they indicate the amount of state aid that schools will receive in a given year, provided that the legislature agrees. It is the governor who either signs the bills that become law or vetoes them. Of importance is the governor's power of appointment. In states where the state board of education is appointed, the governor has this important function. Through the power of appointments, the governor influences policymaking that has an impact on schools.

[3]*The School Code of Illinois 1981* (St. Paul, Minn.: West, 1981), pp. 165–166.

State Board of Education

While the legal authority for education rests in the legislature, the various states have established state boards of education to set educational policies for the state. Although there are variations from state to state, the state board generally has authority over elementary and secondary school districts. For example, forty-eight states give authority to a board of education over elementary and secondary school districts in that state.

Membership on state boards of education also varies from state to state. Membership is by appointment, election, or some combination of election and appointment. In thirty states, members are appointed by the governor; nine states have elected boards; eleven states use a combination of election and appointment. The number of members on a state board of education also varies. Texas is the largest, with twenty-one members; Mississippi has only three members. The usual number ranges between seven and eleven.

The role of the state board of education can be understood best by examining its functions. Its general functions are to carry out the educational responsibilities that must be administered at the state level. As a policymaking body, the state board formulates the educational policies that relate to the implementation, control, and supervision of education throughout the state. Frequently, the state board appoints or elects the chief state school officer, designates the term of appointment, defines the duties, and fixes the salary.

State School Officers

One of the major responsibilities of the state board of education is to select the chief school officer of the state, whose title is usually that of state superintendent of public instruction or commissioner of education. In twenty-four states, the chief state school officer is appointed by the state board of education. In five states this official is appointed by the governor. Twenty-one states continue to elect their superintendents of public instruction.

The chief state educational officer and staff constitute the state department of education. The functions of the state department of education again vary from state to state. However, some of the common functions can be identified. First, the state department enforces the school codes by making certain that the local school districts are in compliance with their provisions. Second, the state department is the agency for the distribution of state and federal funds to local school districts; it also distributes funds allocated to the state by the federal government for specific purposes, such as vocational education, special education, and school lunch programs. Third, the state department is the principal agency for teacher certification by establishing and enforcing certification requirements for teachers at the various levels and in the various subject matters. Fourth, the state department establishes task forces to investigate and propose solutions to specific problems, such as declining enrollments, school vandalism, and other issues, and publishes reports to aid local school districts in dealing with their own special problems.

The state department of education exercises its greatest control over local school districts by establishing and enforcing minimum standards, which are designed to provide pupils with a basic standard of education regardless of their location within a state. Minimum standards include (1) making sure that teachers possess the minimum qualifications needed for state certification, (2) requiring that students be in attendance for a minimum number of days each year, (3) requiring that the curriculum include such subjects as the English language, American history, health education, and physical education, and (4) making sure that school buildings meet certain standards of construction, heating, lighting, and ventilation that protect students' health and safety. If local districts fail to meet the minimum standards established by the state board of education, they face penalties, such as reduction in state financial aid.

The State and Local Control of Schools

While the state legislature and executive branch of state government are charged with establishing and maintaining public schools, they have delegated much of the day-to-day operation of these schools to local boards of education. The delegated responsibilities of local school boards include (1) establishing of attendance areas and schools to serve the children resident in them, (2) construction and maintenance of school facilities, (3) employment of a superintendent of schools, (4) establishing the policies designed to govern and manage schools, and (5) the power to levy and expend money. Although delegated responsibilities are extensive, the powers of the local school board are prescribed and delimited by the state legislature and are recorded in the state school code. A detailed account of the role of the local school district and board of education appears in Chapter 8. Chapter 9, on finance, examines state and local school support.

AREAS OF STATE CONTROL

There is considerable variation among the states regarding the specific areas that they reserve to themselves and that they delegate to local districts. The following sections examine some of the major areas that are subject to direct state prescription.

Curriculum and Instruction

The states are responsible for identifying certain basic curriculum areas that must be offered in the public elementary and secondary schools of the state. Such basic curriculum areas often include the study of the English language, U.S. and in some instances local history, the study of the U.S. and state constitutions, health, and physical education. The states may also require certain minimal standards or levels of competency in these mandated curriculum areas. Many states allow broad discretionary powers to local boards of education in curricular and instructional matters. A recent trend has been for some states to require minimal competency tests as part of the graduation requirement for students.

In the selection of textbooks, most states allow the local school boards to select and purchase books and other instructional materials, but some state boards of education identify and distribute the textbooks used in the public schools.

Compulsory Attendance

Generally, children are required to attend school from ages seven or eight until age sixteen. Most states specify a minimum school term that requires schools be in session a prescribed number of days. The typical mandated school calendar is about 180 days. The states may also specify certain holidays in which schools are not to be in session.

Certification of School Personnel

Most states have specific regulations regarding the certification of school teachers, administrators, and other educational personnel. Certification is a means of maintaining the quality of education.

Many state boards of education have established teacher certification boards that issue certificates to teachers, administrators, and other educational personnel. Many state certification boards also recognize or approve college and university preparation programs and grant certificates to graduates of approved programs. Many states also permit individuals to present their credentials to the state certification board and to request the issuance of a certificate.

Facilities Standards and Requirements

Most states' school codes have provisions relating to the specifications of school buildings and other physical plant facilities. Designed to ensure the life safety of the students, they govern such items as standards for school construction, ventilation, heating, lighting, recreation areas, and other matters connected with buildings and maintenance.

Financial Support

Because the state is responsible for establishing and maintaining public schools, formulas for public taxation must be designed, approved, and implemented. The bulk of the financial support for schools comes from the local property tax and state aid. The states generally have been specific as to the taxing powers and rates that local school districts can levy. The states have developed foundation programs to determine the distribution of state aid.

Most states have established a ceiling on the taxation rate that a local school district can levy. They prescribe the format for the local school budget as well as the assessment and collection of school funds, especially through the local property tax, by county or other units of government.

CONCLUSION

The American educational system is comprised of fifty different state school systems. In each state, the legislature has ultimate responsibility for establishing, organizing, and financing public schools. The states, in turn, have delegated substantial educational responsibility to local school districts. Among the major responsibilities of state government to education is the financing of schools. To this end, state legislatures have established foundation formulas for state aid to schools. The governor of the state has responsibility for implementing the state laws governing education. The state superintendent of instruction or school commissioner has the responsibility for making recommendations to the legislature, governor, and other state officials. The state board of education exercises a variety of educational functions, including the certification of teachers.

As is true of the American political system, the governance of the educational system is divided among the federal, state, and local governments. Of these levels, the state has major responsibility.

QUESTIONS AND ANSWERS

1. Do research on education in France and the United States. Briefly compare and contrast the role of the national government in each country.
2. What is the constitutional basis for the states' role in education?
3. Trace the effects of the common school movement in developing the states' educational role.
4. Read a biography of a leader in the common school system, such as Horace Mann or Henry Barnard. From your reading, ascertain the growing role of the state in educational affairs.
5. Examine your state's school code. Identify the major areas covered in the code.
6. Describe the functions of the state board of education in your state.
7. Enumerate the functions of the state department of education in your state.
8. What is your state's policy on textbook selection?
9. Identify the subjects that are mandated in your state.

FIELD EXERCISES

1. Invite a member of the state legislature to your class to discuss your state's educational role.
2. Maintain a log on newspaper articles dealing with state actions in education.
3. Invite a local school board member to your class to discuss his or her conception of the state's educational role.
4. Invite a member of a local teachers' union or association to your class to discuss his or her conception of the state's educational role.
5. Analyze your governor's statements on education and see if you can identify his or her basic educational policy.
6. Identify your state superintendent of public instruction and members of the state board of education. Prepare short biographical statements for each.

SELECTED READINGS

CAMPBELL, ROALD F., CUNNINGHAM, LUVERN L., USDAN, MICHAEL D., AND NYSTRAND, RAPHAEL O. *The Organization and Control of American Schools.* Columbus, Ohio: Charles E. Merrill, 1980.

CAMPBELL, ROALD F., AND MAZZONI, TIM I., JR.   *State Policy Making for the Public Schools*. Berkeley, Calif.: McCutchan, 1976.

HARRIS, SAM P.   *State Departments of Education, State Boards of Education and Chief State School Officers*. Washington, D.C.: G.P.O., 1973.

KATZ, MICHAEL S.   *A History of Compulsory Education Laws*. Bloomington, Ind.: Phi Delta Kappa Educational Foundation, 1976.

MESSERLI, JONATHAN.   *Horace Mann: A Biography*. New York: Knopf, 1972.

THURSTON, LEE M., AND ROE, WILLIAM H.   *State School Administration*. New York: Harper & Row, 1947.

WIRT, FREDERICK M., AND KIRST, MICHAEL W.   *The Political Web of American Schools*. Boston: Little, Brown, 1972.

8

The Local Role in Education

Although the constitutional authority for education is the state government, American educational patterns historically have been decentralized with important responsibilities being vested in local school districts. Instead of a national system of education, the decentralized pattern of American education takes the form of thousands of local school districts throughout the United States. In these local districts, boards of education make the policies that govern public schools and levy the taxes that pay for them. Chapter 8 examines the historical origins of local control of education and discusses the contemporary forces and trends that shape educational policies in the local school districts of the nation.

HISTORICAL ORIGINS OF LOCAL CONTROL

The origins for the local control of American education date back to the seventeenth century. In New England, particularly in Massachusetts, religious, economic, and social forces made the town the basic social, political, and educational unit. An area of from twenty to forty square miles, the town was generally settled by members of a particular religious congregation. A particular congregation would petition the General Court, the colonial legislature, for permission to settle in a new town. When the General Court granted the petition, the town as a corporate entity was entitled to hold town meetings, elect selectmen or trustees, and send representatives to the General Court.[1] In addition to their attachment to local government, the New England Puritans also were strongly committed to schooling as a means of bringing up a literate and religiously orthodox population. These two factors of town or local control and a commitment to education were important forces in originating the American concept of local control of education.

Laws that reflected the Puritan commitment to civil control of education were those of 1642 and 1647 enacted by the General Court of Massachusetts. The Law of 1642 required the town selectmen to make certain that the children in each town were able to read and to understand the principles of religion; the Law of 1647 required every town of fifty or more families to appoint a teacher to give instruction in reading and writing. Every town of one hundred or more families was to appoint a master to give instruction in Latin to prepare boys to meet Harvard entry requirements. The General Court's action originated the principle that the state government had the authority to control schools. The civil or political authority was to supervise and control schools and to require that children be educated through the expenditure of public funds. In Massachusetts, the laws placed responsibility for education on local town boards of selectmen or trustees who were to (1) examine, commission, and certify the schoolmaster; (2) establish and maintain the school; and (3) levy taxes for the support of the school. As the towns became more populated, colonial legislatures gave towns the right to divide into smaller local districts to direct, conduct, and administer schools. Each district within a township was a separate and independent entity for school governance. In the late eighteenth and early nineteenth centuries, each district with its own elected board of trustees often administered a single school.

Local Control in the Nineteenth Century

After the American Revolution and in the first half of the nineteenth century during the common school movement, the general pattern of school control that emerged remained localized and decentralized in most of the northern states. The school district, with its own elected board, became the most immediate unit of organization and administration of public education. As the midwestern and other northern states entered the Union, they tended to adopt the New England pattern of township or district control. The southern states adopted the county as their unit of educational administration and organization.

Although the states made the local districts responsible for implementing their educational policies, school districts are creatures of and derive their powers from the state. Only by permission of the state legislatures or through powers delegated to it can the local school district control its own affairs.

[1]Newton Edwards and Herman G. Richey, *The School in the American Social Order* (Boston: Houghton Mifflin, 1963), pp. 41–43.

CONTEMPORARY SCHOOL DISTRICTS

The local school district is the basic unit of educational administration, organization, and support in the United States. Relying on historical precedents of local school control, most of the states have created a variety of local districts to educate the children who live in that district. The types of school districts vary in that there are elementary, secondary, and unit districts that combine both elementary and secondary schools. Some local districts are township units; others are county units. There are rural, urban, and suburban districts. Despite these variations, local school districts share some common features.

First, a local school district is a "quasi-corporation" because, while it operates like a corporation, it does not have articles of incorporation. As a state instrument, it operates under state laws and is designed to execute the state's educational policy and to facilitate the administration of public education within that state. The state's authority is executed through an elected board of education that is responsible to the state government. Second, a local school district has the responsibility of educating the children who live within that district, as identified by district boundary lines. Third, a local school district is also a unit for the financial support of schools, through taxes on its residents' property. Fourth, within the local district, citizens, through their elected board of education, establish educational policies to govern the administration, organization, financing, and maintenance of schools.

Before describing the functions of the board of education that governs each local school district, it is useful to examine the number and types of school districts and the relationships existing between school districts and other governmental units.

Number of School Districts

In 1900, there were more than 100,000 local school districts; as of the school year 1975–76, there were 16,376 districts operating in the United States.[2] However, of the thousands of local school districts that still function in the United States, 40 percent are located in the states of Nebraska, Illinois, Texas, South Dakota, California, and Minnesota. Because of the great variety of districts, there are wide variations in area, population, and financial support from district to district.

Since World War II, there has been a trend to consolidate school districts. Although there has been resistance on the part of those who believe that smaller districts mean that control will be closer to and more responsive to the people of the district, the advocates of consolidation have generally prevailed. The arguments for consolidation have generally been as follows. (1) Larger districts make it possible to eliminate the duplication of administrative and support services and results in cost saving to the people of the district. (2) A larger district has a more diverse social, economic, ethnic, and racial population with greater opportunities for a genuinely integrated school population. (3) A larger district

[2]Roald F. Campbell et al., *The Organization and Control of American Schools* (Columbus, Ohio: Charles E. Merrill, 1980), p. 100.

will have a greater tax base that will provide more revenue for educational purposes. (4) The larger tax base and administrative efficiency will enable more resources to be devoted to increasing the program diversity in the curriculum.

Of the more than 16,000 school districts that exist in the United States, a divergent pattern of relationships between these districts and other units of government emerges. In twenty-nine states, the school districts are independent of other government units; in four states, the school district has a dependent relationship with the political division in which it is located; the remaining seventeen states present a mixed pattern of relationships, with varying degrees of dependency to the other government units.

The general argument for having school districts organized independently of other governmental units is that it provides them with greater freedom from partisan politics, political control, and political patronage. In addition, the following advantages are cited frequently: (1) the boundaries of school districts can be defined logically rather than being drawn on the historical and political accidents that have shaped other governmental units, and (2) taxation for school purposes may be viewed more favorably by voters when it is not tied to or related to other government expenditures and budgets.

Several disadvantages arise from having school districts exist independently of other units of government, as when a school district overlaps with several other units of government (e.g., municipalities, townships, and park districts), which may mean that school planning, construction, and use of facilities may have to be coordinated with several agencies of government. Obviously, in these cases, school boards and administrators will have to spend more time and effort in working cooperatively with multiple governmental agencies.

Areas Served by School Districts

Another factor to be considered is that of the populations and residential areas that they serve. Despite the variations that exist, it is possible to distinguish four types of population and residential patterns: the large city or urban, the suburban, the small town, and the rural or agricultural. Each of these population patterns presents unique opportunities and problems.

THE URBAN SCHOOL DISTRICT.   The large-city or urban school districts have boundaries that coincide with the boundaries of the city, as is the case in New York, Chicago, and Los Angeles. Boards of education in the large urban districts are either elected or appointed. In Chicago, the board of education is appointed by the mayor with the approval of the city council. Large-city school boards necessarily deal with large student populations and budgets. The school district of New York City enrolls more than 1 million students and has a budget exceeding $1 billion.

Since the mid-1950s, the problems of education in the larger cities are complex and stem from complicated demographic, sociological, and economic forces. The large-city district has historically been the location of America's greatest social mobility and change. In the late nineteenth and early twentieth centuries, the large-city districts included thousands of immigrant children in their school populations. At that time, the major problems were related to the

The one-room country schoolhouse was common at the turn of this century and is still found in some rural areas. *(Irene Springer)*

The large factorylike school was typical of large-city districts in the early twentieth century. *(Irene Springer)*

In the mid-1950s, many functionally designed schools were built in suburban school districts. *(Irene Springer)*

Three Buildings Illustrating the Historical Evolution of School Architecture and Different Types of School Districts—the One-Room Rural School, the Older Large Urban School, and the More Contemporary Suburban School.

assimilation of immigrant children. Today, the large-city or urban district is the residence of many members of disadvantaged minority groups. The so-called "inner city" is the area in which the black, Chicano, and Appalachian populations are clustered; the residential areas of the white or advantaged social and economic groups are found in the outer edges. Residential patterns found in most of the large cities have contributed to de facto segregation.

Not only do the large-city districts have problems in achieving racial integration, but they also have generally experienced a decreasing tax base as businesses and industries move from the large cities to suburban areas or to other parts of the country.

THE SUBURBAN SCHOOL DISTRICT.   Another demographic and sociological phenomenon that affected American society and education since World War II has been the growth and development of the suburb. The large city, with its equally large single school district, is ringed by numerous suburbs, each generally having its own form of municipal government and its own school district or districts. Of the great variation among suburbs, some are old and exhibit conditions that are similar to the cities that they surround; others are new and are experiencing great population growth. School districts found in the newer suburbs often have a wealthy tax base, growing housing and population developments, and newer school physical plants.

THE SMALLER-CITY OR TOWN DISTRICT.   School districts located in smaller towns and cities serve various populations, from a few thousand people to over a hundred thousand. They differ from the suburbs in that the residents of the smaller city usually work in that city rather than commute to the larger city. The small cities may have one or more school districts at the elementary level and enlarged districts at the secondary level. Some also have unified elementary and secondary districts.

The school populations of the small city, especially in the secondary or high school district, may be more heterogeneous in social background than those of the suburb or large city, however, as large cities are composed of neighborhoods populated by persons of similar social, racial, ethnic, or economic backgrounds. Since schools are attended by children who live in the neighborhood, the student population reflects that of the particular neighborhood.

RURAL OR AGRICULTURAL DISTRICTS.   In the past when the majority of the American population lived on farms and earned their livelihoods in agriculture, the small, often single-school district, was the dominant pattern of school organization in the United States. The one-room schoolhouse with a single teacher and administered by its own school board characterized elementary education in the rural United States. Since the Civil War, there has been a steady movement of population from rural to urban areas. Except in the most sparsely populated regions of the United States, the trend in rural districts has been to consolidate small districts into larger ones, to bring about more efficient operations and provide a wider range of opportunities to students.

LOCAL BOARD OF EDUCATION

The local board of education, or school board, is the legal agent specified by the state legislature with responsibility for conducting education. For convenience, the local board will simply be referred to as the school board in the remainder of this chapter. Although its members are generally elected locally, in legal reality, the school board is a state agency rather than an adjunct to or a subsidiary of local government. As indicated earlier in the chapter, the local school board evolved from the board of selectmen or trustees that governed the New England town and district schools.

School boards are generally granted large latitude by the state in governing their schools and have authority to act in many areas unless they are specifically prohibited from doing so. Despite these broad powers, school boards are subject to numerous state laws and regulations that are specified in the school codes of the various states.

Election or Selection of Board Members

About 85 percent of school board members are elected to their positions by the voters of the district; the remaining 15 percent are appointed to their positions by some other governmental agency. In many of the large-city districts, for example, school board members are appointed by the mayor with the approval of the city council. Because of many intrusions of partisan politics into school matters in the past, reforms were enacted that made the election or appointment of school board members nonpartisan. This means that school board candidates are not the formal nominees of regular or existing political parties. In a real sense, however, many school board members may be supported for election by partisan political groups or may have close ties to them.

Although candidates for school board may simply file the needed petitions to secure a place on the ballot, many districts use some sort of initial screening to identify qualified nominees. Some kind of screening committee or district caucus approves a slate of endorsed nominees to be presented to the voters at the school board elections.

Qualifications of Board Members

The legal requirements for candidacy to a board of education are generally few and simple. The candidate must be a qualified voter and a resident of the school district. However, a number of factors or characteristics are desirable for members of school boards. Among them are

1. Board members should be generally knowledgable about educational needs, problems, issues, and resources. Although they are not expected to be professional educators, they need to demonstrate a sincere and sustained interest in education.
2. They should be able to understand the nature and role of a school board.
3. They should be able to understand and direct the financial and business affairs of the school district.

4. They should know how and desire to cooperate with their colleagues on the board.
5. They should have the ability to see educational issues in broad, general terms that enable them to rise above special interests.
6. Since membership on a school board is time consuming, members should have enough time and energy to devote to the office.

Ideally, members of school boards should try to see the broad issues facing education in the nation and state as well as in their district so that the policies that they enact will serve the general interests of all the children of the district. However, in the realities of policymaking, individual board members will often be representing specific as well as general interests. Board members may often find themselves exercising a transactive role as they mediate between the specific interests present in the district without losing sight of the goal of general policymaking.

The term of office for school board members varies from state to state, but it is generally believed that board members should serve for terms of three to five years so that they can become familiar with their duties and responsibilities. To provide continuity in board matters, the terms of office for board members are staggered.

As noted earlier, the number of members of a board of education varies from state to state. The size of a large-city board often exceeds that of smaller districts. In Illinois, for example, school boards consist of seven members, but Chicago, a large-city district, has eleven members. Although opinions vary as to the desired size of a board of education, it is generally argued that a board should be large enough to be representative but not so large that it is inefficient

School boards establish the policies that govern schools at the local level. *(Cresskill, N.J., Board of Education)*

in conducting its business. Most board members are not paid for their service, but a few city and county boards offer some compensation.

Socioeconomic Background of Board Members

The social and economic backgrounds of school board members tend to reflect the composition of their districts. However, the majority are likely to be members of higher-income and -status groups. For example, boards of education will have a large number of business and professional persons as members. Members of minority groups and laborers are generally underrepresented.

Functions of a Board of Education

Primarily, a school board establishes educational goals and develops the policies by which these goals are attained efficiently. While it is the superintendent's responsibility to operate the schools according to these policies on a day-to-day basis, the board is responsible for seeing that the schools in the district are functioning according to their general policies.

As a policymaking body, school boards may act only at authorized, public meetings as a board. Individual board members may not make decisions that are binding on the district. It is important that both the public and the board members understand that the board members should not assume the tasks that are those of the superintendent and professional staff.[3]

As a policymaking body, the decisions of a local school board should occur at meetings that are held at times and places that are convenient to the general public and open to the news media. All board actions should be recorded in accurate minutes that are open to the public. For the board to be effective, it should adopt and follow procedures that contribute to its efficient operations. The following is a sample agenda that many local school boards follow:

1. A call to order by the president of the board.
2. A roll call of the board members.
3. Approval of minutes of the previous meeting.
4. The recognition of visitors, delegations, and the receipt of petitions from the public.
5. Financial matters, such as the approval of pay orders, the acceptance of invoices, and a review of receipts and expenditures.
6. The superintendent's report.
7. Old business that remains from previous meetings.
8. New business.
9. Adjournment.

While the board has the general functions of establishing a district philosophy and general policies for education within the district, it also has to attend

---

[3]*Guidelines for Effective School Board Membership: A Handbook* (Springfield: Illinois Association of School Boards, 1976), p. 7.

to many specific matters. Among the most important of the board's functions is that of employing a professional educational staff that includes a superintendent, associate or assistant superintendent, a business manager, teachers, custodians, secretaries, clerks, and other support personnel. The key appointment is that of the superintendent, who recommends the hiring of staff members who are in subordinate positions. When it employs a superintendent, the board delegates executive functions to him or her.

The school board also has the function of supporting the schools and the educational program financially. To do so, it must levy taxes, approve budgets, establish salary schedules, and keep account of the funds spent. While it relies on the superintendent, business manager, and other professional staff for advice, it alone has the responsibility for keeping the schools financially solvent.

Within the prescriptions of the state-mandated subjects, the board approves the overall educational program or the curriculum to be followed in the district. In this important function, it has the benefit of the professional staff's expertise. However, the final decision over the choice of instructional programs and materials again rests with the school board.

The school board is also responsible for providing that the children of the district have schools that are physically safe and conducive to learning. While the school codes establish the basic requirements for the "life safety" of students, the school board is responsible for maintaining heating, lighting, and ventilation that safeguard the health and physical well-being of the students who attend the district's schools. School boards, upon the recommendation of the superintendent and professional staff, also have the responsibility for approving the school calendar and the district transportation policy and establishing the boundaries of school attendance areas.

In addition to their general policymaking functions, the school board acts as a mediating agency between the public and the professional staff. It provides the public with information regarding the educational progress and problems of the school district. It also sorts out and discusses the problems that concern the public.

As teacher organizations, such as the NEA and the AFT, have become more action oriented in achieving their goals, school boards have spent more time and energy in negotiations with the bargaining agencies that represent teachers. Usually, these negotiations are conducted through well-defined procedures. Negotiations between school boards and teacher bargaining agents usually involve such matters as salary schedules, sick leaves, fringe benefits, and teaching conditions.

Board-Administrator-Staff Relationships

Although more will be said about the organization of the professional staff in Chapter 15, it is important to make some general observations about board, administrator, and staff relationships in terms of the operations of the local school district.

In any discussion of board and administrator relationships, it should be remembered that the board is the policymaking and governing body of the district and that the superintendent of schools is the chief administrative officer.

When these roles become confused, the district is likely to experience unnecessary controversy and difficulty. That is, the superintendent should not try to make policy, and the board members should not usurp the superintendent's professional role. Both public and staff confidence in the district's school system can be undermined when there is either a lack of trust or a breakdown of communications between the board and the administrator. Effective board-administrator cooperation is undermined when the board attempts to assume administrative authority or when administrators have undermined the board by making policy. Within these general guidelines, it is possible to explore board-staff relationships in greater depth.

If the local school district is to fulfill its major function of providing children with the optimum education of which they are capable, there must be a clearly defined and harmonious working relationship among the board, the superintendent, and the other administrators and staff. Once a board has adopted its policies, it becomes the responsibility of administrators to implement them. The methods used to implement policies should be defined in a handbook of rules and regulations that also contains the job descriptions of all persons who are employed by the district. This handbook should be available to all employees of the district.[4]

As the chief administrator of the district, the superintendent is charged principally with the enforcement of board-adopted policies. This means that administrative decisions should be consistent with these policies. Administrative assignments of principals, assistant principals, and other personnel should be recommended by the superintendent and approved by the board of education. While each administrator should have sufficient autonomy to function in his or her area of responsibility, the board members and the administrators of the district need to realize that a complete educational program requires mutual trust, respect, and a team effort to succeed.

In building a board-staff team, there must be effective communication between the two parties, for at least two reasons. (1) The administration and the staff have the educational expertise needed to make informed and intelligent decisions. The professional expertise that they possess should not be ignored. (2) The board members, as representatives of the public, are aware of the educational concerns of the community. Each group needs to communicate with the other.

CONCLUSION

Prospective teachers will become employees of a local board of education when they secure a teaching position. After initial employment, teachers will continue to be affected by the policies that are made by a local board of education. There will be many occasions when a teacher, often as a member of a committee, will meet with members of a board of education. Whether the teacher works in a large or a small district, it is important to have a clear idea of the role and functions of the local board of education.

[4]Ibid., p. 9.

DISCUSSION QUESTIONS

1. To a degree, contemporary institutions are a product of historical circumstances. To what degree does this statement apply to public schools?
2. What is the definition of a local school district? What is the impact of local control on American public education?
3. What are the social, economic, political, and educational advantages and disadvantages of larger consolidated school districts?
4. Describe the type of school district in which you live. Is it urban, suburban, small-town, or rural? What is the district's socioeconomic and ethnic composition?
5. As a teacher, describe the type of school district in which you would prefer to be employed.
6. Read a newspaper published in a large city and a newspaper published in a suburb or small town. Make a list of the educational issues reported in these newspapers. Compare and contrast the problems that public schools face in these different settings.
7. What is a local school board? What are its powers, responsibilities, and functions?
8. What are the desirable characteristics of school board members?
9. Describe the proper relationship that should exist between a superintendent and a school board.

FIELD EXERCISES

1. Assume that you are seeking a teaching position in a particular school district. Identify that school district. Then, do some basic research about that district. What is its population? What is the socioeconomic, ethnic, and racial composition of the district? Who are the members of the local school board? What is the condition of the schools? What are the educational issues in that district? After having developed a profile of the district based on your research, visit the district. Spend some time in its business district and its neighborhoods. Visit a school. Based upon the information that you have gathered, would you want to accept a teaching position in that district?
2. Assume that you are seeking a teaching position in a large-city (urban) school system. Refer to and use the same questions asked in Field Exercise 1, but adapt them to a subdivision, a district, within that system so that your research has a manageable base.
3. Assume you are a newspaper reporter who is covering a school board meeting. Attend a school board meeting and note the following: (a) Where is the meeting held? (b) Who is in attendance? (c) What items are on the agenda? (d) What decisions are reached? (e) What issues are raised by the public? (f) What are the interactions between board members and between board members and the superintendent and other administrators present?
4. Interview several school board members and through your questions attempt to determine how they perceive their roles and responsibilities?
5. Interview several teachers and through your questions attempt to determine how they perceive the impact that a school board has on their professional roles and responsibilities.

SUGGESTED READINGS

BOWERS, C. A., ED. *Education and Social Policy: Local Control of Education.* New York: Random House, 1970.

BURRUP, PERCY E. *The Teacher and the Public School System.* New York: Harper Row, 1967.

CAMPBELL, ROALD F., CUNNINGHAM, LUVERN L., USDAN, MICHAEL D., AND NYSTRAND, RAPHAEL O. *The Organization and Control of American Schools.* Columbus, Ohio: Charles E. Merrill, 1980.

CISTONE, PETER J., ED. *Understanding School Boards.* Lexington, Mass.: Lexington Books, 1975.

CRONIN, JOSEPH M. *The Control of Urban Schools.* New York: Free Press, 1973.

IANNACCONE, LAURENCE, AND LUTZ, FRANK W. *Politics, Power, and Policy: The Governing of Local School Districts.* Columbus, Ohio: Charles E. Merrill, 1970.

KOERNER, JAMES D. *Who Controls American Education?* Boston: Beacon Press, 1968.

WIRT, FREDERICK M., AND KIRST, MICHAEL W. *The Political Web of American Schools.* Boston: Little, Brown, 1972.

9

Financing
Public Education

The subject of school finance may not seem exciting to a person preparing for a teaching career. But it becomes immediately apparent that school finance is of basic importance to citizens, teachers, administrators, and students. The quality of education depends upon the willingness of citizens to support schools. The availability of teaching positions and salaries, educational programs and services, and facilities depends upon the willingness and ability of communities to support them.

The 1980s appear to be a time in which it will be increasingly difficult to finance public elementary and secondary schools. Since most state financial assistance is based on pupil attendance, declining enrollments have reduced the amount of aid available to local school districts. Moreover, well-organized taxpayer groups have worked to defeat referenda for increased school support and thereby reduce taxes. Finally, the dramatic inflationary cycle of recent years and a sluggish economy have not only increased school expenditures but have also dried up new revenue sources. Because of these economic factors, many school systems will have to cut expenditures. The task is to provide quality education in an era of economic retrenchment.

The three major sources of financial support for schools are the local, state, and federal governments that distribute tax money to school districts.

Throughout most of America's educational history, the bulk of school income has been generated by local taxes, primarily the property tax. Locally generated revenues have decreased from approximately 83 percent in 1920 to the current level of about 48 percent. During the same period, state support for schools has increased slowly but steadily from 17 percent to 44 percent. It is expected that the states' share will increase as school districts experience severe problems in raising needed school revenues locally. The federal government's support of education has grown from less than 1 percent in 1920 to the current level of 8 percent. While the percentages indicated are based on national averages, the revenues generated from each funding source vary tremendously from state to state.

LOCAL EDUCATIONAL FUNDING

The property tax, based on the assessed value of real estate and personal property, generates approximately 98 percent of local school revenue. Real estate includes residential and commercial land and buildings. Personal property includes items such as automobiles, furs, jewelry, and stocks and bonds. The property tax originated in America's frontier past when wealth was measured primarily in land. It remains a widely used tax for historic reasons and because it produces a fairly stable rate of collection since it is difficult to evade.

The income generated by the property tax for schools is based on the assessed valuation of such property. Appraisals of property to establish its assessed valuation include such factors as location, structure, condition, and use. The value of real property is reviewed at regular intervals, usually in a quadrennial assessment, to establish current market value. Although continuing efforts have been made to assess property close to its market value, the assessed value is usually fixed at a percentage of the market value. Underassessment may result from such factors as obsolete assessment practices, lack of expertise on the part of assessors, and political reasons.

Multiple local government units use the property tax to support such varied services as police and fire protection, mosquito abatement, park and library districts, and highway and bridge maintenance. Since the taxable property wealth of communities within a state varies, inequalities of educational opportunity have resulted from a primary reliance on property taxes.

Most of the states specify by law the basic minimum property tax rate that local school districts can levy. Increases in the tax rate beyond this minimum usually require approval by the voters of the district. Since the mid-1970s, local school districts have had great difficulty in raising the property tax as voters continue to defeat referenda for that purpose.

When the local property tax is considered without relationship to state and federal aid, there are great inequalities in the income that can be generated by a local school district. A district that has a high assessed valuation of property can generate more income for schools than can one with a low assessed valuation.

A simple example illustrates the relationship of the property tax to the education of children in two local school districts. The income generated by the property tax can be divided by the number of pupils in average daily attendance.

For example, if school district A has an assessed valuation of $100 million and 1,000 pupils and school district B has an assessed valuation of $50 million for 1,000 pupils, a tax rate of $2 per $100 of assessed valuation would produce $2 million for school support in district A and $1 million in district B. District A would have $2,000 to spend per pupil as compared with $1,000 in district B. Thus, an equal number of students—1,000 in each district—would be likely to receive an unequal education, since the amount of revenue generated in the poorer district would only be half of that of the wealthier district. It should be remembered, however, that state aid—depending upon the particular state formula—would tend to equalize the funds available.

Legal Challenges to the Property Tax

In the early 1970s, litigation in several states challenged the primary reliance on property taxes to finance public education. The most often cited of these cases occurred in 1971 in *Serrano* v. *Priest*, when California's Supreme Court heard a case alleging that the heavy reliance on local property taxes in financing California public schools violated the Fourteenth Amendment. Specifically, the plaintiffs, several parents of public school children in Los Angeles County, contended that:

1. In the wealthy Beverly Hills school district, the assessed property value amounted to $50,882 per student and that a tax rate of $2.38 per $1,000 provided $1,232 per student. In contrast, Baldwin Park, a poorer district, had a property value of $3,706 per student and a tax rate of $5.48 that provided only $577 per student. As a result, Beverly Hills could spend 210 percent more than Baldwin Park on each student, although Baldwin Park's tax load was 230 percent greater.

2. The California public financing law with its primary reliance on local property taxes created large disparities among local school districts in the amount of revenue generated to finance public education. This resulted in gross financial and educational inequalities. Further, this condition violated the equal protection clause of the Fourteenth Amendment to the U.S. Constitution and the California Constitution.[1]

In a 6-to-1 vote that agreed essentially with the plaintiffs, the California Supreme Court ruled that

The commercial and industrial property which augments a district's tax base is distributed unevenly throughout the state. To allot more educational dollars to the children of one district than to those of another merely because of the fortuitous presence of such property is to make the quality of the child's education dependent upon the location of private commercial and industrial establishments. Surely, this is to rely on the most irrelevant of factors as the basis of educational financing. . . .

[1]Charles S. Benson, *The Economics of Public Education* (Boston: Houghton Mifflin, 1978), pp. 339–342.

We find that such financing system as presently constituted is not necessary to the attainment of any compelling state interest. Since it does not withstand the requisite "strict scrutiny," it denies to the plaintiffs and others similarly situated the equal protection of the laws. If the allegations of the complaint are sustained, the financial system must fall and the statutes comprising it must be found unconstitutional.[2]

Following upon the *Serrano* decision, state courts in Minnesota, Texas, New Jersey, Wyoming, and Arizona issued similar decisions. In 1973, however, the U.S. Supreme Court in *San Antonio Independent School District* v. *Rodriguez* upheld reliance on the property tax by a 5-to-4 decision.[3] In the *Rodriguez* case, the Court ruled that (1) while public school finance was chaotic, it was not unconstitutional, and (2) the property tax was not necessarily discriminatory since poor people were not necessarily concentrated in poor districts. The Court did urge fundamental reform, however, in school finance.

Since the 1970s, a great deal of litigation regarding school finance has occurred in the courts. In California, Connecticut, New Jersey, Washington, and Wyoming, for example, existing systems of school finance were found unconstitutional. In Idaho, Ohio, and Oregon, existing financial patterns were upheld. Although reliance on the property tax appears to be continuing, more legal challenges can be expected.

The impact of the judicial decisions on primary reliance on the local property tax to finance public elementary and secondary education is not yet clear. One apparent result is that several states have established commissions or task forces to examine the financing of public education. The trend seems to be that the use of alternative taxes will increase in the future and that the state will assume a larger share of the responsibility for financing public schools.

Criticisms of the Property Tax

Although the property tax is the oldest means of generating revenues for public schools, it is criticized as being inadequate to meet today's economic needs. Among the criticisms of the property tax are

1. It places a disproportionate tax burden on the homeowner.
2. It is very easy for voters to strike out against higher taxes by defeating referenda to raise school rates. Such voter action forces school boards to eliminate needed programs and services.
3. A broader tax base is needed to raise needed school revenue and to create a more equitable distribution of the tax burden.
4. The assessment of property and the collection and administration of the property tax has been inequitable and inefficient in many communities.
5. Since there are vast differences in property wealth among local districts, financial inequalities have led to educational inequalities.

[2]*Serrano* v. *Priest*, California Supreme Court, 96 *California Reporter*, (1971), pp. 601–626.
[3]*San Antonio Independent School District* v. *Rodriguez*, 36 Law. Ed. 2d 16 (1973).

STATE EDUCATIONAL FUNDING

Subject to continuing legislative revision and modification, state methods for financing public schools are extremely varied and complex. Since the state is the unit of government that has primary responsibility for and jurisdiction over education under the "reserved powers clause" of the U.S. Constitution, it is important that citizens, in general, and teachers, in particular, have a basic understanding of state methods of school finance. Although the states have delegated certain powers and responsibilities to local school districts, the state remains responsible for educating its citizens. It appears likely that, as local school districts experience greater difficulties in financing their schools through the property tax, the state will assume more of the financial responsibility.

State Revenue Sources

The major sources of state revenues come from taxes on sales and gross receipts, income, licenses, and other miscellaneous categories. A general breakdown of items included in these taxes is

Sales and Gross Receipts Taxes: on general sales, motor fuels, alcohol and tobacco, insurance, and amusements.

Income Taxes: on individual and corporate income.

Licenses: on motor vehicles and their operators, corporations, occupations, and hunting and fishing.

Miscellaneous Taxes: on property, mineral extractions, deaths and gifts.

Every state uses some form of sales tax that generates more than half its revenue; almost 30 percent comes from income taxes and the remainder from other taxing categories.

Sales taxes are levied by all the states and occasionally by other government units. State sales taxes generally range from 2 to 6 percent. The sales tax is collected by the vendor, the seller, who is responsible for accounting and payment of the tax to the state. Although the collection of the sales tax is relatively easy, the amount of revenue generated depends on economic fluctuations. The sales tax has been attacked as a regressive tax that falls most heavily on lower-income persons, especially when such essential items as food, clothing, and medicines are taxed.

The state income tax is based on personal and corporate income. It can be withheld from wages. Income taxes can be a flat percentage or graduated according to income. With a graduated income tax, individuals in higher income brackets pay at a correspondingly higher rate.

State Aid

In addition to local revenues generated largely through the property tax, the state provides financial assistance—state aid—to local school districts. An often complicated matter, the distribution of state aid varies considerably among the states. The rationale for state aid is partially historical and partially a product of current economic factors. Historically and constitutionally, the state has primary responsibility for educating its citizens. In the era of the common school movement in the nineteenth century, the states sometimes used grants-in-aid to encourage local school districts to organize and to levy a certain minimum taxation rate. It became apparent that local districts within a state varied greatly in their wealth and correspondingly in their financial ability to support schools. As a result, states have devised aid formulas to equalize per pupil expenditures. Historically, major economic changes have occurred. In the agrarian past, wealth was measured by possession of real property, often farmland. Today, wealth is based on other categories in addition to real property.

In terms of its use, state aid is classified as general or categorical aid. General aid is given to the local district to use as it so determines. Categorical aid is distributed to local districts to finance state-determined programs. For example, the use of categorical aid may be restricted to transportation, vocational education, driver training, and special education. Often, the state establishes categorical aid as an incentive to districts to establish specific programs.

GENERAL STATE AID AND FOUNDATION PROGRAMS. General aid rests on the assumption that each child in the state should have basic educational opportunities. To equalize these opportunities, the states have devised various foundation programs to distribute that aid to pupils. The following elements are involved in establishing the foundation program:

1. determining the dollar value of the foundation effort in a state, usually on a per pupil basis;
2. determining the minimum standard of local effort, usually based on revenues generated by the property tax; and
3. determining a means of distributing funds to school districts based on their school population and their local wealth as indicated by assessed valuation of property.

FLAT GRANT MODEL. The flat grant model is the oldest and simplest but also the most unequal method of allocating state aid to local school districts. State allocations to local school districts are determined by a flat grant, usually a fixed amount that is multiplied by the number of pupils enrolled in the district's schools. State aid is a supplement to the amount of revenue generated by local taxes, usually on property. Although the flat grant approach is simple, it means that wealthier districts have more funds at their disposal than poorer districts. Thus, the education received by a child in one part of the state may be grossly unequal to that in another part of the state.

THE FOUNDATION MODEL. Some form of the foundation model is used in about two-thirds of the states to equalize per pupil expenditures across districts. Guaranteeing an equal minimum of aid per pupil, the foundation model provides the amount of state aid needed to supplement a minimum required local tax effort. Generally, the state's contribution is inversely related to local property tax wealth. With the foundation model, each local school district in the state is required to put forth the same minimum local effort to finance its schools. This local effort is a minimum tax rate that produces the local district's share of the foundation level. Since this tax rate will produce more revenue in a wealthy district than in a poorer district, the poorer district will receive more aid from the state than will the wealthier district.

In the foundation model, two crucial and often controversial elements are (1) the degree of local tax effort required and (2) the amount of local leeway permitted. Local leeway permits wealthier districts to use surplus revenues from local taxes to finance schools above the foundation level. At the same time that local leeway has perpetuated inequalities in per pupil expenditure, it has enabled some districts to develop high-quality and often innovative education programs.

EQUALIZED PERCENTAGE GRANTS.   Some states have attempted to provide both fiscal equality between children of different districts and to encourage local districts on their own initiative to levy higher tax rates for school support. In the equalized percentage model, the local school district determines its own rate of expenditure—often with limits set by the state—beyond the required minimum. The local district determines a local property tax rate and the state guarantees equal levels of expenditure for equal tax effort.

Recent Trends in State School Finance

In the 1980s, it appears that several major trends will occur in school financing at the state level. Among them are

1. the strengthening of general equalization aid programs;
2. increased equity of state school finance structures;
3. the development of new methods to expand the fiscal capacity of local school districts;
4. an expansion of state support for special education programs; and
5. the development of aid categories for school districts with special problems.[4]

FEDERAL EDUCATIONAL FUNDING

Although the U.S. Constitution reserved education to each of the states, the federal government has historically provided some financial support for public elementary and secondary education. The initial support by the federal government came in 1785 when the Northwest Ordinance provided land grants of one section of land in each township to support education in each of the new western states. Aid to the Freedmen's schools in the South during Reconstruction, vocational education in the Smith–Hughes Act of 1917, and the National Defense Education Act of 1958 are examples of specific federal aid programs. Always

---

[4]Allan Odden and John Augenblick, *School Finance Reform in the States: 1980* (Denver, Colo.: Education Commission of the States, 1980), pp. 3–6.

controversial, this support has sometimes been enthusiastic but more often re-luctant. Federal aid has usually been categorical and for specific purposes rather than general.

A major change in the federal policy toward the financing of education came in 1965 with the enactment of the Elementary and Secondary Education Act (ESEA). Although still categorical, the ESEA was broad in scope. As part of President Lyndon Johnson's War on Poverty, the major thrust of the ESEA sought to equalize educational opportunities, particularly in inner-city and rural poverty areas. Local education agencies that wished to participate in the ESEA had to prepare proposals within the guidelines of the act's various titles. In the 1970s, federal revenue sharing provided for the return of some revenues to the states. Some of the states used these funds for educational programs.

Until the Johnson programs of the Great Society, the limited amount of federal aid was for specific programs and categories. Among the categories of federal support have been vocational education, manpower development, special education, national defense, and aid to areas impacted by poverty, vet-erans' education, school lunches, educational television, school libraries, eco-nomic opportunity programs, and others. While these categories of special aid have benefited particular programs, they frequently have had negative side effects in increased bureaucracy and red tape. Federal aid—in the form of assistance to particular educational categories—often has been short-lived and poorly planned.

At the same time that basic programs of regular education have lan-guished due to the inability of many local districts to support them adequately, federal programs have tended to overemphasize isolated new and innovative programs. Federal grants have also been superimposed on state and local dis-tricts. In their eagerness to tap the source of federal funds, states and local districts have sometimes devised programs that really do not meet or benefit local needs.

Educators who argue for increased federal aid would prefer to have it without the bureaucracy and confusion that often accompanies it. They argue that federal assistance should be reformed so that (1) the many categories of aid to special programs should be condensed into a few large and comprehensive categories and (2) more revenue sharing with the states would permit a larger amount of federal assistance to be given directly to the local school districts for general program support.

POLITICS OF SCHOOL FINANCING

At the bottom line, the financial support of the public schools rests on the willingness of citizens to support them. Schools are supported at the local level primarily through the property tax, at the state level by aid allocated according to various foundation formulas, and at the federal level through categorical aid programs. A general population trend for the 1980s strongly indicates a con-tinued increase in the sixty-five-and-over age group. This means a decrease in the number of people who have a direct interest—children enrolled—in schools. Unless local school boards and administrators develop strategies to enlist the support of those who are not directly related to schools, the number of voters favorable to increased support is likely to decrease.

Proposition 13

In the late 1970s, there were abundant signs of a taxpayers' revolt against increased taxation. The most dramatic example of a growing fiscal conservatism occurred when a large majority of California voters supported Proposition 13, an initiated referendum to freeze property tax rates and assessments. Proposition 13 restricted taxation in four ways:

1. Property taxes were limited to 1 percent of the market value of real property.
2. The assessed value of real property for tax purposes was rolled back to the 1975–76 level.
3. Increases in sales taxes are permitted only if approved by two-thirds of both houses of the state legislature.
4. Local tax increases—other than property tax—are permitted only with the approval of two-thirds of the voters.

Proposition 13 brought about a dramatic decrease in local revenues in California, estimated at a $7 billion decrease in 1978–79. School districts suffered the greatest loss of revenue of local government units in that they lost over 50 percent of their property tax revenue. The immediate effects of Proposition 13 were blunted somewhat by the use of a state surplus for local government finance. When the surplus is exhausted, severe and drastic cuts are likely.

Special Interests

The rise of special-interest groups is another trend that has affected school financing as well as other areas of American life. Special-interest groups for special, vocational, or bilingual education, for example, may lobby for mandated programs and categorical funding at the state level. Teacher organizations and unions often pursue their own specific "bread and butter" programs for their membership. An unfortunate result is that the ranks of those who argue for general school aid are badly fractured. A properly functioning school system needs adequately supported regular education programs upon which to base special programs to meet particular needs.

A Greater State Role

A third trend of importance is that the states' share of public school support increased dramatically in the 1970s and is likely to increase still more in the 1980s. While local support increased by $19.7 billion in the 1970s, state aid rose by $27.3 billion. Increases in state aid outdistanced local increases by nearly 50 percent.[5] Dislike of and rebellion against the property tax, judicial litigation, and state finance reform are likely to work to increase further the

[5]Odden and Augenblick, *School Finance Reform in the States: 1980*, p. 26.

states' share in financing schools. The federal share has been relatively constant at around 8 percent. It seems likely that federal aid will remain at that level or decrease.

A rising state role in financing public schools suggests strongly that many of the crucial decisions affecting school support will take place in the legislative chambers and governors' offices of the state capitols.

EDUCATION BUDGETING PROCESS

In the broadest sense, a local school district's budget is a planning instrument that establishes educational priorities and allocates the financial resources to be spent to achieve its goals. More specifically, a budget expresses the financial plan of the local school district and its educational program in dollar amounts. The states, in their school codes, generally prescribe the forms and procedures to be used by local school districts in preparing, adapting, administering, and auditing their budgets. School budgets are usually prepared on an annual basis, and they project income and expenditures for a given fiscal year.

The school budgeting process involves three elements:

1. Establishing the priorities of the school district, expressed as goals and objectives, and specifying the programs, staff, facilities, and support needed to achieve them. The setting of educational priorities involves continuing long-range and short-range planning on the part of the members of the community, the board of education, and school administrators and staff.
2. Estimating the revenues available to finance the costs of the total educational program, broken down into its specific components.
3. Ascertaining the financing plan, or expenditures, needed to meet the costs of the educational plan.

A local school district's budgeting process may be divided into four major steps: (1) preparation, (2) presentation and adoption, (3) administration, and (4) appraisal. The district superintendent, assisted by a staff, usually prepares the budget.

Preparation of the Budget

The preparation of the budget is a continuous process in that the financial plan for a given year cannot be isolated from the budgets that have preceded and are likely to follow it. The initial point of budgeting involves both the philosophy and the politics of education. The philosophy shared by the community determines in large part the priorities of the local school district. The willingness of the community to support implementation of that philosophy is expressed in concrete school programs, physical facilities, professional staff, and support services.

After educational priorities—really a sense of educational direction—

have been established in terms of goals and objectives by the board of education, the superintendent and staff have the difficult task of making the abstract goals operational in terms of specific programs and the necessary staff and support services. This operationalizing is accomplished by balancing the revenue available with the anticipated expenditures of the program. A key factor in the process is having the professional staff—principals, department heads, and teachers— prepare and submit budgetary requests to the superintendent.

Presentation and Adoption of the Budget

The school administration—the superintendent, business manager, and their staffs depending on the size of the school district—prepares the budget in tentative form. It is then presented to the board of education and to interested citizens and groups for explanation and perhaps modification. After discussion, the budget is then drafted in final form and presented for public hearing. It is then ratified by the board of education or other appropriate legal bodies. Although in most states the appropriate legal body to ratify the budget is the board of education, a few states require approval by other bodies, such as the city council or the voters of the district.

Administration of the Budget

After the estimated revenues have been transferred to the school accounting ledgers as initial entries, the budget is ready to be implemented. The terms "cost-effective" and "fiscally responsible" are used to identify carefully administered school financing. In the long run, it is crucial that expenditures not exceed income, that purchases be carefully made, and that spending be monitored carefully.

Appraisal

Most directly, appraisal means that the educational results are used to measure the degree to which the planning objectives have been accomplished. The appraisal involves an audit of expenditures and educational results.

Classification of Budgetary Items

The classification of budgetary items varies from state to state and from local district to local district, depending upon the approved budgetary format. The U.S. Office of Education has developed a general format that classifies educational expenditures under three major headings: current operating expenses, capital outlay, and debt services. Current operating expenses include expenditures for operations and maintenance. In nearly all school district budgets, the largest amount of revenue is spent on expenses related to instruction such as teachers' salaries, books, and supplies. Capital outlay items include expenditures for land, buildings, physical facilities, and equipment. Debt service includes repayment of borrowed money and the interest on the debt.

The following outline indicates the various items that may appear in these three categories:

I. Current Operating Expenses
   A. Instruction: teachers' salaries, textbooks, supplies, in-service training and workshops.
   B. Administration: superintendent, central office staff, principals, other administrative staff, clerical and support personnel.
   C. Pupil personnel and auxiliary support services: student health services, guidance, cafeteria and food service.
   D. Transportation services: bus drivers, buses, vehicle leasing, vehicle maintenance.
   E. Operation and maintenance: utilities, fuel, cleaning supplies, maintenance personnel.
   F. Student activities: athletics, student organizations, clubs.
   G. Fixed charges: contributions to retirement plans, social security, health insurance, fringe benefits.
   H. Intersystem and cooperative payments: payments to other school districts for shared facilities or projects; contributions to consortia or cooperatives.
II. Capital Expenses: building construction, remodeling, landscaping, paving (permanent improvements to be paid for on a long-term basis).
III. Debt Services: Redemption of bonds and interest on money owed by the district.

Rather than using the traditional budgetary category of instruction or education, some school districts use planned program budgeting that classifies expenditures by programs, such as the reading, the mathematics, or the industrial arts program. In this way, the costs of a particular program are separated from the costs of other programs. The rationale for planned program budgeting is that it operationalizes the principle of accountability so that the costs of a particular program can be related specifically to educational achievements.

CURRENT ISSUES
IN EDUCATIONAL FINANCING

The recent history of the United States has been marked by economic unrest and anxiety. The major economic trends of this period have been incessant inflation and sporadic recession, spiraling energy costs, and a pronounced unwillingness of citizens to pay higher taxes. Paralleling this, the demographic conditions affecting public education have also changed. The school-aged population has decreased; the number of individuals not related directly to the public schools, especially childless couples and senior citizens, has increased. Tax-conscious citizens groups have charged that the costs of maintaining public schools have not been equalled by educational results. From various and often unrelated sources, there have been demands for retrenchment and greater accountability on the part of public school officials and teachers.

Accountability

Since the 1970s the term "accountability" has been applied to educational financing and outcomes.[6] Accountability implies a direct relationship between educational spending and educational results and asserts that dollars spent on education should be measured by pupil achievement. Those who argue for accountability want schools to be judged by their output in terms of their students' educational accomplishments.

The demand for accountability was stimulated by such recent trends as the rising cost of financing schools, a widely held public assumption that students' achievement has declined, and a growing loss of credibility in public education.

As is true of most public services, the costs of public schooling have increased because of greater demands being placed on schools and because of the high cost of financing schools in an inflationary era. Energy and fuel costs, teacher's salaries, building maintenance, and the cost of support services have risen. When called upon to provide additional support for public schools, taxpayers have demanded specific justifications for added taxes for schools.

In addition to increased costs of schooling, there is a widely held assumption that students' basic competencies in reading, writing, comprehension, and mathematics have declined. Critics of the achievements of the public schools, especially those related to the basic education movement, have charged that, although more money is spent on education today, academic achievement of American students has declined.

Finally, the public schools—as is true for many other social institutions—have been caught up in a crisis of credibility. Many citizens have lost their historic trust in education as a panacea for the nation's ills. The failures of the public schools, particularly in the inner-city schools, have been publicized. Critics have also attributed the increase in vandalism, crime rates, and drug addiction to the public schools' inability to foster positive values.

In practical and operational terms, the movement for accountability has caused many school to define their general educational goals in specific operational objectives. First, the schools must identify their goals; then, they must translate them into specific instructional performance objectives for students. Such goals as reading or mathematical competency must be indicated in terms of specific objectives for each grade level.

Accountability can also be implemented through the budgeting process if the accounting system records expenditures by educational programs. For example, what is the cost of the reading, the mathematics, or the physical education program? What are the measurable results of the particular program in terms of student achievement? When indicated by program, the costs of the program can be determined by the accomplishments of the program's stated performance objectives. In other words, accountability places the responsibility for educational outcomes—for student achievement—directly on administrators and teachers.

[6]For a comprehensive treatment of educational accountability, see Frank J. Sciara and Richard K. Jantz, *Accountability in American Education* (Boston: Allyn & Bacon, 1972).

Performance Contracting

Performance contracting is a system by which a school district enters into an agreement with a private firm that provides instructional or other services to the district. Payment is determined by the degree to which the firm reaches a predetermined outcome, such as raising student achievement in a particular skill or subject such as reading, within a definite period of time. For a specified sum of money, the firm guarantees the school district that its students will achieve a stated performance objective. The fees paid to the firm are determined by and scaled to student achievement. If the firm succeeds in reaching the stated objectives, it receives the money specified. If, however, the students' achievements are less than promised, the firm receives a smaller payment.

The major argument for performance contracting is that, since public schools have failed to achieve noted success, particularly in inner-city schools, other efforts should be attempted. Critics, particularly in teachers' unions and organizations, contend that performance contracting weakens the professionalization of teachers and detracts from the total education of children since it reduces learning to specific but often unrelated tasks.

Educational Vouchers

Educational voucher plans have been proposed to give parents public funds or tax credits to pay the cost of educating their children at the school of their choice, be it public or private. The proponents of the voucher system claim that it is unfair for the public schools to exist as a tax-supported educational monopoly. The voucher system, they contend, would bring greater competition to the educational arena. Public schools would have to compete with private schools. This competition would raise the quality of education in both sectors by forcing the mediocre schools out of the educational business. Vouchers, they insist, would result in greater freedom of educational choice.

Critics of the voucher plans contend that they would weaken and perhaps destroy the public schools as a common school system. Public schools might become the refuge of the economically disadvantaged and of minority groups as more affluent groups abandoned them for private schools. They also charge that vouchers would encourage racial segregation and encourage expensive duplication of schools and lead to many of marginal quality. Aid to parochial schools, they contend, would violate the principle of separation of church and state.

CONCLUSION

This chapter has examined the complex but vitally important subject of school finance. The ability and the willingness of Americans to pay for their schools has long-range social, political, and educational consequences. Poor schools will mean a poorly educated citizenry that will be poorly equipped to maintain the quality of American life.

As an educator, an understanding of the general bases of school finance will help you to recognize the various constituents that contribute to educational financing at the local, state, and federal levels.

DISCUSSION QUESTIONS

1. Prepare an analysis of public financing of education in your state showing the proportion of local, state, and federal funding.
2. Examine the rationale and implementation of state efforts to equalize educational opportunities.
3. Debate the advantages and disadvantages of various taxes used to generate revenue for public schools.
4. Do you agree with the concepts of "accountability," "performance contracting," and "school vouchers"?
5. Describe the general procedures for preparing and administering a local school district budget.

FIELD EXERCISES

1. Invite a local school district superintendent or business manager to speak to your class on the budgeting process.
2. Interview several members of local boards of education on school finance issues and problems. Report to the class on the trends that you discerned in your interviews.
3. Attend a budget hearing in a local school district and report to the class on your reactions to the hearing process.
4. Research the attempt of a local school district to pass a referendum to increase its tax rate. Was the effort successful? If so, why? If not, why?
5. Arrange a debate on the issue of school vouchers.

SELECTED READINGS

BENSON, CHARLES S. *Education Financing in the Coming Decade.* Bloomington, Ind.: Phi Delta Kappa, 1975.

————. *Equity in School Financing: Full State Funding.* Bloomington, Ind.: Phi Delta Kappa, 1975.

————. *The Economics of Public Education.* Boston: Houghton Mifflin, 1978.

BERKE, JOEL S. *Answers to Inequity: An Analysis of the New School Finance.* Berkeley, Calif.: McCutchan, 1974.

BOWLES, SAMUEL, AND GINTIS, HERBERT. *Schooling in Capitalist America.* New York: Basic Books, 1976.

COHN, ELCHANAN. *The Economics of Education.* Cambridge, Mass.: Ballinger, 1975.

COONS, JOHN E., CLUNE, WILLIAM H., AND SUGARMAN, STEPHEN D. *Private Wealth and Public Education.* Cambridge, Mass.: Harvard University Press, 1971.

GARMS, WALTER, FUTHRIE, JAMES, AND PIERCE, LAWRENCE. *School Finance: The Economics and Politics of Public Schools.* Englewood Cliffs, N.J.: Prentice-Hall, 1977.

GOERTZ, MARGARET. *Money and Education: How Far Have We Come?* Princeton N.J.: Education Policy Research Institute, Educational Testing Service, 1979.

HARRISON, RUSSELL S. *Equality in Public School Finance.* Lexington, Mass.: D. C. Heath, 1976.

JOHNS, ROE L., AND MORPHET, EDGAR L. *The Economics and Financing of Education.* Englewood Cliffs, N.J.: Prentice-Hall, 1975.

LINDMAN, ERICK L. *Dilemmas of School Finance.* Arlington, Va.: Educational Research Service, 1975.

ODDEN, ALLAN, AND AUGENBLICK, JOHN. *School Finance Reform in the States: 1980.* Denver, Colo.: Education Commission of the States, 1980.

PRESIDENT'S COMMISSION ON SCHOOL FINANCE. *Schools, People, and Money: The Need for Educational Reform.* Washington, D.C.: G.P.O., 1972.

SCIARA, FRANK J., AND JANTZ, RICHARD K. *Accountability in American Education.* Boston: Allyn & Bacon, 1972.

10

Early Childhood Education

Chapter 10 examines the major theories that have shaped current practices and institutions in early childhood education. It identifies leading pioneers of early childhood education such as Rousseau, Pestalozzi, Froebel, Montessori, Piaget, and Erikson, and it examines the structures and organization of nursery and kindergarten education. The pioneering work of the early childhood theorists has implications for all stages of human growth and development as well as early childhood. The treatment of nursery and kindergarten education should be considered as an institutional prelude to elementary schooling, which is examined in Chapter 11.

CHILD NATURE

It is difficult to treat the rich and complex history of early childhood education in a single chapter. But it is possible to examine some of the major conceptions of childhood that have developed throughout our history and to consider some of the important educators who shaped our changing conceptions of childhood and early childhood education.

Children are born into the human group that reproduces itself biologically, But children do not inherit biologically the knowledge and values of the human group of which they are members. Knowledge and values, customs and beliefs, manners and mores are learned by processes of socialization and enculturation in which the immature members of the group, the children, acquire the culture of the group. The socialization process contains many variables that may alter the intended result. That is, children may not turn out exactly as adults would have them.

A basic cultural tension that has emerged in the education of children and that is reflected in the various theories of early childhood education involves the relationship of the child to the group. This tension is not unique to early childhood but occurs throughout the life cycle.

Throughout history, most of the patterns of early childhood education that developed were designed to bring children into group life in a deliberate and specifically defined manner that encouraged little or no diversity. Children were trained in the mores, folkways, knowledge, and values of the group by parents, elders, or guardians. Usually, the leader of the group and/or head of the family acted as the guardian of the cultural heritage and traditions that were imposed on children. Basically, children were to acquire the standards or norms of behavior of the group into which they were born. Once these standards were learned, then the child became a participant in the group's cultural processes. As an adult, he or she was expected to transmit the heritage to his or her offspring. Such a pattern of cultural transmission and imposition on children was to safeguard the heritage by reproducing it culturally in the offspring of the group. This basic pattern of cultural reproduction through imposing the cultural heritage on children was true in the time before recorded history, in ancient Greece and Rome, during the medieval period, and throughout most of human history.

The theory of cultural imposition—that is, giving the cultural heritage to the young so that it might be perpetuated—is a continuing characteristic of early childhood and indeed of all education. The theory of cultural imposition rests on a strategy of determining what knowledge and values are appropriate for a child to acquire. You might consider the various meanings of appropriate education as it impacts childhood.

There is appropriateness in terms of socioeconomic conditions. In an agricultural society, the children of farmers would be expected to acquire the knowledge appropriate to land tenure and the production of farm products. The same conditions of appropriateness would apply to children born into a sea-faring culture or a mining society. Moreover, there is appropriateness in terms of politics and nationality. Children born in the United States are expected to acquire the political concepts and practices through political socialization or civic education that will enable them to share and participate in American political life and institutions. Children born into the Soviet Union are expected to acquire a Marxist-Leninist view of life, society, and institutions.

In addition to social, economic, and political appropriateness, there are other forms of what is regarded as appropriate learning for children. Such forms of appropriateness are based on the norms required for membership in a particular socioeconomic class or religious, linguistic, or ethnic group. Historically, there were also strongly enforced expectations of what was appropriate to boys and girls. For example, boys were to be wage earners, soldiers, businessmen, politicians, lawyers, physicians, engineers. Girls were to be wives, mothers, cooks, laundresses, and elementary school teachers. Today, sexual stereotyping based on predetermined career roles has been challenged, and career goals and orientations are no longer proscribed because of one's sex. However, much education is based on the expectations that society holds as appropriate for its future members. This means that certain bodies of knowledge, life-styles, and values will be imposed on the young by the adult members of the society.

If you consider your own upbringing and early education, you will discover the degree to which cultural imposition according to some standard of appropriate group norms has shaped your life and attitudes. For example, as a child you learned to speak the language of your parents or guardians. You really had no conscious choice in the matter. Your being born into a certain family meant that you would learn the family's language. At the same time that this language was imposed upon you, learning it also gave you an immense amount of power that enabled you to express your needs and to communicate with those around you. Being born in a particular country meant that you would be a citizen of that nation with all its privileges and duties.

Although cultural imposition occurs in everyone's life and education, the important factor is the degree to which that imposition allows for alternative behavior and choice. Some groups and their cultures permit few alternatives; other cultures permit a variety of choices within a basic context of cultural consensus. All education, and early childhood education in particular, is shaped by the society and the social, cultural, economic, and political expectations that it has for its young.

THE INDIVIDUAL CHILD

While childhood has been imposed upon by social norms and by what the adult members of society have defined as appropriate learning and behavior for children, a number of important educational reformers have sought to liberate childhood from the prescriptions of adult-imposed social control. These advocates of child freedom have ranged from those who sought to free children from social imposition such as Rousseau to those who wanted to enlarge child freedom within a framework of social consensus as did Dewey and many of the progressive educators. Basically, those who sought to liberate the child believed that childhood was an important time of human growth and development that has its own intrinsic patterns. Some early childhood educators had a new vision of society and wanted to liberate children from the norms of the old society so that they could build a new society. Others were interested in children and child nature and culture so that they could develop a more adequate method of child rearing. Regardless of their motivation, the pioneer figures of early childhood education challenged many of the social preconceptions that were imposed upon children.

What the pioneers of early childhood education did was to define appropriateness in a new way. As a reference point, they rejected what adults had defined as appropriate to childhood. For Froebel, Montessori, and Piaget, what was regarded as appropriate to a child's education came from the intrinsic developmental and growth patterns of childhood itself. These pioneers of early childhood education used various means of research that ranged from introspection about their own childhood experiences, to the observation of children, to philosophical and historical inquiry, to clinical studies. They identified stages of child development and sought to develop educational activities and experiences appropriate to them. In varying degrees, the criteria of appropriateness was defined as what was necessary to the child's stage of development and readiness rather than societal expectations. The following sections identify and examine some of these major contributors to early childhood education.

Jean Jacques Rousseau

Jean Jacques Rousseau (1712–1778) was an iconoclast who challenged the conventional wisdom of his day on religious, social, economic, political, and educational matters; in this section, we focus on his vision of the child's education. In his didactic novel *Emile,* published in 1762, Rousseau imagined himself the tutor of Emile, the son of a wealthy family.[1] In *Emile* and his other works, Rousseau attacked the two widely held educational doctrines of child depravity and social imposition.

The doctrine of child depravity, often ascribed to Calvinist Puritanism, perceived human nature to be innately evil. Because of the sin of Adam and Eve, human beings had inherited the afflictive corruption of original sin. While some people were chosen by God for salvation, the vast majority of human beings were doomed to hell. To overcome their inherited corruption, which inclined them to idleness and mischief, children needed discipline and moral training. Play and games, now regarded as desirable children's activities, were then considered to be a nonsensical, childish waste of time. The "good child" was one who looked, dressed, spoke, and behaved like a miniature adult.

Rejecting the concept, Rousseau proclaimed children to be naturally good "noble savages." Since they are born good, children's needs, impulses, and desires are also naturally good. The child's senses and feelings were the best guide to his education. The wise educator, personified by Emile's tutor, did not interfere with his pupil's impulses and emotions.

Rousseau also abandoned the theory of social and cultural imposition. Arguing that there was no evil in the infant at birth, Rousseau said that evil was acquired from a corruptive society. Not knowing how to lie, cheat, or steal at birth, children were taught these vices by adults. If free to follow their natural inclinations and escape the corruption of the society about them, children could grow up as natural men and women. Socially isolated in his early childhood, Emile's growing up is done in natural surroundings, exploring the natural environment, and discovering nature's ways. Only after becoming a genuinely authentic natural person does Emile enter society.

Rousseau also discarded the venerable tradition that acquiring knowledge from the liberal arts and sciences was educationally desirable. Rather, he believed that verbal and literary information, organized in encyclopedic form,

---

[1]William Boyd, ed., *The Emile of Jean Jacques Rousseau* (New York: Teachers College Press, Columbia University, 1966).

was useless and pernicious in that it produced artificial rather than natural men and women. Opposed to vicarious learning in early childhood, Rousseau believed that premature instruction in reading and writing harmed rather than benefited children since it stuffed their young minds with disconnected, often meaningless words. Only after enjoying a wide range of direct experience, should children begin to read and write.

From his challenge to conventional education, Rousseau developed several influential ideas that shaped the course of early childhood education.

(1) *Follow nature.* Born without guile and innocent, children should not be governed by social conventions and artificialities. Human instincts, impulses, emotions, and feelings come from nature itself and are trustworthy. It is undesirable and unhealthy to force children to repress their natural inclinations.

(2) *Learn from the environment.* Nature, again, provides the ideal setting for learning. Rather than acquiring secondhand, indirect bookish information, children should learn directly from the environment. Rousseau emphasized the role of sense experience in learning; our ideas, he believed, resulted from the objects sensed in the environment. Rousseau's admonition that children learned most effectively from their environment stimulated other educational theorists such as Froebel, Montessori, and Dewey to emphasize the environment's educative role and to assert that environmental control or manipulation was the key to learning.

(3) *Develop permissive teacher-learner relationships.* As indicated, the Puritanical conception of child depravity contributed to the psychological and physical coercion of children. Rousseau recognized that adult coercion caused children to repress their interests and emotions. Repressed children tended to become artificial and ingenuine adults. Contrary to the adage that children should be seen but not heard, Rousseau recommended permissive child-adult relationships in which children acting on impulse experienced either success or failure. Children thus learned that their actions had consequences. As the natural and direct consequences of action, rewards and punishments were not bestowed artificially at the pleasure or displeasure of adults.

(4) *Divide childhood into stages of human growth and development.* Rousseau did not consider childhood to be of one piece but rather divided it into developmental stages. Infancy, the first developmental stage, from birth until the age of five, was a time when almost everything had to be done for the virtually dependent child. Attention was given to physical growth and development and to building strong, healthy bodies. The infant's diet was to consist of simple country food. Rousseau was opposed to confining children to playpens. He wanted them to have freedom of movement to develop and exercise muscles. In terms of moral development, Rousseau did not believe that infants were moral beings. Arguing that good and evil had relevance only for those who could reason, Rousseau believed that children—in infancy—were governed only by their feelings of pleasure and pain. In terms of language development, Rousseau stated that the child's first words should be few, simple, and clear and should be names for the objects found in the immediate environment.

Rousseau's second developmental stage was boyhood, from ages five to twelve. At this stage, Emile was physically stronger and was able to do more for himself. The tutor who was to avoid trying to teach virtue by moral preachment was also to keep the environment free of social corruption and vice. The boy's experience was still essentially nonsocial. The emphasis in learning was on physical and sensory training in which Emile observed objects in the environment and their relationships to each other. Sensory training—using one sense to check another sense—involved measuring, counting, weighing, and comparing objects.

Rousseau's third developmental stage, from ages twelve to fifteen, could be termed early adolescence. Now, Emile learned the concept of utility, that is, that objects and actions have purposes and consequences. He learned a manual skill, such as carpentry or gardening, that contributed to the correct combination of mental and physical labor. Emile's continuing interaction with the natural environment led slowly, at this stage, to forming of ideas about science and geography. He also read his first book, *Robinson Crusoe*, where he learned of a man's survival on an isolated island.

Rousseau's fourth stage, that of later adolescence, from ages fifteen to eighteen, is the time when Emile developed social relationships with others. Emile's questions about sexual development and relationships are answered directly by his tutor, with neither mysteriousness or coarseness.

The fifth and last stage treated in *Emile* is from ages eighteen to twenty, called by Rousseau the age of humanity. Emile now studied history, languages, languages, and traveled. He met and fell in love with Sophie, whom he married.

The most important fact about Rousseau's developmental stages is that during them the learner—because of physical and psychological maturation—has a readiness to learn certain things. The teacher's task is to recognize this readiness and to create a situation that provides for the exercise of this readiness.

Johann Heinrich Pestalozzi

Johann Heinrich Pestalozzi (1746–1827) was a Swiss educator whose theory and practice exerted a major influence on both early childhood and elementary education. A shy, introspective, and occasionally eccentric but consistently humane individual, Pestalozzi attempted religious, legal, and agricultural careers before deciding to devote his life to education.[2] An eager and receptive reader of *Emile*, Pestalozzi endeavored to make Rousseau's novel an educational reality. He also saw education, particularly that of children, as an instrument of human regeneration and social reformation.

As was true for Montessori and other early childhood educators, Pestalozzi's educational work began with socially and economically disadvantaged children. From 1774 to 1779, he conducted a farm school at Neuhof for poor children. For a short time he was headmaster of an orphanage at Stans. He then established well-known educational institutes at Burgdorf and Yverdon, where he developed and perfected his insights into early childhood education.

Pestalozzi also wrote on educational themes. Like Rousseau, he was an educational novelist. His *Leonard and Gertrude*, published in 1781, told of the moral, social, and economic revitalization of a fictional Swiss village that had

---

[2]For a systematic treatment of Pestalozzi's life and ideas, see Kate Silber, *Pestalozzi: The Man and His Work* (London: Routledge and Kegan Paul, 1960).

implemented educational reforms. Pestalozzi's *How Gertrude Teaches Her Children,* published in 1801, was a treatise of his philosophy and method of education.

As an early childhood educator, Pestalozzi emphasized the total development of the child. Anticipating what later-day progressives would call the education of the whole child, Pestalozzi gave importance to emotional as well as cognitive development. Conventional schooling, he believed, had often been one-sided in that it stressed cognitive development but minimized or ignored emotional and physical development.

Pestalozzi's educational strategies were based on his concepts of children's growth and development. In the wholesome mother-infant relationship, the infant had basic needs for food, warmth, and affection. The good mother responded to and satisfied her child's basic needs. The child, in turn, responded with a growing love and affection to the mother. From this elemental but crucial mother-infant relationship, the child experienced emotional security and love. Once established firmly in the psyche of the child, the initial feelings of love could be extended outward to others in what Pestalozzi called the widening circles of humanity. The child extended his or her love to other members of the family circle—to the father, brothers, and sisters. Such a loving family situation built an emotionally secure household. Once the child experienced an emotionally healthy and secure family life, he or she could then extend trust and love to the neighbors and other members of the community. Still growing ever outward, the feelings of love could be extended to countrymen, to all members of the human race, and ultimately to God.

Pestalozzi's view of the growth and development of emotionally secure children had several important educational implications. First, his theory of emotional security was based on the child's immediate needs and their satisfaction in the very intimate mother-child relationship. He avoided treating emotional development in abstract terms. Second, at Neuhof and Stans, Pestalozzi attempted to educate emotionally scarred, frightened, and often suspicious children who distrusted adults. Discovering that his initial efforts accomplished little cognitive learning among such emotionally disadvantaged children, Pestalozzi then sought to reshape the school environment into a climate of love, trust, and emotional security. Once the children trusted and loved their teachers, effective instruction could take place. Pestalozzi's stress on the need for creating an educational climate of love and emotional security became known as his General Method, which had to be established prior to physical and cognitive learning. For effective instruction to take place, the emotional security of the General Method had to be maintained.

Once the General Method had been used to cultivate emotional security and growth, then Pestalozzi's Special Method could be employed as an instrument of physical and cognitive development.[3] The Special Method was based on the principle of *Anschauung,* a German word, which Pestalozzi used to signify the process of concept formation. As did Locke and Rousseau, Pestalozzi believed that human knowledge was derived from and based on sense impressions of the environment. Again, as did Rousseau, Pestalozzi attacked the verbalism and memorization of conventional schooling, which he believed was miseducation.

[3]Gerald L. Gutek, *Pestalozzi and Education* (New York: Random House, 1968), pp. 80–128.

Pestalozzi's Special Method was designed to make the direct sensation of objects systematic, effective, and efficient. Known as the "object lesson," Pestalozzi's Special Method consisted of form, number, and name lessons that he claimed should be taught prior to traditional schooling's reading and writing.

According to Pestalozzi, human beings encounter objects in their environment. These objects have a form, a shape, a design. Children should learn to recognize and distinguish the forms of particular objects. They can trace the shapes of smaller objects or can draw larger objects. From drawing would slowly come the process of writing. Objects also have quantity. Children can learn to count real objects, such as beans, peas, stones, or marbles. They can learn to subtract, multiply, and divide these objects. Only after extensive practice with real objects should children be introduced to the numbers that signify the various quantities. The sound or name lessons are to give children practice in using the words used to identify various objects.

The Special Method included a number of instructional strategies that teachers were to observe. Among them were the following:

1. Begin instruction with some thing that is related directly to the child's experience and environment; do not introduce concepts or ideas that are remote to or foreign to the child's experience.
2. Base instruction on concrete objects and proceed gradually to more abstract concepts.
3. Learning should begin with the simplest and easiest element of a particular skill, which should be mastered before the child advances to more complicated learning.
4. Emphasize simple ideas and concepts before going on to those that are more sophisticated and complex.

Pestalozzi's contribution to early childhood education was to recognize and stress the importance of well-rounded emotional, cognitive, and physical development. His attention to the creation of an environment of love and emotional security encouraged more permissive attitudes to early childhood education that recognized the dignity of the individual child.

Friedrich Froebel

Friedrich Froebel (1782–1852), a German educator, developed the early childhood school known as the *kindergarten,* or child's garden. Froebel, whose mother died when he was nine months old, was the victim of a strict and unhappy childhood. After several starts in such varied careers as forester, mineralogist, and museum curator, Froebel turned to education.[4] To gain teaching experience, he went to Switzerland to study with Pestalozzi, whose methods he found useful but not completely satisfactory. Froebel reasoned that Pestalozzi's method needed a more systematic and complete philosophical base.

Froebel established schools at Friesheim in 1816, at Keilhau in 1818,

---

[4]Robert B. Downs, *Friedrich Froebel* (Boston: Twayne, 1975), pp. 11–33.

and at Blankenburg in 1837, where he and his colleagues educated children between ages three and eight in programs featuring games, stories, play, gifts, and occupations. These early preschools were designed to stimulate the child's growth and development by self-activity. As did Pestalozzi, Froebel wrote several books explaining his educational theory and practice. *The Education of Man*, published in 1826, expressed his highly mystical educational philosophy. Related most directly to early childhood education were Froebel's *Outline of a Plan for Founding and Developing a Kindergarten*, in 1840, and *Mother and Play Songs*, in 1843.

Froebel's philosophy of early childhood education, a form of philo-sophical Idealism, came from several sources. Among them were (1) introspec-tion into his own unhappy and melancholy childhood, (2) beliefs and symbolism related to the Lutheran Church of which his father was a minister, (3) the reading of various German Idealist philosophers, and (4) his own impressionistic forays into the natural sciences. From these diverse sources came Froebel's views of human nature, childhood, and education.

For Froebel, all creation had a spiritual origin and destiny in that it originated in God, a supernatural and spiritual being. Humankind came from and was destined to return to God. In every human being, there was, Froebel said, a spiritual essence, a life force, that moved the person to self-activity. Throughout life, this Divinely implanted spiritual force sought externalization. For Froebel, then, the Divine essence in every person endowed human nature with a spiritual worth and dignity. Froebel's view of human nature differed radically from the Puritanical doctrine of human depravity. It also varied from Rousseau's naturalistic doctrine of innate human benevolence. While Froebel concurred with Rousseau that the human infant was innately good, he did so for far different reasons.

Froebel's view of the child was based on his conception of human nature. Children possessed an intrinsic spiritual force that motivated and moved them to self-activity. Using the analogy of plant life, Froebel believed that all that the child was to be was already present within him or her at birth in the same way that the entire plant was already present in the seed. Just as the capable gardener provides plants with sunlight, water, and suitable soil, the good teacher is to provide children with an educational environment that encourages their growth and development. To this end, Froebel developed his kindergarten.

Giving credence to the cultural recapitulation theory, Froebel believed that childhood's stages represented the child's propensity to act out and portray by play the history of the human race in a short time span. Among examples of cultural recapitulation were the following: children may draw on walls to recapitulate that period of human history in which primitive man decorated his cave dwellings; boys who play at hunting or tent-making were re-enacting the nomadic life-style of their ancestors. Although largely rejected today, Froebel's acceptance of cultural recapitulation shaped his kindergarten practices. Many kindergarten songs, stories, and games were intended to unite the individual child with other children. These activities not only socialized children but intro-duced them to the stories and songs of their culture.

One of Froebel's significant contributions to early childhood education

Jean Jacques Rousseau (1712–1778) wrote *Emile*, an influential novel advocating permissive, naturalistic education. *(New York Public Library Picture Collection)*

Johann Heinrich Pestalozzi (1746–1827), a Swiss educational reformer, emphasized the development of the whole child in a homelike school environment. *(New York Public Library Picture Collection)*

Friedrich Froebel (1782–1852) founded the kindergarten which stressed the unfolding nature of the child and play. *(New York Public Library Picture Collection)*

Maria Montessori (1870–1952), an Italian educator, devised an educational method that emphasized a structured and orderly prepared environment. *(American Montessori Society)*

Rousseau, Pestalozzi, Froebel, and Montessori—Pioneers of Early Childhood Education.

was his legitimizing of play. Regarding it as the means by which children externalized their interior nature, Froebel saw play as a means by which children could imitate and "try out" adult roles and behavior.

To prepare the kindergarten's environment for learning, Froebel designed a series of gifts and occupations. Gifts were items or objects given to children in completed form. For example, the ball—representing a spherical shape—and the cube were gifts with which children could play. As they used the gifts, children came to understand the concepts of shape, dimension, size, and their relationships. The occupations were malleable items, such as clay, paints, paper, wood, and cardboard upon which children could imprint their own designs. They could make the figures of animals from clay or externalize their thoughts and emotions with paints, brush, and paper. Through the occupations, children externalized the concepts within their minds.

Maria Montessori

Maria Montessori (1870–1952) was born in Italy to well-educated, upper-middle-class parents. Unlike the typical girl of her social class, she attended a technical rather than a finishing school. Admitted to the University of Rome, she first studied mathematics, physics, and natural sciences and then medicine.

In 1894, she was the first Italian woman to receive a medical degree from the University of Rome.[5]

Montessori was appointed to the staff of the Psychiatric Clinic of the University of Rome, where she specialized in the educational problems of mentally retarded children. At this time, she read and was influenced by the work of Édouard Seguin, a French physician, who was a pioneer in special education. Believing that every child had the right to education, Seguin devised instructional materials to stimulate the learning of children labeled "mentally defective."

As did Pestalozzi in his early career, Montessori worked first with disadvantaged children. From 1899 to 1901, she was directress of the State Orthophrenic School in Rome, where she worked with mentally handicapped children and trained teachers. In 1907, she founded the "Casa dei Bambini," the Children's House, for socially disadvantaged children who lived in the slums of Rome's San Lorenzo district. As a result of her careful observation of these children and her anthropological and psychological research, Montessori devised her method that consisted of using learning exercises and didactic materials in a prepared environment. Children, she concluded, preferred meaningful tasks to play, enjoyed order rather than disorder, and were capable of sustained concentration. Her method was so successful that Montessori schools opened throughout Italy. The Montessori method gained international recognition as schools were established throughout the world.

Montessori was also a prolific writer. Among her works were *The Montessori Method, The Secret of Childhood, The Discovery of the Child, Spontaneous Activity in Education, Education for a New World,* and *The Absorbent Mind.*

Assuming that children possessed a tremendous potential for self-development, Montessori identified a series of crucial transitory periods of special sensitivity to particular learning that children experienced.[6] From birth to age six, children's major work was to absorb and organize environmental stimuli. It was important that the child learn the appropriate skill at the time of greatest sensitivity for that learning.

As did Froebel, Montessori reasoned that self-development occurred most expeditiously when children used the sequential didactic materials and exercises of a prepared environment. In such an environment, the directress or teacher was an observer who assisted indirectly in the child's perceptual, motor, intellectual, emotional, and social development.

Among Montessori's instructional strategies were the exercises of practical life and those based on manipulating didactic materials. The practical exercises involved everyday activities such as washing hands, serving lunch, lacing and buttoning, and dressing, designed to cultivate both motor skills and self-reliance. Montessori warned that adults who performed these activities for children denied them needed practice and stifled their "spontaneous" urge to self-accomplishment.

Montessori's didactic materials consisted of self-corrective and graded items that facilitated sensory awareness and muscular coordination. For example,

[5]E. M. Standing, *Maria Montessori: Her Life and Work* (New York: New American Library, 1962).

[6]Maria Montessori, *The Discovery of the Child* (New York: Ballantine Books, 1972).

Montessori devised sets of cylinders of varying diameters that could be arranged according to decreasing height or decreasing diameter. The didactic materials were to be used in a prescribed manner so that the child would master the specified skill.

The Montessori method enjoys widespread popularity in the United States and elsewhere. It is acclaimed by those who prefer a structured and ordered environment for early childhood education. While it is an organized environment, it also permits children to work at their own readiness and rates of learning.

The critics of the Montessori method, particularly progressive educators, contend that it is too rigid and overly structured. They criticize it for prematurely stressing academic development to the neglect of children's socialization.

Jean Piaget

Contemporary early childhood education owes much to Jean Piaget's research. As was true of those two historical giants of educational theory, Rousseau and Pestalozzi, Piaget was a native of Switzerland. From 1921 on, he was associated with the Rousseau Institute in Geneva, becoming its co-director in 1932. Piaget has been variously a professor at the universities of Neuchatel, Geneva, and Lausanne. He also founded the International Center of Genetic Epistemology in Geneva.

Piaget has made significant contributions to the literature on early childhood education and developmental psychology. Among his important works are *The Language and Thought of the Child, The Child's Conception of the World, The Origins of Intelligence in Children, The Construction of Reality in the Child,* and *Structuralism.* Among the topics of Piaget's research and writing that relate to early childhood are those dealing with children's conceptions of physical causality, moral judgment, number, space, logic, and geometry.

Piaget's major contribution to early child education—that children are the primary agents in their own education and development—is based on his work as a developmental psychologist. In identifying the quantitative changes in cognitive structure occurring during the course of human development, Piaget discovered that mental development takes place through a complex and continuous interactive process between the child and the environment. Human behavior, he asserts, is an adaptation of the person to the environment. Adaptation is a two-way process in which (1) the individual assimilates the factors of the environment and (2) the individual accommodates to the requirements of the environment. Cognitive development is a process in which the individual arrives at a balance between assimilation and accommodation that is accompanied by a growing ability to generalize, differentiate, and coordinate cognitive schemata. In other words, children form mental images or structures that correspond to their experience of the external world and continually modify these structures because of new experiences.

Piaget has discerned that human intelligence develops in stages and in sequence. Piaget's theory emphasizes that because of their mental structures and organization of experience children are ready to learn certain things at specific times and that there are appropriate things for them to learn. Children proceed from one developmental stage to another because of their own activity. Learning is a continuous process in which a person assimilates the external facts of experience and integrates them into his or her own internal mental structures. Each stage, based on a particular organization of cognitive structures, flows from the preceding into the following stage.

Piaget has identified four major stages in the development of human intelligence: (1) sensorimotor, from age eighteen months to two; (2) preoperational representation, from two to seven years; (3) concrete operations, from seven to eleven years; and (4) formal operations, from age eleven to fifteen years.

In the *sensorimotor stage,* initially infants conduct a series of isolated explorations of their environment by using their mouths, eyes, hands, independently of each other.[7] Later, they coordinate these actions for a more concerted and thorough exploration. For Piaget, this exploratory activity is the means that children use to construct an organized view of the world. In the Piagetian mode,

1. An action is represented in the brain by a plan, which Piaget calls a scheme; the child sees and acts upon an object; this interactive experience—a visual configuration—is incorporated into the scheme.
2. Each time the child manipulates a given object in a different way, a new scheme is added to the original one. A compound schema is created, composed of the various ways that the object can be acted upon.
3. The various compound schema become part of a coordinated whole.

The *preoperational representation stage* occurs between ages of two and seven as the child continues to bring order to the environment. Objects are now gradually seen as entities, classified into related groups, and named. The child's organization and classification only approximate that of adults. During the preoperational stage, children continue to build on the schema developed in the preceding sensorimotor stage. They are building on objects to form concepts and on concepts to form classes of concepts. Although their thinking differs from that of adults in many respects, children are beginning to use logical relationships.

The development of logical thought patterns proceeds as children begin to develop a series of hunches about reality. They have difficulty in explaining causal and chronological relationships. Their speech patterns can be both communicative and egocentric. Their egocentric speech is self-satisfying and consists of monologue and mimicry. In their play, children prefer simple and direct games without a great many rules.

Piaget's third stage, *concrete operations,* takes place between ages seven to eleven, as children use schemes involving classes of objects and people. They isolate the general characteristics of objects and people such as size, duration, length and use them in more complex mental operations. While the child's cognitive operations are still rooted in concrete objects, they are becoming more and more abstract.

---

[7]Jean Piaget, *The Origins of Intelligence in Children,* trans. Margaret Cook (New York: W. W. Norton, 1952), pp. 23–42.

At this stage, children can comprehend number signs, processes, and relationships. They can carry out operations mentally but while so doing visualize these operations in concrete terms. They have difficulty in comprehending adequately abstract concepts such as love, honor, dignity, freedom. They tend to argue with each other but not with adults. Although appearing to accept adult authority, they question it in their own minds. They begin to use reason in structuring their arguments. They prefer games and play with rules. More socially inclined, they form clubs and groups.

The *stage of formal operations,* from ages eleven to fifteen, is characterized by the individual's independence of concrete objects in generating abstract, formal conclusions. The person, at this stage, functions at a high level of generality and comprehends and uses the properties of objects such as numbers, quantity, and weight. Since individuals at this stage understand cause and effect relationships, they can appreciate using the scientific method in establishing scientific explanations of reality. For example, they are ready to relate concepts such as mass and number, and they can conjecture cause and effect relationships and apply them to hypothetical situations in the future.

At this stage, individuals enjoy using abstract ideas and are influenced by formal concepts, ideas, classifications, relationships, and logical structures. They are capable of learning complex mathematical, linguistic, mechanical, and scientific processes. They can use moral standards that can be applied fairly. They also enjoy examining and discussing attitudes, customs, and life-styles that differ from their own.

Piaget's cognitive theory has important implications for early childhood as well as elementary education. As did Rousseau and Pestalozzi, Piaget suggested strongly that human growth and development occurs in sequential stages and that certain states of readiness and activities are appropriate to each stage. Since the learning cycles are sequential and cumulative, teacher-assisted learning should begin at an early age. What is to be learned and how it is to be learned should be matched with the child's stage of development.

For Piaget, the role of the teacher is to assist children in their learning processes.[8] Learning cannot be forced until the individual child is ready to learn, nor should it be delayed when the child is ready to learn. Teaching is to create situations in the environment where children can actually discover structures; it does not mean attempting to transmit structures verbally to children. As Pestalozzi admonished more than a century earlier, verbal instruction is likely to stay at this level and be neither understood nor internalized by children. In the Piagetian environment,

1. Teachers should arrange situations that encourage children to explore and experiment.
2. Instruction should be individualized so that children can learn at their own readiness and pace.
3. Children should be provided with concrete materials to touch, manipulate, and use.

[8]For the application of Piaget's theory to teaching, see Hans G. Furth, *Piaget for Teachers* (Englewood Cliffs, N.J.: Prentice-Hall, 1970).

Erik Erikson

Erik Erikson, the eminent psychoanalytical theorist, was born in Frankfort am Main, Germany, in 1902. His early educational career began in 1927 when he taught in the Burlingham School, a private school with a psychoanalytical orientation in Vienna. He also was familiar with the work of the Vienna Psychoanalytic Institute. In addition to his work in psychoanalytical theory, Erikson was also involved in the anthropological study of simple cultures that facilitated his understanding of the interrelationships between culture, family, and children.[9] For a time, Erikson was a psychology professor at the University of California. In 1950, Erikson's major work, *Childhood and Society,* developed his cycle theory. Among his other works are *Young Man Luther: A Study in Psychoanalysis and History* (1958), *Gandhi's Truth* (1969), *Dimensions of the New Identity* (1974), and *Toys and Reasons* (1977).

Erikson's major theory is that stages of human psychosocial development are to a large extent determined biologically. As biological entities, human beings are products of and are guided by genetic and environmental factors. As participants in human history, individuals interact with and change their environment and themselves. Erikson also developed the concept of identity crisis in which a conflict may occur when a person experiences traumatic situations that impede the course of sequential development.

According to Erikson's life-cycle theory, the human race, over time, has always experienced the same sequence of developmental stages. The human life cycle goes through the following succession of eight developmental stages:

1. Trust versus mistrust—birth to eighteen months.
2. Autonomy versus shame and doubt—eighteen months to three years.
3. Initiative versus guilt—three to six years.
4. Industry versus inferiority—six to twelve years.
5. Identity versus role confusion—adolescence.
6. Intimacy versus isolation—youth.
7. Generativity versus stagnation—mature adulthood.
8. Ego integrity versus despair—old age.

As can be noted, each stage presents a specific conflict to the person. If the individual succeeds in resolving the conflict positively, he or she reaches the next higher stage of human development.

In *trust versus mistrust,* tendencies to trusting or mistrusting influence the person's social relationships. Regarding basic trust as the foundation of a healthy personality, Erikson believes that trust facilitates the person's social encounters with others and interactions with the environment. Conversely, mistrust impedes these relationships. The infant's trust grows out of the feeling that there always will be someone present who can be trusted. Erikson's first stage resembles Pestalozzi's circle of love and trust between mother and child. In the case of

---

[9]Maria W. Piers and Genevieve M. Landau, "Erik H. Erikson," in David Sills, ed., *International Encyclopedia of the Social Sciences,* 18 (New York: Free Press, 1979), pp. 172–176.

both theorists, the initial relationship of trust fosters more general feelings of emotional security.

In Erikson's second stage, *autonomy versus shame and doubt,* at around eighteen months, the sense of the self becomes clear as children exhibit tendencies to independent action in wanting to do things for themselves rather than having them done for them. However, children at the "toddler" stage have feelings of doubt that they will be able to accomplish control over their toilet habits and walking on their own. In some respects, the so-called "terrible two's" represent a series of conflicts between parents who must put limits on the child's behavior and the child who wants to have his or her own way. Independent action can foster a sense of autonomy if the child's actions are successful. In large measure, successful consequences depend upon adult approval or disapproval. When adults approve of and encourage a child's behavior, it leads to a greater sense of self-confidence than when such behavior elicits adult disapproval and punishment that brings about self-doubt and shame.

In *initiative versus guilt,* the child's sense of autonomy, if developed supportively, has reached a high state of evolution. Along with the sense of autonomy comes benign aggressiveness in which children actively explore their environment, experimenting with new and different objects and situations. At times, children may experience guilt feelings that their curiosity has caused them to go too far. To nourish the tendency to initiative, children need encouragement to explore actively their environment. Again, it is important that parents, teachers, and other adults encourage rather than impede the child's initiative. If overly controlled or punished for their explorations, children may develop guilt feelings that may plague them throughout life.

In *industry versus inferiority,* children enjoy and experience new powers. Their bodies are developed and coordinated better physically; they are interacting socially with their peers in both cooperative and competitive activities. Children now use advanced language patterns and intellectualize their experiences by using rational thought processes.

To develop a sense of industry, children need to channel their growing energies in constructive, task-oriented directions. The sense of industry stimulates feelings of competence, pride in work well done, and a joy in craftsmanship. Once again, adult disapproval, rejection, and punishment can stifle initiative and create inferiority feelings. It is crucial that individuals in this preadolescent period develop strong feelings of self-worth. Erikson's fourth stage coincides with elementary schooling. Teachers can stimulate industriousness by developing and encouraging children in activities and projects that cultivate a sense of purpose, work, and accomplishment.

In *identity versus role confusion,* childhood ends and adulthood begins. During these storm and stress years, adolescents experience feelings of inferiority, self-doubt, and incompetence. Simultaneously, they experience feelings of power, might, independence, and freedom. This is a crucial stage in making the determinations and clarifications that lead to a sense of personal identity. Diverse attitudes, feelings, roles, and experiences are either integrated into a positive self-concept or they are disintegrated. During this period, adolescents search for, find, and experiment with a variety of models and life-styles, ranging among those provided by parents, by media figures, and by peer group members. The exploratory period of adolescence is simultaneously exciting, painful, and joyful. As adolescents seek their own self-identity and self-definition, it is important that junior and senior high school teachers understand the dynamics of their students' psychological and emotional development.

Erikson's major contributions of the sequential development of personal identity have had significant implications for early childhood education as well as for other periods of human development. They have provided educators with a statement of the need for the positive reinforcement of the concepts of self-worth and self-esteem in children.

CURRENT EARLY CHILDHOOD INSTITUTIONS AND PRACTICES

Thus far, we have identified several of the major contributors to early childhood education. We turn now to some of the institutions and trends that exist in the early education of American children. In particular, we focus on nursery schools and the kindergarten.

The Home in Early Childhood Education

Successful educational efforts at any level depend upon cooperative relationships between the home and the school or educational agency. In recent years, a growing attention and literature have developed on the subject of responsible parenting. Of the many areas of deliberate instruction, education to prepare persons for parental roles and responsibilities has been most neglected.

As stressed by pioneers of early childhood, learning begins in the home environment. A good learning environment is provided by the home that is emotionally secure and has the material requirements needed to foster positive growth and development. Professional educators have recognized that a great deal of important learning takes place in the home before the child enters school and encounters teachers. For example, children learn behavior patterns based on adult norms; they begin to develop patterns of social interaction based on their relationships to siblings and peers; they acquire a conversational command of language that permits them to communicate; they begin to internalize the value syndrome of parents as they acquire preferences for certain foods, dress, words, and actions.

In home-school relationships, particularly those of early childhood, it is desirable that the values of the home and the school be compatible. Later educational efforts are more likely to succeed when children already possess the value predispositions that are conducive to learning.

Most early childhood educators emphasize the role that direct experience exercises in human learning, particularly that of children. These educators stressed that children should have opportunities for direct experience, especially with the world of persons and objects. Family excursions, trips to parks, zoos, and museums, and family projects involving making and doing things all provide children with a network of direct experience.

Since early childhood is crucial in establishing the directions for later learning, recent efforts have been made to identify psychological or physical problems before children enter school. Preschool screenings are used so that children can be examined and tested to identify potential learning disabilities. In many areas of the country, such remedial work involves (1) medical and psychological diagnosis, (2) remedial programs, and (3) parental education.

Parental and Family Education

Since children's first teachers are their parents, parents need to be prepared for their responsibilities and duties. Parenting education may be offered to students before they marry and have children; more often, parenting education is studied by parents or prospective parents. Hospitals, medical centers, and public and private agencies have courses on child care for expectant parents.

Parental and family life education programs are often provided by voluntary organizations, churches, and social agencies; they are not generally offered in a concerted manner by the public schools. Topics that might be discussed in a family life education program include the role of parents and children as a family unit; the impact of family relationships and attitudes on early childhood education and development; family stress and problems; effective parenting; and parents' and children's needs and expectations.

Impact of Television on Early Childhood Education

The entry of television into American homes after World War II has had a continuing and profound impact on American education, in general, and on early childhood education in particular. As with other media, television itself is a neutral instrument that can be used for good or for ill. While it has been educative in bringing into American homes programs of national and international significance, television can be miseducative, particularly when it is grossly commercial.

It is estimated that 97 percent of American homes have television sets. It is further estimated that the average child watches four thousand hours of television programs before entering school. Undoubtedly, television can facilitate learning by giving children a "head start" as is the case with "Sesame Street," but it should be remembered that the programs that children view present values and models that they tend to imitate in their play. It is also true that television viewing is sedentary and provides indirect experience that is conducive to passive rather than active learning.

Since television has easy entry into the overwhelming majority of American homes, educators should reflect on the learning style that it encourages. Television programs rely on the quick and dramatic and television news programs may treat events of major significance in one or two minutes. The kind of learning style fostered by television is superficial rather than in depth. It is noisy rather than quiet. Some educators think that school-based learning should imitate the quickness and drama of television; others argue that the school should stress the more reflective and in-depth learning associated with print rather than the screen.

Head Start Programs

During the Johnson administration, attention was given to educational programs for minority groups and for poverty-impacted areas. The Economic Opportunity Act of 1965 created a number of early childhood educational programs, known collectively as Operation Head Start. As the name implies, these programs were designed to give economically and culturally disadvantaged children an early educational opportunity before entering school.

Head Start programs are designed to provide cultural stimulus and educational experiences to lower-income children that are generally common to middle-class children. They provide story telling; field trips to museums, zoos, parks; group games, songs, and play; and activities that stimulate learning readiness such as drawing, coloring, and painting. Dental and physical examinations are included. Head Start staff members seek to enlist parents in the educational program so that the learning activities will be continued at home.

The results of Head Start programs have been mixed and often controversial. Some observers feel that the programs provide an initial start, as intended, but need to have better designed follow-up strategies to continue this initial impetus when children enter regular school programs. Critics of the program claim that the initial tendency and achievement is lost by the time the child enters the third grade and that other instructional strategies need to be designed for children from disadvantaged groups.

Nursery Education

Nursery school education is one of the most rapidly growing educational sectors today, as a result of numerous social, economic, and educational factors, including the recent favorable findings of psychological and educational research and the entry of more women into the job force. Although nursery schools and day care centers are gaining popularity in the United States, other countries, especially Israel, the Soviet Union, and the Scandinavian countries, have a long and concerted experience in nursery school education.

SCOPE OF NURSERY SCHOOL EDUCATION. The two most common forms of nursery education are day care centers and nursery schools. Often, the services provided by both agencies are so similar that it is difficult to differentiate functionally between them. The day care center is an institution that provides meals, play, and recreation to the children of working parents. Today, more than half the married women in the United States are employed; there are approximately six million working mothers with children under six years of age. As more women enter the working force, the need for trained day care personnel will increase.

The nursery school resembles both a nursery and a school. Some nursery schools have well-developed educational programs designed and staffed by trained early childhood educators. The quality of nursery schools varies greatly, however. Parents should investigate the kind of services provided, especially those of an educational nature, before enrolling their children in a particular nursery school. While some nursery schools provide a carefully designed educational environment, others really perform a strictly custodial, baby-sitting service for working parents. Some nursery schools will accept children as young as two; others at age three or four. Some operate a full-day schedule; others a half-day cycle.

Depending upon the state, day care centers and nursery schools may be inspected and licensed by state welfare departments or by state departments of education.

TYPES OF NURSERY SCHOOLS. More than half the nursery schools in the United States function independently of public school or other educational systems. The typical nursery school is sponsored, supported, and conducted by independent organizations, social welfare agencies, churches, philanthropic organizations, or parent associations. In a few situations, nursery schools are part of the public school system. They can also be found as demonstration and observation laboratories for colleges and universities that offer specialization in early childhood education.

EDUCATIONAL PROGRAM OF NURSERY SCHOOLS. The kind of educational program that is desirable for early childhood education at the nursery school level has been subject to considerable controversy. Upon examination, educational approaches to early childhood education range from the very permissive, activity centered play school to structures that encourage the early introduction of intellectual skills and academic subject matters. Nursery schools that take an Experimentalist-Deweyite approach emphasize a full range of activities designed to involve children directly in problem-solving situations. Typical of these approaches are those that involve children in group projects. Somewhat related to the Progressive educational approaches associated with Dewey are recent developments based on the "open education" philosophy associated with the British primary school.

In the British primary schools, children pursue their interests by using materials placed in learning centers. In these permissive environments, the children structure their own activities and experiences according to their own interests and needs. The Progressive and British primary approaches emphasize a permissive environment in which children are encouraged to learn at their own pace. Attention is paid to socialization so that the individual child learns to relate to members of the group. Formal instruction in academic skills is often delayed until the child has built up an experiential, emotional, and psychological readiness for them.

At the other end of the spectrum are the more structured approaches to early childhood learning such as the popular Montessori method, the underlying assumption being that preschool-aged children have a great curiosity and capacity to learn and that they desire structure and order. It is believed that delayed organized learning activities deny children the educational head start of which they are capable.

Nursery schools conducted under the auspices of churches often have curricula that include religious stories, lessons, and experiences. In addition to the usual range of preschool learning activities, children are introduced to the beliefs and practices of the particular religious denomination supporting the school.

ENROLLMENTS AND CONTROL.   Nursery schools and day care centers serve about 15 percent of the population under the age of six. Although this means that the majority of children in that age range do not attend nursery schools, the number of those who do has increased dramatically since 1970. In 1974–75, approximately 1,600,000 were enrolled in schools at the prekindergarten level.[10]

Most nursery schools are privately controlled and supported. Some, particularly those serving low-income families, receive support from government agencies, especially at the federal level through the Department of Education, the Office of Child Development, and the Social and Rehabilitation Service. It is also expected that private industry will begin to operate day care and nursery schools for their employees. Finally, there is mounting pressure for public school systems to involve themselves in preschooling efforts beyond the kindergarten, which is part of most systems.

STAFF.   Nursery school staffs vary considerably in professional preparation. Day care centers and nursery schools that perform primarily custodial functions are unlikely to have a highly trained staff of professionals. Nursery schools that emphasize the educational development of children enrolled in them require a staff professionally prepared in early childhood education. Such preparation involves study and experience in child growth and development, educational instructional methods suited to young learners, and a knowledge of children's literature, music, and art. It is important, as Pestalozzi and Froebel noted, that those who work with young children be emotionally secure, patient, and warm. It is also important that early childhood educators be able to relate to parents as well as to students.

Kindergarten Education

The kindergarten, developed in the midnineteenth century by Friedrich Froebel, is an example of an approach to early childhood education that was developed in Europe and introduced and adopted in the United States.

The kindergarten was brought to the United States initially by immigrants who left Germany after the failure of the Revolution of 1848. Margaretha Meyer Schurz (1834–1879) is credited with opening the first kindergarten for German-speaking children in Watertown, Wisconsin in 1856. Caroline Louise Frankenburg, who had been trained by Froebel, also established a number of kindergartens in Ohio and Pennsylvania that served German-speaking communities. In cities such as Milwaukee and St. Louis, where the German-American population was concentrated, Froebel's kindergarten principles were used as part of the curriculum for the younger children who attended bilingual schools.

Henry Barnard, who popularized Pestalozzian education in his *American Journal of Education*, enthusiastically advocated Froebel's kindergarten. While attending the International Exhibit of Educational Systems in London in 1854, Barnard saw a display of kindergarten materials. He afterward praised Froebel's principles for their usefulness in early childhood education.[11]

[10]*Digest of Educational Statistics, 1975* (Washington, D.C.: G.P.O., 1976), p. 47.

[11]Evelyn Weber, *The Kindergarten: Its Encounter with Educational Thought in America* (New York: Teachers College Press, Columbia University, 1969), p. 24.

Elizabeth Peabody (1808–1898), a pioneer in kindergarten education in the United States, established an English-language kindergarten in Boston in 1860. After studying Froebelian pedagogy in Europe, she dedicated her life to advancing kindergarten principles through lecturing, writing, and editing the *Kindergarten Messenger*.

William T. Harris, the superintendent of schools in St. Louis, was attracted to the Froebelian method on both philosophical and educational grounds. Harris, like Froebel, was a philosophical Idealist, who believed that the kindergarten was the ideal institution to externalize the child's potentialities. Due to his advocacy of Froebelian education, the kindergarten became part of the St. Louis public school system in 1873. Susan Blow (1843–1916) worked with Harris in St. Louis, where she assisted in training teachers in kindergarten methods. By the turn of the century, other school systems followed the example set by St. Louis and incorporated the kindergarten as part of the public school. By 1900, approximately 5,000 kindergartens were functioning throughout the United States.[12]

The kindergarten is the institution of early childhood education with which most Americans have had some experience. Today, the kindergarten is an important part of the American public school system. Although not a compulsory part of the public school system, many American children enter the kindergarten at age five, their first introduction to formal schooling. The conventional kindergarten pattern enrolls children for half a day, five days a week, for the school year, usually nine months.

Kindergarten education is widely accepted throughout the United States, and the vast majority of school districts include kindergartens in their school system. In 1974–75, 3,100,000 children were enrolled in kindergarten. Of these, 2,600,000 were enrolled in public school kindergartens and 500,000 in parochial and private schools.[13]

KINDERGARTEN PROGRAMS. Although kindergarten practices have changed substantially since the founding of the institution by Friedrich Froebel in the nineteenth century, certain essential features have been maintained. Rather than serving as an institution for academic development in the strictly intellectual sense, kindergarten programs seek to develop a general readiness for learning that emphasizes well-rounded, physical, emotional, social, and mental development.

Activities that kindergartens stress include:

1. Introducing children to a larger social environment in which they encounter children other than siblings and an adult other than parents or relatives—the teacher.
2. Introducing patterns of regularity and a sense of time that is conducive to children's entry into the primary grades.
3. Enriching children's experiences through projects, activities, and field trips.

[12]Nina C. Vandewalker, *The Kindergarten in American Education* (New York: Arno Press and The New York Times, 1971), p. 195.
[13]*Digest of Educational Statistics, 1975* (Washington, D.C.: G.P.O., 1976), p. 47.

Kindergarten programs are designed to promote learning readiness in children. *(Children's Bureau, Department of Health and Human Services)*

4. Enriching children's vocabulary, speech, and reading readiness by books and stories.
5. Stimulating mathematical readiness by introducing arithmetic concepts, numbers, and counting exercises.
6. Developing writing readiness by drawing, cutting, other activities that encourage eye-hand and muscular coordination.
7. Developing aesthetic readiness and creativity through painting, dancing, singing, and dramatic plays.
8. Developing muscular coordination and physical stamina through games, play, and activities.
9. Developing a readiness for science by nature studies, studying nature, plants, and animals.

In addition to cultivating readiness for later learning, the kindergarten is a major agency of initial socialization. It introduces children to the concepts of respect for private and group property, to taking turns in using books and equipment, to respect for others, and to listening to the teachers and to other children.

Although most kindergartens continue to emphasize socialization and learning readiness as primary goals, kindergarten programs have been experiencing change. Factors that have stimulated this change are social, economic, and educational. As more children are enrolled in nursery schools, they will encounter at an earlier age many of the experiences and activities that used to occur initially in the kindergarten. Television, particularly educational television programs such as "Sesame Street," introduce many youngsters to word and number concepts before such exposure occurs in kindergarten. Finally, some parents and parent groups have pressed school districts to begin basic skill development in the kindergarten.

CONCLUSION

This chapter has introduced several major theories of early childhood education along with the institutions designed for early childhood education. Although this introduction has been necessarily brief, it seeks to provide an overview of the theoretical richness of early childhood education. The various theories treated in the chapter have implications for early childhood practice. They are also relevant for elementary education, which is the subject of the next chapter.

The second section of the chapter described the institutions of early childhood education that exist in the United States. Early childhood education is a growing area. Socioeconomic changes have increased the need for day care and nursery services. In the future, the demand for trained professionals will accelerate.

DISCUSSION QUESTIONS

1. Read a biography of one of the early childhood educators discussed in the chapter and trace the development of the educator's theory.
2. Analyze the issue of social imposition versus child freedom.
3. Examine the meaning of "appropriateness" in a child's education.
4. Examine the impact of television on early childhood education.
5. Analyze the factors that have contributed to the growth of day care centers and nursery schools.
6. What are the purposes of the kindergarten?
7. Project the future trends in early childhood education.

FIELD EXERCISES

1. Using the method of recalling early childhood educational experiences, arrange a panel discussion in which the participants examine, share, and analyze their own impressions of their childhood experiences.
2. Arrange visits to private, church-related, and, if possible, public nursery schools. Observe the children and their programs and report your observations to the class.
3. Read a book on the Montessori method of education and then arrange a visit to a Montessori school. Note the extent to which the method is being followed. Report your observations to the class.

4. Visit a kindergarten. Observe the program and report your observations to the class.
5. Watch several television programs intended for children's viewing. Include programs that appear on both educational and commercial television. Note (a) the particular learning strategy being used, (b) the value models being cultivated, and (c) the degree to which the program seeks to shape the child's attitudes.
6. If you are especially interested in exploring early childhood education as a career, volunteer to act as a part-time aide in a nursery school, kindergarten, or other children's program.

SUGGESTED READINGS

ALMY, MILLIE. *The Early Childhood Educator at Work.* New York: McGraw-Hill, 1975.

AUSTIN, GILBERT R. *Early Childhood Education: An International Perspective.* New York: Academic Press, 1976.

BEARD, RUTH M. *An Outline of Piaget's Developmental Psychology for Students and Teachers.* New York: Basic Books, 1969.

BELL, T. H. *Your Child's Intellect: A Guide to Home-Based Preschool Education.* Salt Lake City, Utah: Olympus, 1972.

BOYD, WILLIAM. *The Emile of Jean Jacques Rousseau: Selections.* New York: Teachers College Press, Columbia University, 1966.

DOWNS, ROBERT B. *Heinrich Pestalozzi: Father of Modern Pedagogy.* Boston: Twayne, 1975.

FROEBEL, FREDERICK. *The Education of Man,* trans. W. N. Hailman. New York: Appleton, 1896.

FURTH, HANS G. *Piaget for Teachers.* Englewood Cliffs, N.J.: Prentice-Hall, 1970.

GOODLAD, JOHN, KLEIN, FRANCES, AND NOVOTNEY, JERROLD M. *Early Schooling in the United States.* New York: McGraw-Hill, 1973.

GUTEK, GERALD L. *Joseph Neef: The Americanization of Pestalozzianism.* University, Alabama: University of Alabama Press, 1978.

———. *Pestalozzi and Education.* New York: Random House, 1968.

HAINSTOCK, ELIZABETH G. *Teaching Montessori in the Home: The Preschool Years.* New York: Random House, 1968.

KILPATRICK, WILLIAM H. *Froebel's Kindergarten Principles: Critically Examined.* New York: Macmillan, 1916.

———. *The Montessori System Examined.* Boston: Houghton Mifflin, 1914.

LILLARD, PAULA P. *Montessori: A Modern Approach.* New York: Schocken Books, 1973.

LILLY, IRENE M. *Friedrich Froebel: A Selection from His Writings.* Cambridge: Cambridge University Press, 1967.

MONTESSORI, MARIA. *The Discovery of the Child.* New York: Ballantine Books, 1972.

———. *The Secret of Childhood.* New York: Ballantine Books, 1972.

MONROE, WILL S. *History of the Pestalozzian Movement in the United States.* Syracuse, N.Y.: C. W. Bardeen, 1907.

OREM, R. C. *Montessori Today.* New York: Capricorn Books, 1971.

PESTALOZZI, JOHANN H. *How Gertrude Teaches Her Children,* trans. Lucy E. Holland and Francis Turner. London: Swan Sonnenschein, 1907.

————. *Leonard and Gertrude,* trans. Eva Channing. Lexington, Mass.: D. C. Heath, 1907.

PIAGET, JEAN. *The Origins of Intelligence in Children.* New York: W. W. Norton, 1952.

SILBER, KATE. *Pestalozzi: The Man and His Work.* London: Routledge and Kegan Paul, 1960.

SPODEK, BERNARD. *Early Childhood Education.* Englewood Cliffs, N.J.: Prentice-Hall, 1973.

STANDING, E. M. *Maria Montessori: Her Life and Work.* New York: New American Library, 1962.

VANDEWALKER, NINA C. *The Kindergarten in American Education.* New York: Arno Press and The New York Times, 1971.

WEBER, EVELYN. *The Kindergarten: Its Encounter with Educational Thought in America.* New York: Teachers College Press, Columbia University, 1969.

————. *The English Infant School and Informal Education.* Englewood Cliffs, N.J.: Prentice-Hall, 1971.

11

Elementary Education

Chapter 11 examines American elementary education. It presents a brief historical overview of elementary education and examines the goals of elementary education. It then discusses the elementary school program and patterns of organization and analyzes recent trends in elementary education. Among the general focusing questions that will be answered as you read the chapter are

1. Historically, what has been the major purposes of elementary education?
2. What are the continuing goals of elementary education?
3. What are the basic features of the elementary school program?
4. How are elementary schools organized?
5. What are some of the recent trends in elementary education?

HISTORICAL OVERVIEW
OF ELEMENTARY SCHOOLING

Throughout history, adults have prepared their children to participate in and contribute to their society by giving them the skills and knowledge that they regard as needed for the group's survival. In its oldest sense, elementary education is the means by which the mature members of a society transmit their knowledge, beliefs, methods, and values to the immature members of the society. When this transmission takes place, the group's heritage is preserved in the life of the next generation. The transmission process can range from a static indoctrination designed to perpetuate the status quo to one that encourages change and progress.

In preliterate societies, elementary education of a utilitarian sort was done in families or kinship groups where children learned hunting, fishing, farming, and cooking. Religious values—usually the group's ethical core—were transmitted by tribal priests or elders.

In literate societies, such as those of ancient Greece and Rome, elementary education stressed the process of becoming literate by learning to read and write the language and becoming familiar with its literature. In the school of the "grammatist," the young Athenian boy living in the fifth century B.C. learned his letters, reading, writing, counting, poetry, music, drama, and gymnastics. By the end of the third century B.C., Roman boys were attending an elementary school called the *ludus,* where they learned reading, grammar, and literature. These Greek and Roman elementary schools were private and a teacher taught his pupils for a fee. The important historical development is that elementary education in a literate society became identified with schooling that stressed the learning of language. In the thirteenth and fourteenth centuries, a variety of parish, chantry, guild, and monastic schools provided instruction in reading, writing, arithmetic, and religion under the auspices of the Christian church.

The Protestant Reformation of the early sixteenth century exercised a decided influence on elementary education. Believing that reformed Christians should read the Bible in their own language, Calvin, Luther, and other leaders of the Reformation encouraged the establishment of elementary or vernacular schools in which children learned to read and write so that they would know the Scriptures and the principles of their religion.

At the time of the settlement of North America, the purposes and function of elementary schooling were shaped heavily by the imprint of the Protestant reformers. In Puritan New England, in particular, the town schools incorporated what had become the conventional pattern of elementary education—the learning of the language by reading and writing it. Closely related to the process of becoming literate was a thorough program of religious education or indoctrination, which literally meant to internalize the doctrines of the church so that one could defend it against those who held contrary creeds. Along with reading, writing, spelling, and religion, arithmetic was also taught. The typical methods of instruction were the recitation of memorized lessons and the answering of questions contained in the catechism. Discipline was harsh, and corporal punishment was administered freely by the teacher.

The most direct institutional ancestor of today's elementary school was the common school of nineteenth century America. The creation of the movement led by Horace Mann, Henry Barnard, and others, the common school was a public, elementary school, that (1) was supported by public taxation, primarily the property tax, (2) was open to all children living within the attendance area it served, and (3) offered a curriculum that consisted in most instances of reading, writing, spelling, arithmetic, health, history, geography, music, and art.

The common school was so called because it sought to be the educational institution that was open to all the children, educating them in common without class distinctions. It also was to provide the children who attended it with a common body of skills, knowledge, and values. Since Americans held differing religious beliefs and since the Constitution prohibited the establishment of religion, the common school was nondenominational. While it did not teach the tenets of a particular religion, it did emphasize the values of hard work, industriousness, thrift, and punctuality, which had been prized by the Puritans. In secular form, these values were impressed on thousands of children who learned to read with the help of McGuffey's readers.

By the mid- and late-nineteenth century, elementary school teachers were being prepared for teaching careers in normal schools, where they reviewed the general areas of the elementary curriculum, practiced the methods of teaching, and studied principles of pedagogy. It was during this time that multitudes of women embarked on careers as elementary teachers. Revisionist historians would assert that, in an industrializing country, women were employed because they were a cheap labor force that could be paid low salaries and were willing to teach under restricted conditions. One could also contend, however, that it was elementary teaching that made it possible for women to leave the home and enter the career world. Perhaps, the entry of women into elementary teaching careers was an early step in the womens' liberation movement.

The common schools of the nineteenth century varied from the little one-room school house of rural America to the large factorylike buildings in the large cities. It was in the urban schools that served large numbers of children that the graded pattern of organization was developed by which children were assigned in classes according to their age. This pattern of organization caused many elementary schools to be called "grade schools."

By the beginning of the twentieth century, American elementary schooling was well established and tending to become overly formal. The rote instruction and emphasis on routine sparked the Progressive Movement in American education in which educators such as Francis Parker, John Dewey, and William H. Kilpatrick criticized traditional schooling for being overly literary and formal and too removed from the real needs of children.[1] The impact of progressive education was to introduce activities, projects, problem solving, field trips, and "hands on" laboratory learning into elementary schools.

Today's elementary school is largely a result of the impact of historical forces. Still emphasizing the need for basic, foundational skills and knowledge, modern elementary schools seek to cultivate both the cognitive and affective development of the children whom they educate.

GOALS OF ELEMENTARY EDUCATION

As have most educational institutions, American elementary schools have experienced change. Elementary education has been changed by a number of forces, such as the findings of research into child growth and development, by

---

[1]For a treatment of progressive reform, see the definitive work by Lawrence A. Cremin, *The Transformation of the School: Progressivism in American Education, 1876–1957* (New York: Knopf, 1962).

an evolving sensitivity to the needs of children, and by the rising expectations that society has for its children. In the section that follows, some of the continuing goals of American elementary education are identified and examined.[2]

Preparation in Fundamental Skills and Knowledge

Since the establishing of the earliest schools, elementary education has sought to provide children with the fundamental skills and basic knowledge necessary to function as members of society. In literate societies, this means that organized elementary education prepares children to use language by teaching reading, writing, and comprehension. In the elementary curriculum, the language arts are designed to cultivate this ability to use language.

In a literate society—especially in an industrialized and technological one—the ability to understand information and to communicate effectively is needed for personal development, for social interaction, for participation, for ongoing education, and for employment. In the language arts, reading instruction occupies much of early elementary education, particularly in the primary and intermediate grades. The reading materials used in school convey the values that the society has for its children. For example, an examination of the various readers that have been used in elementary schools will indicate social change, expectations, and values. *The New England Primer* used in the town schools of colonial New England emphasized religious precepts, stern admonitions against the child's tendency to idleness and sin, and the need to practice the virtues of frugality, hard work, and perseverance. The readers and spelling books written by Noah Webster stressed many of the same values but also added themes of American cultural nationalism and patriotism. McGuffey's readers, which enjoyed a long-lasting and wide popularity, reiterated the values of the Protestant ethic and promised children that honesty, patience, diligence, punctuality, and effort would bring them success in life as well as in school. The readers of the late 1940s and early 1950s that featured "Dick, Jane, and Baby Sally" and their parents depicted an American middle-class family that lived in a white frame house and in which the father took a briefcase to his office rather than a lunch pail to a factory. The stories in current readers are about a multicultural and pluralistic society in which children live in cities as well as suburbs, in apartments as well as houses, in which the family may be a single-parent one, and in which the characters are black, Chicano, and Oriental Americans as well as white. A discerning analysis of elementary reading materials will often illuminate not only the purposes of elementary education but of American society as well.

Along with the fundamental skills of reading, writing, spelling, and listening, elementary education also prepares children in basic mathematics—in

[2]From time to time, individuals and organizations have sought to identify the goals of elementary education. For examples of such identifications, see Educational Policies Commission, *The Purpose of Education in American Democracy* (Washington, D.C.: National Education Association, 1938); Educational Policies Commission, *Education for All American Youth* (Washington, D.C.: National Education Association, 1953), pp. 2–4; Nolan C. Kearney, *Elementary School Objectives* (New York: Russell Sage Foundation, 1953), pp. 52–120; George Manolakes, *The Elementary School We Need* (Washington, D.C.: Association for Supervision and Curriculum Development, National Education Association, 1965), pp. 20–21.

LESSON XI.

ĭ'ron (ī'urn)
ĕye' lĭd₂
förġe
in tĕnse'

elĭn'ker ty
shrĭnk
lā'bor
hăm'mer

THE BLACKSMITH.

1. Clink, clink, clinkerty clink!
   We begin to hammer at morning's blink,
   And hammer away
   Till the busy day,
   Like us, aweary, to rest shall sink.

2. Clink, clink, clinkerty clink!
   From labor and care we never will shrink;
   But our fires we'll blow
   Till our forges glow
   With light intense, while our eyelids wink.

(New York Public Library Collection)

Sally said, "Oh, oh, oh.

Come here, Dick.

See what I see.

See my little blue boat now.

See who wants my boat.

My little blue boat.

See who wants it now."

(New York Public Library Collection)

McGuffey's Readers of the Late Nineteenth Century and the "Dick and Jane" Series of the Midtwentieth Century. These readers were used widely in American elementary schools.

counting, number systems, and fundamental processes. The foundations of science, social science, art, music, and physical education are also established in the elementary school years. A continuing goal of American elementary education, then, has been to cultivate fundamental skills and processes.

While most educators concur on the need to emphasize fundamental skills and knowledge in the elementary school, many of the controversies among elementary teachers are about the most effective methods for accomplishing this goal. Essentialists and "Basic" educators call for what they refer to as a "no-nonsense," structured, teacher-directed learning environment, characterized by an emphasis on drill and practice in the basic skills. More progressive educators, influenced by the tradition of Francis Parker, John Dewey, and William Kilpatrick, believe that a hands-on, learning by doing, child-centered approach is not only more humane but also more effective educationally. Progressives argue that children's interests are the best way in which to begin teaching fundamental skills. In most elementary schools, teachers have created a synthesis that incorporates both fundamental skills and experiential activities.

Entrance into a Larger World

Elementary education has personal and social goals as well as academic ones. It has the general goal of expanding the child's perceptions that are based on the home, family, and neighborhood into a world view. To accomplish this goal, elementary education needs to articulate with and relate the early childhood and kindergarten experience that precede with the secondary school experience that follows it. No part of the school sequence can be treated in isolation from its related components. As part of a child's education, elementary education seeks to introduce children to the diversity and also to the commonness of human experience. It seeks to develop a sense of personal integrity, of cooperation with others, and a respect for human values. This means that the child's world needs to be expanded into new dimensions.

Recognizing the Health and Physical Development of Children

The years from six to eleven when most American children are attending elementary school are an important time of physical, mental, emotional, and social development. Programs of health, safety, and physical education that are incorporated in the formal elementary school curriculum are designed to aid the child's development. However, much that occurs in elementary education is of an informal or extracurricular nature. As children learn with other children in groups, intricate patterns of social interaction, friendship, rivalry, competition, and cooperation develop. In addition to academic learning, children are acquiring and practicing the skills that will lead to social success or frustration. The ability to make a series of personal adjustments to different persons and situations is an important learning goal in elementary education. Children learn that other individuals are both like them in many ways but also different from them. In a multicultural society, children need to learn to respect racial and ethnic groups other than their own and also to understand at the same time the commonness of human experience.

Teachers need to be sensitive to the problems that all children have as they are growing up. At times, however, some children may have serious mental and emotional problems that teachers need to recognize and refer to specialists.

Extending the Horizons of Space and Time

The elementary school child often begins school with limited concepts of space and time that are based on his or her small world of family and neighborhood. In the early nineteenth century, Pestalozzi urged teachers to begin instruction with that which was close to, near to, and immediate to the child's experience and then to lead the child outward to the larger world by a series of carefully planned but short steps. In his classic work, *Democracy and Education*, John Dewey wrote that the elementary curriculum should begin with "making and doing" activities that involved children actively in socially significant projects and problems based on their interests and needs.[3] From "making and doing," Dewey stated that the second level of curriculum involved history that helped to create a sense of time and geography that extended the sense of space.

Elementary education has a major role in broadening the child's horizons into time and space. Teachers should be aware that today's elementary children may well bring a different perspective of time and place with them to school

---

[3]John Dewey, *Democracy and Education* (New York: Macmillan, 1916), pp. 228–270.

Elementary education helps to extend children's concepts of space and time. The social studies, in particular, seek to develop concepts about humankind's use of space over time. *(Ken Karp)*

because of their exposure to television. For example, from an astronaut's perspective, photographs of planet Earth taken from the moon give a much different orientation to space than that which children had in earlier times. In the formal elementary curriculum, the social studies, particularly when they include materials from history and geography, give children a sense of their particular time in relationship to the past and of their particular place in relationship to a global society.

Developing Democratic Values

Since the founding of the American republic, elementary education has stressed the cultivation of citizenship and the processes of participating in a democratic society. In their arguments for common schooling, Horace Mann, Henry Barnard, and others saw public education as a necessary instrument in providing the knowledge and values needed for effective citizenship. Today, there has been a strong revival of interest in the role that elementary education plays in developing the values needed for life in a democratic society.

Once again, the social studies have an important role in citizenship education.[4] This role is supplemented by the milieu of the elementary classroom as children learn the processes of sharing, discussing, and reaching decisions in a peaceful and representative manner.

Liberating Creative Impulses

Since the time of Comenius and Froebel, educators have viewed the years of elementary education as a time for children to liberate their creative

---

[4]James P. Shaver, ed., *Building Rationales for Citizenship Education* (Arlington, Va.: National Council for the Social Studies, 1977).

impulses. Music, art, drama, dance, and writing are ways that children can portray and vivify these impulses through artistry in various media. While the fundamental skills contribute to cognitive development, the arts contribute to affective expression. The arts in the elementary curriculum provide a means by which the child can take an idea, a mood, or a feeling and embody it in a picture, drawing, or song. The elementary school program should provide experiences that stimulate creativity, inventiveness, and originality. In the broad sense, it should cultivate both aesthetic appreciation and creativity.

DEFINITION OF ELEMENTARY EDUCATION

In terms of a curricular definition, elementary education educates children in the fundamental skills and primary areas of knowledge. It can be defined broadly but vaguely as that education that takes place before secondary education. The age range of the children who attend elementary schools is from six to twelve, thirteen, or fourteen, depending upon the particular pattern of organization. In many school districts throughout the United States, elementary education includes grades one through six. Some school districts still retain the more traditional pattern of grades one through eight.

Within most school districts and in many teacher preparation programs, elementary education is organized into the following subdivisions: *primary:* grades one to three (kindergarten may also be included); *intermediate:* grades four, five, and six; and *upper:* grades seven and eight. It should be noted that grades six, seven, and eight form middle schools in some districts and that grades seven and eight are designated as junior high schools in still other patterns of organization. Where junior high school patterns of organization are used, grades seven and eight are frequently identified with secondary education. The discussion in this chapter is limited to grades one through six.

ELEMENTARY SCHOOL PROGRAM

The educational program or curriculum in the elementary school is designed to provide the fundamental skills and areas of knowledge needed for participation in society, for personal growth and development, and for ongoing education. In the early years, the program is more generalized and then becomes gradually more specialized in the intermediate and upper grades. To some extent, the curricula of the lower schools have been influenced by that of the higher institutions. For example, graduate and professional schools have influenced the college curriculum, which has influenced the high school curriculum, which in turn has influenced the elementary school curriculum. However, elementary schools generally have been influenced less directly by higher institutions. As a result, elementary schools frequently have been more innovative and experimental than secondary and higher institutions.

Since the curriculum at the primary and intermediate levels of the elementary school is general rather than specific, there is also a greater stress on methodology than in secondary and higher institutions. Although content is important, the methodology of instruction is vitally important at the elementary level. For example, children need to learn to read, and teachers must be able to teach them to read, before it is possible to proceed to other curricular areas.

The typical elementary school curriculum, which emphasizes general education, is organized around the theme of "broad fields" or general areas.

BROAD FIELD	INCLUDES
Language arts	Reading, handwriting, listening, literature, spelling, speech, creative writing, drama.
Social studies	Concepts and materials from history, geography, political science, economics, anthropology and environmental studies.
Mathematics	
Science	Concepts and materials from natural and physical sciences, introduction to the scientific method, environmental studies.
Health and physical education	Health concepts and practices, physical fitness and motor skills, safety, and recreation.
Music and art	

The Primary Grades

The primary division of the elementary school generally consists of kindergarten and grades one, two, and three. Today, the first introduction of schooling for most children occurs in preschools and in private or public kindergartens. For some children, however, first grade may be the initial introduction to organized education. In any event, the work of the primary grades is to build on the work of the family and home and to extend the child's experience into the skills and subjects that comprise the broad fields of the elementary school curriculum.

In the primary grades, the most fundamental and foundational activity is reading, since so much of the school's program depends upon it. The major objectives of elementary reading programs are

1. To begin, develop, and improve reading skills.
2. To develop the skill of gaining information through the printed medium.
3. To cultivate the value of reading for enrichment, enjoyment, and recreation.

Contemporary reading programs are related to and often integrated with the other broad fields of the elementary curriculum. Much of the progress that the children are expected to make in social studies, mathematics, and science depends upon their ability to read. In addition to reading, children are introduced to concepts in the other broad fields of the curriculum. The primary

Group activities and projects in the primary grades of the elementary school develop both academic and social skills. *(Ken Karp)*

grades continue the socialization process in which children acquire and develop their skills of interacting with others and of participating in group activities.

The Intermediate Grades

In most elementary schools, the intermediate grades are grades four, five, and six. The emphasis on reading continues in the intermediate grades, but the informational and enjoyment functions of reading receive greater emphasis than do the mechanics and comprehension stressed in the primary grades. The broad fields of the curriculum—social studies, mathematics, and science—also are pursued in greater depth.

The Upper Grades

The upper grades in the elementary school are grades seven and eight. While some school districts continue to locate the upper grades in the same buildings with the primary and intermediate grades, other districts have created upper grade centers. Throughout the country, many districts use the junior high school or the middle school as the institution for educating children in these grades. Since the junior high and middle school are treated elsewhere, the upper grades receive only a brief discussion here. In the upper grades, pupils are entering adolescence and are in a transitional stage of development. The broad fields that characterized the primary and intermediate grades are often differentiated into more specialized subjects such as English, literature, social studies, history, natural and physical sciences, and mathematics. Of special importance in these grades are vocational, industrial, home arts, career, sex, and drug abuse education.

ELEMENTARY SCHOOL ORGANIZATION

Elementary, and other schools as well, are organized vertically and horizontally. Vertical organization relates to the movement of students in time, usually by grade, through the various levels of the school system. Vertical organization can be viewed as a ladder, with each level being a rung on the ladder and the students climbing from rung to rung until they reach the top. Horizontal organization, to be discussed later, is a lateral form of organization in which students are classified, grouped, and assigned at given educational levels.

The Grade School

Historically, the common school—the early nineteenth-century public elementary school—was often a one-room building, staffed by a single teacher. Within this one-room school, the teacher divided the pupils into groups for instructional purposes, often according to their age.

The graded school, a midnineteenth-century innovation, was introduced first by Francis Parker, in Quincy, Massachusetts. This pattern, which organized elementary schools into grades, was followed throughout the country, first in large urban districts and then in smaller districts. In the grade school, children were assigned to a given grade on an age specific basis. For example, all six-year-olds were placed in the first grade, seven-year-olds in the second grade, and so on. Teachers were assigned to a specific grade level and identified with the grade level they taught. A specific body of skills and subjects were assigned to each grade. At the end of the school year, students who completed the requirements of a given grade were promoted to the next grade. Those who failed were retained. Thus, the following typical graded elementary school pattern emerged:

Grade 1	Age 6
Grade 2	Age 7
Grade 3	Age 8
Grade 4	Age 9
Grade 5	Age 10
Grade 6	Age 11
Grade 7	Age 12
Grade 8	Age 13

At a time when testing and evaluation were at a primitive state of development, the graded system, based on pupil ages, was a simple and specific means of classifying and assigning children and of organizing the instructional program. Unfortunately, as with many educational innovations, the graded system soon became overly formal and routinized. In many schools, elementary education became a lockstep system in which armies of children moved at an inflexible and rigid cadence. A system based solely on age is indifferent to children's individual differences and needs. Although they might have been born within the same year, important differences exist among children of the same age in terms of pyschological and emotional development and learning readiness. The traditional graded system did not recognize the need of gifted children to move at an accelerated pace or of slower learners who needed more time than that allotted by the prescribed syllabus and time schedule.

Since the children assigned to a given grade were heterogeneous in everything except age, creative teachers have turned to grouping—a simple form of horizontal organization—within a grade level. To group children of similar readiness and ability together, homogeneous small groups are used. Children within a given grade are grouped according to their ability within a skill or subjects. For example, those who are progressing in reading at a similar rate may be organized into a particular reading group. Although progressive educators have attacked the rigidity of the graded system over the years, it is still a common pattern of elementary school organization.

Because of dissatisfaction with the inflexibility of the graded system, the multigraded pattern—a fairly recent modification of the more traditional graded school pattern—was introduced. Although grade level designations may still be used, the multigraded patterns combine several grades so that more homogeneous groupings can be organized from the larger number of students. An individual child, then, has the opportunity to work in several ability groups in different subjects. In a fourth and fifth grade combination, for example, a child might be working with a fifth grade mathematics group and a fourth grade social studies group.

The Ungraded School and Individualized Instruction

The nongraded, or ungraded school, plan—an innovation introduced into elementary education in the mid-1960s—is designed to eliminate completely the rigidity of the graded system. Because it uses age-specific assignments, instruction in the graded school is often directed to learners of average ability. The nongraded organization emphasizes that there is no average child and that a good elementary school should meet the individual needs of every learner. The nongraded philosophy stresses that

1. Children are unique and have their own readiness for and rate of learning.
2. Specific learning tasks need to be developed for each child.
3. Pupil progress is not determined by the years spent sitting in a classroom but by an individual's achievement.

The theme of the nongraded school is flexible scheduling of children so that they can move at their own pace from module to module or unit to unit within a given skill or subject. This generally means that individual classroom teachers must be reorganized into teaching teams. The curriculum also must be reorganized. The continuous progress curriculum, found in nongraded schools, is organized into smaller and often more diverse units to permit children to move at intervals of a few weeks and to work with other children who are functioning at their ability level. Ability levels, too, will vary for the same child according to the particular subject or skill. Since small groupings are used, children can be assigned to several groups according to their individual needs, interests, and abilities in a particular subject. The children may move to another group when they are ready to do so rather than be required to spend the entire school year with a single class as in the conventional graded school.

Individually guided education (IGE), another recent innovation in school organization, is used as the instructional program and method in some nongraded schools. Since the mid-1960s, a number of elementary schools were reorganized to implement IGE as the instructional pattern. IGE is a system that individualizes instruction by designing and programming specific learning tasks so that individual learners can progress through the program at their own level of readiness and own learning rate. The implementation of highly individualized instructional programs such as IGE requires a staffing pattern that encourages a team effort by teachers. It also requires a curricular design that permits the continuous evaluation and assignment of pupils.

In the late 1970s, nongraded schools and highly individualized instructional programs came under criticism from some educators and parents. Advocates of basic education were especially disenchanted with these innovations, which they claimed lacked specific academic standards and requirements for pupil promotion. The critics contended that highly individualized instruction also neglected proper order and sequence in the curriculum.

Horizontal Organization of the Elementary School

Elementary schools are also organized horizontally; that is, children within the same educational level may be assigned to a variety of groups at that level. If, for example, there are one hundred children at the third grade level in a given elementary school, these children might be divided horizontally into four classes of twenty-five pupils. Within a particular classroom, the teacher may divide the children further into five reading groups of five pupils. The following diagram illustrates the interrelationship of vertical and horizontal organization.

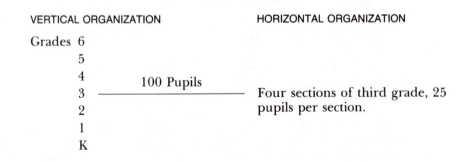

VERTICAL ORGANIZATION

HORIZONTAL ORGANIZATION

Grades 6
5
4
3   100 Pupils
2   Four sections of third grade, 25
1   pupils per section.
K

The conventional unit of horizontal organization in the elementary school is the self-contained classroom in which pupils of a given age level are instructed by a teacher assigned to that classroom. In the self-contained classroom, a single teacher instructs the entire class of pupils for the whole school day. Despite criticism over the years, the self-contained classroom remains a widely used pattern of horizontal organization, since it enables the teacher to become familiar with the needs of the whole child and to make sure that the children's instruction is integrated into a total educational pattern. The successful self-contained classroom teacher needs to be a generalist in elementary education but also must be competent in providing instruction in particular skill and subject areas. The weakness in the self-contained pattern is that particular subjects and skills may be neglected if the teacher is unable to integrate them all into a total learning experience for the children.

In many elementary schools, the self-contained pattern has been modified so that the teacher is assisted by specialist or resource teachers in art, music, physical, and special education. The following illustrates the typical self-contained classroom pattern that uses specialist and resource teachers.

SELF-CONTAINED CLASSROOM

Classroom teacher provides instruction	in	Reading Language Arts Mathematics Social Studies Science Health	to Pupils
Specialist teachers provide instruction	in	Art Music Physical Education Special Education	to Pupils

While the self-contained classroom is found in many elementary schools, the departmentalized pattern of horizontal organization is also used. In the departmentalized model, specialist teachers are assigned to teach a particular curricular field or area. For example, reading and language arts may be assigned to specialist teachers in that subject. Mathematics, science, social studies, physical education, and art also would be taught by specialists.

Some elementary schools also use a combination of the self-contained and departmentalized models. For example, kindergarten and grades one to three may be self-contained, and grades four, five, and six departmentalized.

Horizontal organization can also be arranged on the readiness and ability grouping of children. Children are assigned to heterogeneous groups according to age and other factors such as readiness, ability, and achievement. Proponents of heterogeneous grouping claim that it is a more realistic and democratic arrangement since children are not segregated on any basis other than age. Children of high ability as well as those of lower ability learn to work together and to appreciate individual differences.

In homogeneous grouping, children with similar problems, needs, and, most frequently, ability levels are grouped together for instructional purposes. Advocates of homogeneous groupings contend that instruction can be planned and delivered more efficiently when the pupils who are being instructed are in a similar ability range. Gifted and high-ability learners can move at an accelerated rate and use more advanced materials and not be held back by slower children when they are grouped homogeneously. Pupils who are progressing at a slower learning rate or who may be experiencing learning difficulties also can be grouped so that teachers can address their particular needs.

While there are purists who will argue for either homogeneous or heterogeneous grouping, a sound educational approach often takes a middle ground and uses both patterns of horizontal organization. Pupils can be grouped on the basis of readiness and ability in some skills and subjects such as reading, language arts, and mathematics and then be in heterogeneous groups for social studies, music, art, and physical education. Thus, they can learn with students of the same ability in certain subjects and still share experiences with classmates of differing abilities in other subjects.

CONTEMPORARY TRENDS IN ELEMENTARY EDUCATION

During the past several decades, important trends have emerged in elementary education. Team teaching and programmed instruction are two examples. In curriculum, the trend in the early 1960s was to "inquire" into the "structure of disciplines" and away from the conventional patterns of cumulative sequence. By the end of the 1970s, this trend had been reversed as more sequential programs were being redeveloped and reintroduced. The "open classroom" movement gained popularity in the late 1960s. It, too, has experienced a decline with the resurgence of the "Back to Basics" movement of the late 1970s. This section examines the course of several contemporary trends in elementary education.

Instructional and Organizational Trends

Team teaching, an "effort to improve instruction by the reorganization of personnel," is a form of cooperative teaching in which two or more teachers plan and work together to instruct the same group of students.[5] Team teaching requires organizing the school staff into a close working group in which team leaders, cooperating teachers, and instructional aides form a coordinated instructional team.

While every teacher is not expected to be expert in all subjects, teachers involved in team teaching need a thorough understanding of the entire educational process. Members of the teaching team need to work cooperatively with their colleagues in planning, organizing, presenting, and evaluating instruction. Team teaching tends to reduce the isolation of teachers from their colleagues that often occurs in the self-contained classroom. It also permits and encourages teachers to develop special areas of expertise.

[5]Judson T. Shaplin, "Team Teaching," in Ronald Gross and Judith Murphy, eds., *The Revolution in the Schools* (New York: Harcourt Brace, 1964), p. 93.

Team teaching, which was introduced into both elementary and secondary schools in the mid-1960s, requires a more flexible pattern of organization, scheduling, and staffing. In the elementary school, for example, pupils would be assigned to

1. large groups for demonstrations, presentations, films, television, and field excursions;
2. small groups for discussion, projects, experiments, and group work; and
3. independent reading and study.

Because of the flexibility that team teaching requires, it is more often found in ungraded schools and in situations that encourage individualized instruction. Flexible scheduling provides for modules of twenty to thirty minutes of instruction rather than the longer periods found in conventional arrangements.

While team teaching encouraged a number of changes in elementary schools, such as flexible scheduling of pupils and differential staffing of teachers, it did not have the revolutionary impact that some of its proponents predicted. At times, it was introduced by administrators who did not understand that its successful implementation required a thorough reorganization of the school program. In other cases, teachers were expected to become part of a teaching team without having the necessary commitment or in-service preparation. Merely assigning two teachers to teach the same group of students is not team teaching.

Programmed Learning and Computer-Assisted Instruction

In recent years, programmed learning and computer-assisted instruction has been introduced into elementary as well as secondary schools. Programmed learning is a companion innovation along with the ungraded school, team teaching, and individualized instruction. It is designed to bring pupils to concept formation or skill acquisition through a series of carefully graduated sequences that provide them with a means of instant self-evaluation. Since pupils are given instant "feedback," they recognize their correct and incorrect responses as rapidly as they make them and can progress at their own learning rate. Although the principles of programmed learning can be applied to most skills and subjects, it is particularly adaptable to those that can be reduced easily to elemental steps, such as spelling, language development, and mathematics. Initially, program learning was introduced with teaching machines that are still used widely in elementary schools, especially in learning centers. Textbooks, workbooks, and other printed materials are now available that incorporate the principles of programmed learning.

Another contemporary instructional innovation involves computers. Since the early 1970s, computers have entered the mainstream of American life, especially in science, business, and industry, where they make it possible to store, classify, record, and retrieve vast amounts of information. Computer-assisted instruction is used in elementary schools to (1) individualize instruction so that it relates to pupil needs and skill levels and (2) bring about computer literacy—familiarity with and facility in using computers—in much the same way that literacy is developed in reading, writing, and understanding language.

Many school districts have introduced computer-assisted instruction into their elementary schools to cultivate computer literacy as a basic skill. *(Ken Karp)*

From Open Learning to "Back to Basics"

Many of the curricular innovations of the early 1960s were designed by university professors in mathematics, the sciences, and other academic disciplines who developed new programs such as the "new mathematics," the "new physics," and the "new social studies." Underlying these innovations in curriculum could often be found Jerome Bruner's learning theory, which emphasized identifying the structure of disciplines and using the inquiry or discovery method.[6]

The movement for curriculum revision began first in the sciences and then extended into language arts and social studies. The new curricula were designed to replace the emphasis on facts with the key concepts needed to understand a field. Stressing the inquiry or discovery method, the new curricula sought to introduce students to the methods of investigation used by scientists and other scholars in their research. Rather than the direct presentation of factual information in textbooks or by teachers, the students were to investigate topics or problems and reach their own conclusions.

The curricular innovations of the 1960s were supported by the federal

[6]Jerome Bruner, *The Process of Education* (Cambridge, Mass.: Harvard University Press, 1960).

government that funded special institutes and workshops for teachers through the National Defense Education Act. The Carnegie Corporation, the Ford Foundation, and other private philanthropic organizations also encouraged the new curricula. Commercial publishers promoted the movement by designing and marketing "learning packages" featuring the new programs.

Although professors of education were sometimes involved in designing new programs, the major impact came from professors in academic disciplines. Frequently, the academic innovators were unaware of or neglected already existing research on learning. In some instances, the new curricula were introduced without sufficient attention to the experience of classroom teachers. Some critics contended that the apparent sophistication of the new curricular programs masked a superficiality that neglected needed information and skills. Nevertheless, the concerted efforts of the private corporations, the federal government, and the commercial publishers brought about the introduction of the new curricula into many elementary schools.

In the early 1970s, a group of educational critics emerged who wanted to reform elementary education according to a child-centered philosophy that emphasized the liberation of children's impulses. The new critics argued that many elementary schools were too formal, bureaucratic, and inflexible. A series of books by educational critics such as Herbert Kohl, Jonathan Kozol, George Dennison, and John Holt argued for informal and open learning.[7] As did some of the progressive educators before them, these critics urged that children should be free to follow their own curiosity, interests, and needs. Teachers were to guide the learning process in an enthusiastic, informal, interesting, and exciting way.

The cause of informal and open learning gained a major impetus with the publication of Charles E. Silberman's *Crisis in the Classroom* in 1970.[8] Silberman's book, based on his research as director of the Carnegie Corporation's Study of the Education of Educators, contended that American public schools had become overly formal. Excessive routine and formality had devitalized schools that practiced a mindless routine. For Silberman, the remedy was to create more open, informal, and humanistic schools. He argued that the model of the British primary school, or integrated day school, could be adapted to American elementary education. Informal open classrooms would encourage teachers to follow and guide learners' interests.

Silberman's work as well as that of other educators promoted an American enthusiasm for the British primary school.[9] In its various forms, the British

---

[7]Among the representative critics are George Dennison, *The Lives of Children* (New York: Random House, 1969); James Herndon, *The Way It Spozed to Be* (New York: Simon & Schuster, 1968); John Holt, *How Children Learn* (New York: Pitman, 1967); Jonathan Kozol, *Death at an Early Age* (Boston: Houghton Mifflin, 1967).

[8]Charles E. Silberman, *Crisis in the Classroom: The Remaking of American Education* (New York: Random House, 1970).

[9]The major source on the British primary school is Lady Bridget Plowden et al., *Children and Their Primary Schools: A Report of the Central Advisory Council in Education* (London: Her Majesty's Stationery Office, 1966). Other works on open education are John Blackie, *Inside the Primary School* (London: Her Majesty's Stationery Office, 1967); Mary Brown and Normal Precious, *The Integrated Day in the Primary School* (New York: Agathon Press, 1970); Lillian S. Stephens, *The Teacher's Guide to Open Education* (New York: Holt, Rinehart and Winston, 1974).

primary school rested on the philosophy that children learned most effectively when they were directly involved with their immediate environment in which they pursued their interests with the guidance of teachers. Rather than following the scheduled time sequences of more traditional schools, the British primary school stressed longer blocks of time in which the children worked individually or in small groups at a wide range of activities. The British primary school gained a following among enthusiastic American educators who began to implement it as open space education.

During the late 1960s and early 1970s, the open education movement gained ground steadily in the United States. A noteworthy example of the implementation of open education occurred in North Dakota, where a number of small schools were converted into informal or open schools. Throughout the country, school districts inaugurated open classrooms or open space schools.

By the mid-1970s, the pendulum of educational change had begun to swing away from curricular innovation and open education to basic education. The "Back to Basics" movement was inaugurated by parents and nonprofessionals and then began to influence professional educators. Essentially, advocates argued that the school curriculum should emphasize basic skills and subjects. There was a fear that essential skills of reading, writing, and arithmetic were being neglected. Along with the attention to the basic skills and subjects, advocates urged a return to discipline and order in a structured classroom in which the teacher was the center of authority.

A leading force in the "Back to Basics" movement is the Council for Basic Education, which was organized in 1956 to work for an increased emphasis on the fundamental intellectual disciplines in the public schools. The council has urged that students receive adequate instruction in the basic intellectual disciplines of English, mathematics, science, history, foreign languages, and the arts.[10]

What the impact of the basic education movement will be on American public education is still difficult to assess. It does appear, however, that the trends of the 1960s that produced the innovations in the curriculum, instruction, and school organization have run their course and that most recent developments suggest an emphasis on essential skills and subject matters.

CONCLUSION

In discussing elementary education, Chapter 11 has examined its role as an agency of cultural transmission. In the United States, the common school of the early nineteenth century was the prototype of today's public school. The elementary school has been designed to cultivate fundamental skills and knowledge in the young. While an instrument of cognitive development, it also serves to cultivate social, personal, and aesthetic sensibilities in children. The elementary school is the institution that prepares youngsters for entry to the junior high or middle school, which is the subject of Chapter 12.

[10]For the theory of basic education, see James D. Koerner, ed., *The Case for Basic Education* (Boston: Little, Brown, 1959).

DISCUSSION QUESTIONS

1. Debate the proposition that elementary education's major purpose is to transmit the cultural heritage from adults to children.
2. Prepare your own list of goals for elementary education and provide a rationale defending your statement of goals.
3. Examine the various books that have been used to teach reading at a particular level in elementary schools over a given historical period. Identify the values that are emphasized in these books.
4. Debate the proposition that elementary schools tend to be more innovative than secondary schools.
5. Why is the elementary school curriculum generally arranged into broad fields?
6. Distinguish between vertical and horizontal patterns of organization and provide examples of each.
7. Compare and contrast homogeneous and heterogeneous groupings.
8. Compare and contrast the graded and nongraded elementary school.
9. Identify and analyze the "open education" and "basic education" philosophies. Compare and contrast these educational perspectives.

FIELD EXERCISES

1. Invite an elementary teacher to visit your class and describe a typical school day.
2. Visit an elementary school and observe classes at the primary and intermediate levels. Note the similarities and differences between these levels. Report your observations to the class.
3. Invite an elementary school principal to visit your class and describe the way in which his or her school is organized.
4. If possible, visit both a graded and an ungraded elementary school. Compare and contrast them. Decide in which school you would prefer to teach.
5. Interview several elementary teachers on their reactions to recent curricular changes. Try to elicit their opinions about the new mathematics, new social studies, and other curricular innovations.
6. Visit an elementary school in which team teaching is used. Report your observations to the class.
7. Read a book written by an advocate of informal or open education. Identify the author's critique of elementary education and analyze it for the class.
8. If there is a group in your community that advocates "basic education," invite its representatives to speak to your class on the organization's purposes.

SUGGESTED READINGS

BRUNER, JEROME. *The Process of Education.* Cambridge, Mass.: Harvard University Press, 1960.

FEATHERSTONE, JOSEPH. *Schools Where Children Learn.* New York: Liveright, 1971.

GOODLAD, JOHN I., AND ANDERSON, ROBERT H. *The Nongraded Elementary School.* New York: Harcourt Brace, 1963.

GROSS, RONALD, AND MURPHY, JUDITH. *The Revolution in the Schools.* New York: Harcourt Brace, 1964.

GUTEK, GERALD L. *Basic Education: A Historical Perspective.* Bloomington, Ind.: Phi Delta Kappa Educational Foundation, 1981.

HOLT, JOHN. *How Children Fail.* New York: Pitman, 1964.

———. *How Children Learn.* New York: Pitman, 1967.

JOYCE, WILLIAM W., OANA, ROBERT G., AND HOUSTON, ROBERT W. *Elementary Education in the Seventies.* New York: Holt, Rinehart and Winston, 1970.

KOERNER, JAMES D. *The Case for Basic Education.* Boston: Little, Brown, 1959.

KOHL, HERBERT R. *The Open Classroom.* New York: New York Review Book, 1969.

MANOLAKES, GEORGE. *The Elementary School We Need.* Washington, D.C.: Association for Supervision and Curriculum Development, National Education Association, 1965.

POSTMAN, NEIL, AND WEINGARTNER, CHARLES. *How to Recognize a Good School.* Bloomington, Ind.: Phi Delta Kappa Educational Foundation, 1973.

PERRONE, VITO. *Open Education: Promise and Problems.* Bloomington, Ind.: Phi Delta Kappa Educational Foundation, 1972.

SHAVER, JAMES P. *Building Rationales for Citizenship Education.* Arlington, Va.: National Council for the Social Studies, 1977.

SILBERMAN, CHARLES E. *Crisis in the Classroom: The Remaking of American Education.* New York: Random House, 1970.

STEPHENS, LILLIAN S. *The Teacher's Guide to Open Education.* New York: Holt, Rinehart and Winston, 1974.

WOLF, WILLIAM C., AND LOOMER, BRADLEY M. *The Elementary School: A Perspective.* Chicago: Rand McNally, 1966.

12

The Junior High School

Chapter 12 examines the origins, development, and contemporary condition of the American junior high school. In most instances, the junior high school, which did not appear until the early twentieth century, is a three-year institution that consists of grades seven, eight, and nine; less frequently, it is a two-year school that includes grades seven and eight. There are also variations on these patterns. Within this general framework, it enrolls adolescents ranging in age from twelve through fourteen or fifteen. The following sections on the historical origins and contemporary status of the junior high school examines its objectives, curriculum, and students.

HISTORICAL DEVELOPMENT OF THE JUNIOR HIGH SCHOOL

The period from 1900 to 1920, the era in which the junior high school appeared and took shape, was influenced by (1) massive immigration from southern and eastern Europe to the large cities of the United States; (2) the continuing industrialization of the United States marked by the emergence of a technological society; (3) the recognition, caused by the Spanish-American War and World

War I, that the United States was a world power; (4) the growing impact of behavioral research and science on education and society; and (5) the impact of progressive education and pragmatic philosophy on American schools. These trends, which would eventually result in the reorganization of American life and society, also stimulated reorganization in the way in which Americans ran their schools.

An important source of discontent with the "8-4" school system came from advocates of industrial education who believed that traditional schooling had failed to provide the skilled workers and technicians needed for an America that had become one of the world's leading industrial nations. These critics believed that American schools needed to update and modernize their system of organization, curriculum, and instruction. They contended that the eight-year elementary, or graded, school still reflected rural, nineteenth-century America; they also believed that the high school was still overly oriented to the traditional college preparatory curriculum. The proponents of industrial education were impressed by the role that technical-industrial education had in German schools. They felt that a modernized and industrially competent American economic and productive system also required an economically and socially efficient school system.

In 1907, the proponents of industrial education organized the National Society for the Promotion of Industrial Education (NSPIE) to promote their cause in the schools. NSPIE worked to bring about a reorganization of the school system to create units or institutions that offered programs distinct from the basic literary and mathematical preparation of the elementary schools and also different from the traditional college preparatory secondary school.

While the proponents of industrial education were promoting educational reorganization, some professional educators also were questioning the traditional 8-4 system, for example, educators such as Frank Spaulding and Franklin Bobbitt who urged the application of scientific management to education. They believed that the curriculum should be constructed according to measurable outcomes that had social or economic results. As did the industrialists who wanted an educational institution to respond to economic needs, social efficiency educators wanted schools to be justifiable economically and socially.

The proponents of industrial education were active at the state and national levels. Using the argument that industrial training would open to American youth a wide range of useful occupations, this group and their allies in Congress secured the passage of the Smith–Hughes Act in 1917 to promote vocational education.

While the entry of industrial education was a major goal of certain advocates of educational reorganization, other educators wanted to create new structures to facilitate the transition from elementary to secondary schooling. The major question was the appropriate time at which to begin the transition from elementary to secondary school. They were concerned that the upper years of the elementary schools, particularly the seventh and eighth grades, were too repetitious of the preceding grades. They wanted to replace the repetitious reviews of reading, arithmetic, spelling, and vocabulary exercises with different kinds of educational experiences. While they might agree that different experiences were needed, they could not always agree if these experiences should be the earlier introduction of secondary courses or increased vocational education.

For still other educators, the movement for reorganization developed a new perspective about the nature of adolescence and the need to adapt educational institutions to patterns of human growth and development. Educational psychologists such as G. Stanley Hall (1846–1924) had developed the pioneering studies of adolescent psychology. Hall's two-volume work *Adolescence* (1904) and *Educational Problems* (1911) attempted to outline the educational implications of his theories of adolescent growth and development. While these theorists saw the high school as an institution for adolescents, they also believed that an educational institution was needed for the early adolescent period. They also believed that the years of early adolescence were sufficiently distinct from those of childhood.

Early Junior High Schools

Since a variety of reorganized school patterns developed throughout the country, there were also different kinds of reorganized intermediate schools. In 1910, the Cleveland, Ohio system had established an "intermediate industrial school" for fourteen- to sixteen-year-old boys and girls. The Cleveland curriculum was modified to include vocational work for boys and home arts for girls.

A prototype of today's junior high school was created in 1910 by Superintendent Frank Bunker in Berkeley, California, where grades seven through nine were organized into an "introductory high school." Bunker's concept for this new school was based on (1) the characteristics of adolescence, (2) the need for a more "gradual transition" between elementary school and work, (3) the need to alleviate overcrowded central schools, and (4) the need to develop a curriculum that reflected the future occupational needs of students.[1] The curriculum of the Berkeley "introductory high school" was revised to emphasize vocational courses such as typewriting, bookkeeping, stenography, commercial law, elementary banking, manual training, domestic science, business arithmetic, and business English.[2]

In addition to the early junior high schools in Cleveland and Berkeley, there were others throughout the country. However, there was little agreement as to the scope of instruction or to the grades to be included in a reorganized school plan. Some districts marked off the seventh and eighth grades as the years for junior high school instruction. In other localities, arrangements were based on 6-6, 7-5, 7-4, 6-2-4, and 6-3-3 plans. While there was diversity throughout the country, the general trend was for a six-year elementary school, a three-year senior high school, and an intermediate school—the junior high school composed of the seventh, eighth, and ninth grades.[3]

[1]Frank P. Bunker, *Reorganization of the Public School System* (Washington, D.C.: G.P.O., 1916), pp. 108–109.

[2]W. Richard Stephens, "The Junior High School: A Product of Reform Values, 1890–1920," paper presented at the Midwest History of Education Society, Chicago, October 27–28, 1967, p. 16.

[3]Francis T. Spaulding, O. L. Frederick, and Leonard V. Koos, *The Reorganization of Secondary Education*, National Survey of Secondary Education, Monograph 5, United States Office of Education Bulletin 17, 1932 (Washington, D.C.: G.P.O., 1935), pp. 27–29, 38–44.

By 1920, several educators had written authoritative books about the junior high school.[4] Leonard Koos, in particular, provided an analysis describing the major functions of the junior high school that had emerged in the first two decades of its existence. According to Koos, the junior high school was to

1. Retain students in school by reducing the dropout rate and by easing the transition from elementary to high school.
2. Economize instructional time by the earlier introduction of certain secondary level subjects and by eliminating unnecessary repetition and review of subjects studied in the elementary school.
3. Recognize and provide for individual differences in students' ability, interests, environment, age, and development.
4. Provide more extensive guidance, especially about careers and occupations.
5. Initiate vocational education by providing a range of vocational activities, training, and experiences.
6. Recognize the nature of adolescence and its impact on education.
7. Begin subject matter departmentalization and thereby increase teacher specialization.
8. Increase students' educational and socialization opportunities by providing a variety of physical, social, recreational, athletic, and educational activities.[5]

The trend to school reorganization, including an increase in the number of junior high schools, is demonstrated by the following statistics. In 1930, there were 16,460 regular high schools, 1,842 junior high schools, and 3,287 junior-senior high schools. In 1952, there were 10,168 four-year high schools, 3,227 junior high schools, 1,760 senior high schools, and 8,591 junior-senior high schools. In 1959, there were 6,044 high schools on the 8-4 system, 1,407 high schools on the 6-2-4 system, 1,651 senior high schools on the 6-3-3 system, 5,027 junior high schools on the 6-2-4 and 6-3-3 systems, and 10,155 junior-senior high schools on the 6-6 system.[6] By the midtwentieth century, the junior high school was an important and widely acknowledged part of the American educational ladder. Although there were still school systems based on the 8-4 pattern, the majority of school systems had been reorganized to incorporate the junior high school.

THE CONTEMPORARY JUNIOR HIGH SCHOOL

Now that the historical development of the American junior high school has been examined, we describe its general goals and curriculum.

[4]Noteworthy examples are Leonard Koos, *The Junior High School* (New York: Harcourt Brace, 1920); Thomas H. Briggs, *The Junior High School* (Boston: Houghton Mifflin, 1920).

[5]Koos, *The Junior High School*, pp. 13–85.

[6]Robert E. Potter, *The Stream of American Education* (New York: American Book, 1967), p. 376.

Goals

As indicated, the junior high school's origins were diverse. The following goals still reflect this diversity: namely (1) to provide a transition from elementary to secondary education; (2) to introduce learners to separate subject matters and disciplines; (3) to recognize and provide for the physical, physiological, emotional, and social changes that are taking place in adolescent students; (4) to introduce students to the range of careers and occupations; (5) to provide opportunities for social and physical as well as educational development; and (6) to provide articulation with the senior high school.

Junior High School Curriculum

Unlike the typical elementary school curriculum, the junior high school curriculum is usually differentiated into specific subject matter courses. Similar to senior high school teachers, those in junior high schools are expected to be specialists in the content of and in the teaching of their subjects. Educators who work to construct curricula for junior high schools must answer questions such as

> How can the junior high school curriculum build on skills and subjects learned in the primary and intermediate grades of the elementary school?
>
> What academic skills and subjects are appropriate to and needed by junior high school students?

In junior high and middle schools, subject matter departmentalization encourages greater use of teachers as subject area specialists. *(Ken Karp)*

What physical, social, recreational, athletic, and educational experiences and activities are appropriate to and needed by adolescents enrolled in junior high schools?

What skills, subjects, and experiences are mandated by state authorities?

How does the curriculum and extracurricular program relate to the social and economic realities—including career or occupational possibilities—of the community served by the junior high school?

To what extent should the junior high school curriculum articulate with that of the senior high school? How well does it prepare students to meet the academic expectations of the high school?

What should be the scope (the breadth) and the sequence (the arrangement) of subjects, experiences, and activities that have been included in the junior high school curriculum?

What instruments should be developed and used to evaluate the progress of junior high school students?

Junior high school administrators, teachers, parents, and students have considered and answered these questions in the past. As this curriculum is revised, they will need to address these questions in the future. Today's junior high school curriculum represents a combination of recommended or required and elective courses. Required courses generally are English or language arts, mathematics, social studies, science, health, and physical education. Elective courses are likely to be art, music, home and industrial arts, and foreign languages. Required and elective courses may vary from school district to district.

The following descriptions provide an overview of a "typical" junior high school curriculum.

ENGLISH OR LANGUAGE ARTS.   English, often called language arts, represents a continuation of certain skill-building activities from the elementary level and an introduction to more specialized subject matter content. The techniques and skills of reading may be continued. The study of literature is used to introduce the concepts of genre or type, subject, form, interpretation, and appreciation in prose and poetry. The study of the English language as written and oral expression may be subdivided into units on language structure, grammar, and usage. Basic research skills involving the use of the dictionary, reference books, and the library are also stressed.

MATHEMATICS.   Since the early 1960s when the "new math" was incorporated into the junior high curriculum, mathematics instruction has been in a state of change. The "new math" emphasized the process of mathematical reasoning. In the late 1970s, declines in computational skills and scores on achievement tests caused many school districts to rethink their mathematics programs. Recently, junior high school mathematics curricula have reflected an emphasis on basic computation and application. Units included in the mathematics curriculum at the junior high school include basic computation, fractions, percentages, ratios, decimals, metrics, measurement, graphing, practical problem solving, and an introduction to algebra and geometry.

SOCIAL STUDIES.   As is true in both the elementary and senior high school, the social studies or social science curriculum represents a wide variety of subjects and courses. If the curriculum is organized as separate subjects, the most frequently offered courses are geography, world history, American history (which is typically mandated by the state), local and state history (which again may be mandated), and civics. In many junior high schools, social science courses are multi- or interdisciplinary. Such integrated courses include selected concepts from history, geography, economics, sociology, psychology, and anthropology.

SCIENCE.   While the pattern of science instruction was found in the general science course at most junior high schools until the late 1950s, a great deal of experiment, revision, and development took place in the 1960s and 1970s. This development was stimulated by funds provided by the National Defense Education Act (NDEA) in 1958 and by the National Science Foundation. Among the various projects that stimulated change in the junior high school science curriculum were the Elementary Science Study (ESS), Science Curriculum Improvement Study (SCIS), Intermediate Science Curriculum Study (ISCS), Introductory Physical Science Study (IPSS), Biological Science Curriculum Study (BSCS), Earth Science Curriculum Project (ESCP), and Secondary School Science Project (SSSP). The major impact of these projects was to stimulate revisions in existing science curricula and the creation of new courses in earth, biological, and physical sciences and chemistry. Along with content that reflects the structure of the parent scientific discipline, the new science programs generally emphasized the research and investigative processes used by scientists in laboratory situations.

HEALTH.   Although it may be incorporated into the science or physical education curriculum, most junior high schools teach health as a separate subject. Health education at this level includes units on nutrition, hygiene, cleanliness, disease, dental care, and the organs of the body. Special units, often reflecting state mandates and local community concerns, are often included on the use of tobacco, alcohol, and drugs. Units on the use of tobacco present information about the effects of tobacco smoking on the human body. Units on the use of alcohol tend to discuss the physiological, psychological, sociological, and economic implications of drinking. The impact of alcoholism on the individual and his or her family may also be discussed. Units on drugs are generally intended to create an awareness in students of the effects of drug abuse on human beings and on society. Such topics may be treated as (1) the names and characteristics of certain drugs, (2) drug abuse, (3) legal aspects and penalties of drug abuse, and (4) the availability of medical and psychological rehabilitation for drug users. Health units also include instruction on sex education that describes the physiology of the reproductive organs and that may explore sexual decision making.

PHYSICAL EDUCATION.   The junior high school curriculum includes organized physical education activities. The major objectives of junior high school physical education programs generally are (1) development of physical fitness and the acquisition of useful body skills, (2) development of a desire to participate and enjoy recreational activities as leisure time activities, and (3) provision of experiences in a variety of skills, games, and fitness activities. Activities that may be included in a junior high school physical education program are badminton, basketball, rhythmic exercises, bowling, cross country, football, hockey, gymnastic stunts and tumbling, soccer, softball, square dancing, swimming, tennis, volleyball, weight lifting, and wrestling.

INDUSTRIAL ARTS.   As was indicated, demands for increased industrial and vocational training were a major force in stimulating the junior high school movement. Today's junior high industrial arts program is *rarely* designed to prepare students for an immediate entry into the work force. Social attitudes, economic realities, and child labor laws have deferred vocational preparation until senior high school. Contemporary junior high school industrial arts seek to (1) stimulate interest and skills in industrial arts, (2) introduce students to the range of industrial careers, (3) encourage a sense of design and craftsmanship, and (4) encourage safety habits in using machines and materials. Units included in industrial arts are woodwork, metalwork, plastics, graphic arts, electronics, design, printing, photography, and leather and textile work. While only boys were enrolled in industrial arts in the past, the contemporary junior high school enrolls girls as well as boys.

HOME ECONOMICS.   Home economics, or home arts, is a co-educational subject in today's junior high school. The general objectives of home economics are to (1) introduce concepts and practices needed for family life and home management, (2) develop the basic functional skills needed in home management, (3) examine the responsibilities and roles of family members, and (4) examine the impact of socioeconomic change on family life. Home economics courses may include units in food preparation, sewing, money management, child care, clothing design and construction, grooming, and etiquette.

FOREIGN LANGUAGES.   In the mid-1960s, foreign language instruction in the junior high schools experienced growth. Since the late 1960s, foreign language offerings have declined seriously. Where they remain at the junior high school, they are typically elective courses. The most common foreign language offered is Spanish. Other languages are French, German, Italian, and Portuguese. If a particular foreign language is spoken by large numbers of people in a community, it may find a place in the junior high school curriculum.

MUSIC.   Most junior high schools provide a variety of courses and activities in music, such as instrumental music, vocal music, and music appreciation. Students have the opportunity to participate in band, orchestra, choir, and glee club. They may perform in school and in public musical performances.

ART.   As with music, courses and junior high school activities in art are designed to promote artistic appreciation and creation. While some junior high schools may require art, it is often an elective. Units include art history, art appreciation, painting, crafts, design, weaving, macramé, and sculpture. Junior high schools may sponsor exhibitions where students' work is displayed for other students, parents, and the public.

As can be seen from the discussion about the origins, purposes, and curriculum of the junior high school, teaching junior high school students is challenging and exciting. Junior high school teachers need to understand the physical and psychological transitions that young people experience upon entering adolescence. In many respects, junior high school teachers need to be "bridge builders" between the basic educational skills and subjects of the elementary school and the more complex and differentiated subjects of high school. They need to be expert in adolescent psychology and in organizing instruction to meet the social and educational needs of students entering the early stages of young adulthood. An important feature of high school teaching is that of being a leader in exploratory education.

Junior high school students are introduced to new subjects and experiences. They are consciously and seriously beginning to ponder career choices as they are introduced to business, home economics, agriculture, and various vocations. In addition to academic instruction, junior high school students need counseling about their interests, problems, aptitudes, and educational and career goals and choices.

EMERGENCE OF THE MIDDLE SCHOOL

In the mid- and late 1960s, the middle school concept was developed as a new approach at school reorganization. Middle schools seek to incorporate the intermediate grades—fifth and sixth—with the upper grades—seventh and eighth—into a separate institution. Proponents of middle schools have argued that the social and educational needs of the ten- to fourteen-year-old population can be met more adequately in such a reorganized institution than in either the elementary or junior high school arrangement. In the section that follows, the definition and rationale of one of America's newest educational institutions—the middle school—is examined.

Although definitions of the middle school vary, it is usually agreed to be a school that is intermediate between elementary and high school that combines grades five through eight or six through eight into one organization and facility. Middle schools are also often characterized by team teaching, flexible scheduling, and interdisciplinary institutionalized programs. The proponents of the middle school have tended to view junior high schools as overly imitative of the senior high school and of failing to fulfill its original promise of creating an educational climate and program to meet the needs of youngsters in their early adolescent years. Among the arguments given for the middle school are the following:

1. The middle school is designed to meet the unique requirements of adolescent learners who need the security of the elementary school while gaining confidence and skill through a broad exploratory learning.
2. Because of its unique combination of grade levels, the middle school can serve as a socially and racially comprehensive institution.
3. The middle school facilitates a great deal of individualization in the instructional program to meet the needs of a heterogeneous student

population that includes preadolescents, early adolescents, and older adolescents.

Although the rationale for the middle school appears to resemble that of the junior high school, middle school proponents have pointed out the differences between the two institutions. They allege that many junior high schools have imitated too closely the senior high school in becoming overly departmentalized and overly oriented to subject matter. As junior high schools approximated senior high schools, they tended to neglect the function of aiding students in the transition from elementary to high school. In fact, the middle school proponents have alleged that many junior high schools had become downward extensions of the senior high school. Despite the arguments of middle school advocates, middle and junior high schools often appear very similar to many observers.

Carl L. Midjaas, an advocate of the middle school concept, has argued that the effective middle school should

1. Recognize the very special needs of young people between the ages of ten and fourteen.
2. Emphasize wide exploratory activities in a warm and supportive educational environment.
3. Humanize the learning of young people at a stage in their development when feelings, beliefs, understanding, and social relationships are of critical importance.[7]

Midjaas has also identified the characteristics of the humanistic middle school curriculum as a pluralistic learning program that emanates from the students' personal needs,

1. emphasizing process or "how to learn";
2. providing instruction in learning skills—the abilities to read, write, perform arithmetic computations, use information retrieval technology, and effective communication;
3. providing exploratory opportunities;
4. having class schedules that are arranged flexibly for efficient and effective learning;
5. emphasizing healthy social relationships and development; and
6. evaluating learner achievement in ways that avoid comparing students with one another.[8]

While exaggeration of the differences between junior high and middle schools should be avoided, certain philosophical differences should be mentioned. Middle schools are supposed to be more student oriented, more open

[7]Carl L. Midjaas, "The Middle School: An Opportunity for Humanized Education," address to the Northern Michigan Planning Symposium, Marquette, Michigan, May 1970.
[8]Ibid.

to a process-oriented curriculum, more likely to use flexible scheduling and to individualize instruction. Junior high schools are likely to emphasize departmentalization, a subject matter curriculum, more teacher-directed instruction, and a standard six-period instructional day. Despite these philosophical differences, junior high and middle schools may be more similar than different operationally.

CONCLUSION

The junior and middle school represent a rather recent refinement of the American educational ladder. Designed to meet the educational, social, and vocational needs of the early years of adolescence, the junior high school resulted from demands to reorganize the traditional 8-4 pattern of organization.

Today's junior high and middle schools are transitional institutions that are subject to pressures and demands that come upward from the elementary school and downward from the high school. At the same time that they have eased the transition from elementary to high school, these intermediate educational institutions also have maintained articulation with the high school. While providing articulation and transition, the junior high and middle school has become a unique educational institution that serves the educational and social needs of American young people in the early stages of their adolescence.

DISCUSSION QUESTIONS

1. Identify and examine the major social, political, economic, and educational trends that contributed to the development of the junior high school.
2. Identify and examine the major functions of junior high schools.
3. If you attended a junior high school, reflect on your experiences. Then write a short educational biography about your experiences as a junior high school student.
4. Examine the transitional function of the junior high school in terms of its implications for students, curriculum, and educational institutions.
5. Compare and contrast the concepts of the junior high school and middle schools.
6. Read a book on either the junior high or middle school and review its content for the class.

FIELD EXERCISES

1. Interview a junior high school principal or teacher and ask the following questions:
   a. How does the junior high school curriculum build on skills and subjects learned in the elementary school?
   b. What academic skills and subjects are appropriate and needed by junior high students?
   c. What extra- or co-curricular activities are appropriate to junior high school students?
   d. How does the junior high school relate to the senior high school?
      After obtaining answers to these questions, report and discuss your information with members of your class.

2. Obtain a copy of a junior high school student or parent handbook. Examine its content and answer the questions raised in Field Exercise 1.

3. Interview several junior high school students and try to determine (a) the transitional problems they experienced in going from the elementary to the junior high school and (b) what they enjoy or dislike about their experiences as junior high school students.

4. Visit a junior high school and record your impressions of (a) teachers, (b) students, (c) classroom instruction, and (d) activities.

5. Visit a middle school and record your impressions of (a) teachers, (b) students, (c) classroom instruction, and (d) activities.

SELECTED READINGS

ALEXANDER, WILLIAM M., WILLIAMS, EMMETT L., COMPTON, MARY, HINES, VYNCE A., PRESCOTT, DAN, AND KEALY, RONALD. *The Emergent Middle School,* 2nd ed. New York: Holt, Rinehart and Winston, 1969.

BOSSING, NELSON L., AND CRAMER, ROSCOE V. *The Junior High School.* Boston: Houghton Mifflin, 1965.

BRIGGS, THOMAS H. *The Junior High School.* Boston: Houghton Mifflin, 1920.

EICHHORN, DONALD H. *The Middle School.* New York: Center for Applied Research in Education, 1966.

GROOMS, M. ANN. *Perspectives on the Middle School.* Columbus, Ohio: Charles E. Merrill, 1967.

KOOS, LEONARD. *The Junior High School.* New York: Harcourt Brace, 1920.

POPPER, SAMUEL H. *The American Middle School: An Organizational Analysis.* Waltham, Mass.: Blaisdell, 1967.

PRESCOTT, WILLIAM M., ET AL. *The Emergent Middle School.* New York: Holt, Rinehart and Winston, 1968.

13

American Secondary Education

While it is generally agreed that elementary schools should prepare children in basic literary, computational, and social skills, the purposes of secondary education are often debated. Elementary school controversies often deal with methodological issues about the most efficient way in which to teach a skill such as reading, for example. At the secondary level, controversies are generally curricular and relate to the essential purposes of secondary schooling. Chapter 13 examines (1) the historical development of American secondary education, (2) the goals and curriculum of contemporary secondary schools, (3) types of secondary schools, and (4) continuing issues in secondary education.

The following generalizations are a useful way in which to establish a frame of reference for discussing American secondary education:

1. Secondary education refers to schooling that follows elementary schooling but precedes higher education; in terms of levels of learning and institutional articulation, secondary schooling is transitional between elementary and higher education.

2. Institutionally, in the United States, secondary education generally occurs in the high school. In some instances, however, it may take place in academies and institutes.

3. In the United States, secondary education generally is age specific to adolescence. Apart from these basic generalizations about secondary education, there are few other areas of agreement. A brief foray into the history of secondary education will indicate why this is so.

EUROPEAN CONCEPTS
OF SECONDARY EDUCATION

The European colonists in North America brought with them preconceptions about secondary education as they did about other matters. Traditionally, European schools were organized according to the inherited socioeconomic class structure. By the Renaissance and Reformation, two separate and distinct educational tracks had been developed—primary schools for the children of the masses and classical humanist schools for the sons of the upper socioeconomic and political classes.

The classical humanist schools of the Renaissance that gave an elitist preparatory education to the sons of the dominant ruling class prepared young men for leadership positions in church and state. Graduates of humanist schools would enter higher education, government service, or other leadership positions. Since they attracted and catered to the needs of an elite, the various European classical humanist schools were exclusive and selective. To be a teacher or a student in a humanist school carried prestige and status.

European humanist schools have flourished since the time of their Renaissance origins. In Italy, the schools of Vittorino da Feltre and Guarino da Farrara educated the scions of aristocratic houses to be courtiers, rulers, and diplomats. Their schools became the prototype of the Italian *liceo.* In France, the academic preparatory school was the *lycée,* frequently conducted by religious teaching orders such as the Jesuits. In England, the famous *public schools,* really private schools, such as Rugby, St. Pauls, Eton, and Harrow, educated young English gentlemen to serve king and country. For the Germans, the classical preparatory school was the *gymnasium.* During the Protestant Reformation, leading reformers such as Luther, Melanchthon, and Calvin endorsed classical humanist education as most effective for preparing young men for college and the ministry.

Certain institutional characteristics of the European classical humanist school have shaped our conventional conception of secondary schooling. When the British settled in North America, they imported the Latin Grammar school that embodied the following characteristics:

1. Secondary schooling should be preparatory for more advanced or higher learning. If the student should end his education with secondary school, the classical curriculum would benefit him as much as the student who continued his education.
2. A good preparatory education was based almost exclusively on mastering the classical Greek and Latin languages and literature. This conception persisted until the early twentieth century; knowledge of Latin was frequently required for college entry.

3. Since it focused on the classical languages, knowledge was thought of as originating in the past and was construed in verbal or literary terms. Even when Latin was dethroned as the language of the educated person, learning was still thought of as language mastery. For example, science might be included in the curriculum, but instruction was based on reading scientific books rather than on using experimental laboratory processes.

4. Secondary schooling was to be restricted to a small group of students— to a socioeconomic or academic elite. It was not thought necessary to provide secondary education for most of the age-specific population.

While these prevailing attitudes were brought to North America in the sixteenth and seventeenth centuries, they would be reshaped by time and by the social and educational change caused by living in a new land. To plot these changes, we turn to the historical development of American secondary education.

THE HISTORY OF AMERICAN SECONDARY EDUCATION

Two major developments stand out as greatly significant in the history of American secondary education: (1) the emergence and public acceptance of the comprehensive high school and (2) the role of the high school in completing the American educational ladder. The comprehensive high school resulted from gradual historical processes that defined it as the basic institution of American secondary education. This process of institutional development began when the English colonists imported the Latin Grammar school in the seventeenth century, continued with the appearance of the academy in the nineteenth century, and culminated with the comprehensive high school in the late nineteenth and early twentieth centuries.

Although many states had established common or elementary schools by the Civil War, the public high school did not appear until much later in the nineteenth century. When the public high school became the major institution of American secondary education, the well-known American educational ladder was completed. This meant that American youngsters could proceed from the kindergarten, through the common elementary school, to the high school and eventually enter the state college or university. The development and public acceptance of the high school marked a crucial phase in American educational history since it established the basic institutional framework of the American public school system.

The concept of the "educational ladder" refers to the single, articulated, and sequential school system that characterizes public education in the United States. In contrast to the educational ladder, the traditional European dual system differentiated students into separate tracks, with some schools educating the elite and others preparing the children of the masses. While the American educational ladder provides for upward movement through elementary, secondary, and higher institutions, it should be remembered that this movement is often limited by social and economic variables such as family background, income, degree of tax support, and community attitudes that may limit genuine equality of educational opportunity.

To review the development of the educational ladder, three major periods in the history of American secondary schooling can be identified: (1) that of the Latin Grammar school of the colonial period, (2) that of the academy of the nineteenth century, and (3) that of the public high school of the late nineteenth and twentieth centuries.

Latin Grammar School

The Latin Grammar school, the major preparatory institution, was attended by the sons of the social, economic, and political elite who were intended for leadership positions in Britain's North American colonies. Students in the Latin Grammar school had already learned to read and write in English and knew some mathematics prior to their admission. Entering the school at age eight, they usually remained another eight years. The Latin Grammar school curriculum formed a direct cultural link between the New and the Old Worlds. Its emphasis on the Latin and Greek classics was inherited from the Renaissance classical humanist tradition and a strong denominational religious influence came from the Protestant Reformation. Students studied Latin classical authors such as Cicero, Terence, Caesar, Livy, Vergil, and Horace. Advanced students read Greek authors such as Aesop, Hesiod, Homer, and Isocrates. Little attention was given to utilitarian subjects such as mathematics, science, and modern languages.

By the eighteenth century, the Latin Grammar school—losing much of the intellectual vitality of its Renaissance origins—had become increasingly formalized and sterile. When it was established in North America, the Latin Grammar school curriculum narrowly emphasized mastery of grammatical and stylistic mechanics.

Even before the American Revolution, critics of the Latin Grammar school such as Benjamin Franklin objected to the limited curriculum. In 1749, Franklin proposed the establishment of an English academy in Philadelphia to offer more modern utilitarian studies. There were also a number of private venture schools that offered a more utilitarian educational alternative. Usually conducted by a single teacher, these schools offered modern languages, navigation, bookkeeping, and surveying in trade locations such as New York, Philadelphia, and Charleston. The political impact of the American Revolution and the economic impact of the Industrial Revolution contributed to the decline of the Latin Grammar school. The public began to demand a more utilitarian education that would prepare young people for citizenship in the new nation and for the more practical skills needed in industrial society. The academy was the educational institution that appeared to fill these needs of a changing society.

The Academy

Although appearing in the late eighteenth century, academies enjoyed their greatest popularity in the period of nation building that occurred in the nineteenth century in the decades between the Revolution and the Civil War. In the Jacksonian era of individualism, mobility, and expansion, the academy seemed ideally suited as the institution that would provide the needed educational opportunities through its easy admission requirements and unstructured curricula. In that time of "free enterprise" entrepreneurship and economic growth, the privately controlled academy extended the competitive spirit into education.

The academy either replaced or absorbed the Latin Grammar school. In many respects, it combined the functions of the Latin Grammar school and the private venture school. As did the former, it provided the classical Greek and Latin preparation needed for college entry. As did the private venture school, it offered such practical subjects as bookkeeping, navigation, surveying, and modern languages. The academies attracted, as students, the sons and daughters of the middle-class businessmen, professionals, and entrepreneurs. The popularity of the academy was demonstrated by its growth. Sizer, the historian of the academy movement, reports that by 1855 more than 263,000 students were enrolled in 6,185 academies.[1]

The academies met three major needs: (1) they made it possible for more people to attain more formal schooling, (2) they satisfied the industrial and commercial demand for individuals with utilitarian skills, and (3) they continued to exercise the college preparatory function that was traditional to secondary education. The American academies satisfied these needs by their wide course offerings that were usually fashioned into three basic curricula: the classical (college preparatory); English (terminal); and the normal (teacher preparation). Within these three major curricula, a number of curricular hybrids such as the English-classical, English-scientific, English-commercial, and English-normal could be found. Among the course listings that were included in the prospectuses of the academies were

Classical languages: Greek and Latin and their literatures.

English language: English grammar and composition, English and American literature, rhetoric, composition, oratory, declamation.

Modern languages: French, Spanish, Portuguese, German, Italian.

Mathematics: arithmetic, algebra, geometry, trigonometry.

Sciences: geology, biology, botany, chemistry, physics, natural philosophy, optics, astronomy, phrenology.

Commercial subjects: bookkeeping, accounting.

Geography and history: English history, American history, ancient history, regional geographies.

Philosophy: moral philosophy, political philosophy, logic.

Agriculture.

Domestic sciences and needlework.

Art and music.

Pedagogy: art of teaching, principles of teaching, review of common school subjects.

Military drill and tactics.

---

[1]Theodore R. Sizer, *The Age of Academies* (New York: Teachers College Press, Columbia University, 1964), p. 12.

The attempt to offer such a wide range of courses often exhausted the academies' energies. While some academies sought to offer as many courses as possible, others were satisfied with a restricted curriculum. As the curriculum varied, so did the quality of instruction. Some of the academy "professors" were well trained and highly competent scholars and teachers; others were superficially prepared and diffused their energies by trying to teach all subjects. Methodology, based on mental discipline, stressed the acquisition of factual information by drill, memorization, recitation, and repetition. Since there were no recognized standards for certifying teachers or accrediting academies, the quality of secondary education was uneven at best. There was a chaotic proliferation of courses, and some of the weaknesses in the academies were later inherited by their institutional successor, the high school.

Since they were private institutions, academies were controlled by independent boards of trustees. Although a few academies received state subsidies at their inception, the trustees usually were responsible for building the academy, hiring the staff, and attracting students. Most of the financial support came from the students' tuition fees.

The academy was often maintained by particular religious denominations. Methodists, Episcopalians, Baptists, Roman Catholics, Presbyterians, Congregationalists, and other denominations established academies to teach the principles of their faith and prepare students for college. Many small denominational colleges existing today were originally chartered as academies.

Some academies were also downward extensions of colleges and universities. When colleges found that applicants were inadequately prepared, they sometimes established preparatory branches, or academies, to prepare students for admission to their undergraduate programs.

By the 1870s, academies were slowly being replaced by public high schools. The trend in favor of the high school was partially a product of the process of urbanization. Large cities were often able to support an extensive public secondary school system because of their larger tax base. In addition, a more technically inclined industrial society also needed more systematically organized secondary education than that provided by the loosely structured academy.

Emergence of the High School

Although high schools had existed in the United States since the early nineteenth century, it was in the latter half of that century that the high school replaced the academy as the dominant institution of American secondary education. In 1889–1890, the U.S. commissioner of education reported that the 2,526 public high schools enrolled 202,063 students in contrast to the 94,391 enrolled in the 1,632 private secondary schools and academies.[2]

The emergence of the comprehensive high school as the dominant form of secondary education can be attributed to a number of factors, some of which can be related to socioeconomic, political, and educational change. Perhaps the most obvious factor was that the United States was ready for a more extensive secondary school system. The expressed political philosophy emphasized the

---

[2]Edward Krug, *The Shaping of the American High School*, Vol. I (New York: Harper & Row, 1964), p. 5.

responsibility of the individual to participate in political life. If America was truly the land of opportunity, then its educational institutions should further that opportunity by being open to larger numbers of people. The country was also ready economically to support a more extensive school system. Industrialization, with its attendant urbanization, had created a larger and more concentrated tax base—a wealth—that could be used to pay for high schools. While industrialists had come to see the need for more highly trained workers, labor leaders saw the high school as a means of providing greater opportunity to the children of working men and women.

If the nation was ready politically and economically for the high school, it was also entering a state of educational and psychological readiness that was receptive to the institution. The system of elementary schools, generally kindergarten through grade eight, was recognized as necessary to the national well-being. Elementary schools were flourishing throughout the states and were preparing thousands of children for continuing and more extensive schooling. Furthermore, professors in normal schools and university departments of education were working to develop a science of education to rationalize the educational process. The research of psychologists, such as G. Stanley Hall, had developed a theory of adolescence that pointed to the need for an education designed to meet the needs of adolescents. In many respects, then, the United States was ready for the public high school.

At the same time that the country was generally ready for the high school, there were many groups that were unable, unwilling, or unprepared to attend the high school. Those who would attend the high school in the first two decades of the twentieth century generally came from the more economically and socially favored groups; they were the children of businessmen, professionals, and wealthy farmers. The sons and daughters of immigrants, especially those from southern and eastern Europe, frequently dropped out of school as soon as it was legally possible. The children of immigrants often went to work in factories, mines, and small family-owned shops to earn money to augment the family's income. Black children, too, went to work rather than to high school. The rural poor were also usually not among those attending the high school.

Kalamazoo Case

If the country was ready for the high schools generally, there were still some who challenged its legitimacy as a tax-supported institution. Although several court cases are applicable to legally establishing public taxation for high schools, the decision of Justice Thomas C. Cooley in the *Kalamazoo* case of 1874 is cited as precedent making. A taxpayer's group sued to prevent the Kalamazoo board of education from levying a tax to finance a high school. Arguing that the primarily college preparatory high school curriculum benefited only a small minority, the claimants contended that the majority was being taxed to support the education of the college-bound minority.

Upholding the right of the Kalamazoo school district to tax for high school support, Justice Cooley found that the state was obligated to provide not only elementary education but also to maintain equal educational opportunity for all. Since public funds were already supporting elementary schools and colleges, Cooley ruled it inconsistent to fail to provide the transitional stage whereby students could move from elementary to higher education. He affirmed the right of the school board to tax for the support of high school, the transitional institution. The *Kalamazoo* and similar cases made it possible for students to attend a complete sequence of tax-supported and publicly controlled educational institutions from kindergarten, through elementary and high school, to the university.

The Committee of Ten

The basic identity of the American comprehensive high school was shaped from 1880 to 1920 when many issues related to the high school were debated. Was it a college preparatory institution as had been true traditionally of secondary education? Or was the high school a terminal institution for those completing their formal education? Should it stress traditional college preparatory subjects, or should it offer industrial, commercial, vocational, and agricultural education?

Initially, the high school inherited some of the curricular weaknesses of its predecessor, the academy. It offered a multiplicity of ill-defined curricula, bearing names such as ancient classical, business-commercial, shorter commercial, English-terminal, English-science, and scientific. College and university administrators, in particular, wanted to standardize the high school curriculum so that they had some standard means of evaluating the transcripts of high school graduates.

To resolve the problems of curricular standardization, the National Education Association (NEA) established the Committee of Ten in 1892. Composed of five college representatives, one public school principal, two private school headmasters, and William T. Harris (the U.S. commissioner of education), the committee's chairman was Charles Eliot, Harvard's influential president.[3] Known for introducing the elective principle at Harvard, Eliot wanted generally to improve the efficiency and the quality of high school instruction. The committee developed its policies around two of Eliot's basic concepts: (1) the early introduction of the fundamentals of subjects into the upper elementary grades and (2) standardization of subject matter for all high school students.[4]

The Committee of Ten recommended an eight-year elementary and a four-year high school. Directing its report to the issues in secondary education, the committee sought to end the proliferation of courses that had weakened the quality of instruction in the academies. It recommended that the high school offer a small number of subjects and that each subject be studied intensively for a longer period of time. Further, each subject should have the same content and be taught in the same way for both terminal and college preparatory students. The committee's recommended list of courses was significant in that it shaped the basic outlines of the high school curriculum. The curriculum recommended was

1. English language and literature;
2. foreign language, such as Greek, Latin, German, French, and Spanish;

---

[3]*Report of the Committee on Secondary School Studies* (Washington, D.C.: G.P.O., 1893).
[4]Krug, *The Shaping of the American High School*, p. 17.

3. mathematics, such as algebra, geometry, and trigonometry;
4. natural sciences, such as astronomy, meteorology, botany, zoology, physiology, geology, and physical geography; and
5. physical sciences, such as physics and chemistry.

The report of the Committee of Ten demonstrates the tendency of the higher institution, the college, to dominate the lower, the high school. Although the committee claimed that the high school was not exclusively a college preparatory institution, it emphasized the subjects needed for college entrance. Justifying its orientation on the mental discipline theory, it claimed that its recommended subjects were well suited to the needs of terminal and college preparatory students since it trained their powers of observation, memory, expression, concentration, and thinking.

High School Accreditation

In the 1890s, one of the major problems facing high schools was to establish curricula that satisfied college admission requirements. To deal with accreditation issues, the North Central Association was established in 1895 with a combined membership of secondary schools and colleges in the north central states.[5] In 1899, the NEA's Committee on College Entrance Requirements proposed a set of constant subjects as a core of courses for all high school students without regard to their educational destination. The constants recommended in the core were four units of foreign languages, two of mathematics, two of English, one of history, and one of science. The remainder of the courses was to be elected by the student. A unit was defined as a subject studied for four or five periods of at least forty-five minutes per week. Furthermore, all high school curricula were to include as constants three units of English and two units of mathematics.[6]

In addition to the North Central Association, other regional accreditation agencies were established: the New England Association, the Middle States Association, the Northwest Association, the Western Association, and the Southern Association. Historically, the accreditation associations developed two patterns for admitting students to college: by examination, such as that of the College Entrance Examination Boards, or by graduation from an accredited high school.

Commission on the Reorganization of Secondary Education

In 1918, the NEA established the Commission on the Reorganization of Secondary Education to re-examine the function of the high school. Under the leadership of its chairman, Clarence Kingsley, the commission issued the "Cardinal Principles of Secondary Education," which proclaimed objectives of health, command of fundamental processes, worthy home membership, vocational preparation, citizenship, worthy use of leisure, and ethical character.

[5]Calvin O. Davis, *A History of the North Central Association of Colleges and Secondary Schools* (Ann Arbor, Mich.: The North Central Association of Colleges and Secondary Schools, 1945), p. 7.

[6]Ibid., p. 49.

The commission saw the high school as both an academic institution and an agency of social integration. The comprehensive public high school would bring students of different racial, religious, ethnic, and economic backgrounds together in the same institution. A comparison of the reports of the Committee of Ten and the Commission on the Reorganization of Secondary Education reveals some of the major changes that occurred in social and educational attitudes between 1893 and 1918. In this short span of twenty-five years, significant social and economic changes in American life and education had affected the high school curriculum. Whereas college professors of academic disciplines had dominated the Committee of Ten, the Commission on the Reorganization of Secondary Education was influenced by professors of education and educational administrators. Whereas the academic professors saw the high school as a college preparatory institution, the members of the commission saw it in a larger social, economic, and political perspective. The commission members regarded the high school as an institution in which a diverse adolescent population would define its goals and interests.

CONTEMPORARY SECONDARY EDUCATION

By the 1880s, the vast majority of Americans had attended the common elementary school. One hundred years later the education of most Americans had extended upward to the high school. Although many factors contributed to this phenomenal increase in high school attendance, the most compelling ones were social and economic. Modernization and its attendant need for persons who possessed more sophisticated knowledge and technical competencies made at least a high school education a necessity for most jobs. Furthermore, state laws that set a minimum age for beginning employment and that required compulsory school attendance also worked to keep most of the appropriate age group enrolled in school. At the beginning of the 1980s, more than 95 percent of the population between the ages of fourteen and seventeen were enrolled in school. Although the number of high school dropouts continues to be a serious problem among some groups in some communities, more than 80 percent of students who begin secondary school will graduate. In contrast to the high level of attendance in American secondary schools, the average attendance at the secondary level in most European nations is less than 20 percent. It is clearly apparent that a major characteristic of American secondary education is mass attendance.

The Comprehensive High School

As a multifunctional institution serving a widely diverse adolescent population, the comprehensive American public high school (1) provides a general education for all students, (2) prepares some students for college entry, (3) prepares some students for jobs, and (4) acts as an agency for civic, social, and personal development and integration. In the vast majority of communities, the comprehensive high school strives to satisfy the needs of all youth of secondary school age. The curricular pattern in most comprehensive high schools is to (1) have all students enroll in a common core of general education courses so that individuals of varying interests and career goals have the opportunity for common association and learning; (2) provide parallel curricular tracks such as the college preparatory, industrial-vocational, commercial, general, and, in rural areas, the agricultural, to satisfy the special needs of students; and (3) provide a number of elective courses to permit students to exercise freedom of choice in satisfying particular interests. Comprehensive in a social as well as an educational sense, the comprehensive high school brings students of varying social, economic, religious, racial, and ethnic backgrounds together in a single institution. The important principle regarding the comprehensive high school is to avoid segregating students on either academic or nonacademic grounds into separate, specialized schools.

The Conant Reports

While the comprehensiveness of the comprehensive high school has long been a guiding principle of American secondary education, observers such as James B. Conant have warned that its force as an integrating agency in American society is being weakened.

In *The American High School Today,* Conant, a former university president, scientist, and diplomat, made a number of recommendations designed to restore the vitality of the comprehensive high school.[7] Public schools, he wrote, should educate all of the nation's children regardless of their social and economic class.

James B. Conant, a former president of Harvard University, conducted extensive research on the nature and purpose of the American comprehensive high school. *(New York Public Library Picture Collection)*

[7]James B. Conant, *The American High School Today* (New York: McGraw-Hill, 1959).

They should both provide a common core of learning for all students and also meet individual academic and vocational needs.

For Conant, the comprehensive high school is the secondary institution that best meets the needs of American democracy. He used the term "comprehensive" in two ways. First, a public high school should be socially comprehensive so that it enrolls students from a wide range of social, family, ethnic, economic, and racial backgrounds. The comprehensive school should neither segregate nor isolate any group but should bring students together in an institution that satisfies common social as well as individual needs. Second, a public high school should be large enough to provide broad curricular possibilities that encompass programs to meet the vocational needs of terminal students as well as those of academically oriented, college-bound students.

In Conant's conception of the American comprehensive high school, it serves three broad purposes. (1) It should provide a sound general education for all future citizens, regardless of socioeconomic background and career expectations. Such a general curriculum should consist of English, social studies, mathematics, and science. (2) It should provide a rigorous program for academically talented students (the top 30 percent in achievement) who are likely to enter college. (3) It should offer a range of elective programs to meet the needs of terminal students. Based upon their appropriateness to the economic realities of each local community, vocational programs should be diversified enough to encompass training in agriculture, business, trade, and industry. Thus, Conant sought to preserve and to strengthen the comprehensive high school as the basic institution of American secondary education.

Conant's *Slum and Suburbs*, appearing in 1961, correctly predicted the coming of a crisis that would have a pronounced impact on urban schools.[8] He feared that "social dynamite" was building up in the large cities as unresolved social, economic, and racial tensions accumulated and festered as white families fled to the suburbs and were replaced by black and Hispanic families.

Urban high schools were unprepared to meet the educational and economic needs of minority group students. The high school curriculum was often irrelevant to preparing students for jobs. Unemployed and underemployed youths tended to become not only economically disadvantaged but socially alienated as well. Conant's call for the infusion of funds to support special programs for minority youth was prophetic of what would become "compensatory education" later in the decade. Unless concerted efforts were made to restore the social and educational comprehensiveness of the public high school, Conant predicted that a dual school system would develop with suburban schools catering to the needs of an affluent elite and urban schools being used by a segregated and disadvantaged minority.

Goals of Secondary Education

As indicated in the discussion of the origins and development of American secondary education, the high school as a multifunctional institution has been subject to conflicting interpretations about its role and function—its mis-

---

[8]James B. Conant, *Slums and Suburbs: A Commentary on Schools in Metropolitan Areas* (New York: McGraw-Hill, 1961).

sion—in American society. Some critics—such as Arthur Bestor and Admiral Rickover in the 1950s and the current "Back to Basics" advocates—have argued that the high school should be a strictly academic institution that emphasizes the learning of academic skills and subject matters. Others, such as those associated with the life adjustment education movement of the late 1940s and early 1950s, de-emphasized the academic role of the high school and argued that the high school should meet the personal and social needs of adolescents. Still others want the high school to be an institution for career development and vocational preparation that will provide graduates with immediately useful and salable skills in the economic marketplace. It is difficult to specify the general goals of American secondary education because of these varied voices that plead for the satisfaction of their special interests.

Despite the diversity of opinion regarding the mission of the high school in American society, the National Commission on the Reform of Secondary Education, in 1973, sought to provide a statement on the general goals of American secondary education. This commission, sponsored by the Charles Kettering Foundation, conducted hearings and visited high schools throughout the country. It analyzed the goals statements of thirty-seven states to identify common goals. According to the commission, secondary students should

1. Acquire the essential communication skills of reading, writing, speaking, listening, and viewing that contribute to functional literacy.
2. Acquire those computational and analytical skills needed to solve practical, personal, and business problems.
3. Acquire proficiency in critical and objective thinking skills through research, analysis, and evaluation.
4. Be prepared to make competent career choices and possess the work skills needed for entry into occupations.
5. Have a clear understanding of the relationship between human beings and their natural environment.
6. Understand the American economic system as both a producer and consumer of goods and services.
7. Understand the American political system to participate purposefully in the political process with a respect for other's opinions, be able to discuss controversial issues intelligently and rationally, have a respect for public and private property, and accept political responsibility.
8. Be able to assess their mental, physical, and emotional capacities to manage their lives, their health, and their leisure.
9. Develop an understanding of the differences and similarities of the human race's common humanity and multi-cultural, ethnic, racial, and religious diversity.
10. Learn to deal with, adjust to, and direct the course of change to live satisfying lives in the present and future.
11. Acquire a knowledge of and a respect for duly constituted law and authority and also know how to generate change by democratic processes.

12. Be able to clarify their values to discover values and ethical standards that promote their own self-respect as well as that of other human beings and the environment.

13. Appreciate the human race's historical achievement in art, music, drama, literature, and the sciences and acquire reverence for the cultural heritage.[9]

Stated in very general and global terms, the goals of the National Commission on the Reform of Secondary Education enable local school boards, administrators, parents, teachers, and students to redefine these goals more specifically in terms of the high schools that serve their local community.

The Three- and Four-Year High School

The traditional organizational pattern of American public secondary education has been the four-year high school with its well-known freshman, sophomore, junior, and senior years—grades nine, ten, eleven, and twelve. In some states, particularly California, Illinois, and New Jersey, the four-year high school remains the basic organizational pattern. In these states, the high school district may function as a separate entity with its own board of education and is distinct from the elementary district. There is a trend to combine elementary and secondary schools into a combined or unit district. Large urban systems typically combine elementary and secondary schools into a unified district.

In other states, the senior high school follows a three-year pattern of organization that includes grades ten, eleven, and twelve. Three-year senior high schools are linked institutionally to junior high, grades eight and nine. In some communities, the junior high or middle school is regarded as a part of secondary education; in other communities, it is viewed as an upward extension of elementary education. Since the junior high school has become an increasingly important institution in American education, it has been treated more fully in Chapter 12.

Whether the pattern of organization is three or four years, the high school can be comprehensive. The crucial determinant is whether or not the school follows the philosophy and provides the curriculum needed for a comprehensive social and educational institution.

The Comprehensive Curriculum

The three- or four-year comprehensive high school seeks to offer a curriculum that provides a range of courses designed to satisy the general education, college preparatory, and vocational needs of students. The following curriculum areas offered by the high school also indicates the areas in which prospective high school teachers may prepare.

ENGLISH.   Courses in English language and literature are required of all high school students. While some high schools may require students to enroll

---

[9]These goals are adapted by the author from the National Commission on the Reform of Secondary Education, *The Reform of Secondary Education* (New York: McGraw-Hill, 1973), pp. 32–34.

in English courses each year, other high schools may require two or three years of study in the subject. Instruction in English is subdivided into such courses as practical English, reading skills, grammar, composition, creative writing, expository writing, journalism, American literature, English literature, world literature, business English, speech, and drama.

MATHEMATICS. The majority of American high schools generally require two or more years of mathematics. The range of courses includes general mathematics, algebra, advanced algebra, plane geometry, analytical geometry, trigonometry, and calculus. Some high schools may also offer work in statistics and computer mathematics.

SOCIAL SCIENCE. The area of social science, also known as social studies or social education, may consist of courses in the separate disciplines of history and other social sciences or various interdisciplinary courses combining elements from several of the social sciences. Social science courses in the high school curriculum are American history (usually a required subject), world history, African or Asian history, state history (which may be required in certain states), geography, regional geography, physical geography, government, economics, sociology, psychology, personal development, anthropology, peace studies, and international studies.

NATURAL SCIENCE. Courses in the natural sciences, like those in the social sciences, range from interdisciplinary introductory courses to advanced courses in particular disciplines. Among the courses offered are natural science, physical science, general science, earth science, biology, botany, chemistry, and physics. Certain high schools, particularly large schools, may also offer courses in physiology, geology, and zoology.

HEALTH. Most high schools require a course in health education that includes such topics as general hygiene, diet and nutrition, sex education, dental care, drug abuse, and information about the health problems that may be caused by using tobacco and alcohol.

PHYSICAL EDUCATION. Physical education is also a required subject. This area may include a range of experiences such as team sports, physical fitness activities, and recreational activities. Among the areas offered are football, baseball, basketball, soccer, tennis, swimming, dance, body building, bowling, rhythmic activities, weightlifting, gymnastics, wrestling, and track and field.

BUSINESS EDUCATION. Business education may also be called commercial education in some high schools. A concentration of courses in this area may form the program of students enrolled in specialized career preparation. Students enrolled in other programs may elect courses in this area. Among the courses that the large high school may offer in business education are general business principles, business mathematics, business law, business English, typing, shorthand, bookkeeping, office management and organization, consumer education, career education, data processing, and key punch and office machines.

INDUSTRIAL ARTS.   Industrial arts courses originated in the manual arts in the early years of this century. In some schools, industrial arts may be a separate area or may be combined with the larger and more encompassing area of vocational education. Course offerings include woodworking, metalwork, plastics, automobile mechanics, drafting, mechanical drawing, graphic arts, manufacturing, construction, and architectural home planning.

VOCATIONAL EDUCATION.   This area of instruction often combines organized in-school training with on-the-job experiences. The following areas may be offered: machine shop, electricity, food preparation and service, carpentry, nursing, child care, plumbing, painting, sheet metal and welding, cosmetology, drafting, automobile maintenance, printing, television repair, building construction, retailing, refrigeration and air conditioning, distributive education, and marketing.

AGRICULTURE.   In rural high schools, courses in vocational agriculture are an important part of the curriculum. This area provides instruction in farming, ranching, animal husbandry, soils, forestry, landscape gardening, horticulture, and maintenance of farming implements and equipment.

FOREIGN LANGUAGE.   As indicated earlier, foreign language instruction has long been a part of the secondary school curriculum. When it was required for college entry, foreign language enrollments were large. In recent years, enrollments in foreign language courses have responded to international trends. In the Sputnik era, enrollments accelerated and then declined in the late 1960s and 1970s. The president's commission on foreign languages and international education is expected to stimulate greater activity in this area.

Traditionally, the classical languages of Greek and Latin formed the core of foreign language instruction. By the turn of the century, Greek had largely disappeared. Although still offered, Latin has suffered a substantial decline. Among the modern languages, Spanish and French have enjoyed sustained popularity followed by German and Italian. Today, some high schools also offer courses in Russian and Chinese.

MUSIC.   High school music courses are generally elective. Offerings may include wind ensemble band, orchestra, marching band, piano, choir, chorus, glee club, general music, and music theory appreciation. Students in music education are often involved in extra- or co-curricular activities such as concerts, band, and orchestra that perform at school and civic activities.

ART.   Art or fine arts education forms another area of elective courses. Among the offerings are design, art appreciation, drawing, painting, weaving, crafts, leather work, ceramics, photography, commercial art, illustrating, jewelry, and cartooning.

DRIVER EDUCATION.   The driver education course involves classroom instruction and range and street driving.

While the areas indicated constitute the formal curriculum of the three- or four-year comprehensive high school, a great deal of learning also occurs in the extra-curricular or co-curricular activities. As well as being an academic institution, the comprehensive high school is also an agency for the socialization of American adolescents. Students can participate in activities such as student government, intramural and interscholastic athletics, drama, debate, the school newspaper and yearbook production, dances, and a wide range of clubs and organizations that reflect their academic and career interests.

Public Vocational, Technical, and Specialized High Schools

In addition to the three- or four-year general or comprehensive public high school, there are also public vocational, technical, and specialized high schools. These schools, usually found in large urban systems, offer terminal programs for students who will enter the labor force upon graduation or preparatory study that leads to advanced technical education.

While they include general education courses, the curricula in vocational, technical, and specialized high schools are designed to prepare students for particular occupations such as clerical workers, technicians, and tradespersons. Often, the curricula are based on the particular labor needs found in the areas where the schools are located. For example, a commercial high school will have a curriculum that specifically prepares students for clerical, secretarial, data processing, bookkeeping, and office work; a technical school's curriculum may emphasize design, drafting, and related courses. Trade schools may prepare students in appliance repair, automobile mechanics, machine-shop operation, radio and television servicing, welding, and refrigeration and heating maintenance and repair. Among the newer areas being offered in specialized high schools are chemical technology, marketing, computer technology, and practical nursing.

Periodically, the federal government has stimulated vocational education by aid through such legislation as the Smith–Hughes Act of 1917, the National Defense Education Act of 1958, and the Vocational Education Act of 1963. Vocational education appeals to students because it provides specific training that may have an immediate economic payoff for students who are not interested in entering college.

At the same time that vocational technical schools have their defenders, they also have their critics. Those opposed allege that they erode the comprehensive high school's role as an agency of academic and social integration. They also contend that job-related training at the secondary level is premature and may actually restrict the student's later range of career choices. Critics also allege that specific vocational and technical training tends to become obsolete very quickly, whereas general education provides the knowledge base and intellectual skills that can be used in a variety of occupational, technical, and vocational situations in later life.

Private Secondary Schools

As indicated in the historical sections of this chapter, the antecedents of today's private secondary school can be traced to the colonial Latin Grammar school and the nineteenth-century academy. In many respects, the academy was the common ancestor of both the public high school and private secondary school. The general types of private secondary schools are (1) those operated under the auspices and control of religious denominations, (2) those operated under independent boards of trustees of a nonreligious or nondenominational nature, and (3) various private trade, technical, and commercial schools.

Private high schools that are controlled and operated under the auspices of religious denominations may be parochial or nonparochial. A parochial high school is related to a particular parish or church. While an occasional Roman Catholic parish may maintain a high school, it is more usual for private religious high schools to enroll students from a number of parishes. Such schools are better termed independent religious high schools rather than parochial high schools.

High schools, supported by religious denominations, constitute the largest sector of private secondary schooling, enrolling 75 percent of nonpublic secondary schools. The largest number of these schools are Roman Catholic, and their enrollment is about 85 percent of those attending private secondary schools. Roman Catholic secondary schools are usually operated by religious teaching orders such as the Dominicans, Franciscans, Sisters of Mercy, Sisters of Charity, or Christian Brothers. While Roman Catholic high schools still continue to be operated by religious teaching communities, they now include large numbers of lay teachers who are not members of religious communities. In addition to the Roman Catholic secondary schools, there are also Lutheran, Jewish, Episcopal, and Christian independent schools. The number of schools operated by these religious groups is much lower than that of the Catholics. It should be noted, however, that the number of Christian schools has increased rapidly. A Christian high school may be maintained by a number of religious denominations, usually of a fundamentalist orientation, who oppose the secular orientation of the public schools and who prefer a more strictly disciplined atmosphere for their children.

Private independent high schools of a nonreligious type may reflect a wide range of educational philosophies. They may range from very traditional, well-endowed, prestigious preparatory schools such as Phillips, Groton, Andover, Exeter, and Choate, which generally adhere to a highly structured curriculum, to independent schools that are very progressive and feature experimental programs. Still others are military academies.

Among the private secondary schools are technical, trade, and career schools. Usually, they do not offer a complete curriculum of general studies but rather concentrate on a particular specialty. Examples of such schools are business, modeling, dancing, acting, beauty, and computer programming schools. These schools are profit-making institutions that charge tuition for a particular course of study.

CONCLUSION

The comprehensive public high school is a unique product of American education. Attempting to serve a diverse adolescent population, the history of the high school has been marked by debate, conflict, and frequent attempts to redefine and restructure. The challenges that face secondary school teachers and administrators in the future are not unlike the issues that were raised in the past. Namely, is it possible to have a single institution that can

> Provide an education for the vast majority of American adolescents?
>
> Provide programs of academic excellence for talented American youth?
>
> Provide the practical training needed for useful and productive vocations and occupations?
>
> Provide an atmosphere that will encourage worthwhile personal and social development?

DISCUSSION QUESTIONS

1. Identify and describe the major traditional functions of secondary education.
2. Trace the historical development of American secondary education from the Latin Grammar school, to the academy, to the high school.
3. To what degree is the American educational ladder fact or fiction?
4. Compare and contrast the function of the high school as viewed by the Committee of Ten and the Commission of the Reorganization of Secondary Education.
5. Reflect on your high school education. To what degree was your education comprehensive?
6. Examine the general goals of the National Commission of the Reform of Secondary Education and make them specific to the high school that serves your community.

FIELD EXERCISES

1. Interview an experienced high school teacher and attempt to get his or her views of (a) the changes that have taken place in his or her subject matter specialty and (b) the changes that have occurred in student aspirations and attitudes.
2. Visit a high school in your community and report your observations to the class.
3. Read a novel or see a motion picture that has a high school as a setting. Describe and analyze the author's perception of the high school environment.
4. Interview several high school students and elicit their perceptions of (a) their curriculum, (b) their teachers, and (c) their peers.
5. Consult the classified (Yellow Pages) of your phone directory. Identify the types of for-profit private schools.

SUGGESTED READINGS

COLEMAN, JAMES S. *Youth: Transition to Adulthood.* Chicago: University of Chicago Press, 1974.

CONANT, JAMES B. *The American High School Today.* New York: McGraw-Hill, 1959.

———. *Slums and Suburbs: A Commentary on Schools in Metropolitan Areas.* New York: McGraw-Hill, 1961.

FISH, KENNETH L. *Conflict and Dissent in the High Schools.* New York: Bruce, 1970.

GROSS, RONALD, AND PAUL OSTERMAN, EDS. *High School.* New York: Simon & Schuster, 1971.

KAUFMAN, BEL. *Up the Down Staircase.* Englewood Cliffs, N.J.: Prentice-Hall, 1964.

KRUG, EDWARD A. *The Shaping of the American High School.* New York: Harper & Row, 1964.

———. *The Shaping of the American High School, 1920–1941.* Madison: University of Wisconsin Press, 1972.

National Association of Secondary School Principals. *The 80s: Where Will the Schools Be?* Reston, Va.: NASSP, 1974.

National Commission on the Reform of Secondary Education. *The Reform of Secondary Education.* New York: McGraw-Hill, 1973.

National Task Force for High School Reform. *The Adolescents, Other Citizens, and Their High Schools,* New York: McGraw-Hill, 1975.

SIZER, THEODORE R. *The Age of Academies.* New York: Teachers College Press, Columbia University, 1964.

14

Patterns of American Higher Education

Chapter 14 examines the origins, development, and patterns of American higher education, the major aim being to provide an overview of American colleges and universities. Among the topics examined are the historical evolution of American colleges and universities, the types of institutions, and the governance of higher education.

THE HISTORICAL DEVELOPMENT

The conceptions of higher education in the colonial period were primarily European and were brought to the New World by the English colonists. The major European influences that helped to shape the early American colleges were (1) the scholasticism of the medieval university, (2) Renaissance classical humanism, and (3) the denominationalism of the Protestant Reformation.

In the colonies, collegiate education was modeled on Oxford and Cambridge, the major English universities, which offered the liberal arts and professional curricula in law, medicine, and theology. The institutional structures of Oxford and Cambridge were inherited from the medieval universities of Paris, Salerno, and Bologna. The traditional liberal arts curriculum consisted of the *trivium* (grammar, rhetoric, and logic) and the *quadrivium* (music, astronomy, geometry, and mathematics). Catering to the educational needs of England's wealthy families, Oxford and Cambridge sought to "train up" cultured, well-rounded gentlemen who would be comfortable and adept in drawingroom and playing field. In addition to educating gentlemen for service to king and country, the English universities also prepared classically educated scholars, theologians, lawyers, and physicians. English higher education was designed for a favored elite, not for the masses.

After completing the liberal studies, medieval students might enter professional study in theology, law, or medicine. Instruction in the medieval university was the scholastic method developed by Abelard and Thomas Aquinas. Latin was the language of educated discourse and instruction.

The fourteenth- and fifteenth-century Renaissance period revitalized humanistic studies. Classical humanist educators stressed Greek and Ciceronian Latin as the languages of the educated man. With the Protestant Reformation, religious studies dominated higher education as various churches sought to build doctrinal loyalty and prepare educated ministers.

Harvard College, chartered by the Massachusetts General Court in 1636, was modeled on the English conception of liberal education. *(New York Public Library Picture Collection)*

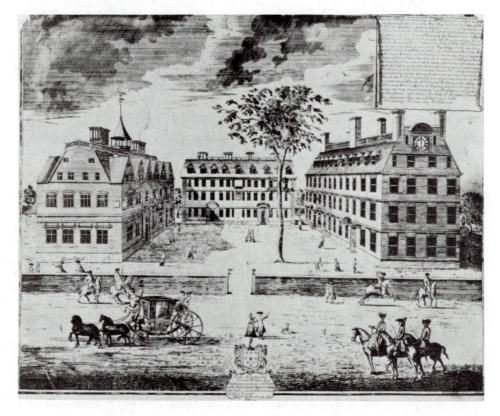

Almost as soon as they had arrived in Massachusetts, the Puritans sought to establish a college to prepare ministers for their churches. On October 28, 1636, the Massachusetts General Court created Harvard College and appropriated an endowment for its support. Harvard's curriculum followed the traditional liberal arts model of the medieval universities. True to its task of preparing an educated clergy, the college emphasized Hebrew, Greek, and Latin, which were useful for scriptural study. As good Congregationalists, the Harvard professors were to adhere to John Calvin's theology.[1] When Harvard's faculty appeared to be liberalizing their theological persuasion, more traditional Congregationalists established Yale at New Haven in 1701 to preserve religious orthodoxy.

The plantation-owning southern gentry at first sent their sons to England for collegiate education. When Virginians demanded their own college, a royal charter was granted in 1693 for the establishing of William and Mary. In 1779, Thomas Jefferson stimulated reorganization of William and Mary's curriculum to include the more secular subjects of science, mathematics, law, anatomy, medicine, moral philosophy, fine arts, and modern languages.

In the Middle Atlantic colonies, Presbyterians chartered Princeton in 1746 in New Jersey. King's College, later Columbia, was chartered in 1754 to serve New York's Anglicans. By the outbreak of the Revolutionary War, Dartmouth had been established in New Hampshire and Brown in Rhode Island. The University of Pennsylvania received its charter in 1799.

The following generalizations characterize the colonial colleges: (1) they resembled their European institutional counterparts, (2) they were founded by religious denominations, and (3) they offered a liberal arts curriculum. Although it varied from institution to institution, the colonial college curriculum had the following general sequence:

Year 1: Latin, Greek, logic, Hebrew, and rhetoric.
Year 2: Greek, Hebrew, logic, and natural philosophy.
Year 3: Natural philosophy, metaphysics, and moral philosophy.
Year 4: Mathematics and review in Latin, Greek, logic, and natural philosophy.[2]

The colonial colleges were small institutions that were attended by the sons of the wealthier classes. Young women were excluded from the male-dominated institutions. The presidents of these early colleges, usually well-known ministers, acted as father figures for both faculty and students. Despite the generally paternalistic atmosphere, the students occasionally complained about lodging, food, and the quality of instruction.

[1]For the history of Harvard, see Samuel Eliot Morison, *The Founding of Harvard College* (Cambridge, Mass.: Harvard University Press, 1935), and *Three Centuries of Harvard* (Cambridge, Mass.: Harvard University Press, 1936).

[2]Frederick Rudolph, *The American College and University: A History* (New York: Knopf, 1962), pp. 25–26.

The Scottish University Influence

While the most direct influence on the colonial colleges came from the English universities of Oxford and Cambridge, the Scottish universities also helped to shape American higher education.[3] Immediately prior to the American Revolution, large numbers of Scots and Scotch-Irish immigrated to North America. The Presbyterian ministers who accompanied these immigrants wanted to establish colleges that were modeled on such universities as Saint Andrew, Glasgow, Aberdeen, and Edinburgh in Scotland. The Scottish universities that stressed utilitarianism and scientific research attracted American students, such as Benjamin Rush, a founder of American medical education. Rush, who studied medicine at Edinburgh, introduced the new learning at the College of Philadelphia and the University of Pennsylvania.

The College of New Jersey, founded in 1742, particularly reflected the educational ideas of the Scottish universities. While retaining the classics and theology, New Jersey's curriculum was reorganized to include mathematical and scientific studies. The methods of instruction also emphasized experimentation. The major contribution of the Scottish universities to American higher education was that the college was viewed as a center for scientific and applied research.

The Early National Period

During the Constitutional Convention, establishment of a national university was proposed. Although supported by Washington, Jefferson, and Madison, the proposal failed. In the early national period, state colleges were chartered. Among the new state colleges were the University of Georgia established in 1785, the University of North Carolina in 1789, the University of Tennessee in 1794, and South Carolina College in 1801.

The University of Virginia, established in 1825, was one of the first major American institutions of higher learning to deviate in organization, control, and curriculum from the pattern found in the older colonial colleges. Conceived of by Thomas Jefferson, the University of Virginia was free of religious denomination and was to promote scientific progress. The University of Virginia exemplified several characteristics of the new state universities: (1) it was publicly controlled and supported; (2) it had a scientific rather than a classical curriculum; (3) it had several curricula rather than a single one prescribed for all students; and (4) it was a nonsectarian institution.[4] These factors were found in other state-established and -maintained universities such as Indiana, founded in 1820, Michigan in 1837, and Wisconsin in 1848.

In addition to the newly established state universities, many of the churches also established colleges. Church-related colleges were established as the various denominations followed the path of westward migration.

---

[3]Douglass Sloan, *The Scottish Enlightenment and the American College Ideal* (New York: Teachers College Press, Columbia University, 1971).

[4]John S. Brubacher, "A Century of the State University," in William Brickman and Stanley Lehrer, eds., *A Century of Higher Education: Classical Citadel to Collegiate Colossus* (New York: Society for the Advancement of Education, 1962), pp. 70–71.

Presbyterians, Congregationalists, Roman Catholics, Methodists, Lutherans, Christian Disciples, Baptists, Episcopalians, Quakers, and Mormons were among the churches that established colleges. Several factors worked to involve religious denominations in higher education: (1) it was already part of the American tradition since the days of the colonial college; (2) the great majority of the churches valued a well-educated ministry; (3) the proliferation of religious sects during the great revivals of the nineteenth century stimulated a competition that was also felt in education; and (4) the churches had assumed a social service as well as a religious role that extended into matters educational.

The Dartmouth College Case

In the early national period, it was already clear that the United States was developing two parallel systems of higher education: state and private. The *Dartmouth College* case of 1819 reinforced the existence of these two approaches to higher education. The *Dartmouth* case resulted from a controversy over the control of Dartmouth College. In 1816, the New Hampshire legislature attempted to take control of Dartmouth by changing its charter and establishing a new institution called the University of New Hampshire. The Dartmouth board of trustees contended that the state's action was unconstitutional. Arguing the case before the U.S. Supreme Court, Daniel Webster won a decision that affirmed the original charter, restored the college to the board of trustees, and returned it to its earlier status as a private educational institution.

The *Dartmouth College* decision was significant in that it protected the existence of the independent, privately controlled college and ended state efforts to establish control over such institutions by legislative action. It sanctioned the duality of higher education in the United States, which has since produced two great academic systems, one private and the other state supported.

Land Grant Colleges and Universities

As western areas such as the Northwest Territory and the Louisiana Purchase were organized and then admitted as states, the state governments established their own state universities. State initiatives were encouraged by the federal policy of granting land from the national domain for education. The use of federal land grants for education dates back to the Ordinances of 1785 and 1787 by the Continental Congress. The Ordinance of 1785 reserved the sixteenth section of each township of the Northwest Territory for education; the Ordinance of 1787 expressed a federal commitment to encourage "schools and the means of education." The use of the abundant frontier land as a source of financial aid to education was an obvious step for the federal government, since it did not require increased taxation. The establishment of state universities was also encouraged by the federal land grant policy that granted land for establishing institutions of higher learning to each state as it entered the Union.

In addition to the land grant provisions contained in the enabling acts under which states were admitted to the Union, the federal government also had contributed to several special projects to achieve specific objectives rather than provide aid to higher education in general.[5] For example, the military academies at West Point and Annapolis were established to train army and naval officers, respectively. In 1857, the Columbia Institute for the Deaf, later named Gallaudet College, was established with federal assistance. After the Civil War, Howard University was established to provide higher education for the former black slaves. By the 1850s, a strong demand had been generated, particularly in the western states, for federal assistance in establishing agricultural and mechanical colleges and universities. Finding the existing liberal arts colleges unresponsive to their needs, a number of agricultural and industrial organizations wanted a new institution of higher education.

Justin S. Morrill, a Vermont congressman, introduced a land grant act to encourage the establishment of agricultural and mechanical institutions. The enactment of the Morrill Act of 1862 granted each state 30,000 acres of public land for each senator and representative it had in Congress according to the apportionment of the census of 1860.[6] The income from this land was to support at least one college whose primary purpose was agricultural and mechanical instruction. In states lacking adequate acreage of public land, the grant was given in federal scrip (i.e., certificates based upon the public domain that could be sold by the state). The proceeds that accrued were then used to establish the land grant college. The Second Morrill Act, passed in 1890, provided a direct cash grant of $15,000, to be increased annually to a maximum of $25,000, to support land grant colleges and universities. This act also provided aid to institutions for black students in states that prohibited their enrollment in existing land grant institutions. The federal government required that land grant colleges provide instruction in agricultural and mechanical subjects and in military training. The Morrill acts were a response to the rapid industrial and agricultural growth of the United States in the nineteenth century.

Since the passage of the First Morrill Act, land grant institutions have been established throughout the United States. In a number of states, these agricultural and mechanical schools are part of the state university.

Examples of such universities are Maine, founded in 1865, Illinois and West Virginia in 1867, California in 1868, Nebraska in 1869, Ohio State in 1870, and Arkansas in 1871. A more recent example is the University of Hawaii, founded in 1907. In still other states a number of agricultural and mechanical colleges were established as separate institutions, such as Purdue University, founded in 1869, the Agricultural and Mechanical College of Texas in 1871, and the Alaska Agricultural College and School of Mines in 1922. Seventeen southern states established separate land grant colleges for black students under the provisions of the Second Morrill Act of 1890.

---

[5]For additional reading related to the federal government's role in education, see Hollis P. Allen, *The Federal Government and Education* (New York: McGraw-Hill, 1950); Richard G. Axt, *The Federal Government and Financing Higher Education* (New York: Columbia University Press, 1952); Homer D. Babbidge and Robert M. Rosenzweig, *The Federal Interest in Higher Education* (New York: Columbia University Press, 1962).

[6]Benjamin F. Andrews, *The Land Grant of 1862 and the Land-Grant College* (Washington, D.C.: G.P.O., 1918), pp. 7–8.

Land grant colleges emphasize agriculture as a blending of science and practice. They also provide research and teaching in areas closely related to agriculture, such as home economics and veterinary medicine. Maintaining their commitment to industrial development, they stress technology, engineering, and applied science. In addition to agricultural and industrial education and research, they offer liberal arts and teacher education programs. Many land grant universities also maintain large extension and continuing education programs.[7]

The German Research Influence

German universities, which emphasized specialized scholarly and scientific research, had a significant impact on American higher education in the late nineteenth century. Universities such as Berlin, Halle, Gottingen, Bonn, and Munich encouraged scholarship by having a graduate faculty guide the research of students by the seminar method. American professors, who had studied at German universities, sought to introduce the German model into American higher education. For example, Daniel Coit Gilman sought to make Johns Hopkins University a center of graduate study and research by imitating its German counterpart. Johns Hopkins used the seminar method in which a professor and a select group of graduate students researched specific topics in a given scholarly discipline. The methods of Johns Hopkins were emulated by the graduate schools at Harvard, Yale, Columbia, Princeton, and Chicago.[8] The German emphasis on scholarship and research came to dominate American universities as graduate faculties devoted themselves to the pursuit of truth and advancement of knowledge.

The American university reached its basic pattern in the late nineteenth century. The focal point of the university was the undergraduate college of liberal arts and sciences, which eventually was surrounded by the graduate college and the professional schools of law, medicine, agriculture, education, nursing, social work, theology, dentistry, commerce, and engineering.

TYPES OF HIGHER EDUCATION

As the historical section indicated, American higher education has taken a variety of institutional forms. American colleges and universities include (1) two-year junior or community colleges, (2) four-year private liberal arts colleges, (3) four-year multipurpose institutions that often originated as teachers colleges, (4) state land grant universities, and (5) a variety of professional schools and institutes. Although many states recently have established boards of higher education to coordinate higher education planning, development, and financing, the historic origins of American higher education were virtually unplanned. This section examines the major types of institutions.

[7]Hugh S. Brown and Lewis B. Mayhew, *American Higher Education* (New York: Center for Applied Research in Education, 1965), pp. 26–27.

[8]Abraham Flexner, *Universities: American, English, German* (New York: Oxford University Press, 1930), pp. 73–74.

The junior college concept originated in the late nineteenth century when several university presidents suggested that the first two years of undergraduate education be provided in an institution other than the four-year college or university. Henry Tappan of Michigan, William Follwell of Minnesota, and William Rainey Harper of Chicago believed that junior colleges would free university professors from the teaching of basic undergraduate courses and allow them to concentrate their efforts on scholarly research.

The junior college concept won support slowly. The first junior college was established in 1901 in Joliet, Illinois. Directed by Superintendent J. Stanley Brown, the Joliet Junior College enrolled high school graduates in postgraduate courses without additional tuition.[9] Brown's experiment at Joliet was imitated elsewhere as junior colleges appeared throughout the country. During the 1920s, 1930s, and 1940s, the number of junior colleges increased steadily.

As a new institution, the junior college faced the problem of establishing an institutional identity. According to the concept of the university presidents who proposed it, the junior college would offer general liberal arts courses to students who were planning to enter four-year institutions. In 1925, the American Association of Junior Colleges expanded its institutional definition by stating that its members would offer two years of collegiate instruction of a quality equivalent to the first two years of a four-year college and also serve the social, civic, religious, and vocational needs of the surrounding community.[10]

During the 1930s and 1940s, junior colleges began to give greater emphasis to vocational and technical training programs for students who were not college bound. For example, the Los Angeles Junior College introduced extensive semiprofessional curricula that included fourteen separate terminal programs in 1929, its inaugural year. Junior colleges throughout the country increased their offering of terminal programs.

Today, the junior or community college is the fastest-growing sector in American education. Although the terms "junior" and "community" college are often interchanged, they describe the same institution but illustrate differing institutional conceptions. The term "junior college," based on the institution's historic origins, signifies that the institution provides the first two years of undergraduate education, after which the student who has earned an associate of arts or science degree transfers to a four-year college. When viewed as a junior college, the institution is a downward extension of the four-year college.

In the 1960s, many junior colleges were transformed into community colleges. While still remaining two-year institutions, the term "community college" designates a broader range of educational activities, such as postsecondary terminal education, technical training, community service, and noncredit continuing education. In many ways, the community college resembles the "people's college" that was urged by some of the nineteenth-century advocates of popular education. As such, it becomes an upward extension of the public elementary and secondary school systems.

[9]Elbert K. Fretwell, Jr., *Founding Public Junior Colleges* (New York: Teachers College Press, Columbia University, 1954), pp. 11–12.

[10]James W. Thornton, *The Community Junior College* (New York: John Wiley, 1966), p. 51.

Today, the junior college is an important link in the educational systems of many of the states. California is an example of a state that has established an extensive junior college system. In 1907, its legislature authorized high school districts to offer postgraduate courses. Ten years later, in 1917, state financial aid was provided for such programs. Then, in 1921, the California legislature authorized the formation of junior college districts.[11] In planning for higher education, California has provided an extensive community college system that serves a large student population. The presence of this system has enabled the state to provide the opportunity for higher education for many students and also maintain a selective university admissions policy.

Florida has also developed an extensive community college system. In 1955, its legislature provided funds for junior colleges already existing and authorized appointment of a community college council to plan for future development. In 1956, it recommended establishing a community college system to provide a broad range of educational programs. In addition to California and Florida, New York, Texas, Illinois, and other states have developed extensive junior college systems.

The increase in enrollment in community colleges has been one of the striking phenomena of American education. In 1960, approximately a half-million students were attending community colleges. Five years later, in 1965, enrollment had doubled, with 1,152,086 students on community college class rolls. At the beginning of the 1980s, more than 5,000,000 students were attending community colleges. Today, more freshmen enter two-year colleges than four-year institutions. The more than 1,200 community colleges enroll approximately one-third of all college students. It has been projected that by the year 2000, half the undergraduate student population will attend two-year community colleges.[12]

More than an academic institution offering the first two years of liberal arts courses for transfer into four-year colleges, the contemporary junior college is a comprehensive, multipurpose institution. While continuing to offer basic undergraduate liberal arts and science courses, it also offers a wide range of vocational, technical, and adult education programs, among them data processing, communications, electronics, medical technology, recreation, food preparation, and dental hygiene.

As one of the most recent additions to the American educational ladder, the junior or community college is still in the process of institutional self-definition. As time goes on, it will probably cease to be either an upward extension of the secondary school or a downward extension of the college and will define its own unique institutional identify. The major purposes of the community college have been defined as providing

1. Academic programs for students planning to transfer to four-year colleges.

[11]Leland L. Medsker, *The Junior College: Progress and Prospect* (New York: McGraw-Hill, 1960), p. 210.

[12]Edmund J. Gleazer, ed., *American Junior Colleges* (Washington, D.C.: American Council on Education, 1971), p. 7.

2. Technical and preprofessional programs for postsecondary students.
3. General education for all students who attend.
4. Continuing education in general, cultural, and vocational education for adults.
5. Part-time education.
6. Community service.
7. Counseling and guidance of students.[13]

State Colleges and Universities

Although a few four-year colleges may be municipal, most public colleges and universities are state supported and controlled. While most states have a number of state colleges, every state has at least one state college or university. State colleges and universities have had a variety of origins. Some state colleges began in the nineteenth century as two-year normal schools for teacher education and were later transformed into four-year state teachers colleges. Most of these institutions have now become multipurpose state colleges that offer a broad

This view of Washington State University illustrates the campus of the large, multipurpose state university. *(United Press International)*

[13]Thornton, *The Community Junior College,* p. 59.

range of degree programs. Other state institutions were established originally as four-year liberal arts and science colleges. Still other four-year colleges and universities resulted from the Morrill Act of 1862 that provided land grants to the states to establish agricultural and mechanical colleges. Today, state universities have established graduate and professional schools and colleges.

Historically, state colleges and universities have been governed by individual and autonomous boards of trustees that serve as policymaking bodies. While this is still true in some states, the most recent trend has been to establish state boards of higher education that act as a statewide coordinating agency to establish policies, coordinate development, and allocate finances to the colleges and universities in that state. In some states, each university or college is fairly autonomous; in other states, the colleges and universities are integral units of a single system. For example, New York state represents an example of an integrated and coordinated state university system. In New York, the community colleges, state colleges of arts and sciences, agricultural and technical institutes, university centers, and professional schools are governed by a single board of trustees.

Land grant institutions refer to the sixty-nine state colleges and universities that were established with funds from the Morrill Act. They were established to provide instruction in agricultural and mechanical arts. Today, land grant colleges and universities educate about 20 percent of American undergraduates. They are also centers for graduate and professional education and research.

Some land grant institutions are state universities as in Minnesota, Illinois, Arizona, and Nebraska. Other land grant institutions still retain their agricultural and mechanical arts designations, such as the Alabama Agricultural and Mechanical College. In a few instances, such as Cornell University, a land grant institution is part of a private university.

Private Colleges and Universities

As indicated, the American system of higher education originated in the privately established religious institutions of the colonial era. During the nineteenth century, religious denominations established colleges—often four-year liberal arts institutions—to prepare youth in the beliefs of the particular faith and to provide higher education within a religious context. Today, there are approximately eight hundred private church-related institutions of higher education. In addition, approximately five hundred private liberal arts colleges operate under private and independent but nonreligious auspices.

Private colleges and universities exist in a variety of institutional forms as do their public counterparts. Although many of these colleges and universities have received federal aid in the form of specific grants or state aid in scholarships to individual students, they are governed by self-perpetuating boards of trustees. Among the various private and religious institutions of higher education, one can find

1.   The small four-year liberal arts college. In the past, some of these institutions enrolled either men or women; today, most of them are co-

educational. Their curriculum is designed to educate undergraduate students.

2. The technical or specialized institute or college. There are a number of colleges or institutes that specialize their educational efforts to prepare persons in engineering, the performing arts, music, art, nursing, or other fields.

3. The private university. A number of private universities offer a full range of higher education programs, from the liberal arts to graduate and professional education. Some of these institutions, such as the University of Chicago and Johns Hopkins University, have distinguished reputations for scholarship and research. Other universities, often associated with religious denominations, particularly the Roman Catholic Church, provide higher and professional education in urban settings.

The rising cycle of economic inflation of the 1970s and early 1980s has produced strains and stresses on the financial resources of private colleges and universities. It is estimated that the cost of attending a private college or university is almost $3,000 per year higher than that of attendance at a public institution. Because of rising tuition costs, more students are attending public institutions. For example, in 1950, private colleges and universities enrolled about half of the student population. By the mid-1980s, it is expected that they will enroll less than 25 percent of the student population.

Because of declining enrollments and rising expenses, some private institutions have been forced to close. Other institutions have joined into consortia or mergers to create larger and supposedly more cost-effective operations. Unless private institutions receive greater support—through grant programs or extended state scholarships to students—more of them will cease to exist. Advocates of private education argue that the presence of a variety of institutions of higher education has provided a desirable diversity that would be lacking should the surviving institutions of higher education be exclusively state supported.

Proprietary Institutions

Proprietary institutions are private schools operated for profit. Proprietary postsecondary schools prepare persons for specialized careers in such fields as business, performing arts, commercial art, music, fine arts, computer technology, electronics, refrigeration, and many other fields. Historically, these institutions developed from the tradition of the private venture schools of the colonial and later eras that offered instruction neglected by more academic institutions. They fill an educational need in that they are usually able to respond to the changing supply and demand relationships of the marketplace. If in a technical area, they may be more responsive to innovation; if in the fine arts area, they may engage professionals as part-time or adjunct instructors to offer training that directly relates the aspiring performer to the stage or concert hall.

While proprietary schools have filled a definite need, not all of them have maintained quality instructional standards. Some have engaged in misleading advertising, exaggerated promises in recruitment efforts, and inferior instruction.

Since the Middle Ages, universities have offered professional study. Although the patterns vary from institution to institution, most universities offer both undergraduate and graduate programs. The major universities have a college or school of liberal arts and sciences that provides undergraduate education—usually in a four-year program of study leading to the bachelor's degree. Upon completing undergraduate study, certain students—usually of high academic potential—continue their education in professional schools. Originally, the three professional schools were theology, law, and medicine. Over the course of time, the number of professional schools has multiplied because of the impact of social and technological change on higher education. Today, the modern university includes undergraduate education in liberal arts and sciences and in professional areas at both the undergraduate and graduate levels. Large universities have professional schools such as medicine, law, education, business, social work, veterinary medicine, agriculture, journalism, architecture, fine arts, nursing, engineering, music, and library science. Some of the professional schools offer both undergraduate and graduate programs. For example, the typical college or school of education offers undergraduate instruction leading to the bachelor's degree and graduate programs leading to the master's and doctoral degrees. Schools of business administration, nursing, and social work also follow the pattern of providing both undergraduate and graduate education. In medicine, law, and dentistry, the pattern differs in that students admitted to these schools typically must already possess the bachelor's degree as a prerequisite to professional study.

The relationship between undergraduate and professional study has been enriched further and made more sophisticated but also more complicated by the evolution of graduate education. As indicated in the historical section, the development of graduate education in the United States was influenced greatly when the concepts of the research and seminar approach were introduced to the United States by American professors who had studied in German universities in the late nineteenth century. Although a few American universities, such as Johns Hopkins, concentrated exclusively on graduate education, most universities developed graduate programs that had an impact on both their undergraduate and professional schools.

By way of illustration, a college of liberal arts and sciences in a university contained departments of English, history, and chemistry, for example. In the late nineteenth and early twentieth centuries, universities began to offer post-baccalaureate work in these areas that led to the master's or doctoral degree, usually the Ph.D. (doctor of philosophy), in these academic areas. To develop, coordinate, and maintain the quality of these advanced academic programs, graduate schools—with graduate deans at their head—were established within universities. At the same time that academic departments were developing graduate programs, professional schools, such as law, medicine, education, and others mentioned earlier, were offering programs beyond the undergraduate or baccalaureate level. From this development came graduate programs and degrees, such as the Ed.D (doctor of education), M.D. (doctor of medicine), M.S.W. (master's of social work), and others. The coordination, development, quality control, and articulation of professional programs at the graduate level brought about a variety of administrative arrangements in universities. They may be administered through the dean of the professional school involved, the dean of the graduate school, or cooperatively by both deans.

Examination of the catalogues of various institutions indicates the bewildering variety of graduate and professional degree requirements that exist from institution to institution. Several factors must be considered by institutions that develop professional or graduate programs. Among them are the following:

1. The general education requirements at the undergraduate level that constitute a necessary preparation for entering such study.

2. The areas of professional or graduate study regarded as necessary components by the disciplines or professions involved; for example, what does the American Medical Association regard as the necessary preparation of the physician? What does the American Library Association regard as necessary for the librarian? What do political scientists regard as appropriate preparation in that field? Frequently, these components of a professional degree program are specified by accreditation bodies that represent the profession. In professional education, the National Council for the Accreditation of Teacher Education (NCATE) has established standards for both undergraduate and graduate preparation.

3. Entry into professions such as medicine, law, architecture, teaching, and nursing is also governed by state certification requirements and examinations. Programs of professional preparation are designed to meet the certification requirements and to prepare students to sustain successfully state certification examinations.

4. In addition to professional and certification requirements, there may be requirements pertinent to the particular institution offering the degree. Private and religious institutions offering graduate and professional programs may have requirements based on the educational philosophy that is unique to them.

Because of the complexity and variety of degree programs, it is difficult to generalize about them. However, the general outlines of the master's (M.A. and M.S.) and doctor's degrees (Ph.D.) will illustrate degree requirements. The typical master's degree program includes (1) completion of an undergraduate degree, with appropriate courses relating to the subject of graduate study, and an academic average that promises success in graduate work in the field, required for admission; (2) completion of a specified number of graduate courses—typically thirty semester hours of graduate credit—in the area of study requiring at least a year, the fifth year, beyond the bachelor's degree; (3) comprehensive examinations, which may be written or oral or a combination of both; and (4) completion of a field experience, a research project, or a thesis. In professional education, for example, the degrees commonly awarded at the master's level are the master's of arts or master's of science in education (M.A. or M.S.), the master's of education (M.Ed.), or the master's of arts in teaching (M.A.T.).

The doctor of philosophy (Ph.D) or equivalent professional degree, such as the doctor of education (Ed.D.) or doctor of science (Sci.D.) is the highest degree awarded by American universities. Although it is called the doctor of philosophy because of medieval origins, the recipient may have studied any number of academic areas other than philosophy. The typical doctoral program involves (1) completion of an undergraduate degree program and usually, but not always, a master's level program for admission; (2) an academic record in previous work that promises success at the doctoral level; (3) completion of from seventy-five to ninety semester hours of graduate course work, depending upon the particular program and institution; (4) passing written and oral examinations, or a combination of both, that admit the student to doctoral candidacy; (5) the research and writing of a doctoral dissertation on an original topic; and (6) the successful defense before a committee of professors on the dissertation. Doctoral work is a challenging undertaking requiring the ability to do independent research. The completion of doctoral study may take from three to five years, depending upon the student's time and ability and the institution's requirements. In professional education, many institutions may award either the Ph.D. or the Ed.D. degree. Although there were originally distinctions between the two degrees, they have tended to become blurred over time. Generally, the Ph.D. degree is preferred by students seeking to become professors of education or educational researchers, as its focus is often specialized on a particular discipline in education, such as educational history, philosophy, or psychology. The Ed.D. degree (doctor of education) frequently exposes students to the various fields of education and may include field work or applied research. The Ed.D. is often preferred by students who are preparing for careers in educational administration, supervision, or curriculum development.

GOVERNANCE OF HIGHER EDUCATION

Although the role and structure of the state governance of higher education is a highly complex matter that varies widely from state to state, two general patterns emerge. (1) There is the single university pattern in which all the institutions of higher education are part of one system governed by a single board of higher education, usually appointed by the governor. (2) There is a more decentralized pattern that provides for a state board of higher education that acts as planning and coordinating agency for all institutions of higher education in the state but that allows considerable autonomy to be exercised by boards of trustees of each of the colleges and universities included in the statewide system. In both patterns, state boards of higher education (1) review requests for capital budget outlay of the colleges and universities within the system, (2) provide general reviews of institutional budgets, (3) interpret functional differences between various institutions, (4) approve new programs and modifications of existing programs, and (5) plan for the orderly growth of higher education and make recommendations concerning needs and locations of new facilities.

In performing these functions, the state board of higher education exercises a general role of being a statewide planning and coordinating body for higher education. Since the 1950s, when state colleges and universities experienced tremendous growth in their student enrollments, faculties, and physical facilities, the states have sought to eliminate needless duplication of programs, personnel, and facilities. Although the growth of public higher education was not as well coordinated as it might have been in the period of growth during the 1950s and 1960s, it was crucial to avoid needless expenditure and duplication of efforts in the inflationary decades of the 1970s and 1980s. State boards of higher education have discovered that it is much more difficult to allocate resources in a period of scarcity and retrenchment than it is in a period of growth and abundance.

Although state boards of higher education have sought a larger role in private higher education, their functions remain generally limited. They may grant charters to private institutions and approve programs relating to professional licensure and certification.

Boards of Trustees

Private institutions and many state institutions are governed by their boards of trustees. These boards of trustees are generally self-perpetuating; that is, as a board, they appoint their own successors. Their functions are to (1) exercise ceremonial roles connected to university observances, commencements, and events; (2) establish and approve general governing policies; (3) approve operating and capital budgets; and (4) appoint the president of the institution. In addition, the board of trustees can also facilitate communications between the institution and the communities or publics that it serves. Boards of trustees of state or public institutions can provide a vehicle of communications for the general public, taxpayers, citizens groups, and alumni. Those of private institutions can facilitate communications with foundations, benefactors, and alumni. Boards of trustees of private institutions are often active in fund raising. In both state and private institutions, boards of trustees generally confine their activities to general policymaking and delegate implementation of policies to the president and other university administrators.

Administrators

Appointed by the board of trustees, the college or university president is the institution's chief executive officer. His or her powers depend upon the nature of the institution and its governing policies. The president is the chief institutional spokesperson to the public, the faculty, the students, the state legislature, and the alumni. Depending upon the style of the administrator and the institutional traditions and policies, the president may be the chief educational leader, or the principal manager, or the agent by which consensus is established. Frequently, contemporary institutional presidents have found themselves in the difficult role of the chief adjudicator of conflicts.

Although the specific functions of the university president are not well defined, the general responsibilities include (1) enforcement of corporate rules and regulations governing the institution; (2) appointment and removal of executive, administrative, and academic officers of the institution; (3) approval or disapproval of policies and procedures of institutional committees; (4) communication between the board of trustees and the university community; and (5) preparation of reports on the university.

The changing role of the university presidency can be illustrated by comparing the perspectives that two university presidents have provided on their role. Charles Eliot, Harvard's president in the late nineteenth century, and Clark Kerr, president of the University of California in the midtwentieth century, provide two models that illustrate the changing nature of the university presidency.

CHARLES ELIOT.   The career of Charles Eliot, president of Harvard from 1869 to 1909, reveals how one major American university was transformed from a classically dominated institution into one that met the needs of a modern and technological society.[14] Eliot, a Harvard graduate, was trained in the classics, mathematics, and chemistry. On a European tour in 1863, Eliot visited French and German universities and polytechnic institutes. Returning to the United

Charles W. Eliot, president of Harvard University from 1869–1909, transformed the role of the university president from paternalistic figure into skilled executive leader and manager of a complex institution. *(New York Public Library Picture Collection)*

[14]Hugh Hawkins, *Between Harvard and America: The Educational Leadership of Charles W. Eliot* (New York: Oxford University Press, 1972), pp. 30–32.

States, he urged the selective adaption of certain aspects of European higher education. However, he also believed that American universities should grow out of their own unique environment and respond to their own changing society.

During his forty-year presidency at Harvard, Eliot's leadership influenced both his own institution and American higher education as well. Traditionally, college and university presidents had been distinguished churchmen who conducted their offices in a highly ministerial or paternalistic fashion. Eliot, in contrast, saw himself as the manager of a highly complex educational corporation. He gave equal attention to undergraduate, graduate, and professional education and sought to achieve more efficiency, higher standards, and greater freedom.

Committed to freedom of choice in higher education, Eliot introduced the elective principle at Harvard in the 1870s. Students were to be free to choose or "to elect" a certain number of courses rather than follow a totally prescribed curriculum. The elective principle, Eliot believed, would encourage undergraduate specialization. It would stimulate new fields of specialized study by freeing professors to teach in their areas of expertise rather than in mandatory general courses.

Since a technological society requires highly trained specialists, Eliot saw the university's role to be that of efficiently preparing well-educated and highly trained specialists. Regarded as one of America's leading educational statesmen, Eliot helped to make American higher education more responsive to the needs of a modernizing nation.

CLARK KERR.   In the 1960s, Clark Kerr, then president of the University of California, commented on the difficult and complex role that had to be exercised by a president of a large university. In fact, Kerr said it was no longer possible to speak of a university governed by a single person. In fact, the modern university had become a "multiversity," composed of often conflicting special-interest groups.

Writing in 1963, Kerr described the University of California as an institution with a total operating budget of nearly half a billion dollars, spending nearly $100 million for construction, employing over 40,000 persons, maintaining operations in over 100 locations, conducting projects in more than 50 foreign nations, listing 10,000 courses in its catalogues, and anticipating an enrollment of 100,000 students. Such an institution, Kerr said, could no longer be described as a single community of scholars and students. It was rather a loose collection of subcommunities united only by a common name and governing board. Coining the term "multiversity," Kerr said,

> The multiversity is an inconsistent institution. It is not one community but several—the community of the undergraduate and the community of the graduate; the community of the humanist, the community of the social scientist, and the community of the scientist; the communities of the professional schools; the community of all the nonacademic personnel; the community of the administrators. Its edges are fuzzy—it reaches out to alumni, legislators, farmers, businessmen, who are all related to

one or more of these internal communities. As an institution, it looks far into the past and far into the future, and is often at odds with the present. It serves society almost slavishly—a society it also criticizes, sometimes unmercifully. Devoted to equality of opportunity, it is itself a class society. A community, like the medieval communities of masters and students, should have common interests; in the multiversity, they are quite varied, even conflicting. A community should have a soul, a single animating principle; the multiversity has several—some of them quite good, although there is much debate on which souls really deserve salvation.[15]

Composed of a number of often conflicting special interest subcommunities, the multiversity was difficult to govern. As California's president, Kerr found several competitors for power in the multiversity: first, the students who, through the elective system, determine which disciplines the university will develop; second, the faculty who have achieved some control over admissions, programs, examinations, degree granting, appointments, and academic freedom; third, public authorities, such as the board of trustees, the state department of finance, the governor, and the legislature, who scrutinize organization and expenditures; fourth, special interests that exert pressures on the multiversity, such as agriculture and business organizations, trade unions, public school groups, and mass media; and, fifth, the administration, which has become a prominent feature of the multiversity.

In the modern university, the president's office is often the place of collision between the conflicting demands of students, trustees, alumni, faculty, and deans. Today's college or university president has the difficult assignment of developing consensus among the various interest groups comprising the institutional community and of providing leadership and direction for the university as a whole.

As with the modern corporation, college and university administration also has become more elaborate, functional, and bureaucratized. Universities have an array of vice presidents who are responsible for various administrative, service, and academic functions. Usually directly responsible to the president, the academic vice president is responsible for faculty appointment and dismissal, academic programs, and the operations and coordination of general instructional activities. Indirectly, he or she may also be responsible for the supervision of admissions, registrations, records, and other academic functions. The vice president for finance has general jurisdiction over the institution's financial and budgetary affairs. The vice president for student services is responsible for nonacademic matters relating to students, such as counseling services, residence halls, and student activities and organizations. The vice president for development is charged with working with public relations, alumni, and benefactors and with fund-raising activities. The vice president for personnel has responsibility for developing policies relating to nonacademic personnel such as administrators

[15]Clark Kerr, *The Uses of the University* (Cambridge, Mass.: Harvard University Press, 1963), pp. 18–19.

with nonfaculty appointments, secretarial and clerical staff, grounds and maintenance staff, and other nonacademic personnel. He or she is responsible for hiring, promoting, and dismissing nonacademic staff.

Academic Deans

The academic deans are the chief executives and administrators of the various colleges and schools of the university. For example, the College of Liberal Arts and Sciences, the College of Education, the College of Fine Arts, the School of Medicine, and other colleges are headed by a dean, appointed by the president of the institution. As the chief executive officer of the college that provides academic instruction, the dean performs such functions as (1) executing universitywide policies established by the board of trustees and the president within their school or college, (2) preparing the budgets for their school or college and the direction and supervision of the expenditure of approved funds, (3) supervising the quality of instruction within the school or college, (4) chairing of meetings of chairpersons and faculty of the school or college, and (5) recommending faculty in their school or college for appointment, promotion, tenure, and termination.

Department Chairpersons

The chief administrative officer for organizing instruction at the departmental level is the chairperson. Chairpersons are generally appointed by the academic vice president or president upon the recommendation of the dean of the unit in which the department is located. They report to the dean who in turn reports to the academic vice president. Among the responsibilities of department chairpersons are (1) organizing the schedules of courses within their departments and assigning faculty to teach them, (2) evaluating faculty within their department and recommending them for tenure, promotion, salary increments, and termination, (3) executing university, college, or school policies within their departments, and (4) calling and presiding over meetings of the members of their department.

Faculty

College and university faculty members are usually members of departments within a college or school. They are usually holders of a Ph.D. degree. The initial appointment may be at the rank of instructor or assistant professor. Upon the completion of a specified number of years at the rank of assistant professor, the faculty member may be promoted to associate professor. With appointment to associate professor, the faculty member is usually granted tenure, depending upon the particular institutional policies. The highest rank, which is awarded to senior members of departments, is professor.

The granting of tenure and promotion through the various professional ranks is earned by faculty members who have distinguished themselves by scholarly contributions to their discipline and by excellence in instruction. Tenure means that a faculty member is a member of the faculty of the college or university for an indefinite period of time, generally from the time tenure is awarded until retirement, unless the specialty that the tenured faculty member teaches is no longer offered by the university. Tenure gives the faculty member who receives it a great deal of independence and security since dismissal of tenured faculty members rarely occurs. Tenure was designed to protect academic freedom and to free the faculty member from the vicissitudes of changing administrations and public pressures. Critics of tenure allege that tenured faculty members may not maintain the same degree of scholarly and instructional activity throughout their careers; they also charge that large numbers of tenured faculty limit entry of younger scholars into teaching positions at the college or university levels.

Promotion through the various academic ranks of the university depends upon factors such as scholarship, teaching competence, and service to the profession and the university. An important element in both promotion and tenure is peer review, in which already tenured faculty members review the accomplishments of colleagues who seek tenure and promotion. These review committees then recommend tenure and promotion to appropriate university committees or administrators.

In the modern university or college, tenure and promotion depend largely on scholarly productivity. University faculty members are expected to do research and to publish the results of this research in scholarly journals and books. These publications are then reviewed by other experts in the discipline. Competency in teaching is another factor affecting tenure and promotion decisions. Here student and peer evaluation of the faculty member's teaching skill is important. Criteria used to verify teaching competency are subject to more debate and discussion since they are not as precise as those that relate to scholarship and publication. Service to the profession and the university usually means that the faculty member has contributed to professional associations and university committees.

FINANCING HIGHER EDUCATION

Institutions of higher education are supported financially by various sources. All colleges and universities derive a part of their income from student tuition and fees. It is estimated that private colleges rely on tuition to pay 60 percent of their expenditures. Tuition-generated income is, however, generally inadequate to support an institution of higher education. At state institutions, student tuitions and fees cover about 20 percent of the costs. Public institutions—community colleges, colleges, universities, and professional schools—receive a substantial amount of their support from public tax monies. Junior and community colleges, depending upon the state, are supported by a combination of local tax support and state funding. State colleges and universities are supported by funding at the state level, generally by appropriations by the state legislature. Private and independent institutions of higher education are supported by foundations, alumni donations, and other philanthropic funding. The federal government has aided both state and private institutions to some degree by the funding of special programs.

As is true of most educational institutions, colleges and universities have been hard pressed by the inflationary trends of the 1970s and early 1980s. The costs of faculty salaries, library and laboratory additions and support, and maintenance costs have forced colleges and universities to increase tuitions. Spiraling costs have had a great impact on the smaller, independent liberal arts colleges that must struggle to survive. Since 1960, for example, approximately two hundred institutions have been forced to close. Most were private colleges. Throughout the 1970s, tuition rates increased dramatically. At the close of this inflationary decade, the average tuition at private institutions was $3,403 as compared with $741 at public institutions.[16] These figures do not include the costs of room and board, books, and other expenses related to college attendance.

ENROLLMENT TRENDS IN HIGHER EDUCATION

Although much effort has gone into the prediction and projection of enrollment trends in higher education, expert prognostications have not always been accurate. One major factor to be considered is the decline of the birth rate in the United States. Since the mid-1970s, elementary schools have felt the impact of a declining birth rate. In the first half of the 1980s, secondary schools will experience declining enrollments. It is anticipated that colleges and universities will experience enrollment declines in the mid- and late 1980s due to the general decline in the birth rate.

However, other trends in college attendance have blunted and offset the anticipated decline in college attendance due to a declining birth rate. Among these are (1) the extensive community college system, which enables more people to attend college in locations convenient to their homes and for a relatively low cost and (2) the fact that the college population is growing increasingly diverse as more women, minority group members, and older people attend.

CONCLUSION

The American system of higher education is unique among those of the world in that it has attempted to provide mass education on both a quantitative and qualitative basis. While the basic institutional structures of American higher education developed without a great deal of planning in the past, the future will not permit Americans to have the luxury of unplanned college and university growth. The future of American higher education will require the careful setting of educational priorities and the judicious allocation of financial resources.

The college student of the future is also likely to be different from the stereotyped carefree sophomore of the 1920s, the G.I. of the late 1940s, and the political activist of the 1960s. The college campus of the 1980s will have more women attending professional schools, more members of minority groups enrolled, and more older students preparing for second careers or for the pure pursuit of knowledge.

---

[16]Gene I. Maeroff, "Private vs. Public College: The Scramble for Students and Money," *Saturday Review*, May 13, 1978, pp. 18–19.

Although some basic changes will occur, it is also prudent to recall that American higher education will blend continuity with change. It will still be possible to find the medieval origins of the university operative in its modern form.

DISCUSSION QUESTIONS

1. Identify and examine the major factors shaping American higher education in the colonial and early national periods.
2. What was the First Morrill Act and how did this legislation shape American higher education?
3. Identify a college or university of your choice and write a brief history of that institution.
4. Read an autobiography or biography of a college or university president and prepare an analysis of his or her style of administration.
5. How do the entry requirements for graduate and professional study have an impact on undergraduate education?
6. Identify the major problems facing your college or university. Arrange them in priority and speculate on possible solutions.

FIELD EXERCISES

1. Identify a community college in your locality. Obtain a copy of its catalogue. Arrange a visit to the institution and report to the class on the various programs offered by the college.
2. Arrange a debate on the issue: "Resolved, the first two years of undergraduate education should take place in a community college."
3. Invite a professor of one of the arts and science disciplines to speak to your class on his or her preparation for a career in higher education.
4. Invite a chairperson or dean in your college or university to speak to your class on his or her perceptions of the problems facing higher education.
5. Examine your local phone directory and identify the postsecondary proprietary schools in your area.
6. Identify the various degrees offered by the institution that you are attending.
7. Consult the catalogue of a college or school of education. Identify the requirements for master's and doctoral programs of that college.

SELECTED READINGS

ALTBACH, PHILIP G. *Student Politics in America: A Historical Analysis.* New York: McGraw-Hill, 1974.

ANDREWS, BENJAMIN F. *The Land Grant of 1862 and the Land-Grant College.* Bulletin No. 13. Washington, D.C.: G.P.O., 1918.

AXT, RICHARD G. *The Federal Government and Financing Higher Education.* New York: Columbia University Press, 1952.

BABBIDGE, HOMER D., AND ROSENZWEIG, ROBERT M. *The Federal Interest in Higher Education.* New York: Columbia University Press, 1962.

BERNHARD, JOHN T., ET AL. *The Changing Role of the College Presidency.* Washington, D.C.: American Association of State Colleges and Universities, 1974.

BRICKMAN, WILLIAM F., AND LEHRER, STANLEY, EDS. *A Century of Higher Education: Classical Citadel to Collegiate Colossus.* New York: Advancement of Education, 1962.

BROWN, HUGH S., AND MAYHEW, LEWIS B. *American Higher Education.* New York: The Center for Applied Research in Education, 1965.

BRUBACHER, JOHN S., AND RUDY, WILLIS. *Higher Education in Transition: An American History: 1636–1956.* New York: Harper & Row, 1958.

BRUNNER, HENRY S. *Land-Grant Colleges and Universities, 1862–1962.* Washington, D.C.: G.P.O., 1962.

BUTTS, R. FREEMAN. *The College Charts Its Course: Historical Conceptions and Current Proposals.* New York: McGraw-Hill, 1939.

DANFORTH, EDDY, JR. *College for Our Land and Time: The Land Grant Idea in American Education.* New York: Harper & Row, 1956.

FEVER, LEWIS S. *The Conflict of Generations: The Character and Significance of Student Movements.* New York: Basic Books, 1969.

FLEXNER, ABRAHAM. *Universities: American, English, German.* New York: Oxford University Press, 1930.

FRANKEL, CHARLES. *Education and the Barricades.* New York: W. W. Norton, 1968.

FRETWELL, ELBERT K., JR. *Founding Public Junior Colleges.* New York: Teachers College Press, Columbia University, 1954.

GALLAGHER, BUELL G. *Campus in Crisis.* New York: Harper & Row, 1974.

GROSS, PATRICIA. *Beyond the Open Door.* San Francisco: Jossey-Bass, 1971.

HAWKINS, HUGH. *Between Harvard and America: The Educational Leadership of Charles W. Eliot.* New York: Oxford University Press, 1972.

HOFSTADER, RICHARD, AND HARDY, C. DEWITT. *The Development and Scope of Higher Education in the United States.* New York: Columbia University Press, 1952.

HOOK, SIDNEY, ED. *In Defense of Academic Freedom.* New York: Pegasus (Bobbs-Merrill), 1971.

KAHN, ROGER. *The Battle for Morningside Heights: Why Students Rebel.* New York: William Morrow, 1970.

KELMAN, STEVEN. *Push Comes to Shove: The Escalation of Student Protest.* Boston: Houghton Mifflin, 1970.

KERR, CLARK. *The Uses of the University.* Cambridge, Mass.: Harvard University Press, 1963.

MCCLUSKEY, NEIL G., ED. *The Catholic University: A Modern Appraisal.* Notre Dame, Ind.: University of Notre Dame Press, 1970.

MCCONNELL, T. R. *A General Pattern for American Public Higher Education.* New York: McGraw-Hill, 1962.

MEDSKER, LELAND L. *The Junior College: Progress and Prospect.* New York: McGraw-Hill, 1960.

MOOD, ALEXANDER M. *The Future of Higher Education.* New York: McGraw-Hill, 1975.

NEVINS, ALLAN. *The State University and Democracy.* Urbana: University of Illinois Press, 1962.

PERKINS, JAMES A. *The University in Transition.* Princeton, N.J.: Princeton University Press, 1966.

ROSS, EARLE D. *Democracy's College: The Land Grant Movement in the Formative State.* Ames: Iowa State College Press, 1942.

ROSZAK, THEODORE. *The Making of a Counter Culture.* Garden City, N.Y.: Anchor Books, 1970.

RUDOLPH, FREDERICK. *The American College and University: A History.* New York: Knopf, 1962.

SLOAN, DOUGLASS. *The Scottish Enlightenment and the American College Ideal.* New York: Teachers College Press, Columbia University, 1971.

THORNTON, JAMES W. *The Community Junior College.* New York: John Wiley, 1966.

TIEDT, SIDNEY W. *The Role of the Federal Government in Education.* New York: Oxford University Press, 1966.

TRIVETT, DAVID A. *Proprietary Schools and Postsecondary Education.* Washington, D.C.: American Association for Higher Education, 1974.

WILSON, ROBERT C., ET AL. *College Professors and Their Impact on Students.* New York: Wiley-Interscience, 1975.

15

The School System and Staff

Chapter 15 examines the school system by identifying its major staff components: the school board, administrators, teachers, and other personnel. Preliminary to this discussion, a brief review of certain basic principles governing American education is useful:

1. Education, when defined in its organized sense as schooling, is a state prerogative.
2. States have delegated substantial authority in organizing and administering schools to local boards of education (i.e., the local school board).
3. Local school boards establish the general policies governing schools and their employees and engage professional educators such as superintendents, principals, and teachers to provide instruction to the students residing in the school district.

While they are state agents, local school board members are also responsible to the public, the community members residing in the school district. Since school policies are a community concern, school issues are open and discussed and debated publicly. Local control of schools is designed to encourage community involvement and participation in the public schools.

Although the local district is the immediate location and focus of school governance, the matter is not so simple. The state—through its school code and through legislation—exerts many controls over education, ranging from mandated curriculum areas to statutes regulating teacher tenure, employment, and dismissal. Although education is a state function, the federal government, over time, has assumed an educational role through legislation such as PL 94-142, which establishes guidelines for educating the handicapped and through court decisions such as the *Brown* case of 1954, which outlawed de jure racial segregation in public schools. These factors should be kept in mind when considering the nature of a school system. While the structural components of a school system can be identified, such a system does not exist in isolation from other social, political, and economic systems and variables.[1]

Although political scientists and sociologists have developed extended analyses of "systems," Chapter 15 uses a limited and necessarily simplified view of a system. Our discussion concentrates on the staffing pattern found in most school systems.

A major purpose of the chapter is to identify the staff members with whom prospective teachers will work. The basic orientation is that teachers are part of a system that requires the cooperative efforts of all its members if it is to succeed in performing its primary educational mission.

SUPERINTENDENT OF SCHOOLS

Most of the 16,000 school districts in the United States employ a general superintendent of schools as the chief executive officer of the district. While the local board of education is responsible for creating the policies governing the district schools, the superintendent is responsible for implementing those policies. The general superintendent's position can be defined by the following major responsibilities that he or she performs for the board of education:

1. Implementing and supervision of the district's educational program.
2. Preparing the annual budget and managing the district's finances.
3. Recommending the employment of teachers, administrators, and custodial, secretarial, and other support staff.
4. Preparing reports and recommendations on the district's relationships to state, federal, and other educational authorities.
5. Supervising the general operations and physical facilities of the district.

In small, usually rural, school districts, the superintendent may perform all these duties and also serve as a building principal as well. In districts of an intermediate size, the superintendent generally works directly with the school building principals and a small number of central office personnel. In large,

---

[1]For a discussion of the school subsystem in relationship to larger systems, see Frederick W. Wirt and Michael W. Kirst, *The Political Web of American Schools* (Boston: Little, Brown, 1972).

usually big-city, districts, the superintendent heads a large central office staff and often has deputy superintendents as administrative subordinates in the various regions or areas of the district. Regardless of the district's size and complexity, the superintendent heads the administrative hierarchy and has ultimate responsibility for implementing the policies enacted by the board of education.

Historically, the position of the superintendent appeared first in the urban areas of the United States, especially in the large eastern and midwestern cities. When the management of a number of schools became too difficult and demanding for a citizen board of laypersons, it was determined that a professional educator was needed to coordinate the administrative functions of the schools. By the end of the nineteenth century, large school districts typically employed a general superintendent.[2] As the rural school district consolidation proceeded in the twentieth century, superintendents were also hired in these areas. Three phases occurred in the historical development of the general superintendency:

1. Initially, the superintendency was essentially a clerical and information office that dealt with the minor but detailed administrative tasks assigned by the board of education.

2. Gradually, the superintendent emerged as the district's educational leader and expert. As educational issues and problems became more complex, boards of education came to recognize and value the expert professional opinions of superintendents who prepared policy recommendations for them.

3. In the third stage, the superintendent, who was now recognized as the district's educational leader, was given the added responsibility of managing its financial and business affairs. The superintendent was now not only responsible for curriculum and instruction but also for managing the district's property, finances, investments, and budget.

As a result of this historical evolution of the superintendency and because of the complexity of contemporary American education, the modern superintendent is expected to fill many demanding roles and complete many difficult assignments. The superintendent is expected to be an educational leader, a political leader, a business manager, and a human relations expert. The following paragraphs examine these demanding dimensions of the superintendency.

EDUCATIONAL LEADERSHIP. As an educational leader, the superintendent is expected to have knowledge and skill in curricular design, development, and implementation. While many curricular matters must be delegated to the professional staff, the superintendent has final responsibility and is accountable for the success or failure of the school district's educational program. The superintendent is expected to assist the board of education in developing

---

[2]For an historical analysis of the development of superintendent-board relations, see David B. Tyack, *The One Best System: A History of American Urban Education* (Cambridge, Mass.: Harvard University Press, 1974), pp. 126–176.

policies that govern the district's educational program. As the foremost educator in the district, the superintendent is accountable for the performance of the district's building principals and teachers.

POLITICAL LEADERSHIP.   Effective superintendents need to be skilled in political leadership and public relations. It is often the superintendent who explains policies and decisions to the professional staff, the public, and the news media. It is the superintendent who has to reconcile the interests of conflicting groups without jeopardizing the primary educational mission of the schools. The modern superintendent needs political and human relation skills of tact, diplomacy, and patience in implementing an educational program for the children of the school district. If the superintendent lacks these skills, conflicts with the board, staff, and public may develop that will affect the district's educational mission.

BUSINESS MANAGEMENT.   The superintendent is responsible not only for educational leadership but also for managing and monitoring the financial affairs of the district. The superintendent is expected to be an expert on tax rates, the state funding formula, investments, and bonds. It is the superintendent's responsibility to prepare and present the annual budget to the school board. Often, the superintendent is involved in negotiations with the teachers' organization on matters of teachers' salaries and fringe benefits. Further, the superintendent is responsible for maintaining the physical facilities of the district.

PERSONAL AND PERSONNEL RELATIONS EXPERT.   In any institution, problems involving the individuals employed to perform the functions of that organization will occur. These problems often relate to the interpersonal relationships of administrators, teachers, and other personnel employed by the school district. These time-consuming problems often come to the desk of the superintendent for solution. The superintendent needs to have the skills in stimulating teachers and other staff members to work at their optimum levels. To a large extent, the educational and working environment of the district is shaped by the superintendent's attitudes.

The Superintendent's Functions

The district superintendent has a direct influence on the teacher's professional career. As the district's chief executive officer and educational leader, the superintendent has a crucial role to play in staff hiring, supervision, and development. If teachers are to be granted tenure, it is on the superintendent's recommendation. If they are to be dismissed, it is also with his or her recommendation. It is important, therefore, for the classroom teacher to be aware of the various specific functions that the superintendent exercises in the school district. Among them are

1.   meetings with community groups, parents of pupils, representatives of the media, and agents of companies doing business with the district;
2.   planning and attending board of education meetings;

3. meetings with the professional staff, subordinate administrators, teachers, and noninstructional personnel;

4. attending to instructional matters such as program objectives, curriculum and instruction, organization and scheduling, and materials and equipment;

5. supervising pupil personnel matters such as guidance, health, discipline, and related legal items;

6. dealing with staff personnel matters such as recruitment, assignment, records, welfare, policies, and in-service education;

7. attending to school physical plant facilities matters such as construction, maintenance, repair, heating, lighting, ventilation, and energy conservation;

8. conducting the financial and business affairs such as budgeting, purchasing, and accounting;

9. attending to school-community relations and services of a public relations nature such as appearing at public events, making speeches, and participating in public service activities and organizations; and

10. involvement with professional activities and organization.[3]

THE SCHOOL SYSTEM HIERARCHY

The roles and responsibilities of various staff members of the school system are discussed in the sections that follow. However, it is important to consider first the flow of authority within the school system. In terms of authority, the school staff is organized in a hierarchy, in which positions and their attendant responsibilities are arranged so that those exercising the greater and more general authority are placed higher in the staffing pattern.[4] Since the superintendent is accountable to the school board for all the district's operations, he or she ranks highest in the school system hierarchy. The flow of authority is downward in a line from the superintendent to subordinate administrators. If the district is large enough to have area or regional deputy superintendents, they occupy the next rung in the administrative hierarchy. In terms of line authority, the building principal comes next. As a teacher, the most frequent encounters will be with the principal who has line authority and responsibility for the operations in a school. Teachers are next in the flow of authority and responsibility in that they are accountable for implementing the district's educational program in their classrooms. The hierarchical pattern should not be viewed as a coercive bureaucracy by teachers. It is a means of identifying and clarifying areas of responsibility within a school system. It simply means that someone is responsible

[3]Roald F. Campbell, Luvern L. Cunningham, Michael D. Usdan, and Raphael O. Nystrand, *The Organization and Control of Schools,* 4th ed. (Columbus, Ohio: Charles E. Merrill, 1980), pp. 217–220; 233–246.

[4]For a discussion of the school system hierarchy, see Campbell et al., pp. 251–274.

for a particular set of functions in the school system. The following is intended to illustrate hierarchical line patterns in the school system.

LINE AUTHORITY IN A SCHOOL SYSTEM

Board of Education
(makes policy for entire district)

Superintendent
(implements policy for entire district)

Deputy Superintendents
(in large districts)
(implement policy in subdivisions of the district)

Building Principals
(implement policy in a single school of the district)

Teachers
(implement policy—the educational program
in a particular classroom of a school)

In addition to and supportive of the line positions in the administrative hierarchy of the school, there is also staff personnel, such as program directors, special service personnel, and curriculum specialists who report to, assist, and advise administrators, such as the superintendent and principal who hold line positions. The recommendations of staff personnel must be accepted by line administrators before they are implemented. Personnel in staff positions are specialists who provide expert opinion to the line administrators that are accountable for operating the schools and implementing the district's educational program. Figure 15–1 illustrates line-staff relationships in the school system hierarchy.

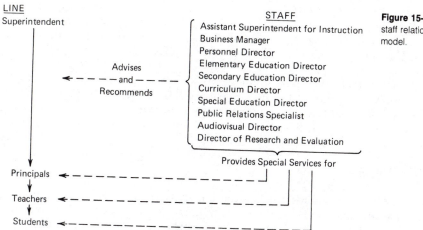

Figure 15-1 School system line-staff relationships: Large district model.

CENTRAL OFFICE STAFF

Subordinate to the superintendent in the administrative hierarchy of the school system is a central office staff that assists in the operations of the district. The success or failure of the superintendent in achieving district goals depends on his or her ability to select capable subordinates and to organize them into an effective administrative team. The school district's size determines to a large extent the number and functions of subordinate central office administrators and personnel. In a very small district, the central office might consist of only the superintendent and a secretary. In the large urban district, it might consist of a large number of subordinate administrators, such as deputy superintendents, administrative assistants, managers, program directors and curriculum specialists.

For example, the central office staff of a large urban school district might include the following:

1. Assistant superintendent for instruction.
2. Assistant superintendent for business.
3. Assistant superintendent for personnel.
4. Assistant superintendent for pupil personnel services.
5. Director of elementary education.
6. Director of curriculum.
7. Director of special education.
8. Director of audiovisual and media services.
9. Public relations and information specialist.
10. Director of research and evaluation.
11. Director of buildings, grounds, and maintenance services.
12. Director of health services.
13. Director of cafeteria and food services.
14. Director of transportation.
15. Specialists, supervisors, and consultants for elementary education, music, art, physical education, mathematics, science, social science, foreign language instruction, and other special subjects.

Most central office personnel are in staff positions insofar as they perform specific tasks assigned by the superintendent in their area of specialized expertise. They also advise the superintendent on the recommendations to be made to the board of education.

THE BUILDING PRINCIPAL

A school district is subdivided into attendance areas with a particular building designated as the school serving the educational needs of students who live within the boundaries designated by the board of education. The typical pattern is to have a principal designated as the administrative officer of that building. Depending upon the size of the building and its enrollment, the principal may have a number of assistant principals, to aid in administering the school. Junior high and high schools may also have a registrar, director of guidance, and department chairpersons for various subject matter areas. Figure 15-2 illustrates the division of a district into attendance areas.

Historically, the position of building principal evolved from the concept of the principal teacher of the school. Regarded as a school's most knowledgeable and experienced teacher, the principal teacher was a master educator who could assist, advise, and often supervise less experienced or beginning teachers. In Europe, the master teacher who administered the school was called a headmaster or headmistress. Private schools, particularly academies, in the United States still use the titles of headmaster or headmistress to designate the chief administrator. As the principalship evolved in American public education, the principal, while still being regarded as the educational leader of the school, also was assigned many other responsibilities of an indirect educational nature. As public schools assumed more social services such as providing transportation, meals, and health services, the principal was expected to administer these added assignments.

In most elementary schools, the building principal is the administrator with whom teachers have the greatest contact. Just as the district or general superintendent plays many roles and performs many functions in the school

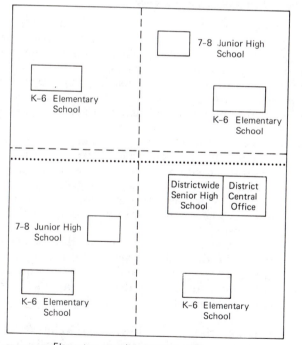

Figure 15-2 Attendance areas and schools within a district.

— — — — Elementary attendance area boundary.
•••••••••• Junior high attendance area boundary.

district, the principal exercises a wide range of functions within the attendance area served by the school under his jurisdiction. It is the principal's duty to implement district policies and administer the instructional program for children attending the school. School planning, staff development, and supervision are also areas of responsibility that the principal is expected to perform. The principal maintains student records, schedules sections of grades or subjects, and deals with staff and student problems.

TEACHERS

The school system of a district exists to educate children. Empowered to do so by the state, a board of education develops the general policies needed to perform this primary function and employs a superintendent to implement its policies. In the hierarchical structure of the school system, the building principal executes policy decisions in his or her particular school. However, the key to a successful educational program is the classroom teachers who actually instruct the students assigned to them. Chapters 19, 20, and 21 examine teacher preparation, certification, employment, and organizations. In the school system, it is the teacher who, following the approved curriculum guides of the school district, instructs children.

Teachers' Instructional Role in the School System

In performing their instructional responsibilities, the teachers' role and functions in the school system are diverse, demanding, and complex. Although the teacher has the district's curriculum guides and instructional handbooks that accompany particular programs and textbook series, much of the planning, organizing, and delivering of instruction is a responsibility that only the teacher can perform. Within the school system as a whole and within the classroom in particular, competent instruction requires the teacher to perform as follows.

1. DETERMINING LEARNING OBJECTIVES. Precisely what is it that the teacher is attempting to teach and the children are expected to learn? Learning objectives provide the teacher with a focused rationale for instruction as opposed to unfocused, scattered dissemination of information. In focusing instruction, objectives help the teacher and the learners to define what is the subject of instruction and to include what is necessary and exclude what is unnecessary and often extraneous and confusing.

Consciously identified learning objectives are useful in determining if instruction has been effective and if the desired learning has taken place. If the objectives are not fulfilled, the teacher can determine if another approach or method should be used or if more time is needed by students. If learning objectives are met, the teacher can go on to the next phase of instruction.

2. IDENTIFYING LEARNERS' NEEDS, INTERESTS, AND READINESS. At the same time that the teacher is determining the objectives of a particular instructional phase, it is necessary to diagnose the particular needs, interests, and read-

iness of the children who will receive that instruction. This means that the teacher must first know the students in order to design instruction for them. Among the questions to be asked in getting to know learners are (a) Are there children who might have particular emotional, physical, or psychological problems in dealing with the material being planned for instruction? (b) Are the children educationally ready—are they prepared by previous instruction—for the new learning that is planned?

Since children's education is cumulative, the entire school system has a role to play in identifying learners' needs, problems, and readiness. The results of previous instruction, at earlier grade levels, the comments of former teachers, and the diagnosis of guidance and special education staff members are especially useful in assessing the learner's readiness.

3. PLANNING INSTRUCTION. When objectives have been framed and learners diagnosed, the teacher can plan the actual instruction that is to occur. The questions to be answered in planning instruction are, What am I going to teach? To whom will I teach it? How will I teach it? How will I know if my teaching has resulted in learning? The following instructional flow chart is helpful in planning instruction:

INSTRUCTIONAL PLANNING CHART

What?	To Whom?	How?	Assessment?
What is the subject or skill?	Who are the learners?	What method will I use? Or what combination of methods will I use?	How will I evaluate my instruction and my students' performance?
What is its relationship to previous or following units of instruction?	What is their level of readiness and previous experience?	What materials will I use?	
	What are their problems?	What instructional aides or resource materials are available?	
	What are their interests?		

Instructional planning, while it centers on and is the responsibility of the individual classroom teacher, requires the assistance of various components of the school system. The identification of the subject or skill that will be taught needs to be integrated into the school district's curriculum plan. The materials and the resources that will be used depends upon the school board's allocation of funds for their purchase and efforts of the administrative staff to provide them for classroom instruction.

4. IMPLEMENTING INSTRUCTION. To a considerable extent, successful instruction depends on the care with which preparatory planning is done. Teaching and learning, however, are an intensely human encounter that is subject to

the "unplanned" elements that are part of human experience. Skillful teaching depends on both planning and also on the ability to improvise when necessary. Obvious examples of the need to improvise occur when the bulb in the projector burns out or the tape recorder malfunctions. Although most successful teaching appears to be done by the experienced teacher with ease, instruction requires knowledge, method, and effort. Implementing instruction means that the teacher is actually teaching and the children are actually learning. It means that something is taking place—a transaction among teacher, learners, and subject matter is occurring. It means that the theory involved in planning is being put into practice.

5. EVALUATION.   It is obviously important for teachers to determine if the students in the classroom have learned some knowledge, skill, or attitude as a result of instruction. In this last stage of the instructional task, the teacher returns to the learning objectives that were framed to focus and guide the lesson. Were the objectives fulfilled? Teachers have a variety of means to evaluate students' learning. Among them are formal examinations or tests, teacher observation of performance, and student demonstration of a skill or operation. In the evaluation process, teachers should be sensitive to both the learning of the overtly stated objectives and to the more subtle concomitant learning that may also occur. For example, learning to share books or playthings is an important concomitant learning in the kindergarten and primary grades. The acquiring of social skills and using democratic decision-making processes are desired concomitant learnings throughout school.

Evaluation is meant not only for students but for teachers as well. The teacher should be prepared to use student performance outcomes as a guide to revising instructional objectives and instruction.

In addition to instructional responsibilities, teachers have a number of other related roles to play in the school system. For example, the teacher often is an informal counselor and academic advisor to students. The teacher may be assigned to perform certain administrative and supervisory tasks and to participate on curriculum committees. Because they have direct responsibility for instruction, teachers also become public relations persons for the school district as they meet with parents and other community members. The following sections explore the various roles that teachers exercise in the school system.

The Teacher as Counselor

In addition to the immediate role of instructing children, the teacher who truly knows his or her students becomes a person who assists their learning, growth, and development as individuals and as members of society. Students not only have a cognitive side to their personalities; they also have emotional, physical, and social needs as well. For successful learning to take place, the teacher needs to be aware of the physical condition, mental health, and emotional needs of his or her students. Frequently, the gaining of such insights takes the teacher out of the classroom into the community since many of the factors affecting a child's learning originate in the home. For example, sickness, illness, or death in the child's family will affect that child's school behavior and learning. Children who have a drug or alcohol abuse problem need to be identified and given help. In addition to the serious problems that children face in today's pressure-ridden society, there are always the important but common problems that arise as a child grows and develops: shyness, lack of acceptance in a social group, and peer group conflicts. To recognize and deal with children's emotional and interpersonal problems, teachers need both an academic preparation in courses in educational psychology, human growth and development, and interpersonal relations and communication and also on-site observation of children and experience in working with them prior to teaching.

In dealing with the emotional, psychological, and social problems of children and adolescents, teachers need to establish some guidelines to govern their counseling responsibilities. Probably, the most important function that the teacher can exercise is to recognize problems and to know to whom to refer serious problems in the school system. Although it is often tempting for teachers to assume the role of psychiatrist or therapist, it is an inappropriate response. It is inappropriate because teachers may become involved in situations in which they lack professional competence. Most junior high, middle, and high schools have professionally prepared counselors on their staffs. In many elementary and secondary school systems, the school district employs school psychologists to deal with severe problems.

The most important aspect of informal counseling that the teacher can exercise is that of being sensitive to children's and adolescent's needs and being available to listen to and talk with them. Teachers have always played the role of a helper in the "growing up" process. They can be an important source of help, advice, and information about how to deal with personal problems, peer group relations, and career decisions.

Teachers' Role in Administration

In many popular novels and motion pictures about teaching, the hero or heroine is portrayed as a humane and concerned young teacher whose efforts are thwarted by an unfeeling and rigid bureaucratic administration. Although there are examples of heavy-handed school officials sapping the energy and initiative of creative teachers, the reverse is often true. At times, individual teachers neglect to follow the policies and guidelines established to govern the school system to create a functioning educational environment for learners. For any system, it is necessary for its various components to function cooperatively in an atmosphere of mutual support. Just as superintendents, principals, and department chairpersons are responsible for allocating instructional resources and materials, teachers have a responsibility to perform certain semiadministrative tasks that the system requires. For instruction to take place, it is important that these delegated administrative tasks do not overwhelm teachers and prevent them from performing their primary function, however.

The following are some of the semiadministrative tasks that teachers may be called upon to perform within the school system:

1. Maintaining and completing records for the students assigned to his or her particular class.
2. Ordering instructional materials, films, tapes, and other classroom aids.
3. Maintaining accurate daily attendance records since state aid formulas are based on the average daily student attendance.
4. Developing and maintaining an accurate reporting system of students' academic progress.
5. Adding to the student's cumulative file such information as health data, test scores, grades, and other necessary information.

While the "paperwork" may not seem related directly to day-to-day instruction, it is needed to record the child's educational progress as well as for legal and administrative purposes. Just imagine how difficult it would be for the teacher to "get to know" the children in her or his classroom if their previous teachers had not provided information relating to their learning readiness, academic progress, and special problems.

The Teacher as Curriculum Maker

Chapter 16 will discuss the complexities of the curriculum construction process. It is the curriculum—its content, activities, and experiences—that constitute the heart of the school's learning process. In terms of the formal school structure, the school board approves the curriculum that is presented to it by the superintendent. The superintendent, in turn, arrives at his or her curricular recommendations through the combined efforts of the curriculum specialists and consultants and the advice of the classroom teachers. Once a curriculum is approved, it is expected that teachers will implement it in the instruction they provide to students.

While the preceding is a brief and formal statement of the curriculum adoption and implementation process, it tells only part of the story of curriculum making. Much of the important work is often done by teachers in curriculum committees that examine and revise existing instructional programs or develop new ones. These committees also identify and recommend the textbooks, materials, and learning resources needed to implement the instructional programs that are approved by the school board.

Service on a curriculum committee for the school district can be challenging, exciting, time consuming, and occasionally frustrating. Such service assumes as a prerequisite that the teacher has acquired in her or his professional preparation and ongoing experience a general knowledge of the nature and organization of the curriculum and of the particular subject or grade level that she or he is teaching. The following represents questions that teachers assigned to curriculum committees need to consider:

THE CURRICULUM COMMITTEE PROCESS

1. *A Review of the General Curriculum*
   What is the general nature of the curriculum?
   What is the particular curriculum that exists in the school district?

2. *The Particular Subject or Skill*

What is the particular subject or skill that is being reviewed by the committee?

What grade level?

What is the subject's or skill's sequence?

How does it relate to preceding and subsequent grade levels, courses, or units?

3. *Students*

Who are the students who will receive instruction in the subject or skill?

What is their age range, ability, and grade level?

What is their previous educational experience in this subject and skill or in related subjects or skills?

4. *Availability of Materials*

What materials are available in the subject or skill in terms of textbooks, workbooks, audiovisual materials?

What materials are suited best to the curricular philosophy of the school district, its students, and its staff?

What is the expected cost of the materials?

5. *Teachers*

What are the particular strengths and weaknesses of the professional staff in instruction in the particular subject or skill?

What are the staff preferences and professional judgments about the particular curricular area under consideration?

What in-service training will be needed should a given program be adopted?

The curriculum committee is generally composed of teachers in the field under review, curriculum consultants and specialists, and often an administrator from the central office staff. As the committee meets, it investigates, researches, and discusses the curricular area under review. During the review process, the teachers involved will need to consider and often reconcile differing perspectives among the committee members. Such a sharing of professional opinion contributes to the individual teacher's professional growth, self-knowledge, and knowledge of colleagues. Once the committee has completed its report, it is reviewed by the superintendent, who suggests modifications if necessary, before presenting it to the board of education for action. At this point, members of the curriculum committee may appear before the board of education to provide further information or to explain its recommendations. As can be seen, the teacher's role as a curriculum maker relates to the school system as a whole.

The following are some of the ways in which teachers can be effective spokespersons for the school system:

1. Become familiar with the community that the school serves. Know its racial, ethnic, social, and economic composition so that you can relate to and listen to parents and other community members.

2. Attend meetings of the Parent-Teacher Association (PTA) or Parent-Teacher Organization (PTO) and work to build constructive relationships with their members.

3. Develop a systematic but informal means of communicating with parents about their children's progress through notes or brief messages that tell about the child's progress and achievements as well as problems.

4. Be aware of your own social, economic, ethnic, racial, and class biases and do not let them prevent you from relating to the community and the children that you serve.

OTHER STAFF MEMBERS

The superintendent, building principals, and teachers are key members of the school system. There are other members of the school system that exercise important supportive roles to those key members. Some of these positions are identified now. The size of the particular school district determines how many of these significant others will be present in the system. It is useful for prospective teachers to have an idea of the role and function of these staff colleagues.

Counselors

School counselors are found in most secondary schools, in both junior and senior high schools. Less frequently, counselors are members of the professional staff of elementary schools. Unlike the classroom teacher, who is usually instructing groups of students, the school counselor works with the individual student on a variety of matters, ranging from career choice and academic decision making to solving personal and behavioral problems. The counselor serves such functions as

The school counselor aids students in planning their academic schedules and in making career decisions. *(Ken Karp)*

1. Providing information and guidance about careers, vocations, and colleges.
2. Providing advice about elective courses.
3. Listening to and helping students to deal with parental, peer group, or teacher-related problems.
4. Listening to and helping students to recognize and cope with a range of emotional, psychological, or behavioral problems.

Often, the school counselor is the member of the school staff to whom teachers refer students who have persistent and serious behavior problems that lead to violations of classroom discipline. While counselors seek to alleviate immediate discipline problems, they also work toward long-range solutions to these problems. The school counselor, usually an experienced teacher who has a master's degree in school guidance and counseling, needs to have a background in educational and counseling psychology and possess a wide repertoire of counseling skills and techniques. When the counselor identifies a student with a severe emotional or psychological problem, the student should be referred to an appropriate specialist such as a clinical psychologist or psychiatrist.

School Psychologist

Since the late 1960s, school psychologists have joined the staffs of many school districts, especially those of intermediate or large size. Usually assigned to the central office staff, school psychologists have a districtwide assignment rather than a location within a single school. The school psychologist's role in the school district is to provide psychological diagnoses of students. Among the functions performed by the school psychologist are

1. Administration and interpretation of tests used in assessing intelligence and identification of students for gifted, mentally retarded, and educationally handicapped programs.
2. Diagnosing students' emotional or psychological problems and suggesting remediation and therapy for these problems.
3. Preparing diagnostic profiles for students requiring special assistance or remedial work. Although some school psychologists are experienced classroom teachers, many are not. They frequently hold a master's or a doctoral degree in psychology.

School Social Worker

The school social worker, who possesses a master's degree in school social work, works closely with staff members who are responsible for guidance and student personnel services within the school district. Specifically, the school social worker, who works cooperatively with counselors and the school psychologist, is frequently involved in case work with parents and students at the home and family level. For example, if, in diagnosing a student's problems, it seems that home factors or conditions are causing the problem, the school counselor or psychologist will refer the matter to the school social worker. The social worker then arranges to visit the home and seeks to work closely with family members to resolve the problem.

School Librarian

Over recent decades, the functions of the school librarian have been enlarged and expanded in most school districts. While in the past, the school librarian was in charge of identifying, ordering, and cataloguing books, periodicals, and other printed materials, the modern librarian's assignment has become more complex as libraries have been converted into learning resource centers with tapes, filmstrips, cassettes, tape recorders, computers, learning machines, and programmed learning materials that can be used independently by students. As a learning resource center specialist, the librarian both provides materials and helps students to learn to use these resources in independent study. The school librarian also serves as a resource person for teachers who

The school librarian today must be a learning center specialist who is skilled in using a variety of instructional materials. *(Ken Karp)*

may need books, periodicals, and other materials in developing their instructional plans and to supplement in-class textbooks and materials.

The school librarian, or learning resource director, is usually a trained, certified school librarian, who has had training in research, in organizing and using reference materials, and in organizing card catalogues and library collections. The school librarian is an important participant in the school system and its staff since the learning resources that he or she provides are a necessary support and supplement of classroom instruction.

Curriculum Specialists and Consultants

In districts that range from intermediate to large, curriculum specialists are generally employed. While attached to the central office, they also provide specialized service to the various schools in the district. Depending upon the particular practice in the district, curriculum specialists have the following designations: curriculum coordinator, curriculum director, or curriculum consultant. Depending on the size and complexity of the school district, curriculum specialists may have the following assignments at various grade levels or subject matters or a combination of both factors:

> *Specialists for curriculum at grade levels* such as director of primary education, director of intermediate education, director of junior high school education, director of senior high school education.
>
> *Subject matter curriculum specialists* such as consultants for social studies, mathematics, reading, science, language arts, music, physical education, art, and so on.

The number and function of curriculum specialists, such as directors or consultants, varies greatly from school district to school district. The district's size and financial capability to support a staff of specialists is a key factor in determining the number of curriculum specialists. In very small districts, curriculum review and development may be assigned to the superintendent. In medium-sized districts, an assistant superintendent may be assigned to curricular matters. In small districts, certain experienced classroom teachers may be given reduced teaching loads to serve as curriculum consultants. In large urban districts, a large department of curriculum specialists may work at reviewing, designing, and constructing the district's curriculum.

The following are activities carried out by curriculum specialists:

1. Reviewing, redesigning, and constructing the curriculum in cooperation with central office administrators and teachers' curriculum committees.
2. Visiting schools to supplement or advise teachers in particular curricular areas.
3. Planning institute days and in-service workshops for teachers in particular curricular areas.

Within the school system, curriculum specialists play an advisory and consultative role for administrators and teachers. Curriculum specialists are typically experienced teachers who have earned advanced degrees, masters or doctorates, in the field of curriculum, often with a specialization in a particular subject matter.

Media Specialists

Intermediate and large school districts often employ media specialists who are trained in the educational uses of various kinds of media such as television, motion pictures, audiovisuals, filmstrips, overhead projectors, record players, transparency makers, cameras, photocopy machines, and other such instructional "hardware." Many districts have discovered that it is more efficient to provide a central location for the storage of "hardware" when it is not in use or is being repaired and then to allocate particular items to schools on the basis of need and frequency of use. Among the functions performed by media specialists are to

1. Identify and advise the administration on the "hardware" that should be purchased to augment district instructional programs.
2. Assist teachers in using media by providing in-service training sessions and demonstrations.
3. Organize, catalogue, and maintain equipment. In small school districts that cannot afford to employ a media specialist, this work often falls on the building principals or teachers as a special assignment. This sort of arrangement often causes problems in coordinating the use of media and in maintaining equipment with the result that it sometimes goes unused. To overcome these problems, small school districts have joined together to employ a specialist to provide services for the various affiliated districts.

Regardless of the availability of a media specialist, it is important that classroom teachers be aware of, know how to operate, and can integrate media instruction. Since the advent of television, educators have used increasingly multimedia aids to enhance instruction. The media specialists performs services, which, like those of the librarian, complement and support the classroom teacher's work.

School Nurse

The school nurse, a health care professional, is found in most elementary and secondary schools. While schools provide limited health service to students, the primary responsibility for health care remains with parents. The school nurse usually administers hearing and vision tests at regular intervals. He or she also is alert to observing symptoms of contagious diseases or problems of a physical nature among students. In cases of emergency or illness at school, the school nurse performs such duties as taking students' temperatures, cleansing wounds, and giving first aid. The school nurse generally has an office or station in which students who are ill may rest until they recuperate, are taken home, or are attended by a physician.

The kinds of services that a school nurse can provide are defined by law and often by school district policies. Districts have developed specific guidelines and regulations governing the school nurse's activities to avoid litigation and

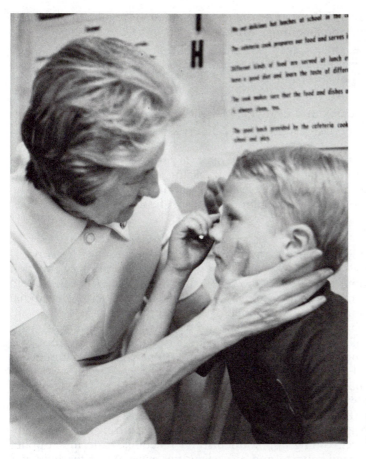

The school nurse is a health care professional who provides limited health care to students. *(Kenneth P. Davis)*

legal suits. Generally, the school nurse may not dispense medications to students unless directed to do so by a physician with the expressed consent of parents.

The school nurse also provides educational as well as health care services. She or he may give instruction on hygiene and health education to students and may serve as a resource person to teachers who are providing instruction in these areas.

Paraprofessionals

The paraprofessional, also often referred to as a teacher aide or assistant, assists teachers in performing routine work and clerical tasks or provides tutorial instruction to individuals or small groups. This assistance enables the teacher to concentrate on the major phases of instruction. Among the tasks performed by paraprofessionals are

1. Readying instructional materials for use by the teacher and students.
2. Assisting teachers in using audiovisual equipment.

3. Serving as an assistant in art, science, vocational, or home arts and other subjects involving laboratory work.
4. Assisting the teacher in working with children who may have learning deficits in reading, mathematics, and other subjects where individual instruction is of special help.
5. Assisting on field trips.
6. Assisting teachers with examinations and in record keeping.
7. Serving as supervisors in libraries, cafeterias, playgrounds, and hallways.

The qualifications for paraprofessionals vary from state to state and from district to district within a state. In some districts, the aides hired may be parents or others who assist on a part-time basis. Other districts employ only those who have had two years of college and some work in professional education.

Support Staff

A school system, as with any other system, depends on the support services of individuals who are not charged directly with the primary function of the system. Without their efforts, however, the system would not be able to function. Among members of the support staff are clerical, food service, custodial and maintenance, and security personnel.

Clerical personnel include secretaries, receptionists, clerks, and typists who prepare reports, make arrangements, handle appointments and schedules, and attend to the other office details. Within a school system, clerical personnel are found in a variety of offices, such as the central office.

The principal's secretary is one of the key persons in managing the noninstructional side of the school. An efficient secretary is indispensable to a principal in operating a well-run school. Among the tasks performed by the principal's secretary are serving as an office manager, organizing and maintaining school records, scheduling appointments and meetings, ordering supplies and materials, preparing reports, and answering the questions of teachers and parents.

Food service personnel staff the cafeteria, plan menus, prepare food, and serve meals to students and teachers. Some large districts employ a chief dietician or director of food services who coordinates the activities of the division. Since the school curriculum emphasizes the importance of a healthy and well-balanced diet, it is important that the food served in the school cafeteria meet the standards stressed in instruction. Attention needs to be paid to providing students with nutritious and balanced meals, particularly in the current era of "fast food" and "junk food."

Food service patterns vary. Despite the general trend for school districts to provide hot meals to students, some small school districts merely provide a place for students to eat a sack lunch brought from home. In larger school districts, food is often prepared in a central location and is then distributed to cafeterias in the various schools in the district. Another recent trend is for the school district to contract with commercial food service corporations that prepare food for students.

Custodial and maintenance personnel are key persons in doing the house-keeping, cleaning, and repair work that is vital to keeping a school in operation. An attractive and well-maintained school presents not only a pleasing appearance to the public but is important to the comfort of students, teachers, and staff members. Often, custodial work and maintenance is taken for granted until a problem occurs such as a leaking roof, a breakdown of the heating plant, or a failure of the electrical system. When these events take place, little or no instruction can occur until damage is repaired. A good deal of the board of education's time and the taxpayer's money are spent on building or maintaining facilities. Once again, the size of the district determines the number and specialization of maintenance and custodial workers. In the small school district, the school custodian may be a "jack-of-all-trades" whose singular efforts keep the building in operating condition. Large school districts may employ a range of custodial and maintenance personnel such as carpenters, electricians, plumbers, painters, heating and ventilation experts, and gardeners.

Security personnel are a recent addition to the school system. In the past several decades, violence and vandalism have plagued school systems, particularly those in large urban areas. Certain schools have had epidemics of gang warfare and other schools have had isolated break-ins in which property has been stolen or damaged. Violence in schools is a serious and debilitating force that erodes public confidence and creates severe stress and anxiety for administrators, teachers, and students. An environment in which persons fear for their safety is not a place in which teachers can teach and students can learn. Of the various forces that threaten academic freedom, violence is one of the most pernicious. Vandalism, too, has weakened schools in recent decades. Money that could be spent on teachers, books, and instructional materials has been diverted to repairing the damage to buildings and facilities. Large-city school systems have spent considerable sums on the continual task of replacing broken windows that are smashed not by the occasional baseball but by vandals.

To offset violence and vandalism, some school systems have employed security forces, off-duty police officers, and nighttime guards. When security personnel are added to the school staff, it is important that school board policy be framed carefully to specify their duties and responsibilities. It is equally important that security personnel not intrude on the instructional and educational environment of the school and that they be trained to perform their responsibilities without infringing upon the privacy and rights of either teachers or students. On the other hand, unless the tendency to violence and vandalism ends, more school districts are likely to use security persons to "police" schools so that violent persons are not allowed to destroy the school as an environment for teaching and learning.

CONCLUSION

This chapter has identified the key persons involved in staffing a school system. It is important that prospective teachers have the information to define their own job requirements and responsibilities in relationship to the other professionals in the school system. Teachers do not work in isolation but are members of a staff that is engaged in the common purpose of educating students. To fulfill this major function, they need to unite their efforts with those of their co-workers.

DISCUSSION QUESTIONS

1. Describe the role and functions of the district superintendent of schools.
2. Distinguish between line and staff authority in a school system.
3. Describe the functions of a school district central office.
4. Describe the role and functions of a school building principal.
5. Analyze the teacher's role and functions in the school system.
6. Define the role and functions of the following members of the school system: counselor, school psychologist, school social worker, librarian, curriculum specialist, media specialist, school nurse.
7. Identify the functions of the paraprofessional.

FIELD EXERCISES

1. Invite a superintendent of schools to visit your class and describe his or her functions in the school system.
2. Invite a building principal to visit your class and discuss his or her work with the building staff and students.
3. Invite the following members of a school system to visit your class and to discuss their roles and functions with you: counselor, school psychologist, school social worker, librarian, curriculum specialist, media specialist, school nurse.
4. Invite several elementary or secondary students to visit your class and to discuss their relationship to the school system.
5. Visit an elementary or secondary school and identify the various members of the school system and observe their functions.

SUGGESTED READINGS

CAMPBELL, ROALD F., CUNNINGHAM, LUVERN L., USDAN, MICHAEL D., AND NYSTRAND, RAPHAEL O. *The Organization and Control of Schools.* Columbus, Ohio: Charles E. Merrill, 1980.

COPPOCK, NAN, AND TEMPLETON, IAN. *Paraprofessionals.* Arlington, Va.: National Association of Elementary School Principals, 1974.

GOLDHAMMER, KEITH, ET AL., *Elementary School Principals and Their Schools.* Eugene, Ore.: Center for Advanced Study of Educational Administration, 1971.

GRAMBS, JEAN D. *Schools, Scholars, and Society.* Englewood Cliffs, N.J.: Prentice-Hall, 1965.

HABERMAN, MARTIN, AND STINNETT, T. M. *Teacher Education and the New Profession of Teaching.* Berkeley, Calif.: McCutchan, 1973.

JACOBSON, PAUL B., LOGSDON, JAMES D., AND WIEGMAN, ROBERT B. *The Principalship: New Perspectives.* Englewood Cliff, N.J.: Prentice-Hall, 1973.

TYACK, DAVID B. *The One Best System: A History of American Urban Education.* Cambridge, Mass.: Harvard University Press, 1974.

WILSON, ELIZABETH C. *Needed: A New Kind of Teacher.* Bloomington, Ind.: Phi Delta Kappa, 1973.

WIRT, FREDERICK W., AND KIRST, MICHAEL U. *The Political Web of the American Schools.* Boston: Little, Brown, 1972.

16

Curriculum Construction

In considering the major issues relating to the curriculum, which is at the heart of the educational enterprise, Chapter 16 answers such questions as, What is the curriculum? Who makes the curriculum? What forces shape the curriculum? What are some of the issues involved in curriculum decision making? What are the basic types of curriculum?

WHAT KNOWLEDGE IS OF MOST WORTH?

In his well-known essay of 1856, the English sociologist, Herbert Spencer, asked, "What knowledge is of most worth?" In answering his own question, Spencer, who found scientific knowledge most valuable, established a priority of knowledge areas that emphasized science but neglected music, art, and literature.[1] Although you may have your own immediate reply to Spencer's question, upon reflection you will see that the question is difficult to answer. If you raise this question with your friends, fellow students, family members, and teachers, you

[1]Andreas M. Kazamias, *Herbert Spencer on Education* (New York: Teachers College Press, Columbia University, 1963), pp. 121–159.

are likely to hear a variety of answers. The matter becomes complicated further when you attempt to reconcile or integrate the various viewpoints.

Spencer's question is still relevant today in that it is being debated around the country and will continue to be discussed as long as human beings are concerned with organized education. University, high school, and elementary school curriculum committees still debate this question; school board members must consider it when they approve and purchase instructional materials; teachers face this question every time that they plan, organize, and prepare instructional units.

WHAT IS THE CURRICULUM?

The word "curriculum" comes from the Latin word, *currere,* which means to run. In its linguistic origins, curriculum meant running, a race, the pattern of one's career, or the following of a course. Webster's *New World Dictionary* defines the curriculum as a "fixed series of studies" required for graduation from a school or as "all of the courses" offered collectively by a school. While this definition may seem simply to mean the program of studies taught to and learned by the students in a school or college, it is not satisfactory to all people. Some educators, such as the pioneer curriculum expert, Franklin Bobbitt, believed that it was too narrow and restrictive. Bobbitt, arguing for a much broader definition of curriculum, claimed that the curriculum encompassed all of a student's school experiences, even the many unorganized and unscheduled experiences that may have an educational impact upon learners.[2]

In contrast, Essentialist educators find Bobbitt's definition to be too broad and nonspecific. Inclined to a more basic education orientation, Essentialists, who see the school's primary function as academic, want the curriculum to consist of needed skills and subjects. Even if a more limited definition of the curriculum were accepted, there is still much controversy about what subjects and skills are necessary and appropriate to learners, the schools, and society.

To make our discussion more manageable, we will use Lindley J. Stiles's definition of curriculum as "the entire body of courses offered by a school including the selected, refined and organized knowledges, understandings, attitudes, skills, values, and behavior to be transmitted to the student."[3] Our focus will be, What is being taught to students?

Ralph Tyler, a leading curriculum expert, has asked four questions that are basic to curriculum discussions:

1. What are the school's educational purposes?
2. What educational experiences can schools provide to achieve these purposes?

[2]For Bobbitt's view of curriculum, see Franklin Bobbitt, *How to Make a Curriculum* (Boston: Houghton Mifflin, 1924), and *The Curriculum* (Boston: Houghton Mifflin, 1918).

[3]Lindley J. Stiles, "Instruction," in *The Encyclopedia of Educational Research,* 3rd ed. (New York: Macmillan, 1960), p. 710.

3. How can these educational experiences be organized effectively?
4. How can educators determine if these purposes are being achieved?[4]

Tyler's rationale for curriculum construction involves (1) an identification and agreement on the school's educational role; (2) a determination of how educators can design experiences, such as courses or units of instruction, to achieve the purposes that have been identified; (3) the development of strategies to organize educational experiences into effective teachable and learnable units of instruction; and (4) the development of evaluative instruments to determine that these educational purposes are being achieved.

Scope and Sequence

In discussing what should be taught and how it should be organized for instruction, educators use the terms "scope" and "sequence." Scope refers to what should be covered in the curriculum; namely, What is it that is worth teaching and learning? Once there is agreement on what should be included in the curriculum, it still remains to decide how much of that subject or skill should be taught.

The determination of the scope of the curriculum inevitably involves such philosophical questions as, What is true? What is knowledge? What is good or ethical? What is beautiful or aesthetically valuable? Philosophers of education have responded to these questions in different ways. For example, the philosophical perspective of Essentialism or Basic Education argues that the school's specific function is primarily intellectual or academic. Accordingly, the scope of the curriculum is limited to the tool skills of reading, writing, and arithmetic and to such academic subjects as history, geography, mathematics, language, and science. In contrast to Essentialism, Progressive educators prefer a broadly construed curriculum based on learners' interests, needs, and problems. Students should be encouraged to follow their interests even if they are not immediately academic.

Once the curriculum scope has been determined, it is possible to turn to sequence, or the order and arrangement of instruction. How is the experience, the skill, or subject matter to be arranged for program and instructional purposes?

Program sequencing refers to the order of arranging skills, experiences, and concepts that a student needs to progress from one learning situation to another or from one grade to another. The development of the program relates to prerequisite skills and knowledge. There are a number of ways in which to determine program sequencing or progression.

Obviously, the learner's psychological, cognitive, and physiological maturity and readiness to perform certain skills or to understand certain concepts are crucial factors in proper sequencing. That is, the teaching of a particular skill or subject should take place only when students are capable of learning it.

Although traditional curriculum arrangement and state guidelines may

---

[4]Ralph W. Tyler, *Basic Principles of Curriculum and Instruction* (Chicago: University of Chicago Press, 1950), pp. 1–2.

strongly influence program sequencing, additional factors are the psychology of the learner and the logic of the subject matter. In terms of such skill areas as handwriting, typing, or swimming, it is necessary to determine the sequence or arrangement of basic motor movements needed for more complicated movements. In historical subjects, the usual sequencing is chronological, from the oldest to the most recent. In the teaching of geography, the preferred sequencing may be from the near, the local community, to the far, or more remote, regions.

Balance, Integration, and Articulation

Scope and sequence relate to questions of balance, integration, and articulation. If the education of the person is to be in harmony and balance, it is necessary that the curriculum also be integrated or orchestrated harmoniously. A well-integrated curriculum is orchestrated when its components relate to each other to produce a whole. The curriculum should not exclusively stress one aspect of learning yet neglect other important skills and subjects.

Articulation refers to the relationship that exists between lower and higher levels of programs and between institutions. Does skill learning and concept development progress smoothly from one grade level to the next? Also, is there a relationship in the learning that is specific or appropriate to certain institutions? For example, is there a conscious relationship between the educational experiences of the kindergarten and the first grade, between the primary and the intermediate grades of the elementary school, between the elementary school and the high school, and between the high school and the college? The lower stage, grade, or institution should prepare the learner for the next higher one. It is also important that various levels do not duplicate each other.

GENERAL FORCES INFLUENCING CURRICULUM CONSTRUCTION

As indicated earlier, education in the United States is a state prerogative. Unlike the systems that prevail in many other nations, the United States does not have a uniform national curriculum. While the states may mandate the teaching of certain subjects, they have granted many discretionary matters to local school districts. Because of historic patterns of local control, a variety of curricula exists since the approval of a given curriculum is the responsibility of local school boards in most instances. In a few states, statewide curricular patterns exist. Thus, the curriculum of most elementary and secondary schools in the United States is based on both local and state approval. Although noticeable curricular variations exist from state to state and even from district to district within a state, there are forces that contribute to curricular uniformity in the United States. The next section examines some of these forces.

Continuity and Change

John Dewey, a leading American philosopher, observed that there is a continuity in human experience in that the past guides and gives direction to the future.[5] When change occurs, it arises out of past experience. There is a flow of human experience that unites past, present, and future. The same continuity that exists in human experience is found in man's educational experience, especially in curricular affairs. In Western civilization, the liberal arts curriculum that originated in ancient Greece was transmitted to the present so that higher educational institutions in Western nations, including the United States, continue to stress the arts and sciences.

Many traditional secondary school programs were college preparatory and emphasized learning bodies of knowledge designed to ready students for their future academic work. As a result, much of the conventional secondary curriculum stressed studying information recorded in books. This caused traditional education to be language and book centered.

Many of those designated as educational "reformers," such as Rousseau, Pestalozzi, Francis Parker, and William H. Kilpatrick, opposed conceptions of schooling that were dominated by the mastery of language and the exclusive study of books. These reformers stressed direct learning through projects, activities, observation, or problem solving rather than the acquiring of knowledge from indirect sources. Much curricular controversy has been between traditionalists who value book-centered learning and proponents of more activity-centered and direct learning.

Despite the ebb and flow of curricular reform, schooling has remained, to a large extent, subject matter, academic, and book centered. Along with this continuity of the traditional curriculum, the reformers have had a limited success in that their innovations have had an impact in changing parts of the curriculum and in changing instructional methods. Thus, curriculum making involves both continuity and change.

While continuity and change are curriculum components, both elements require balance and integration. Several tendencies can upset the balance between tradition and change. One of the most obvious is an unreflective traditionalism that calls for preserving the status quo merely because it exists; the opposing—but equally simplistic—alternative advocates innovation out of an enthusiasm for novelty or change for the sake of change. If subjects are taught merely because they are part of an existing curriculum, they tend to become formal and sterile. At times, the curricular status quo is maintained unconsciously by those who are comfortable with the existing state of affairs. The desire to maintain the status quo can be a powerful impediment in blocking any kind of change, especially curricular.

Teachers, who are identified with the various subjects found in the curriculum, can also become a strong vested interest group opposing change. When a subject is deleted from the curriculum or when it is made an elective rather than a required course, those who teach it may lose their positions or may be forced to teach other subjects. For example, in the late nineteenth century, Latin teachers were a powerful lobby that fought successfully to keep that subject in the curriculum for many decades. Today, as new subjects are included in school programs, there is a tendency to add to the curriculum without a corresponding tendency to delete from it. In recent years, new subjects such as environmental

[5]John Dewey, *Experience and Education* (New York: Collier Books, 1963).

education, drug abuse programs, ethnic studies, legal studies, career education, consumer education, and many others have been added to the curriculum. Despite these additions, financial, time, and staff resources have not increased proportionately. The length of the school year has remained much the same; inflation has decreased the real value of funds available to schools; and numbers of professional staff have not generally increased. As a result of the tendency to add new subjects without restructuring the older ones, the balance between curricular continuity and change often has been upset.

The interaction of continuity and change also has had a strong impact on curricular innovation. The decade of the 1960s was often called the era of the "educational revolution" in that innovative programs such as the "new math," the "new chemistry," the "new physics," and the "new social studies" were introduced into the curriculum. By the late 1970s, many of the new programs had been dropped or so redesigned that they resembled the older subjects that they were intended to replace. Although there are many explanations for this phenomenon, several can be identified to illustrate the effects of continuity and change on the shaping of the curriculum.

A particular curricular innovation can be distorted when a new program is introduced with enthusiasm but without the careful and proper preparation of the professional staff, parents, and the community. Frequently, a great deal of enthusiasm exists for the innovation at the experimental center where it was designed or on the part of administrators and teachers who wish to introduce it into a particular school district. If the professional staff has not been prepared or is reluctant to reorganize its teaching to meet the requirements of the innovation, teachers may teach the new program and materials as they did the old. The results will be that the new program soon will resemble the old.

Parents and other citizens may also be resistant to curricular change. Since nearly all adults have attended school, they have definite opinions on what constitutes a good education and will express these views. A new program such as the "new math" may cause them to question their own education. At the same time that parents may resist change because of psychological uncertainty, those who wish to introduce curricular changes should also be aware that the curriculum acts as a bridge between the generations. When the curriculum is perceived as an organized means of transmitting the cultural heritage, it unites the older and new generations by providing common cultural knowledge and understanding. To act as such a transitional device, the curriculum must contain skills and subjects that are common cultural elements to both generations. If a new program produces a radical break with the past, then it can create a gulf, or a "generation gap," between parent and child and between old and young.

The Cultural Ethos

The cultural ethos, or milieu, while a very broad and somewhat vague term, has an important bearing on curriculum. It refers to those political, economic, social, religious, and aesthetic characteristics that distinguish one people from another. The cultural ethos gives Americans their unique character. While there are philosophical considerations that transcend cultural differences, the culture is a powerful determinant of the general curriculum. To a large extent, the school curricula of various nations work to shape the character of the people of that country. For example, the language, history, and literature found in the curricula in Great Britain are part of the cultural process of creating a Britisher. The language and historical and political ideology found in the Soviet school curricula help to shape the Russian child's character. The same process of national cultural formation that occurs throughout the world also operates in American schools.

While the United States exhibits strong cultural, ethnic, religious, and racial pluralisms, there is also a cultural commonality that identifies a person as an American. The sense of "Americanness" has been shaped by the long common national experience. In the United States, there is a common political tradition and structure that emphasizes representative institutions, government of law, equality before the law, majority rule, and respect for minority rights; there is a shared history that involves common themes such as immigration, settlement, and the experience of a westward-moving frontier; economically, there is a general commitment to private property and to the free enterprise system; educationally, and socially, there is a general commitment to social mobility based on achievement and not ascribed by membership in a specially privileged group, caste, race, or ethnic group. These generalized political, economic, and social values are mirrored in the curricula found throughout schools in the United States.

While this very general cultural character exists, there are also many particular publics, groups, and interests in the United States. Frequently, interest groups have special programs that they want included in the public school curriculum. Special-interest groups, representing some particular organization or association, may attempt to influence curricular development. Such organizations as the American Legion, the League of Women Voters, the National Association of Manufacturers, the AFL–CIO, and many others lobby to bring about curricular change by including subjects, materials, or programs that explain and promote their interests. At other times, they may seek to remove subjects, courses, or materials that they find contrary or injurious to their interests. For example, business interests may want the curriculum to emphasize the free enterprise system; labor unions may want an emphasis on the history, development, and objectives of organized labor in the United States. Members of ethnic groups and organizations frequently propose that special attention be given to the achievements and contributions made by members of their particular group. Among the various interest groups that seek to influence curriculum development are proponents of the conservation of natural resources and opponents of the use of tobacco and alcohol; there are groups that are for and against the presence of sex education and drug abuse education in the curriculum.

Although special-interest groups operate at the local, state, and national levels, they generally try to secure the adoption of statewide guidelines in the form of the mandating of particular subjects from the state legislature. Sometimes, the various special-interest groups are united in national organizations or federations. At times, very localized groups arise to seek adoption or elimination of programs, books, or materials.

So, while a generalized ethos functions in the broad school program, curriculum development is also influenced by special-interest groups. Those who make the curriculum have the responsibility to determine through inquiry, investigation, and discussion which of these competing interests are educationally valuable and which are not. They also have the difficult task of reconciling conflicting interest groups and of seeking to arrive at balance and harmony insofar as that is possible.

Academic Forces and Interests

While curriculum making is a public matter and thus a political affair, it is also an academic concern. For example, the area of language arts is based on the scholarly research of college professors in such related fields as linguistics, literature, and language studies. The same relationship also exists in the other curricular areas, such as the natural and social sciences. Since teachers are prepared in the colleges and universities and since many of the textbooks and instructional materials used in the elementary and secondary schools are prepared by college professors, academic experts exercise a role in determining curriculum content. It should not be assumed that the academic experts always agree. They often disagree strongly on questions of what content is appropriate, on the most effective instructional methodology, and on the validity of interpretations. When faced with matters of academic disagreement, the curriculum makers need a competence that enables them to identify, recognize, and use authorities in a given field.

Impact of the Higher Institution on the Lower One

In curricular decision making, the higher institution usually has a decided impact on the lower one. There is almost a chain reaction from the higher institution to the lower one. For example, professional schools such as law, medicine, and dentistry shape the undergraduate college curriculum as it prepares students to meet the entry requirements for professional study. College-entry requirements have an impact on secondary schools in that preparatory programs are designed to meet these entry requirements. To a lesser but nevertheless discernible extent, the high school has an impact on the elementary school.

Although educational theorists such as John Dewey have attacked the doctrine that education is preparation for further study, this doctrine still operates effectively. Changes in the curricula of higher institutions often have a decided impact on those who teach in lower institutions. For example, when many colleges eliminated foreign language entry requirements, enrollments in foreign language courses in high schools experienced a sharp decline.

General Education versus Specialized Education

Since the classical period in ancient Greece when the sophists who claimed to be able to teach specialized skills debated with the advocates of general education such as Plato, there have been arguments regarding the degree to which education should be general or specialized. In *Building a Philosophy of Education*, Harry Broudy clearly defined the problem of general and special education. For Broudy, a general education was that which all human beings needed because of their common human nature and a specialized education was that which some people needed because of their particular career requirements.[6] The major issue, then, that faces curriculum developers is to determine to what extent the curriculum should be general, that is, for all students, regardless of their career destination, and to what extent it should be specialized and consist of specific career training.

The question of general versus specialized or career training is crucial in the high school curriculum, although this question is also relevant to the junior high school. Those who give priority to a general education, consisting of a common learning core, argue that there are certain skills and subjects that every person needs as a literate and educated human being. Those who give priority to general education include Jacques Maritain, William Chandler Bagley, Robert Hutchins, Arthur Bestor, and Harry Broudy. Philosophically, proponents of general education have been classified as Perennialists, Essentialists, and Classical Realists. Advocates of general education emphasize the tradition of the liberal arts and sciences and oppose premature specialization.

In contrast to the proponents of general education, there are those who argue that a strictly general or liberal arts curriculum is unsuited to the interests, needs, and career goals of large numbers of students. Advocates of specialized education argue that the secondary curriculum should provide commercial, industrial, vocational, and other career preparation to provide the salable skills that people need to earn a living. In the late 1940s, the proponents of "life adjustment" education argued that the curriculum should satisfy students' personal and career goals. Currently, many educators argue that the curriculum should provide high school graduates with skills that are relevant to the job market. Since the controversy between general and specialized education has been a long one, it will continue to generate educational debate.

Demands for Relevance

During the student activism of the late 1960s, especially in colleges and universities, the issue of a relevant curriculum was raised. At that time, the demand for relevance was related to social, economic, political, and international issues. In particular, many students opposed American involvement in the war in Vietnam. Since the 1970s, the concern for relevance has shifted to career preparation.

The issue of what constitutes a relevant education is closely related to the general versus specialized education debate. Most directly, relevance relates to the relationship between what a student is learning in school and what he or she is doing and will do outside of school. Relevance means an observable and direct connection between schooling and life. If it is related to career goals, relevance is most observable in precise or specific skill learning. Those who demand immediate relevance frequently contend that a very general education is unrelated to life. In contrast, proponents of general education claim that the arts and humanities are generally relevant to persons as human beings.

In seeking to develop a relevant curriculum, educators have to ask, Relevant to what and to whom? Is the curriculum relevant to personal needs,

---

[6]Harry S. Broudy, *Building a Philosophy of Education* (Englewood Cliffs, N.J.: Prentice-Hall, 1961). p. 292.

political needs, or community needs? The list of relevant needs is a long one, indeed, that cannot be satisfied easily.

The child has needs. Those who take a child- or student-centered perspective argue that the curriculum should come from the child. The child-centered Progressive educators of the 1920s and some of the contemporary critics of the school have sought to structure the curriculum around the learner's needs. Should the curriculum be relevant to these needs? Are there some needs of children that can be best met by the school and other needs that can be satisfied by the home or family? Or should the school attempt to satisfy all of the child's needs?

Those who favor a subject matter approach argue that children's needs are too limited a basis for a curriculum. They question if the child's range of needs and interests is sufficiently broad and mature to be the sole constituent of the curriculum. Although they recognize that the child's readiness and interest are important factors, the subject matter advocates argue that the long experience of the human race is the most important base for curriculum building.

Other dimensions of the issue of relevance are social, economic, cultural, and political. Now, the question becomes, How does the school's curriculum relate the individual to these needs? In the United States, it is regarded as important that people be competent to participate in government, to vote in elections, to serve on juries, and to perform the duties needed in a democratic society. There is also the question of economic relevance. Does the curriculum prepare individuals who are economically and occupationally competent? To what extent should the law of supply and demand operate in curriculum planning? As changes occur in technology, should these changes be evident in the curriculum?

Thus, it can be seen that the question of relevance has a great bearing on the curriculum. The advocates of general education take the view that liberal studies are always relevant to human needs in that they are theoretical enough to be applied to specific issues and problems and to changing circumstances. In contrast, others would base the curriculum on changing social, economic, and political requirements of society.

CURRICULAR ORGANIZATION

Now that we have discussed the meaning of the curriculum and have examined some of the general issues associated with curriculum construction, we look at several of the various types of curricular organization. Some of these curricular patterns can be found in their pure form in only a few American schools. Most likely, the patterns found in the schools reflect some combination of the basic patterns discussed in the following section.

Fundamental or Basic Skills and Subjects

One of the oldest curricular patterns stresses basic skills and subjects. At the elementary level, a basic skills curriculum focuses on reading, writing, arithmetic, and use of the library. These skills are regarded as foundational in that they prepare children for subsequent learning. Along with an emphasis on the basic computational and literary skills, such a basic curriculum will encourage attitudes that promote obedience to authority, respect for property, patriotism, and perseverance.[7]

It is in the junior high school, grades seven and eight, and in the high school that the subject matter curriculum assumes its basic form. Each subject, such as English, mathematics, biology, chemistry, history, and foreign language, for example, is organized and taught separately by a teacher trained in that academic discipline. The professional staff is organized into departments based upon their academic specialization. A typical pattern of departmental organization would consist of departments of English, foreign language, mathematics, science, and history, or social science.

The proponents of a subject matter curriculum argue that knowledge is transmitted best when it is organized into separate categories by experts and is taught by those who are well versed in the subject. A good teacher is identified as a person who is knowledgeable in that subject, and instruction follows the logic or chronology of the subject. In a subject matter arrangement, there is a strong emphasis on the role of the school and the teacher as a transmitter of the cultural heritage.

The following arguments are used to defend the subject matter arrangement:

1. The recognized academic disciplines represent the organized and funded wisdom of the human race.
2. Organized subject matter has been the product of the research and investigation of experts.
3. Subject matter is a clearly defined and efficient means of instructing the young.
4. Fundamental skills and basic subjects are the best preparation for further education and adult life.

Among the proponents of fundamental or basic skills and subjects are persons who subscribe to the Idealist, Realist, Perennialist, and Essentialist educational philosophies. Individuals such as Arthur Bestor, Max Rafferty, James Koerner, and Hyman Rickover are often associated with the subject matter curriculum. The Council on Basic Education also generally subscribes to the subject matter mode of organization.

Criticisms of the Subject Matter Curriculum

While the subject matter curriculum has enjoyed a sustained historical longevity, it has had numerous adversaries. These critics, who range from the progressive educators of the 1920s to Humanistic educators of the late 1960s,

---

[7]For the Basic Education rationale, see Carl F. Hanson, *The Amidon Elementary School: A Successful Demonstration in Basic Education* (Englewood Cliffs, N.J.: Prentice-Hall, 1962); James D. Koerner, *The Case for Basic Education* (Boston: Little Brown, 1959); William M. Pursell, *A Conservative Alternative School* (Bloomington, Ind.: Phi Delta Kappa Educational Foundation, 1976).

have attacked the subject matter curriculum on numerous grounds. In this section, we identify some alternatives to the subject matter curriculum.

1. The subject matter curriculum is imposed on learners and disregards their interest and needs.
2. The logic or chronology of a particular subject may not be based on the child's readiness or agree with the psychology by which children learn.
3. Subject matter tends to be based on the past or on tradition. It may ignore the issues and problems of the present and future.
4. Rather than exciting the learner's curiosity, the subject matter approach can degenerate into studying inert bodies of information that have little or no real meaning or relevance for the learner.

The Activity or Problem Curriculum

The alternatives to the subject matter curriculum developed by the twentieth-century educational progressives took the form of the "problem-oriented" or "project or activity" curriculum, which is identified closely with the pragmatic or experimentalist philosophy of John Dewey and his followers, such as William Heard Kilpatrick and Harold Rugg.

The problem-oriented curriculum is based on the idea that the most effective way in which to learn is to solve problems that are based on the learner's interest and needs and that have social significance. Since problem areas are transdisciplinary, the solving of a particular problem involves using a variety of skills and subjects. Generally, the methodological strategy for problem solving is to have learners (1) recognize their involvement in a problematic situation, (2) define the problem, (3) do research into the problem, (4) structure various hypothetical solutions to the problem, and (5) test the preferred solution.

To illustrate the problem-oriented curriculum, the issue of environmental pollution can be used as an example. Students generally recognize that environmental pollution is an important problem that has both personal and long-range social significance. To define the problem, students might be organized into task forces or committees to identify various phases of the problem and to assemble evidence regarding the problem. Certain focusing questions can be posed to guide research into the problem. For example, what are the various types and sources of pollution? What are the consequences of environmental pollution? What action is needed to solve the problem? What governmental agencies have responsibility for environmental protection? These questions require multidisciplinary research that transcends the limits of a particular subject. For example, a student task force might investigate the history of the conservation movement and prepare a report based upon its research. Another task force could investigate the effects of pollution on water, land, air, and other natural resources. Although the focus is in the natural sciences, the research required transcends any particular scientific subject matter. Still another task force might identify the jurisdiction and responsibility of various government agencies that deal with environmental problems.

Each of the task forces or committees charged with investigating a particular aspect of the problem would be expected to use a variety of research skills, such as library research, questionnaires, interviews, and field trips. They would also be expected to organize their efforts to make individual or group reports. Reading and writing skills would be used as the groups prepare their reports.

Finally, the various task forces might unite to pool their information and to make recommendations for the solution of the problem. Eventually, it is important that students structure possible alternative solutions and act on them to test them. A most desirable outcome would be that the students' behavior be changed so that they do not become polluters of the environment and work to correct situations that lead to environmental pollution.

Among the possible solutions that might be recommended by the students are (1) student projects or activities designed to clean polluted areas, such as streams or parks, (2) letters to public officials and newspapers to encourage antipollution legislation or campaigns, and (3) programs and newsletters to share their information with other students, parents, and community members.

While pollution of the environment has been used as an example, many other problem areas might be regarded as appropriate for problem solving, such as energy conservation, racial discrimination, drug abuse, vandalism, recreation, war, and so on. The problems might also be ones that have a more direct immediacy to the students' age and interests, such as planning and planting a school garden; planning a field trip or excursion; planning and organizing a student talent show, program, or community event; preparing, writing, and disseminating a student newspaper.

The proponents of the problem-solving or activity-oriented curriculum claim that (1) it is stimulating or exciting to the learners since it arises from their interests and needs; (2) it is a realistic approach to learning since it is multidisciplinary and requires research that involves a number of subjects; (3) it integrates a wide range of skills; and (4) valuable social skills are encouraged through cooperative and democratic group activities.

Opponents of the problem-solving or activity approach argue that sole reliance on this method is (1) an inefficient way in which to learn, since students may neglect needed skills and already existing bodies of knowledge; (2) wasteful, in that time may be dissipated in nonacademic activities; and (3) superficial, in that it assumes that students can take or "raid" information from a subject without really understanding the principles and basic concepts that underly that particular academic discipline.

Other Curricular Patterns

The subject matter and problem-solving curricula, in their pure forms, are two extremes of curricular organization. In between these two poles of the curriculum continuum, other alternative patterns of organization exist that incorporate some of the features of both approaches. This section examines some of these.

BROAD FIELDS.   The broad fields curricular design attempts to reorganize a large number of skills and subjects into a few large integrated areas of instruction. Much contemporary curricula follows the broad fields design. For example, in a strictly subject matter curriculum, history, geography, economics, anthropology, and sociology might be taught as separate subjects. In the broad fields curriculum, subjects that deal with the human social experience are reorganized into a single area called social studies or social science. The skills and subjects of composition, spelling, reading, handwriting, grammar, punctuation, usage, and literature are reorganized into an integrated field called language arts. Botany, biology, chemistry, and physics are reorganized into general science, life science, earth science, or physical science. Generally, the broad fields curriculum is found in elementary and junior high schools.

CORRELATED CURRICULUM. The correlated curriculum is another modification of the subject matter curriculum. Although similar to the broad fields curriculum, correlation involves planned efforts to integrate related fields or subjects around a unifying theme. For example, the teaching of American history and literature might be correlated into American studies. In this case, literature and poetry is studied simultaneously with the social, political, and economic history of a given period. Similarly, various regional studies might be organized in which the language, history, politics, economics, geography, literature, and art of a particular area would be studied in a correlated manner. Examples of such regional studies are Latin American studies, Asian studies, and African studies. Recent examples of other correlated curricula in high schools and colleges are black studies, women's studies, peace studies, ethnic studies, and environmental education.

CORE CURRICULUM. Still another type of curricular organization is attained by combining core and elective studies. The core curriculum includes common subjects, based upon a common body of knowledge and experiences required of all students. A certain part of the instructional sequence is, then, devoted to these core or common learnings. For example, all students may be required to enroll in courses such as language arts, social studies, natural and physical sciences, and physical education to provide them with a common educational base. In addition to the common learning experiences provided by the core, students may also enroll in elective subjects that meet their individual needs and interests.

SPIRAL CURRICULUM. Certain recent trends in educational research and development suggest new curricular patterns. For example, the term "spiral organization" or spiral curriculum has attracted substantial contemporary attention. The origins of the spiral curriculum are attributed to Jerome Bruner who pioneered the "structure of disciplines" orientation in curriculum reorganization.[8] Bruner has argued that instruction should be based on the key concepts that are foundational to a particular academic discipline. Once students have learned these basic concepts, they can progress to more complex areas within that subject. By expanding and refining their ideas, students move in a spiral

---

[8]Jerome Bruner, *The Process of Education* (Cambridge, Mass.: Harvard University Press, 1962).

fashion to increasingly higher levels of complexity. It was Bruner who provided a basis in cognitive research for a psychology of learning that supported much of the curricular innovations of the 1960s.

BEHAVIORAL OBJECTIVES. Another recent curriculum trend in many school districts is to base instruction on behavioral objectives. The term "behavioral objective" means to identify an educational goal and then to operationalize it by reducing the goal to a number of specific objectives. Each of these objectives is stated so that its outcomes can be verified. Behavioral objectives are designed to clarify instructional intentions so that they can be stated clearly and measured precisely. For example, if the general goal is to learn to swim, precise behavioral objectives may be identified for learning specific strokes. In much the same way, it is possible to organize instruction in the language arts into specific objectives such as learning to read at a given level, to use commas and punctuation properly, to write a complete sentence, and so on.

Although many factors stimulated the behavioral objectives movement, the demand for accountability in education was a major cause. According to accountability advocates, schools and teachers should be held accountable for both the success and failure of instruction. If a child failed to learn a particular skill or subject, the precise deficiency could be located and corrected if the learning objectives were stated specifically.

The impact of behavioral objectives has been to make instruction more specific and less general. As with most curricular proposals, the trend to behavioral objectives has sparked controversy. Some critics argue that some behavioral objectives are so specific that instruction is reduced to numerous small objectives that do not constitute an integrated whole. Proponents argue that, if learning is broken down into specific objectives, the degree of learning can be measured.

COMPETENCY-BASED EDUCATION. Competency-based education (or CBE) was a curricular movement that developed in the mid-1970s. To the extent that CBE emphasizes specific skill learning, it is related to behavioral objectives. In many ways, however, CBE is designed to make certain that public school graduates, particularly at the high school level, have mastered basic literary and computational skills. As of 1978, thirty-four states required some type of competency-based education requirement. Several other states are considering the adoption of such a requirement. The Elementary-Secondary Education Act of 1979 assists states to develop minimum competency standards.

In *The Case for Competency-Based Education,* Dale Parnell states that competency-based education emphasizes results and "calls for agreed-upon performance indications that reflect successful functioning in life roles."[9] Since the goal is to educate persons who can function effectively, CBE stresses learning specific skills and knowledge. Competency is defined as the demonstrated ability to apply knowledge and skills learned in school to the life situations that a person encounters as an individual, wage earner, consumer, and family member. To make sure that their graduates are competent, CBE causes schools to identify,

[9]Dale Parnell, *The Case for Competency-Based Education* (Bloomington, Ind.: Phi Delta Kappa Educational Foundation, 1978), p. 7.

teach, and measure the skills and knowledge needed to function in life. Drawing together data from various state systems, Parnell has suggested a competency-based curriculum that focuses on seven roles that a person has as (1) an individual, (2) a learner, (3) a consumer, (4) a citizen, (5) in a career, (6) in leisure, and (7) as a family member.

A brief examination of these roles will illustrate what is encompassed in building a competency-based curriculum.[10]

As an individual, a person who functions successfully should understand the principles of mental and physical health. The individual also needs to develop a sense of ethical sensibility to make responsible moral choices.

As a student in a school setting and as a person who must engage in lifelong continuing education to cope with an ever-changing technological society, one must master basic learning techniques and skills. For example, the person should be able to read, write, compute, memorize, analyze and interpret data, and communicate with others by conversing and listening. Because it emphasizes basic literary and computational skills, CBE has gained support from some of the advocates of the Basic Education movement.

In the role of consumer, the individual faces myriad economic decisions and choices. Among the minimal competencies required in a modern economy are (1) the ability to evaluate the quantity and quality of goods, (2) the ability to use consumer protective agencies, (3) an understanding of the implications of purchasing on credit, (4) an ability to understand the provisions of standard insurance policies, (5) an ability to compute interest rates, and (6) an ability to understand such basic legal documents as contracts, warranties, and bills of sale.

Citizenship is another important competency. Although good citizenship has been a general goal of American education since the foundation of the common school, the objective of a competency-based curriculum is to analyze and specify this basic goal. The person should understand and be able to explain the basic units and divisions of the American political and judicial system and the functions and relationships of federal, state, and local governments. Since the most immediate contact is often with local government, the individual should know and explain local government operations and be able to locate community resources. He or she should have some idea of how to deal with bureaucracies, be able to identify and make some decisions on issues, and understand the basic principles of government.

For economic welfare and survival, individuals need to function effectively in a career. Parnell has identified eight necessary areas of career competency: (1) the ability to analyze employment trends, (2) the self-knowledge needed for career planning, (3) an understanding of production and consumption processes, (4) skill in preparing job application forms, (5) facility in developing effective interviewing techniques, (6) an understanding of the meaning of "inflation" and wages, (7) an understanding of payroll deductions, and (8) the development of salable skills.

Modern technology has produced many time- and labor-saving techniques that have increased leisure time for many Americans. Among the com-

---

[10]Ibid., pp. 23–27. The discussion of a competency-based curriculum is adapted from Parnell's schemata. However, the author has made some revisions and additions.

petencies needed in modern society is the ability to use leisure for worthwhile personal development. Individuals who use leisure time effectively need a range of avocational or hobby skills. They should have some skill and interest in the creative arts and should have the skill and knowledge that enhances aesthetic appreciation. Also, they should have some recreational skills in sports activities.

Since everyone is a family member, it is important that the individual be able to function effectively in a family role. Individuals should have some knowledge of the interpersonal relationships and of the communication skills needed within the family setting. They should understand the legal and social responsibilities of being a parent. It is also necessary to be able to plan for the long-range economic security of the family and be able to deal with such family crises as divorce, illness, and death.

Since the goal of CBE is to specify learning outcomes so that the degree to which particular competencies are achieved can be measured, the competency-based curriculum has also led to competency-based examinations and testing. School systems have developed or are developing programs of evaluating their students to determine that they have the minimal competencies to function effectively. In several states and in many school districts, achievement of minimal competency in a given skill or knowledge area is needed for promotion at certain grade levels for high school graduation.

CONCLUSION

This chapter has examined the general nature of the curriculum to familiarize prospective teachers with the theoretical issues that are involved in curriculum making. As indicated, decisions affecting the curriculum are often complex, since they involve philosophical, cultural, and ethical questions as well as those that are strictly educational. Although curriculum matters are complicated, it is necessary that professional educators be prepared to make the decisions that are necessary since the curriculum is the very heart of the educational enterprise.

As a result of studying this chapter, you should be ready to pursue Spencer's challenging question of "What knowledge is of most worth?" Facility with such basic concepts as scope, sequence, balance, and articulation will help you to answer this question.

It should be remembered that curriculum making does not occur in a vacuum. Such forces as tradition and change, the cultural ethos, and special and academic interests all exert influence in shaping the curriculum. Many questions will arise as you face the issues of curriculum decision making. Chapter 16 was designed to familiarize you with some of the most important of these issues. Chapter 17 examines some of the areas of instruction found in American schools.

DISCUSSION QUESTIONS

1. In your own words, answer the question, What is the curriculum?
2. In terms of the curriculum, define the concepts of "scope" and "sequence" and examine their relationships.

3. Reflect on your educational past and compare your experiences with some of the recent curricular trends in education. Cite examples and evidence of both continuity and change.
4. Describe the American cultural ethos in general terms and indicate its impact on the public school curriculum.
5. Define a special-interest group. Then identify a particular special-interest group and indicate its impact on the public school curriculum.
6. In terms of a specific subject matter, study the problem of curriculum articulation between higher and lower institutions. Is the impact of curriculum shaping from the lower to the higher institution, or vice versa?
7. In class discussion, examine the question, What should be the common core of a general education for all students?
8. Explore the issue of a relevant curriculum.
9. Compare and contrast the subject matter and the problem-solving or activity curriculum. Which do you prefer? Why?
10. Define the following curricular concepts: (a) broad fields, (b) core, (c) spiral, (d) behavioral objectives, (e) competency-based education.

FIELD EXERCISES

1. Examine the school code of a particular state and identify the areas of the public school curriculum that are mandated subjects.
2. Visit several schools and identify the curricular pattern that appears to be used. Then consult the curriculum guide of the schools and determine the degree to which classroom instruction followed the written guides.
3. Interview a teacher and an administrator and ask questions to determine who makes the curriculum and how it is made.
4. Interview a member of an advocacy or special-interest group and identify that group's educational or curricular objectives.

SUGGESTED READINGS

BEAUCHAMP, GEORGE A.   *The Curriculum of the Elementary School.* Boston: Allyn & Bacon, 1964.

BOBBITT, FRANKLIN.   *How to Make a Curriculum.* Boston: Houghton-Mifflin, 1924.

BOOTH, WAYNE C.   *The Knowledge Most Worth Having.* Chicago: University of Chicago Press, 1967.

BRUNER, JEROME.   *The Process of Education.* Cambridge, Mass.: Harvard University Press, 1962.

CLARK, LEONARD H.   *The American Secondary School Curriculum.* New York: Macmillan, 1965.

DEWEY, JOHN.   *The Child and the Curriculum.* Chicago: University of Chicago Press, 1902.

DOLL, RONALD C.   *Curriculum Improvement: Decision-Making and Process.* Boston: Allyn & Bacon, 1974.

DOUGLASS, HARL R.   *The High School Curriculum.* New York: Ronald Book, 1964.

HANSON, CARL F. *The Amidon Elementary School: A Successful Demonstration in Basic Education.* Englewood Cliffs, N.J.: Prentice-Hall, 1962.

INLOW, GAIL M. *The Emergent in Curriculum.* New York: John Wiley, 1973.

KOERNER, JAMES D. *The Case for Basic Education.* Boston: Little, Brown, 1959.

PARNELL, DALE. *The Case for Competency-Based Education.* Bloomington, Ind.: Phi Delta Kappa Educational Foundations, 1978.

RODGERS, FREDERICK A. *Curriculum and Instruction in the Elementary School.* New York: Macmillan, 1975.

SCIARA, FRANK J., AND JANTZ, RICHARD K. *Accountability in American Education.* Boston: Allyn & Bacon, 1972.

SHUSTER, ALBERT H., AND PLOGHOFT, MILTON E. *The Emerging Elementary Curriculum: Methods and Procedures.* Columbus, Ohio: Charles E. Merrill, 1970.

TABA, HILDA. *Curriculum Development.* New York: Harcourt Brace, 1962.

TYLER, RALPH W. *Basic Principles of Curriculum and Instruction.* Chicago: University of Chicago Press, 1950.

VENABLE, TOM C. *Philosophical Foundations of the Curriculum.* Chicago: Rand McNally, 1967.

17

Curriculum and Instruction

Chapter 16 defined curriculum and examined the general issues related to curricular construction. Chapter 17 identifies and describes the major instructional areas found in American schools. Specifically, it deals with the skills and subjects that you may be preparing to teach as a prospective elementary or secondary teacher. In reading this chapter, you should focus attention on the following questions:

What are the major components of the elementary and secondary school curriculum?

What are some of the recent curricular trends?

What is the relationship between curricular and co-curricular activities?

How do teachers function as curriculum decision makers?

LANGUAGE ARTS AND ENGLISH

Most generally, language arts are designed to assist children to become literate, to communicate effectively, and to appreciate literature in its various forms. In the contemporary elementary school, language arts are fused into an integrated core that interrelates the various language skills rather than treats them in isolation as was frequently done in the past. The elementary language arts curriculum seeks to develop the essential modes of communication of speaking, listening, reading, and writing. It is generally agreed that the elementary school program in language arts should provide

1. Systematic instruction in listening necessary for both academic success and for effective lifelong communication.
2. Instruction and opportunities for effective speaking to enable students to express and to share ideas and experiences.
3. An introduction to the structures and patterns of the English language.
4. Experiences designed to develop both functional and creative writing skills.
5. Opportunities to become familiar with and to use basic research tools such as libraries, dictionaries, encyclopedias, and reference books.
6. An introduction to literature and poetry that develops a critical sensitivity and sense of appreciation.[1]

The language arts program in the elementary school prepares students for and leads them to the high school English curriculum. It also develops the ability to locate, read, and use printed information needed for academic, economic, and social success both as a student and as an adult. The skills acquired in the language arts curriculum are highly related to developing competency in all the other areas of the curriculum. A well-developed elementary school language arts program and high school English program should provide experiences appropriate to the learners' readiness and interests at a given stage of development and also prepare them for the next higher level of instruction. This means that there must be articulation, planning, and coordination among grade levels within a school and among the elementary, junior, and senior high schools.

The outline that follows identifies the skills and subjects that are usually found as areas of instruction at the elementary and junior and senior high school levels. As you examine this outline, notice how the skills and subjects in the elementary school lead to and relate to those at the secondary level.

Elementary School Language Arts Curriculum
(typically grades kindergarten through six)

The skills and subjects are taught as an integrated core and generally are not separated into specific subject matters.

Listening and oral communication skills
Reading: word recognition, oral reading, silent reading, narrative and expository reading

[1]William W. Joyce, Robert G. Oana, and W. Robert Houston, *Elementary Education in the Seventies: Implications for Theory and Practice* (New York: Holt, Rinehart and Winston, 1970), pp. 367–368.

Handwriting: printing in primary grades and cursive in intermediate grades

Spelling: integrated with reading and writing

Composition: sentence building, capitalization, punctuation, expository creative writing

Literature: integrated with reading, introduction to basic literary forms such as stories, myths, plays

Research skills: use of libraries and reference sources such as dictionaries and encyclopedias

Junior High School Language Arts Curriculum
(typically grades seven and eight;
a middle school may also include grade six)

The skills and subjects of the junior high or middle school language arts curriculum are transitional between the elementary and senior high school. They continue the skill development begun in the elementary grades and prepare students for the more specialized and departmentalized high school program.

Reading: emphasis on either remedial or accelerated reading, depending on needs of students

Speech and dramatics: introduction to forms and style of speech such as discussion and debate

Literature: further elaboration of literary themes and types. Emphasis on appreciation of literature

Writing: more extensive report, research, narrative, and creative writing

Grammar: structure of the English language

Research skills: further experience in using reference sources

High School Curriculum
(typically grades nine, ten, eleven, and twelve,
although variations exist)

The high school English curriculum is more specialized than the elementary school language arts curriculum. It is generally organized into subject matter courses. In general, there is a continuing emphasis on grammar, writing, and literature. Among the courses offered are

Basic and remedial English
American, English, and world literatures
Business English
Composition
Journalism
Creative writing
Speech
Drama
Radio and television scriptwriting and broadcasting

Reading

Although all language arts are important educational components, it has long been recognized that good reading skills are needed for both academic achievement and success in life. Throughout history, primary or elementary schooling has stressed reading and writing, and recent trends have not lessened this emphasis. Both professional educators and the public have recognized that the United States has a national reading problem in that an estimated one million students cannot read well enough to progress satisfactorily in school. It is also estimated that another million adults are functionally illiterate. Reading improvement programs range from those initiated by local school districts to the federally funded National Reading Improvement Program.

Reading instruction has long been controversial. In the United States, reading experts are divided between advocates of phonics, in which students associate the spoken sounds of letters with printed symbols, and the "look-say" method, in which students recognize whole words through association with pictures, context clues, or intuition. Some reading programs combine both phonics and word recognition.[2]

In the past decade, many developments have occurred in reading instruction. For example, more sophisticated techniques have been developed to identify, diagnose, and remedy reading problems that result from physical or psychological disabilities. School districts employ reading specialists to assist classroom teachers in dealing with reading problems. Several of the states have also increased the course preparation in reading methods for both elementary and secondary school teachers.

MATHEMATICS

Mathematics instruction seeks to develop an awareness of arithmetical and computational relationships in a logical manner. Mathematics instruction and materials should integrate understanding, computation, and application. A basic goal of mathematics instruction is to develop facility in the four basic arithmetical operations of addition, subtraction, multiplication, and division and to cultivate an understanding of their interrelatedness.[3]

Mathematics at the elementary level of instruction seeks to achieve the following general objectives: (1) to develop readiness for mathematics, followed by concept acquisition and the development of computational procedures and problem-solving skills, (2) to provide practice whereby children learn to estimate and compute with accuracy, and (3) to develop a mathematical sensitivity that can be a basis for further study. The mathematics curriculum generally follows careful sequencing so that the skills and knowledge acquired by students are cumulative. Throughout the various levels of the curriculum, problem-solving skills and logical thinking should be emphasized.

[2]Jeanne Chall, *Learning to Read: The Great Debate* (New York: McGraw-Hill, 1968).
[3]Calhoun C. Collier and Harold H. Lerch, *Teaching Mathematics in the Modern Elementary School* (New York: Macmillan, 1969).

Elementary School Mathematics Curriculum
(typically grades kindergarten through six)

The following listing of units provides an idea of program sequencing in the elementary school mathematics curriculum.

Counting and developing facility with the real number system

Experiences with grouping to establish the concept of place value numerals

Developing the concepts of set, set membership, and set combinations

Developing the concept of inequalities and the symbols < and >

Developing basic skills of addition, subtraction, multiplication, and division

Using fractions and decimals

Measuring units: length, area, volume, weight, time, money, temperature

Using measuring instruments: rulers, calipers, scales, thermometers, abacus, and calculators

Dealing with problems of latitude and longitude

Using, understanding, and developing graphs

Developing skills of estimation and approximation

Introduction to simple algebra and geometry

Junior High School Mathematics Curriculum
(typically grades seven and eight;
a middle school may also include grade six)

The junior high school mathematics curriculum is transitional between the elementary and the high school programs in that it develops skills begun at the lower level and prepares students for more advanced and specialized work at the higher level. Among the skills and subjects included are

General mathematics with special emphasis on fractions, decimals, percentages, and graphs

An introduction to algebra and geometry

High School Curriculum
(typically grades nine, ten, eleven, and twelve,
although variations exist)

The high school mathematics curriculum is generally more specialized and arranged into separate courses. Most high schools require at least one course, or credit unit, in mathematics. Students may enroll in general mathematics, typically a terminal course, or algebra, which leads to further course work in mathematics. Among the courses offered are

General mathematics: dealing with percentages, ratios, proportions, graphs, insurance, banking, investing, consumer purchasing, and taxation

Algebra: factoring, powers and roots, polynominals, fractional expressions, quadratic equations, and linear equations
Advanced general mathematics
Advanced algebra
Geometry: plane and solid
Trigonometry

Trends in Mathematics Education

Since the early 1950s, mathematics education has experienced dramatic changes. At that time, scholars in the liberal arts and sciences, education, and engineering devised new mathematics courses and trained teachers in new methods of instruction. By the mid-1950s, "new math" programs were introduced in schools throughout the country. Generally, the "new math" programs stressed the understanding of mathematical concepts and processess through the use of the discovery method. An explicit objective of the "new math" was to have students understand the processes that they were using.

By the late 1960s, a concerted reaction set in as some parents and teachers became disenchanted with the "new math." A generation gap had developed as parents experienced difficulty in relating to their children's work in mathematics. Critics also charged that an emphasis on abstract reasoning had detracted from learning basic mathematical skills.

Current revisions of the mathematics curriculum show a tendency to effect a synthesis of the new mathematics and some of the more traditional approaches. The movement to competency-based education is likely to have a pronounced effect on mathematics instruction in that students will be expected to cope with the practical application of mathematical skills and knowledge to concrete life situations. In addition to a general revision of the mathematics curriculum, those involved in this field have also begun to include the metric system in their instructional programs.

SCIENCE

The modern natural science curriculum has emerged slowly from what was called "natural philosophy" in the early nineteenth century. Today, a knowledge of both scientific concepts and an understanding and ability to use the scientific method are considered to be of vital importance in living in a modern and technological civilization. A knowledge of and an appreciation of science is important not only as part of the general education of the educated person but is also of practical necessity in preparing for careers in engineering and the health fields of medicine, nursing, and dentistry. It is generally accepted that the science curriculum should

1. As a part of general education, provide students with an understanding of the natural and physical universe in which they live.
2. Acquaint students with the scientific method of problem solving and provide experience in using that method both in solving science-related and general life problems.

3. Develop both a humanistic and a technical understanding of science as an instrument for dealing with national and world problems, such as environmental pollution, disease, famine, and poverty.

4. Provide knowledge of basic scientific concepts and methods in the various natural and physical sciences, such as botany, biology, chemistry, physics, astronomy, and zoology.

5. Acquaint students with the application of basic science to the applied sciences and professions, such as engineering, medicine, nursing, and dentistry, as well as other fields.[4]

In the primary and intermediate grades of the elementary school, science is usually taught in an integrated and undifferentiated manner. Elementary science instruction integrates concepts and materials from the biological, earth, and physical sciences. The general emphasis is to create an awareness of the interactions of animal, vegetable, and human life with the environment. Plants and animals are usually used to demonstrate these interrelationships. In the junior high and middle school, the science curriculum generally exhibits greater differentiation into life and earth sciences. The high school science curriculum shows still further differentiation into well-defined subject matter areas, such as biology, botany, chemistry, physics, and astronomy. There are also programs in high school science that represent a fusion of concepts and materials from the various sciences. In various states, the science curriculum at the junior and senior high school levels also includes units on the effects of using tobacco, alcohol, and drugs. The following outline of the science curriculum at the elementary, junior high, and high school levels indicates some of the skills and knowledge areas related to this area of instruction.

Elementary School Science Curriculum
(typically grades kindergarten through six)

Until the 1950s, science instruction at the elementary school level was generally underdeveloped. Since that time, the elementary science curriculum has developed but also has remained integrated and undifferentiated. Among the frequent themes found in elementary science programs are living things, the earth and the universe, energy, and the seasons. Although science programs vary, the following representative units illustrate scope and sequence in elementary science instruction:

Growing plants such as beans and peas

Observing animals in the classroom such as gerbils, hamsters, fish, and lizards

Measuring lengths, areas, and volumes

[4]These general objectives of the science curriculum represent the views of the author. Other representative statements of objectives can be found in Paul E. Blackwood, "Science Teaching in the Elementary School: A Survey of Practices," *Journal of Research in Science Teaching*, 3 (September 1965), p 180; National Science Teachers Association Curriculum Committee, *Theory into Action in Science Curriculum Development* (Washington, D.C.: National Science Teachers Association, 1964); Eugene C. Lee, *New Dimensions in Science Teaching* (Belmont, Calif.: Wadsworth, 1967).

Observing and recording changes caused by natural processes, such as rusting, melting, molding, and decaying

Collecting and classifying rocks and minerals

Using the microscope and other scientific apparatus

Studying electricity and magnetism

Observational astronomy relating to the earth, sun, moon, and other planets

Preparing and collecting gases to discover their properties

Junior High School Science Curriculum
(typically grades seven and eight;
a middle school may also include grade six)

As is true in the case of most junior high school curricula, the science program is transitional between the elementary and high school. In some schools, the science course is called general science; in other schools, it is differentiated into several science areas. The following course listing illustrates the kind of program arrangement found in junior high schools:

General science: a core curriculum that integrates concepts and materials from various sciences

Biological science

Introductory physical science

Life science

Earth science

High School Science Curriculum
(typically grades nine, ten, eleven, and twelve)

Once again, the secondary school curriculum is differentiated into specific subject matter courses. For example, the following might be found at the high school level:

General science

Biology

Chemistry

Physics

Applied science

Physiology

Geology

Advanced chemistry and physics

Botany

Zoology

Physiology

Since the 1950s, a number of important changes have occurred in science education. A number of new programs were stimulated by the National Science Foundation, a federal agency created in 1950, "to develop and encourage the pursuit of a national policy for the promotion of basic research and education in the sciences." The foundation encouraged the examination and reorganization of the science curriculum and instruction. Grants from the National Science Foundation and the National Defense Education Act were used for research, institutes, development of materials, and improvement of school and college laboratory facilities.

A general result of the reorganization of the science curriculum was a series of new programs that were styled the "new physics" or the "new chemistry" in imitation of the "new math." These various new scientific programs were designed to emphasize the structure of the various sciences by identifying their key or "necessary" concepts. Through the use of the discovery method, students were to approach their study in the same way that a scientist used the scientific method. The objective was to have students actively involved in the processes and methods of science rather than to be passive memorizers of scientific terminologies and information. The result of these curricular innovations encouraged science instruction to be more process oriented with much of the learning being laboratory or experimentally based. Those who see these curricular changes in positive terms claim that the process-oriented approach to science instruction has contributed to a more exciting, more unified, and better coordinated program. The criticisms of those who have reservations about the new science programs are similar to the attacks on the "new math." They allege that an overreliance on process has led to a neglect of scientific content. They further charge that much of what appears to be an inquiry approach in science is superficial and neglects building a basic foundation that rests on scientific principles.

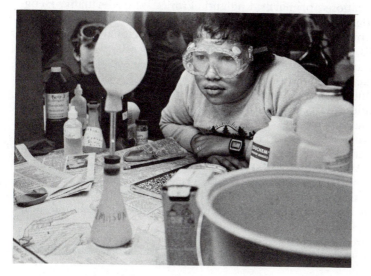

The contemporary science curriculum involves students with more "hands-on" process-oriented experimentation. *(Ken Karp)*

SOCIAL STUDIES

The nature, scope, and sequence of the social studies curriculum has always been difficult to define.[5] Generally, the social studies, or social sciences, encompass the disciplines and fields of inquiry that explain the interactions of human beings and groups with the social, political, and economic environments. Since the social experience of the human race can be examined from a variety of perspectives, the social studies curriculum embraces a multidisciplinary, interdisciplinary, and even a transdisciplinary approach. Among the problems of definition that social studies educators face are the following:

1. What is the nature of the social studies? How should they be defined?
2. Of the various social sciences, which are most significant for inclusion in the elementary and secondary curriculum?
3. How should the social studies be organized for program and instructional purposes? What should be the sequence of social studies instruction?
4. What is the appropriate relationship between content and values in the social studies?

A brief historical examination of the evolution of the social studies curriculum may illustrate the often-changing definition and rationale of the social studies. In the early nineteenth century, the areas of the social studies that emerged as common school subjects were history and geography. History was organized primarily as the study of the American past, with an orientation that was political, military, and literary. At the secondary level, there were courses in ancient and medieval history. By the early twentieth century, history as the dominant social studies subject was represented by courses in American and world history. World history was viewed as the historical experience of the Western European nations, primarily England, France, and Germany. Geography was the standard companion course to history. Instruction usually emphasized the geography of the United States and world regional geography.

By the 1920s, the dominance of history and geography was challenged by other curricular approaches in the social studies. Since social studies were regarded as instruments of building citizenship, civics and American problems courses were introduced that focused on political, economic, and social issues. These courses included materials from political science, economics, and social psychology as well as history and geography. At times, the interdisciplinary approach was referred to as "social education." As new programs evolved, the traditional courses that relied solely on history and geography began to decline.

After World War II, the social studies became still more interdisciplinary. Concepts, materials, and strategies from political science, economics, sociology, social psychology, anthropology, and law have been incorporated into the curriculum. In addition, more attention has also been given to international, mul-

[5]For a recent effort to define the social studies, see Robert D. Barr, James L. Barth, and S. Samuel Shermis, *Defining the Social Studies* (Arlington, Va.: National Council for the Social Studies, 1977).

ticultural, minority, ethnic, black, and Hispanic studies. The scope of the social studies has also broadened from an emphasis on American and Western societies to include Asian, African, and Latin American cultures as well. Since the post-Watergate period, some educators have called on social studies educators to stimulate a renewal of civic education and values. A long-standing controversy in social studies education has been the degree to which this area should reflect social values or seek to change or reconstruct these values.

Although the scope and sequence of the social studies curriculum varies greatly across the nation's school systems, the following outline represents some of the topics and units that might be found in the social studies curriculum.

Elementary School Social Studies Curriculum
(typically grades kindergarten through six)

At the elementary level, there is a great variation from school district to school district and from state to state in social studies curriculum. The curriculum is highly undifferentiated and includes materials from a number of the social sciences. The general focusing themes found in many elementary social studies programs are the following: From history, what has been the human past? From anthropology, how did human beings become what they are? From economics, how do people earn a living? From sociology, how do people relate to each other? From psychology, why do people behave as they do? From political science, how are people governed? From geography, how do people interact and live in their environment? In answering such thematic questions, elementary social studies programs often include such units or topics as

> Family life
> Home and school
> Neighborhood and community
> Community workers and services
> Concepts of culture, social organization, and social processes
> Environment, society, and economics
> Political organization and processes
> The American political system: local, state, and federal governments
> American history
> Technology and modernization
> Rural and urban life
> People of other countries

Junior High School Social Studies Curriculum
(typically grades seven and eight;
a middle school may also include grade six)

Although the social studies curriculum is transitional at the junior high school to the elementary and high school, it varies greatly in terms of sequence from school district to school district and from state to state. No definite pattern emerges. The following kinds of courses may be found at the junior high level:

Social studies: a continuation of themes from the elementary school
World geography: an introduction
United States history
Regional studies: such as Latin America, Asia, Europe, Africa
State and local history: may be required in certain states

High School Social Studies Curriculum
(typically grades nine, ten, eleven, and twelve)

As is usual at the high school level, the curriculum in social studies becomes more differentiated into specific subjects. Most schools require from one to three courses in social studies, one of which must be in American history. The most frequently offered courses are American history, American government, and economics. A recent trend has been to increase the number of elective courses and also to create a wide range of "minicourses." Among the courses offered in social studies at the secondary level are

American history
World history
Modern history
Ancient and medieval history
Civics
World Geography
Economics
American government
Problems of democracy
Sociology
Psychology
State and local history: may be required in certain states
International relations
Anthropology
Current events
Ethnic history
Black studies
Hispanic studies
Personal development: may incorporate career choices and drug abuse, alcohol abuse, and other state-mandated units

FOREIGN LANGUAGE

Historically, foreign language instruction has occupied a prominent place in the curriculum, especially in secondary and higher education. Until the end of the nineteenth century, knowledge of the classical languages of Latin and Greek was required for admission to many colleges. The curricula of the Latin Grammar schools of the eighteenth century, the academies of the nineteenth century, and the high schools of the early twentieth century emphasized Latin as both a college-entry requirement and as an area of general culture. By the end of the nineteenth century, modern foreign languages, such as French, Spanish, and German, were admitted to the secondary school curriculum. Correspondingly, Greek virtually disappeared. Although it lost its dominating position, Latin continues as a subject in the foreign language curriculum. Today, many high schools offer instruction in such languages as Latin, French, Spanish, Russian, and Italian.

The presence of certain foreign languages in the curriculum has been based, to some degree, on the ethnic composition of the communities served by the school. In several instances, bilingual programs existed in German and English in the St. Louis and Milwaukee school systems. Today the largest bilingual programs are in Spanish and English. These programs are found in areas of the country that have large Spanish-speaking populations, such as the western and southwestern states and the urban centers. While the Spanish-English programs are most evident, it is also possible to find programs in Polish, Greek, Czech, and others.

Although foreign language instruction has been found traditionally in secondary and higher education, there have been efforts periodically to introduce it to the elementary school. The American tendency to reserve foreign language instruction to secondary education contrasts sharply to that of other countries, particularly those of Europe, where it begins much earlier. In the late 1950s and early 1960s, concerted efforts were encouraged by the federal government to introduce foreign language instruction into the elementary school curriculum. A study group of the Modern Language Association known as FLES (Foreign Languages in Elementary School), which led the movement, argued that younger children have fewer inhibitions in learning and using a foreign language than do older students and adults. Also, an early beginning would facilitate more sustained study in a given language. In the 1960s, there was an increase in foreign language study in elementary schools among children without a second language. Instruction was given in languages such as Spanish, French, German, Russian, Italian, and Latin. Throughout the 1970s, however, the trend to foreign language study in elementary school was reversed dramatically. Because of financial retrenchment and a declining interest among the public, many of these programs were eliminated. An exception to this general trend has been in bilingual programs, where Spanish is the first language of many children. In some schools, with a large bilingual population, English may actually be taught as a second, or foreign, language.

In contrast to other countries, American efforts in foreign language instruction have been rather weak and sporadic. At several crucial periods in the country's history, it was recognized that American competency in foreign languages was sadly deficient. This weakness has become more and more apparent as the United States assumed a greater international involvement. The NDEA programs of the late 1950s and early 1960s attempted to improve the state of foreign language instruction in the United States.

Despite the general recognition that foreign language instruction needs to be improved, the emphasis in this area has actually decreased. Today, the vast majority of colleges no longer require units in foreign language for admission. This trend has caused a severe decline in enrollments in foreign languages courses at the high school level.

Although the number of students studying foreign languages in secondary and higher education has decreased, the quality of instruction has generally improved in recent years. The stress on grammar that often dominated foreign language instruction in the past has yielded to more informal methods that maximize conversational skills. Multimedia instruction, including the use of sophisticated language laboratories, is also more common. Some high schools also include opportunities for field study in a foreign country to provide immersion of the student in the language. Many colleges maintain overseas centers where students can live in a foreign country, assimilate the culture, and use the language that they are studying. It is hoped that we will see a greater awareness of the need for more American involvement in foreign language study.

Based upon these trends, the following outline identifies the pattern of foreign language instruction in American elementary, junior high, and high schools.

Elementary and Junior High School Foreign Language Curriculum
(typically grades kindergarten to eight)

Since foreign language instruction is not common to many elementary schools, it is included here with the junior high and middle school. In some instances, instruction may be found at the kindergarten through eighth grade level in the following languages:

Spanish
French
German
Russian
Italian
Others

High School Foreign Language Curriculum
(typically grades nine, ten, eleven, and twelve)

In American high schools, the leading foreign language courses traditionally have been Latin, French, and Spanish. Latin, however, has declined steadily in favor of modern foreign languages. Although some high schools offer a four-year course sequence, the usual pattern for students is to study a foreign language for two years. Among the languages that may be offered are

Latin
Spanish
French
German
Russian

Chinese
Japanese
Hebrew
Arabic
Portuguese
Swedish
Greek
Polish
Norwegian
Italian
Czech
African languages
American-Indian languages (in some western states)

PHYSICAL EDUCATION AND HEALTH

Since the early nineteenth century common school movement, American schools have given attention to health and physical education. In the modern elementary school, physical education programs have the general goals of

1. Promoting proper growth and development with physical activity.
2. Developing physical skills and coordination for work and leisure.
3. Developing the proper attitudes between play, exercise, recreation, and relaxation.
4. Improving balance, rhythm, and posture.
5. Providing opportunities for participation in various activities and sports.

In some small elementary schools, the regular teacher of the self-contained classroom may be responsible for the physical education and health program. The general trend in most districts, however, is to employ specialist teachers who are responsible for instruction in this area.

Since the objectives and activities of the physical education program are so diverse, a selective listing serves to illustrate the scope and sequence in this curricular area: understanding instructions and rules of simple games; appreciating the need for group success and teamwork; learning to take turns; developing an improved sense of balance, basic physical movements, and coordination; developing rhythmical patterns in running, walking, skipping, and hopping; learning to accept both defeat and victory; developing self-control to overcome awkwardness and self-consciousness; and learning that guided practice improves performance. Activities undertaken to achieve these objectives include games, folk dancing, square dancing, ballroom dancing, tumbling, track and field events, softball, basketball, volleyball, soccer, tennis, swimming, badminton, football, and calisthenics.

While many of the skills and attitudes that are introduced at the elementary level are developed and refined further at the secondary level, individual and team sports become more diverse. Activities such as dancing, golf, tennis, skiing, swimming, boating, bowling, yoga, and bait and fly casting may be offered as well as the conventional team sports of field and track, basketball, football, baseball, and soccer. The enrichment of the physical education curriculum seeks to develop interest and skills in recreational and leisure activities that will continue throughout life rather than be limited to the school years. The major goal is that of preparing individuals who will be interested in maximizing their recreational and physical fitness potentialities.

Often closely related to the formal curriculum in physical education are the co- or extracurricular interscholastic athletics and sports. It is a long-standing tradition in American education that the football, baseball, and basketball teams are often focal points for school pride and morale.

A recent development has been the efforts to provide equal opportunity and service to both boys and girls in the physical education curriculum. Title IX of the Education Amendments of 1972 prohibits discrimination on the basis of sex in schools and colleges. Schools and colleges are to provide instructors and equipment for female teams. As a result of the impetus of Title IX, co-educational physical education classes are common in many schools.

Health education is often related to the physical education curriculum. The scope of health education includes physical fitness, nature of disease, aware-

Contemporary instruction in physical education is coeducational and is designed to promote health, physical development, and recreational skills. *(Ken Karp)*

ness of environmental hazards, prevention of accidents, safety, first aid, knowledge of community health services, recreation, mental health, sex education, and an understanding of the health risks that may result from the use of tobacco, alcohol, drugs, and narcotics. Driver education is also often included in the secondary school health and physical education curriculum. The outline that follows is intended to illustrate the physical education and health curriculum.

Elementary School Physical Education and Health Curriculum
(typically grades kindergarten through six)

In the elementary school, physical education and health programs often include the following:

Games
Rhythm and coordination activities
Balancing, running, skipping, and hopping
Dancing
Calisthenics
Sports
Safety and accident prevention
Health and diet

Junior High and High School Physical Education and Health Curriculum
(typically grades seven through twelve;
a middle school may also include grade six)

Many of the physical education activities and individual and team sports that are begun in the junior high school are continued through the high school. Among these activities and health education units are

Physical Education
Dancing: square, folk, ballroom, and disco
Track and field events
Softball, baseball, basketball, and football
Volleyball
Soccer
Tennis
Swimming
Badminton
Camping
Golf
Bait and fly casting

Health Education
Nutrition
Dental care

Sex education
Drug and alcohol abuse education
First aid
Safety and Accident prevention
General health and health services

Driver Education

HOME ARTS

The home arts curriculum, also called home economics or domestic science, is generally offered at the junior high or secondary school level as either a required or an elective course. Although some educational experiences relating to home arts occur in the elementary school, most of the structured courses and more organized learning takes place in secondary schools. At the end of the nineteenth and beginning of the twentieth century, home arts—then termed domestic science—were designed exclusively to prepare girls to be homemakers. The early domestic science courses stressed household management, cooking, sewing, and child care. The Smith–Hughes Act of 1917, which provided federal funds on a matching basis to the states, stimulated the concerted entry of home economics courses in the high schools. Contemporary home arts programs assist both boys and girls in understanding and solving the problems of personal, social, and family life. Although the units treated vary from program to program, home arts courses typically include

Clothing design, sewing, and textiles
Food preparation and serving
Career choice and planning
Home and family management
Preparation for marriage
Housing and interior decoration and design
Social and community relations
Child development and care
Consumer economics
Clothing selection and grooming
Personal and family income management
Time management

INDUSTRIAL, VOCATIONAL, AND TECHNICAL EDUCATION

The contemporary curriculum in industrial, vocational, and technical education evolved from the manual training programs of the early twentieth century. When apprenticeship training failed to keep pace with the needs of an increasingly industrialized society, manual and industrial training programs were introduced.

The contemporary industrial arts curriculum provides coeducational activities for boys and girls. *(Ken Karp)*

In 1917, the federally enacted Smith–Hughes Act aided the growth of vocational education by providing matching funds to the states for such programs.

The contemporary industrial arts curriculum emphasizes the processes of industrial design and creation as well as the end product. Among the objectives of the modern industrial arts curriculum are the following:

1. To develop an understanding and appreciation of the role of industry and technology in modern society.
2. To develop safety techniques in using machines, equipment, and materials.
3. To develop an understanding of the application of mathematics and science to industrial and technological processes.
4. To develop a sense of appreciation and pride for design, craftsmanship, and workmanship.
5. To develop planning skills to understand and cope with industrial and technological change.

The scope of industrial and vocational education curricula varies from school system to school system. One can find conventional courses in printing, woodworking, metalworking, and clerical-secretarial skills. In addition, some schools provide training in cosmetology, television repair, automobile maintenance, and the operation of sophisticated business machines. In recent years, there have been demands that high schools should provide training in salable skills to enable graduates to compete successfully in the job market.

Although they deal with related subject matter, important distinctions generally exist between the junior high school industrial arts curriculum and vocational and industrial education at the high school level. In the junior high school, grades seven and eight, industrial arts education is intended to be an exploratory introduction to industrial courses. Of a general nature, programs in industrial education in junior high schools are nonvocational in that they do not provide specific career training.

Junior High School Industrial Arts Curriculum
(grades seven and eight)

The junior high school industrial arts curriculum provides a general introduction to industry and technology rather than specific vocational training. General areas included in industrial education at this level are introductory shopwork, mechanical drawing and drafting, graphic arts and printing, handicrafts, and an introduction to careers. The following listing of units indicates the curricular possibilities at the junior high school level:

> Drafting procedures and equipment
> Organization of manufacturing industries
> Introduction to manufacturing careers
> Use of hand and power tools
> Introduction to the construction industry
> Introduction to transportation
> Power and energy resources
> Engines, turbines, rockets
> Electricity
> Electronics
> Leather, jewelry, metal, ceramics, textiles, wood, weaving

High School Vocational and Industrial Education Curriculum
(grades nine, ten, eleven, and twelve)

At the high school, vocational and industrial education is intended primarily for specific career preparation, but it may also provide experiences that are introductory to the general area of vocational and industrial careers. Despite the usual curricular variations characteristic of American schools, the following broad areas can be found in the vocational programs at the secondary level:

> Clerical, secretarial, and business office preparation
> Technical education
> Agricultural education: animal husbandry, forestry, gardening, horticulture, landscaping
> Allied health education

Trade and industrial education: air conditioning, auto mechanics, brick-laying, cabinetmaking, carpentry, drafting, electricity, food trades, machine shop, printing, sheetmetal, welding

Distributive education: marketing, sales promotion, advertising

The problems of industrial and vocational education have grown with the increasing complexity of American technological society. The modernization process has caused greater specialization; it is difficult for schools to provide sufficient specialized training to keep pace with technological change. The shops, equipment, and laboratories needed for industrial education are expensive and become outdated quickly. To offset the obsolescence of equipment, many schools are making a greater use of business, industry, and community facilities to provide practical work experience and on-the-job training for students.

In 1975, a major impetus was given to career education when the U.S. Office of Education established a Center for Career Education. The rationale for career education emphasizes that schools should (1) identify the various careers and provide students with information about career preparation and entry and (2) develop comprehensive career development programs that include work observation, work experience, and skill development. Career education, while related to vocational and industrial education, is generally seen as a broad and integrated program in career preparation rather than a specialized vocational course.

HUMANITIES, ARTS, AND MUSIC

In elementary and secondary schools, humanities education generally has emphasized art and music. In recent years, the conception of humanities education has grown, however, to include a wide variety of plastic, dramatic, and graphic art forms. There has been a greater recognition that a broadly conceived conception of art education will enable students to realize their creative potentialities. Stated most generally, humanities education seeks to (1) cultivate a sense of appreciation for the various art forms so that students can enjoy them and (2) develop skills in the various art forms so that students can, themselves, create works of art. To examine humanities or aesthetic education, we focus on music, art, and other related art forms.

Music Education

Since the time of the ancient Greeks, music has been an integral part of the curriculum. Today, it is an important means of enjoyment, appreciation, and communication. As a part of general education, it is important that all students enjoy worthwhile experiences in music and be provided with opportunities to develop skills for musical expression. In school settings, the curriculum should introduce students to their musical heritage and also provide the means for artistic expression through vocal and instrumental music. Among the general objectives of music education are (1) introducing students to a range of music that enables them to appreciate the role of this art form in human culture; (2) providing musical activities, such as the development of vocal and instrumental skills, that correspond to the stages of human growth and development; and (3) developing sensitivity in singing, playing, and listening.

Music education is a recognized component of elementary and secondary schooling. At the primary and intermediate levels, music instruction is the responsibility of the classroom teacher or special teacher. From the junior high school years upward, music instruction becomes the responsibility of special teachers of music, who are often located in music or fine arts departments.

The following sample of units in music is intended to illustrate the scope and sequence of the elementary school music curriculum: recognition of basic types of music; recognition of the direction of melodic movements; awareness of rhythm, harmony, and tone patterns; singing songs of different types; clapping or playing simple instruments; developing meaning and sensitivity for music concepts such as melody, rhythm, harmony, form, and dynamics; becoming aware of basic differences and similarities in various musical styles; becoming familiar with a variety of musical compositions such as symphonies, operas, and ballets; having a familiarity with folk dances.

Music education in the junior and senior high school often relates the curricular to the co- or extracurricular. Students may participate in musical and vocal groups, choruses and glee clubs, marching bands, jazz bands, and orchestras. Contemporary trends in music education emphasize techniques that encourage students to play compositions early in their study. This approach avoids many of the often tedious exercises that discourage students from continuing with music. There is also a greater emphasis on creativity that encourages students to write and perform their own musical compositions.

Art Education

As with music education, the fine arts curriculum is designed to encourage both aesthetic appreciation and creativity. It introduces learners to the role of art as a means of human expression in the cultural heritage and also encourages students to express themselves creatively in art forms and objects. Among the general objectives embodied in the art curriculum are (1) to provide opportunities that encourage students to think, feel, and act creatively with art forms and materials and (2) to introduce students to the art works of the past and present to cultivate aesthetic sensitivity and appreciation. The traditional concepts and media of the fine arts have broadened from the conventional coloring and water and oil painting to include sculpture, ceramics, plastics, carving, block and silk-screen printing, and photography.

The following list of topics serves to illustrate the scope and sequence of the art curriculum: noting details and distinguishing relationships pictorially; using tempera paint, crayon, chalk, and pencils; using and arranging shapes imaginatively; combining threads, yarns, and fibers; using clay to explore texture and shapes; developing construction, cutting, and pasting skills; making prints by cutting out designs from linoleum or vinyl tile; carving objects in wood or clay; portrait drawing; becoming familiar with and using the concepts of abstraction and realism; and painting from nature and still life.

Other Humanities and Arts

Although music and art continue to occupy a major position in the humanities and fine arts curriculum, some contemporary humanities programs extend beyond these two areas. Expressive dancing, ballet, and modern and folk dancing are also important forms of individual and group expression. Drama in its various forms should also have a place in the fine arts curriculum. Many high schools have courses in theater and film to provide opportunities for creative expression.

NEW CURRICULAR MOVEMENTS

In the preceding sections of this chapter, the major components of the conventional curriculum were identified and examined. The curriculum, however, is not a static body of skills and subjects. It is subject to forces of change. Some of these pressures for change come from forces that are internal to the school and others are stimulated by external social, economic, and political factors. In this section, some of the recent tendencies for curricular change are identified and examined.

Ethnic and Bilingual Education

Since the late 1960s, programs emphasizing the ethnic, racial, and linguistic diversity of the United States have been incorporated into the curriculum. Chapter 6 examined these developments in multicultural education. Multicultural education encourages students to develop an attitude of cultural pluralism that respects their own ethnic group as well as members of other ethnic groups.

The Bilingual Education Act of 1968 provided federal funds to aid local school districts in meeting the needs of students of limited English-speaking ability. Approximately three million children between the ages of three and eighteen are members of non-English-speaking families. Stimulated by either federal initiatives or responding to their own needs, most states have required bilingual programs. The U.S. Office of Education has estimated that federally assisted programs exist in forty-one states, serving 165,000 children in sixty-eight languages.

Bilingual education is usually defined as instruction that involves using two languages for part or all of the school day. The study of the history and culture associated with a student's mother tongue is also regarded as part of bilingual education. Although the definition of bilingual education is clear, there has been considerable controversy regarding the general objective of these programs. Some educators have argued that bilingual instruction should be transitional; that is, instruction in the student's mother tongue should be carried on to the point that the student can use English effectively. Others argue that bilingual education should maintain facility in the mother tongue and also provide for the learning of English.

Bilingual education programs exist in many languages, depending upon the language composition of the school population. They range from native

American-Indian languages to Chinese, Japanese, Greek, and Spanish. The largest group participating in bilingual programs are students whose mother tongue is Spanish. California and the southwestern states have traditionally had large Spanish-speaking populations, primarily Mexican American. The major urban areas also have large Hispanic communities, particularly Puerto Rican and Cuban.

In the 1960s and 1970s, the elementary and secondary school curriculum, as well as that of higher education, experienced the addition of units or courses relating to black and ethnic studies. Black studies, designed to correct the traditional neglect and stereotyping of the Afro-American experience, emphasized the antecedents of blacks in Africa and their contributions to the American experience. These programs gave black students a greater awareness into their cultural heritage and also introduced white students to the Afro-American experience.

Stimulated by a growing consciousness that the United States is a multicultural nation, Congress passed the Ethnic Heritage Studies Act in 1973, which provided funds for program development. New curriculum materials were prepared and disseminated that illustrated the traditions of ethnic groups in the United States. For example, curriculum materials were prepared that dealt with Polish Americans, Italian Americans, Chinese Americans, Mexican Americans, and other ethnic groups.

Environmental Education

Since the 1960s, there has been pronounced concern about the dangers of environmental pollution. This concern was stimulated by scientific research and a growing public awareness that the environment was being impacted by the misuse of natural resources and by the pollution of air and water. Not only was the quality of human life being harmed but species of certain plants and animals were threatened with extinction.

The general concern that was expressed for the protection and preservation of the natural environment led educators to develop courses and curriculum materials for environmental education. Although environmental education has received a new impetus since the 1960s, curriculum units have existed on conservation education since the early 1900s. Current environmental education programs generally are more comprehensive and multidisciplinary, however. In its broadest perspective, environmental education views the earth as an ecosphere, a total life system. The problems of environmental pollution are then regarded as global concerns that affect the whole planet and its inhabitants. Because of its nature, environmental education is interdisciplinary and draws its materials from the various physical, natural, life, and social sciences.

Although some school systems have developed specialized courses in environmental education, the general trend is to integrate environmental study into the established curriculum by means of units that can be incorporated into the natural and social sciences courses. In addition to classroom instruction, environmental education programs include learning through direct observation of the environment and by having students involved in field study projects that enable them to actually work in restoring or protecting the natural environment.

Sex Education

Sex education is a curricular area that is often subject to controversy since it relates to basic human drives and values that have personal, social, and moral significance. Sex education also is connected to the family and to the home.

The presence of sex education in the elementary and secondary school curriculum relates to social changes that have taken place in modern society. While it was once reserved to the family or the church, sex education is now regarded by many persons to be appropriate for the school. The increase in premarital pregnancies, venereal disease, and abortions among the teenaged population was a major factor that prompted the development of sex education programs.

Sex education is an interdisciplinary subject that involves the integration of materials from a number of academic disciplines such as biology, physiology, sociology, and medicine. In the elementary and secondary school curriculum, it can be taught as a separate subject, or it can be correlated with health education.

Since it includes materials that are not only physiological but also value laden, the curriculum in sex education should be planned carefully and involve cooperation between the school, the home, and community health agencies. It is particularly important that both teachers and communities are prepared for the introduction of sex education into the curriculum and that there is cooperation between all interested groups in developing the curriculum.

Drug Abuse Education

Since the 1960s, there has been a marked increase in the use of narcotics and habit-forming drugs among the American population. Abuse in drug use has been particularly pronounced among youth. The acute nature of the problem has led federal, state, and local government agencies to provide funds for drug education programs, the development of curricular materials, and the training of teachers.

As with many recent curricular innovations, drug abuse education is interdisciplinary, drawing materials from biological and social sciences. Drug abuse programs include units on the physical and psychological effects of drugs on persons; information on the legal aspects of drug use; and information on resources and agencies available to assist students with drug-related problems. As is true of sex education, drug abuse education is often controversial and requires close cooperation between teachers and community members such as pharmacists, physicians, social workers, lawyers, and scientists.

Drug abuse education programs were introduced first at the high school level but have been extended into the junior high and occasionally the elementary school. Since many drug abuse problems begin before adolescence, many educators believe that preteen students need information on drug abuse.

Other Recent Trends

In addition to bilingual, ethnic, environmental, sex, and drug abuse education programs, many other new programs have been prepared and seek a place in the curriculum. There are those who argue that consumer education deserves a place in the school, since young people, especially adolescents, are a major sector in the American economy. Since all Americans are consumers of goods and services, it is important to prepare them to have knowledge of the economy and of regulatory agencies.

It is also argued that moral education needs to have a definite curricular status. While all education is value laden, advocates of moral education believe it is necessary that students should be exposed to the strategies needed in making moral and ethical decisions. Value clarification exercises have been introduced in some schools in which ethical and moral dilemmas are presented to students who decide what action is needed to resolve the issue. The moral decision-making strategy is usually presented in an open-ended rather than closed framework so that students must recognize and clarify their own values. Proponents argue that value clarification enhances the moral sensitivity of students to their own value predicaments. Critics attack value clarification as contributing to a sense of moral relativism that is without clearly defined standards of behavior.

One of the major issues facing educators is to decide what can be added to the curriculum without jeopardizing the skills and subjects needed for a balanced education. An unfortunate tendency has been to add new subjects or materials without deleting others. As a result, the curriculum is often continually growing but unintegrated.

Co- and Extracurricular Activities

The preceding sections have examined the nature, organization, content, and issues of the formal curriculum. Now, we examine briefly the co- or extracurricular program. Teachers will often find that, although instruction in a formal area of the curriculum is their major responsibility, they also are involved in co- or extracurricular activities. The words co-curricular and extracurricular are often used interchangeably. Co-curricular means that the activity, although not part of the formal program of instruction, is related to and enhances it. Extracurricular refers to activities that may be sponsored by the school but are not required by it. The participation of students in co-curricular and extracurricular programs is usually voluntary. To simplify the discussion, the term co-curricular will be used.

In the United States, athletics and sports are prominent and popular co-curricular activities. Football, baseball, basketball, hockey, swimming, soccer, tennis, track and field, wrestling, and fencing are some of the co-curricular activities of an athletic nature that are found in most American high schools. These activities are related closely to physical education programs.

While music is part of the formal curriculum, it is also co-curricular in that schools sponsor and organize a wide variety of musical groups, such as glee clubs, choruses, bands, orchestras, and jazz and rock groups. These groups perform in programs in the school or community. Music is an area in which the curricular and co-curricular are mutually reinforcing.

Speech clubs and societies are also a popular form of co-curricular activity. Since the colonial period, debating societies have existed in American schools. In addition to debating, panel discussions, extemporaneous speaking, and orations, newer types of speech activities are radio broadcasting and telecasting. Drama clubs stage and present plays as school and community events. In preparing plays, dramatics clubs are responsible for preparing stage settings, costumes, lighting, advertising, and selling tickets.

Literary societies and journalism clubs represent co-curricular organizations that relate to the formal curriculum by providing opportunities for improving literary and writing skills. Student organizations often prepare and disseminate the school newspaper, yearbook, and literary magazine.

There are also various forms of student government. There are class officers, such as a class president, vice president, secretary, and treasurer, who conduct class meetings and plan social events. Most schools, especially high schools, have student governments, student councils, and student courts. Student governments often establish policies governing student organizations and conduct. Participation in student government provides students with experience in democratic processes and procedures.

In addition to the general kinds of extracurricular activities identified in the previous sections, there are student organizations that relate to a wide variety of interests and vocations. Representative organizations are the Future Teachers, Future Farmers, Four H, photography clubs, Student Education Association, various language clubs, and ethnic societies.

There are many reasons for schools to sponsor and encourage co-curricular activities and organizations. They may stimulate interests that are not satisfied by the formal curriculum or may reinforce and expand interests that are related to the formal curriculum. They provide occasions and experiences for developing friendships and social skills. They promote a sense of cooperation among students that often goes beyond that found in the classroom. Finally, the co-curricular dimension fulfills recreational and leisure needs that may grow into avocations in adult years.

The Teacher and the Curriculum

Now that we have examined the nature of the curriculum and of curriculum making, you may want to consider some direct curricular responsibilities that you may have as a teacher. As a teacher, you are responsible for implementing the curriculum guide or syllabus that has been adopted in your school district. Therefore, it is important that teachers be familiar with the general curriculum guide of the school district and also with those dealing specifically to the subject or grade level of immediate responsibility.

Teachers also serve on committees when particular subjects are being reviewed. Chapter 15 provides a detailed discussion of the teacher's role in the curriculum process as a member of the school system's professional staff. In brief, the general procedure for curriculum review is (1) when a particular curriculum area is being reviewed, the administrator responsible for curriculum appoints a staff committee to study and recommend additions, deletions, revisions, or general updating; (2) the committee prepares a statement of the philosophy, objectives, content, and evaluative procedures that will guide the review process; (3) the committee recommends the adoption of a particular curricular program and identifies the books and other instructional materials needed to implement it; (4) upon the recommendation of the superintendent, the particular curricular program is adapted by the board of education and implemented in the school system.

Curriculum revision and implementation involves important cost factors. What will it cost to purchase the textbooks, workbooks, films, tapes, and in-service training to implement or revise a curriculum? While it is a crucial factor in determining the educational quality in a given school district, curriculum revision is also expensive and time consuming. In most instances, curriculum development and adoption of materials is a responsibility of the local school district. In a few cases, such as that of Texas, state committees recommend statewide adoptions of textbooks. The state purchases large quantities of approved textbooks and stores them in book depositories. Local districts in these states receive the books from the state and, in turn, lend them to students.

The teachers and administrators who serve on curriculum committees then examine the textbooks and materials that are provided for review by publishers. Often, the curriculum materials are part of a series designed to maintain sequential continuity from grade to grade. The shaping of the curriculum is, then, also influenced heavily by the publishing companies, which are involved in preparing and marketing educational materials. It may also be necessary for curriculum committees and curriculum specialists to design and prepare their supplementary materials.

CONCLUSION

The process of curriculum making is long and involved but is crucial to the educational mission of the school. It involves theoretical questions of great cultural, intellectual, philosophical, and moral significance. It also requires a skilled plan and procedure for practical implementation. The professional educator needs to be both a skilled theoretician and practitioner in dealing with the curriculum of the schools.

DISCUSSION QUESTIONS

1. Examine recent curricular trends in language arts, mathematics, science, social studies, foreign language, physical education, home and industrial arts, vocational and technical education, art, and music.
2. Examine the impact of the theories of Americanization, the "melting pot," and cultural pluralism on American education.
3. Should bilingual education be used for purposes of maintenance or transition?
4. How has curriculum change resulted from attempts to solve major social and economic problems?
5. Examine the recent trend to include such interdisciplinary studies as environmental education, sex education, and drug abuse education in the curriculum. What social problems have led to this trend? Why are these new curriculum areas interdisciplinary rather than disciplinary?
6. Examine the relationship between curricular and co-curricular activities.

FIELD EXERCISES

1. Study the curricular organization of a particular elementary school and determine how articulation is achieved from grade level to grade level.
2. Interview an elementary and a secondary school principal. In each interview, attempt to determine how articulation is achieved between the higher and lower institutions.
3. Examine the curriculum guides and then observe classroom instruction in a particular school district or system in one of the following: language arts, mathematics, science, social studies, foreign languages, physical education, home and industrial arts, art, and music.
4. Interview a classroom teacher and through questioning attempt to discern how the curriculum in his or her area of specialization has changed.
5. Interview several high school students and attempt to discern the degree to which they participate in co-curricular activities. Give special attention to their motivations for participation and the relationships that they perceive existing between the curriculum and co-curricular activities.

SUGGESTED READINGS

AMERICAN PHARMACEUTICAL ASSOCIATION. *A Guide for the Professions: Drug Abuse Education.* New York: American Pharmaceutical Association, 1969.

BANKS, JAMES A. *Multiethnic Education: Theory and Practice.* Boston: Allyn & Bacon, 1981.

BANKS, JAMES A. *Teaching Ethnic Studies: Concepts and Strategies.* Washington, D.C.: National Council for the Social Studies, 1973.

BARR, ROBERT D., BARTH, JAMES L., AND SHERMIS, S. SAMUEL. *Defining the Social Studies.* Washington, D.C.: National Council for the Social Studies, 1977.

BEGLE, EDWARD G., ED. *Mathematics Education.* The Sixty-ninth Yearbook of the National Society for the Study of Education. Chicago: University of Chicago Press, 1970.

BIRD, THOMAS E., ED. *Foreign Language Learning: Research and Development.* New York: Modern Language Association, 1968.

BUFFIE, EDWARD G., WELCH, RONALD C., AND PAIGE, DONALD D. *Mathematics Strategies of Teaching.* Englewood Cliffs, N.J.: Prentice-Hall, 1968.

CHALL, JEANNE. *Learning to Read: The Great Debate.* New York: McGraw-Hill, 1968.

COLLIER, CALHOUN C., AND LERCH, HAROLD H. *Teaching Mathematics in the Modern Elementary School.* New York: Macmillan, 1969.

DONOGHUE, MILDRED R. *Foreign Languages and the Elementary School Child.* Dubuque, Iowa: W. C. Brown, 1968.

FENTON, EDWIN. *The New Social Studies.* New York: Holt, Rinehart and Winston, 1967.

GROBMAN, ARNOLD. *The Changing Classroom: The Role of the Biological Sciences Curriculum Study.* Garden City, N.Y.: Doubleday, 1969.

HOWES, VIRGIL M. *Individualizing Instruction in Science and Mathematics.* New York: Macmillan, 1970.

HUNTER, WILLIAM A., ED. *Multicultural Education Through Competency-Based Teacher Education.* Washington, D.C.: American Association of Colleges for Teacher Education, 1974.

JOHNSON, DONOVAN A., AND RAHTZ, ROBERT. *The New Mathematics in Our Schools.* New York: Macmillan, 1966.

JOYCE, WILLIAM W., OANA, ROBERT G., AND HOUSTON, W. ROBERT. *Elementary Education in the Seventies: Implications for Theory and Practice.* New York: Holt, Rinehart and Winston, 1970.

KRUG, MARK M. *History and the Social Sciences: New Approaches to the Teaching of Social Studies.* Waltham, Mass.: Blaisdell, 1967.

LARSON, LEONARD A. *Curriculum Foundations and Standards for Physical Education.* Englewood Cliffs, N.J.: Prentice-Hall, 1970.

LEE, EUGENE C. *New Dimensions in Science Teaching.* Belmont, Calif.: Wadsworth, 1967.

MOFFETT, JAMES. *A Student-Centered Language Arts Curriculum, Grades K–12: A Handbook for Teachers.* Boston: Houghton Mifflin, 1968.

NATIONAL COUNCIL OF TEACHERS OF MATHEMATICS. *The Continuing Revolution in Mathematics.* Washington, D.C.: National Council of Teachers of Mathematics, 1968.

NATIONAL SCIENCE TEACHERS ASSOCIATION CURRICULUM COMMITTEE. *Theory into Action in Science Curriculum Development.* Washington, D.C.: National Science Teachers Association, 1964.

SCHWAB, JOSEPH J., AND BRANDWEIN, PAUL F. *The Teaching of Science as Inquiry.* Cambridge, Mass.: Harvard University Press, 1966.

SHAVER, JAMES P., ED. *Building Rationales for Citizenship Education.* Arlington, Va.: National Council for the Social Studies, 1977.

TOFFLER, ALVIN, ED. *Learning for Tomorrow: The Role of the Future in Education.* New York: Random House, 1974.

U.S. ADVISORY COUNCIL ON VOCATIONAL EDUCATION. *Vocational Education: The Bridge Between Man and His Work.* Washington, D.C.: G.P.O., 1968.

18

The Education of Special Learners

In the 1970s, both the general public and professional educators directed greater attention to the educational needs of special learners. This new direction was stimulated by several national trends. The civil rights activism and judicial decisions of the 1960s to foster racial integration drew attention to the rights of people in other categories who had been denied equal educational opportunities. Among these groups were the handicapped.

In schools, the segregation of children on the basis of race and handicap was sometimes interrelated. Large numbers of children from minority groups were labeled as handicapped and were placed in isolated special schools and classes.

The medical and psychological professions had advanced further in studying physiological and behavioral problems; their discoveries were translated into educational practice. Persons especially interested in the problems of the handicapped, such as parents, guardians, and others, had organized strong advocacy groups to identify and promote educational opportunities for handicapped children.

It was in this context of greater attention being given to the rights of handicapped children that a U.S. district court decision in 1971 ordered Pennsylvania school districts to educate all retarded learners between the ages of four and twenty-one. The concept of the "right to education" was now expanded to include mentally and emotionally handicapped learners.

FEDERAL LEGISLATION

Congressional legislation complemented the action of the courts regarding the education of the handicapped, with two federal laws being especially relevant: the Vocational Rehabilitation Act of 1973 (PL 93-516) and the Education of All Handicapped Children Act of 1975 (PL 94-142). These laws had far-reaching implications for education at all levels.

The intention of federal legislation was to remove restrictions that prevented handicapped individuals from participating in the opportunities of American education. The Vocational Rehabilitation Act of 1973, especially Section 504, provided for (1) vocational training in mainstream settings, (2) the promotion and expansion of employment opportunities, and (3) the removal of architectural and transportation barriers. This legislation was designed specifically to encourage the entry of more handicapped persons into the job force and to eliminate unnecessary obstacles in their hiring and job performance.

In 1975, Congress enacted the Education of All Handicapped Children Act (PL 94-142). This law established a national policy that the nation's handicapped children (individuals between the ages of three and twenty-one) would be assured of a "fine, appropriate public education," designed to meet their unique needs. PL 94-142 has had far-reaching consequences in that it directly affects the approximately eight million handicapped children in the United States. The law defines handicapped children as

> mentally retarded, hard of hearing, seriously disturbed, orthopedically impaired, or children with specific learning disabilities, who by reason thereof require special education and related services.

The law, particularly its provisions for mainstreaming, affects virtually every child, teacher, and school in the United States. Indeed, the impact of PL 94-142 may equal or exceed that of the *Brown* case of 1954.

Since PL 94-142 has had such pervasive ramifications for American education, it is useful to identify its key provisions and requirements:

1. Each state is to identify and locate all its handicapped children and to provide a curriculum responsive to the needs of each child.
2. Each state is to establish an advisory board—composed of handicapped individuals, teachers, and parents of handicapped children—to advise and comment on needs, regulations, and evaluative procedure.
3. Handicapped children are to be mainstreamed, that is, educated whenever possible in the least restrictive environment, preferably a regular classroom, with nonhandicapped children. Handicapped children are to be placed in the more restrictive environment of special or separate classes only when their exceptionality makes it impossible to educate them in regular classrooms.

4. Due process provisions are to be observed to protect handicapped children against improper placement and to give their parents or guardians the right of access to pertinent records. According to due process provisions, parents or guardians have the right to participate in the placement of their children and to protest and appeal decisions by school officials.

5. School personnel are to prepare an individualized educational plan (IEP) for each handicapped child. The plan is to be developed by a support team that includes a school representative, usually the building principal, the teacher, and the child's parent or guardian. Whenever appropriate, the child is to be included. The plan, which is to reviewed and revised annually according to the child's growth and development, is to specify long- and short-term educational goals and needed services.

6. Instruments and methods used to test and evaluate handicapped children must be racially and culturally nondiscriminatory and must be in the child's primary language or "mode of communication." Also, no single test or evaluative procedure is to be used as the exclusive basis for determining a child's educational program.

7. Related transportation and developmental, corrective, and supportive services are to be provided to handicapped children. These include speech pathology, audiology, psychological seminars, physical and occupational therapy, recreation, and counseling and medical services needed for diagnosis and evaluative purposes.

8. If handicapped children cannot be educated with other children, then they must be educated in their homes, hospitals, or other institutions. The placement of children in private institutions is to be done at no cost to parents. Private school programs must meet the same standards the law requires of public school programs.

9. If states fail to comply with the law, federal funds can be withheld after a reasonable notice and hearing.

10. If local school districts are unable or unwilling to comply with the law, the state can suspend payments to them. The state must then use the funds to provide direct service to the children.

The federal legislation of the 1970s had a pronounced impact on American public education. It meant that regular classroom teaching had to be redesigned to meet the needs of handicapped learners. Not only did the new responsibility fall on teachers who were already in service, but it also fell on teacher education departments and colleges who needed to redesign many of their teacher preparation programs.[1] In the sections that follow, attention will be given to the concept of "mainstreaming" and to identifying the various categories of handicapped learners.

---

[1] *A Common Body of Practice for Teachers: The Challenge of Public Law 94-142 to Teacher Education* (Washington, D.C.: American Association of Colleges for Teacher Education, 1980), pp. 3–5.

SPECIAL EDUCATION
AND REGULAR EDUCATION

Before identifying and discussing the various classifications of exceptionality, it is useful to examine the relationships of special and regular education. First, it should be remembered that public schools were established and are supported to educate all American children. The general guidelines that relate to teaching and learning are applicable to all children. Those who decide to pursue careers in special education should be knowledgeable about the curriculum and methods of instruction that apply to schooling in general so that their work is integrated with the general institutional program. Second, it also should be remembered that each individual child has unique as well as general needs. Teachers, both regular and special, need to know and to be alert to the unique needs of individual boys and girls. Teachers who are sensitive to the economic, social, racial, and ethnic diversity of students will be better prepared to meet both their general and their specific needs. Multicultural education attempts to prepare teachers to recognize and deal with racial and ethnic differences. In much the same way, regular classroom teachers need to recognize the various kinds of physical, psychological, and emotional needs of children so that they can benefit from a public education. In other words, just as children should not be isolated because of race or handicap, neither should teachers work in educational isolation from each other—regardless of their specialization.

In examining the relationship between regular and special education, the term "exceptional children" is often used. The exceptional child has been defined as differing from the normal or average child in mental characteristics, sensory abilities, neuromuscular or physical characteristics, social or emotional behavior, communication abilities, or a combination of these characteristics and abilities so that a modification of regular school practices or special education services is required.[2] The degree of exceptionality determines the degree to which the individual child will be educated by regular classroom teachers or special education teachers. Mildly handicapped children, for example, are likely to have more contact with the regular classroom teacher than with the special education teacher; conversely, profoundly handicapped children are likely to have more contact with the special education teacher than with the regular classroom teacher. The majority of exceptional children, falling in the middle between the poles of mildly and profoundly handicapped, will have contact with both regular and special education teachers.

Now that the term "exceptional child" has been defined, it is possible to examine special education—the field of professional education designed to meet the educational needs of these children. Exceptional children, particularly the handicapped, have been educated by special education. Although gifted and highly talented academic achievers also are exceptional learners, much of their instruction has been done by regular teachers.

Special education refers to instruction that is designed specifically to meet the unique needs of handicapped children. Those responsible for designing and implementing this instruction are special educators who have been prepared

---

[2]Samuel A. Kirk, *Educating Exceptional Children* (Boston: Houghton Mifflin, 1972).

and certificated to carry out their specific functions in educating the handicapped. Special educators include teachers, counselors, teacher educators, and administrators such as special education directors who possess training and competencies for educating certain categories of exceptional children.

In addition to the professional personnel responsible for the education of exceptional children, the term "special education" also has relevance for curriculum, methodology, and materials. Some exceptional children may require a curriculum that differs in content from the regular curriculum; that is, deaf learners may require speechreading and blind learners may need braille. The instructor of certain categories of exceptional children may also require particular methods of instruction; for example, behavior modification techniques are often used with students who have severe learning disabilities. Exceptional children may also need instructional materials that are designed specifically to meet their needs. Among the instruments and materials that are available are braille and large-type books for the visually impaired and special typewriters for the physically handicapped.

SCHOOL PROGRAMS FOR EXCEPTIONAL CHILDREN

School programs for exceptional children (handicapped learners) generally consist of three major and related components: identification, evaluation, and remediation.[3]

Identification

The usual methods of identifying exceptional children are screening and teacher referrals. Many school districts conduct comprehensive preschool screening programs that seek an early identification of cognitive, motor, and communicative problems. Early in the school year, special education personnel may interview or observe children to identify those who have possible problems. Regular classroom teachers, in daily contact with children, are able to observe and assess the child's behavior in various social and academic situations. Of course, obvious and known disabilities are referred to school personnel by parents and physicians.

Evaluation

Interdisciplinary teams that include psychologists, special educators, medical personnel, administrators, social workers, and classroom teachers help in the process of evaluation. The major purpose of evaluation is to compile information about the child that can be used to develop remedial plans and IEPs. Comprehensive evaluations require the collection and coordination of data obtained through (1) the child's case history, (2) specialized standardized tests and procedures, and (3) the observation of the child's behavior.

[3]This discussion is adapted from Gerald G. Freeman, *Speech and Language Services and the Classroom Teacher* (Reston, Va.: Council for Exceptional Children, 1977), pp. 25–48.

Remediation

Specific strategies designed to modify behavior and improve performance will vary with the nature and degree of the handicap or disability. A general program of remediation is likely to involve (1) establishing a success level for the child in terms of specific skills or learning, (2) identifying target behaviors for modification, (3) outlining plans to develop the recommended behavior or learning, (4) implementing the plans, and (5) revising the plans to meet the child's changing needs as development and learning take place.

Educators of exceptional children have tended to use behavior modification or management as an instructional strategy. Since behavior modification tends to focus on specific skills and behaviors, general goals are broken down or are reduced to specific learning. The careful working out of sequence is important so that the learning of a skill grows out of one learned previously and leads to one that is slightly more complex and cumulative. The following techniques of behavioral management are often used in remediation and in teaching handicapped children: (1) identifying the desired behavior, (2) isolating of the behavior, (3) mastering the isolated behavior, (4) transferring the skill to the classroom setting, and (5) fixing or stabilizing the use of the skill in a variety of life situations.

The remediation of disabilities caused by handicaps requires an interdisciplinary team approach. Such a team may include medical personnel, special educators, learning specialists, psychologists, social workers, administrators, parents, and the classroom teacher. The effective interdisciplinary team should (1) coordinate their roles, responsibilities, and functions; (2) integrate the competencies of each member into a remedial program; and (3) relate the child's needs to the educator who is best able to satisfy them.

MAINSTREAMING

It will be recalled that PL 94-142 required that handicapped children be educated in the least restrictive environment and that each handicapped child have an individualized education plan, or IEP, prepared by a support team that includes regular and special educators as well as other professionals. Although regular and special educators need to cooperate throughout the entire process of schooling, it has been "mainstreaming"—the integration of handicapped learners—into the regular classroom that has made such cooperation imperative.

In describing mainstreaming, Maynard C. Reynolds says that

> mainstreaming is based on the principle of educating most children in the same classrooms and providing special education on the basis of learning needs rather than categories of handicaps. Thus, under mainstreaming, children with learning problems can receive the expert help of special education teachers without being labeled or excluded from association with their peers. Furthermore, under mainstreaming conditions, regular and special classroom teachers share their skills and knowledge to teach the same children. Indeed, mainstreaming is distin-

guished by the amalgamation of regular and special education into one system to provide a spectrum of services for all children according to their learning needs. Consequently, special education is a resource for the entire school population rather than an isolated body of skills and knowledge.[4]

In some respects, mainstreaming is not a new concept. Prior to the professional development of special education, handicapped children were often included in the regular classrooms in the nineteenth and early twentieth centuries. Unfortunately, these children, who usually received no special attention, were classified as "problem children" or "dullards" by teachers who lacked sufficient expertise. As special education developed in the twentieth century, many children with handicaps were identified and placed in special classes or institutions that isolated them from students and experiences in regular classrooms. Although they received a "special education" in these special environments, they were segregated because of their exceptionality. By the 1950s and 1960s, several serious questions were raised about the isolation of exceptional children in special classrooms. (1) If a handicapped child is given a special education in a socially and educationally segregated environment, does that situation provide for equality of educational opportunity? (2) Does not the isolation of the handicapped foster many of the same social attitudes that racial segregation promotes? By the 1970s, "mainstreaming" was promoted to provide for the education of the handicapped children in regular classrooms to avoid not only social and educational isolation but also to meet the child's special needs.[5]

In addition to the legal mandate for mainstreaming, social and educational developments have also contributed to the development of the concept. Jack Birch, an early advocate and expert in mainstreaming, has identified the major social and educational reasons that support the concept of mainstreaming:

1. The improvement of the capability to deliver special education services to exceptional children in regular classrooms.

2. Parental demands that exceptional children be provided high-quality special education in regular classrooms.

3. The general public and professional rejection of the notion that children needing special education should be socially and educationally isolated because of labeling. Mainstreaming minimizes the need for labeling and eliminates many of its undesirable effects on children.

4. The legal recognition that the courts have given to the right of all children to have a full and free education regardless of handicap.

5. Historically, psychological tests of intelligence and achievement were major determinants in identifying children for special education classes

---

[4]Maynard C. Reynolds, "Foreword," in Jack W. Birch, *Mainstreaming: Educable Mentally Retarded Children in Regular Classes* (Reston, Va.: Council for Exceptional Children, 1974), p. iii.

[5]John G. Herlihy and Myra T. Herlihy, "Why Mainstreaming?" in *Mainstreaming in the Social Studies* (Washington, D.C.: National Council for the Social Studies, 1980), pp. 2–7.

In the "mainstreamed" classroom, both handicapped and nonhandicapped children learn in the least restrictive environment. *(United Nations/W.A. Graham)*

and special schools. Today, spokespersons for minority children have challenged the application and appropriateness of such tests in placing children in special educational arrangements.

6. A general recognition that nonhandicapped children are deprived of important educational experiences if they do not associate with handicapped children.

7. The compatibility of the concept of mainstreaming with the American belief in equality of educational opportunity for all children.[6]

Mainstreaming Procedures

Since most teachers will be involved in mainstreaming, the following general procedures can help to understand and implement the process:

[6]Jack W. Birch, *Mainstreaming: Educable Mentally Retarded Children in Regular Classes* (Reston, Va.: Council for Exceptional Children, 1974), pp. 2–7.

1. Mainstreaming can be done at any grade level.
2. Handicapped students should be selected for mainstreaming in terms of their educational needs and capabilities rather than on the basis of clinical categories or diagnostic labels such as mentally handicapped, learning disabled, hearing or sight impaired, or physically handicapped.
3. Exceptional (handicapped) children are assigned to regular classes, and special educational services are provided for them while they remain in the regular classroom for as much of the day as possible; mainstreamed handicapped students leave the regular classroom only for essential small-group or individual special instruction or assessment.
4. Regular and special education teachers and educational administrators and supervisors need to cooperate in educational planning and pro-gramming so that handicapped children—as well as nonhandicapped children—can benefit academically and socially from participation in the regular classroom. It will be necessary to clarify the responsibility of each professional who is involved in the mainstreamed educative process.
5. Regular and special education teachers work together to plan individual schedules and assignments needed by handicapped students; the regular classroom teacher or subject matter teacher is responsible for the grading and reporting of handicapped children in consultation with the special education teachers.
6. Mainstreaming needs should be considered by school boards, educational cooperatives, and administrators in planning and organizing instruction, allocating space, providing materials, and designing facilities.

Individual Education Program

While Public 94-142 mandates the mainstreaming of most handicapped children into the regular classroom, it also requires that their instruction be individualized. The law requires that an individual education program, the IEP, be prepared at least annually for each child by a support staff or committee composed of regular and special teachers, administrators, ancillary professional personnel, and the child's parents or guardian. Directly stated, an IEP is "a written statement about the objectives, content, implementation and evaluation of a child's educational program."[7]

In its most general terms, an IEP includes such information as, What is to be taught to the child? Who is to do the teaching? How is the material to be taught? How will the effectiveness of the child's instructional program be evaluated? More specifically, an IEP involves[8]

1. A *description and analysis of the student's educational status*, which includes formal and standardized test data, informal school reports, physical and

[7]Maynard C. Reynolds and Jack W. Birch, *Teaching Exceptional Children in All America's Schools* (Reston, Va.: Council for Exceptional Children, 1977), p. 157.

[8]This description of an IEP is based on John C. Herlihy and Myra T. Herlihy, "The IEP—Individualization of an Institution," in *Mainstreaming in the Social Studies* (Washington, D.C.: National Council for the Social Studies, 1980), pp. 23–25.

medical data, and other related information. From this information, a status report is compiled in performance terms that identify the child's academic, physical, and psychological strengths and weaknesses. The status report is used to identify needs so that appropriate instructional strategies can be devised.

2. A *statement of annual goals,* which are behavioral outcomes that reflect the skills and content of the grade level or subject matter.

3. A *statement of instructional objectives,* which describes the particular schedule and process for achieving the stated annual goals. The objectives may relate to skills, content, or remediation of the handicapping condition. The instructional objectives are derived from the statement of annual goals and represent short-term and specific ways of achieving them.

4. A *statement of instructional and service requirements,* which describes the various support services and professional personnel needed to educate the handicapped child. This may involve the special education teacher and the use of special equipment and facilities.

5. A statement indicating the *degree, time, and nature of the mainstreaming and support service,* which specifies the time that the handicapped child will require special education services.

6. An *evaluation,* which is used to measure the student's success in achieving stated program goals. The evaluation should be formative so that it can contribute to needed modifications of instruction designed to achieve goals more effectively.

7. *Due process* is interwoven into the design and execution of the IEP. Students and their parents have the right to review and to monitor the IEP. They also have the right to legal action if they believe that the system is failing to achieve stated goals. School administrators and teachers also have the right to due process.

The IEP represents a new effort to seek a solution to an old educational problem. How can teachers provide for the child's individual needs and differences in a group institutional setting? On the one hand, the homogeneous group that is comprised of students of the same abilities, achievement levels, or interests is often an effective and efficient vehicle for institutions. The group is also an agency for socialization as well as specific academic learning. While group instruction has these advantages, it often sacrifices individual needs for the good of the majority. Individualized instruction—long a goal of many educators—provides for the unique needs of each child. Unfortunately, it may isolate children from the social relationships and developments that they need. The IEP is designed to satisfy both the individual and social needs of the exceptional learner.

As an essentially cooperative educational effort, mainstreaming requires the participation of school administrators, regular classroom teachers, and the special education staff. Its central theme is that regular classroom teachers can educate exceptional children in the regular classroom with the support and consultative services of special education personnel. Mainstreaming requires partnership on the part of all teachers—both regular and special—in educating all children.

TOWARD A TERMINOLOGY OF EXCEPTIONALITY

Experts in the field of special education have developed a terminology to identify and define the various categories of exceptionality. Since special education has been a rapidly developing field, its expanding terminology has been subject to frequent redefinition and change. The terminology that has been devised is designed to describe more accurately and precisely the various forms of exceptionality. In using the terminology that follows, be aware that changes and further definition are likely.

Learning Disabilities

Although the term "learning disabled" (LD) is used frequently in the language of special education, its definition is subject to considerable controversy. Historically, the term was used to identify learners with perceptual disorders that were caused by neurological impairment. Today, it is used to refer to a wide range of learning deficits or disabilities. In PL 94-142, a "specific learning disability" refers to

> a disorder in one or more of the basic psychological processes involved in understanding or using language spoken or written, which may manifest itself in an imperfect ability to listen, think, speak, read, write, spell or to do mathematical calculations.

According to the law, the term learning disability includes perceptual handicaps, brain injury, minimal brain dysfunction, dyslexia, and developmental aphasia. It excludes learning problems resulting primarily from visual, hearing, or motor handicaps, of mental retardation, or of environmental, cultural, or economic disadvantages.

It is very important to distinguish between learners who are neurologically handicapped and those who are mentally retarded. The learner with a neurological handicap may be intellectually capable of normal academic progress; the mentally retarded is not. Thus, it is imperative that neurologically impaired students be diagnosed correctly so that they receive an appropriate education.

The general term "neurologically handicapped" refers to persons with an impairment of the central nervous system. This impairment can be congenital or be caused by accident; it may be mild or severe. Among the causes of neurological dysfunction are injury to the fetus, injury or oxygen deprivation during pregnancy or birth, malnutrition, chemical or blood irregularities, genetic aberration, and illness of the mother during pregnancy. Often, the symptoms of neurological handicap may not become apparent until the child enters school. It is important that the regular classroom teacher be alert to the following symptoms of neurological impairment:

1. erratic performance in schoolwork
2. easy distractibility
3. swift changes in mood
4. clumsy psychomotor skills
5. ineptness in play activities

Mental Retardation

The term "mental retardation" describes significantly below-average intellectual functioning that ranges from mild to profound. Mental retardation may result from such causes as German measles during pregnancy, poor prenatal or postnatal care, oxygen deprivation at birth, physical injury, or genetic-chromosomal disorder. Mental retardation is a permanent condition that adversely impacts a learner's cognitive abilities such as association, comparison, comprehension, generalization, and symbolization. Among the general learning problems of the retarded child are

1. a limited vocabulary and reading ability that impedes learning in other basic subjects
2. short attention span and limited retention
3. difficulty in learning from experience
4. less capability for making social adjustments

Retarded learners can be aided by proper diagnosis and appropriate instruction that often involves behavior modification and programmed instruction. Behavior modification is based on the strategy that rewards will reinforce desirable behaviors and that the failure to reward undesirable behaviors will reduce them. Programmed instruction in which lessons are reduced to small, sequential steps is also used with retarded as well as other learners. The general educational goal is to assist retarded learners to develop adaptive behaviors that will make them as self-sufficient as possible.

There are three general categories of mentally retarded persons: educable mentally retarded (EMR), with IQs of between 50 and 75; trainable mentally retarded (TMR), with IQs below 50 who are capable of learning some academic skills; and custodial, with IQs below 30 who are capable of only the rudimentary learning of nonacademic skills. The Children's Bureau has estimated that thirty out of every one thousand persons are retarded. Of these thirty, it is estimated that twenty-five are educable, four are trainable, and one is custodial.

Educable mentally retarded children are capable of learning academic skills but with limited facility. They are increasingly being mainstreamed into regular classrooms rather than in special education classes. Teachers who are instructing EMR children should be certain that

1. content and materials are within the child's capacity to learn;
2. materials relate directly to the child's environment and experiences;

3. assignments are within the child's ability range; and

4. visual aids are used to illustrate more abstract concepts.

Trainable learners are children who are unable to benefit from regular classroom experience but who do not need to spend their lives in special institutions. With appropriate instruction, trainable children are able to learn to take care of themselves, to make a reasonable social adjustment, and to learn simple occupational skills. They may or may not become economically self-sufficient. Some public school systems have provided special ungraded classrooms for trainable youngsters; others may be placed in residential schools.

Custodial children have a very limited range of intelligence and require close supervision and care at home or in residential institutions. They can be subdivided into the severely retarded and the profoundly retarded. The severely retarded are capable of learning only rudimentary self-care skills and elementary speech. They may perform simple tasks at home or in sheltered workshops. The profoundly retarded are incapable of speaking and need permanent nursing care.

Behavioral Disabilities

"Behavioral disabled" (BD), a general term that has not been defined precisely, includes the psychologically disordered and the socially maladjusted. Among the behaviors exhibited by BD youngsters are conduct disorders; hyperactivity; extreme physical and verbal aggression; extreme fear, anxiety, and feelings of inadequacy; and social delinquency. Behaviorally disabled youngsters exhibit atypical and extreme forms of behavior.

The Physically Handicapped

Physical handicaps range from congenital birth defects to injuries caused by accidents. Since it is beyond the scope of this book to classify the various categories of physical handicaps in detail, we will discuss only the most common types that have a general impact on education.

SPEECH AND LANGUAGE IMPAIRMENT. Learners with speech and language impairments constitute the largest group of physically handicapped children.[9] Speech impairment refers to any acoustic variation from an accepted speech standard that is so extreme as to be conspicuous in the speaker and confusing to the listener. A speech impairment can be defined as a disorder in the mechanics of speech, such as articulation, voice, and fluency. Among the common kinds of speech defects are stuttering, lisping, cluttering, nasality, thick speech, baby talk, hoarseness, and impairments caused by organic difficulties such as cleft palate and cerebral palsy. Language impairment refers to a student's inability to understand, express, and use language.

Voice problems can be caused by physical abnormalities or from vocal

---

[9]For a discussion of recent developments, see Freeman, *Speech and Language Services and the Classroom Teacher.*

misuse. School speech pathologists and speech-language therapists should refer students with voice problems to medical personnel, usually with a specialty in otolaryngology, for diagnosis and treatment before initiating a remedial program. In cooperation with the speech pathologist or therapist, the regular classroom teacher should plan a program to remediate the speech or language difficulty. Although specific objectives should be tailored to the individual child's needs, teachers should observe the following general guidelines:

1. Enter into full cooperation with the speech pathologist and interdisciplinary support team.
2. Enlist the assistance of parents in carrying out the program of remediation and in-class participation.
3. Encourage children to speak and to participate in speech activities despite their disability.
4. Refrain from threatening or ridiculing students who are speech or language impaired.

HEARING IMPAIRMENT.   Hearing impairment, a very broad and general term, encompasses hearing problems (auditory or acoustical) that interfere with learning. Hearing-impaired children may be deaf or hard of hearing.

Deafness refers to the absence of hearing in both ears. A major educational problem in the instruction of the deaf is that they may have never heard speech and may lack the normal use of language as a means of communication. The difficulty with language development is likely to extend to the learning of basic skills and may adversely affect academic learning. The absence of a normal language foundation means that deaf children require special education services. Often, one or more of the following special educators may be involved in providing services to deaf children: hearing clinician, speech therapist, teacher of the deaf or hearing impaired.

The term "hard of hearing" refers to individuals who once had sufficient hearing to acquire the basic foundations of language with special teaching but who later lost part or all of their hearing.[10] Hard-of-hearing children may experience distortion in language development and have difficulties in acquiring additional communication skills. While hard-of-hearing children have significant hearing losses, they have learned language in the usual way. Special educators have developed a range of effective techniques for providing effective instruction to hard-of-hearing youngsters. It is also possible and desirable to mainstream many hard-of-hearing students into regular classrooms.

Deaf and hard-of-hearing children can be identified in the usual ways that other cases of exceptionality are identified: by physicians and parents, through preschool screening, and by the administration of annual hearing tests as part of the school program. In addition to these standard procedures, the classroom teacher should be alert to the following symptoms of hearing impairment:

[10]Jack W. Birch, *Hearing Impaired Pupils in the Mainstream* (Reston, Va.: Council for Exceptional Children, 1975), p. 8.

1. Repeated failure to respond to one's name.
2. Consistently cocking the head to one side.
3. Difficulty in understanding, interpreting, and following directions.
4. An inability to determine the source of a sound.
5. Persistently watching others and following their movements.
6. Frequently asking to have a word or a direction repeated.
7. Persistently mispronouncing common words.

Regular teachers need to develop sensitivity and skill in instructing hearing-impaired children who are mainstreamed into their classes. As is true of the mainstreaming of other exceptional children, it is necessary for special and regular teachers to cooperate in developing plans and strategies for the education of hearing-impaired students. Birch, an authority on mainstreaming, has identified the following factors that have an impact on the education of hearing impaired students[11]:

1. What is the nature of the hearing defect? Is it in the speech range? While loss of hearing for high- and low-pitched sounds creates some problems in instructing hearing-impaired children, the most serious difficulties occur when the child cannot hear the sounds of ordinary conversation.
2. What is the degree of the hearing impairment? Where does the hearing defect fall on a scale from a total to a relatively limited loss? A total hearing loss creates serious instructional problems as it closes off oral communication and renders a hearing aid useless. If the hearing impairment is limited, a hearing aid is of great value. The proper use of a hearing aid can be of immense use in the education of a hearing-impaired child.
3. When did the hearing loss begin? At what age was hearing lost or impaired? The later the time of the hearing impairment, the greater the opportunity to acquire a language foundation. The earlier in childhood that the hearing impairment occurred, the more serious—depending on the degree of hearing loss—the instructional problem.
4. What is the hearing-impaired child's level of intelligence? As is generally true with all children, the more intellectually able child—including the hearing-impaired child—will have a greater probability of academic success. So that the hearing-impaired child's academic potential can be assessed accurately and realistically, the interdisciplinary support team should have the professional evaluation of a school psychologist. It is important that teachers do not underestimate the intelligence of hearing-impaired children.
5. What kind and amount of stimulation should be given to hearing-impaired children? Unless efforts are made to encourage the hearing-impaired child's comprehension, use, and communication of language,

[11]Birch, *Hearing Impaired Pupils in the Mainstream,* pp. 11–17.

the child's language development and speech quality is likely to deteriorate. Sustained, concerted, and regular stimulation of language comprehension and communication can minimize the efforts of hearing impairment and can maximize the constructive impact of special instruction.

As in other areas of special education, a technology has developed to aid in the education of hearing-impaired persons. The audiometer, an instrument that emits tones of different frequencies at controlled loudness levels, is used to help identify students with impaired hearing and to measure the degrees of hearing. The hearing aid, an electronic device, is used to pick up and amplify sound for hearing-impaired persons who have residual hearing. The radio ear is an instrument that is used to magnify the human voice so that students can hear.

Ameslan, or American Sign Language, is a separate and distinct language used to communicate with the deaf. In Ameslan, actions represent concepts. The manual alphabet, in which the letters are spelled by different finger positions of the hand, can also be used. In the manual alphabet, each position of the fingers represents one of the twenty-six letters.

VISUAL IMPAIRMENT. Millions of Americans have visual impairment. Visual impairment, a term denoting restricted vision, includes both the blind and the low-visioned person. Fortunately, milder impairments such as myopia (nearsightedness), hyperopia (farsightedness), and astigmatism (imperfection in the thickness and curvature of the cornea) can be alleviated by corrective lenses.

Visually impaired children are often identified by parents, physicians, and preschool screenings. Since there may be changes in vision as the child matures, periodic examinations are useful both in the school setting or as part of a regular physical checkup. The following brief terminology is useful to teachers who will encounter students with vision problems in their classrooms:

Visually impaired child: blind and low-visioned children with restricted vision.

Low-visioned child: visually impaired children who use print as a primary learning medium.

Blind child: visually impaired children who use braille as a primary learning medium.

Functional vision: information about a child's vision that has educational relevance. It refers to the child's effective use of the vision that she or he possesses.

Vision teacher: a special educator who provides service to visually impaired children.[12]

[12]This terminology is based on Glenda J. Martin and Mollie Hoben, *Supporting Visually Impaired Students in the Mainstream* (Reston, Va.: Council for Exceptional Children, 1977), p. 28.

A special education teacher assists a blind child in learning recreational and physical coordination skills. *(United Nations/S. DiMartini)*

The regular classroom teacher can be alert to recognizing children who have vision problems and can refer them for further examination. The incidence of children who need some eye care is large and is estimated at approximately 25 percent of the school-aged population. Teachers should be aware of vision problems, such as children who

1. make frequent and repeated mistakes with words or numbers;
2. are unable to study without eye discomfort or who complain about headaches;
3. hold their heads in peculiar and awkward positions and who frequently squint or frown;
4. hold their books very close or very far from their eyes;
5. are able to see objects at a distance more clearly than those at close range;
6. are unable to see objects at a distance; and
7. exhibit redness or swelling of eye lids or inflamed or watery eyes.

As in teaching other handicapped children, teachers who have visually impaired youngsters in their classes should use the general principles and procedures that govern sound instruction. For example, each child should be re-

Visually impaired learners practice activities to improve their sense of feeling by using wooden objects.
(United Nations/S. DiMartini)

garded as a unique individual who has basic human needs. All children should be treated fairly and consistently. Teachers need to be flexible enough to adapt their methods to the needs of the children for whom they have educational responsibility. While these pedagogical guidelines apply to teaching generally, it will be necessary for teachers to make some adaptation for visually impaired children.

The following suggestions may be helpful to teachers who have visually impaired students in their classrooms:

1. Develop an attitude in which you give reasonable assistance to visually handicapped children but avoid pity or too much help. Do not underestimate the ability of the visually handicapped child to learn and to cope with school.
2. In planning seating arrangements, locate visually impaired children in areas that have adequate light. They may need to be seated near the front of the room so that they can see the teacher and the chalkboard.
3. Read assignments, instructions, and explanations that are written on the chalkboard.

4. Provide occasions for visually impaired children to use and to exercise their existing and unused vision.

5. Be familiar with the technology that can be used to assist in the instruction of visually impaired children such as books and typewriters with large type, voice tapes, and audio equipment.

GIFTED AND TALENTED LEARNERS

Although there has been much research on identifying and educating gifted and intellectually talented children, the development of gifted education programs in many American public school systems has been slow and uneven. In the late 1950s, educational critics such as Admiral Hyman Rickover chastized American schools for their failure to challenge the educational potentiality of gifted learners. Financial retrenchment and the urgency of many immediate education problems have often diverted school administrators from implementing programs of gifted education. Critics of American public schools often have asserted that the massiveness of the system and the emphasis on equality of educational opportunity have contributed to an attitude that stresses sameness and the average rather than the unique. Most observers of American education would agree that the education of the nation's gifted children is a neglected area that needs attention, financial support, and curricular development.

Because of their very own creativity and uniqueness, it is difficult to catalogue and categorize the characteristics of gifted children. Although listing of the characteristics of gifted children is difficult, a statement of some of the obvious qualities of gifted children is useful to teachers. Gifted children generally

1. Have keen powers of observation, abstraction, and conceptualization; they are interested in understanding cause and effect relationships and enjoy inductive learning and problem-solving situations.

2. Are adept at and enjoy divergent thinking; they resist the tendency to a premature closure of a problem that sees only a single solution; they prefer to hypothesize and structure alternative solutions to a problem.

3. Enjoy reading and exhibit verbal proficiency, facility in expression, and an extensive vocabulary.

4. Tend to be intellectually curious and enjoy individualized study and independent work.

5. Are critical thinkers who challenge commonly accepted styles of thought. While this list of characteristics can be extended, it should also be stated that giftedness is found throughout the various races, nationalities, and ethnic groups of humankind. Neither is giftedness a matter of color, creed, or sex.

The Academically or Intellectually Gifted

While there is no universal definition of the mentally gifted that is generally accepted by educators, IQ as measured by the Stanford-Binet or Wechsler Intelligence Scale is often used to identify mentally gifted persons. An IQ that exceeds 125 is often used to identify the gifted person. In addition, teacher's judgments and academic records may be used to identify gifted children. It has been estimated that approximately 5 percent of the school population is within the gifted range.

Giftedness may exhibit itself in a particular academic area but not in all areas. For example, a child may be gifted in mathematics but not in art or in music but not in history. While the greatest attention has been devoted to the intellectually gifted, consideration also needs to be given to the creatively gifted and the psychosocially gifted. These last two categories are not well defined, but teachers will recognize students who exhibit creative and leadership potential. The creatively gifted demonstrate consistent superior ability in originative, flexible, and productive thinking. Those who are socially gifted exhibit a strong tendency to political and social leadership. They have skill in interpersonal relationships and in determining and facilitating the attainment of group goals.

Instructing Gifted Learners

There are various approaches to organizing instruction for gifted learners. Among them are grouping, acceleration, enrichment, and independent study.

Grouping of students is not new in education. One of the oldest patterns, historically, has been to group students according to age. Homogeneous grouping is used to cluster students in terms of intellectual readiness and ability and skill. Some high schools may schedule students into ability tracks. Other schools may use more flexible scheduling in which an individual student may be placed in a lower- or higher-level group in a particular subject.

Homogeneous grouping has long been the subject of considerable controversy among teachers. Those who favor homogeneous grouping argue that it makes it possible to organize materials and instruction according to the ability of a particular group of students. Opponents contend that it fosters intellectual elitism in that students in the higher-ability group may develop attitudes of superiority to those in lower groups. They also claim that ability grouping does not encourage realistic socialization.

Acceleration is an arrangement in which gifted students are promoted through school more rapidly than others. Gifted students may enter certain grades at an earlier age than the average student and may skip grades. In ungraded situations, it is also possible to accelerate or advance students into more complex areas of subjects in which they demonstrate proficiency. The major argument used against acceleration is that it may place students in social situations for which they lack adequate social and emotional readiness and maturity.

Enrichment is designed to provide gifted students with a broad and varied experience within a given subject. If a student has mastered the essentials of a given subject matter, then he or she can broaden his or her knowledge by readings or assignments that add to the core knowledge. For example, if a student in a high school course in American history has mastered the material relating to the Civil War and Reconstruction, then he or she can pursue other topics that relate to the central theme such as biographies of military and political leaders, military campaigns, or civil rights legislation.

Independent study can be used to individualize instruction for all students, including the academically gifted. It can provide for in-depth learning in a particular skill or subject that is part of the regular curriculum. Independent study projects or problems can also be interdisciplinary and related to several subject matter areas.

CONCLUSION

Public schools in the United States exist to educate the children of all the American people. Historically, this has meant that public education has served the needs of an increasingly diverse student population. To maximize the educational opportunities of the students, educators have designed instructional programs and patterns of school organization that meet the needs of individual students. Today, public schools, their administrators, and teachers are working to meet the needs of special learners in settings that not only maximize their educational opportunities in schools but integrate them as productive citizens in the larger society.

DISCUSSION QUESTIONS

1. Identify the major provisions of the Education of All Handicapped Children Act of 1975 (PL 94-142) and comment on their implications for education.
2. Discuss the various components of an individualized education plan and devise a model to be used in developing such plans.
3. Define the concept of "exceptionality." Is this term adequate or inadequate for use in school situations and in parent-teacher conferences and meetings?
4. Read a recent book on one of the categories of exceptionality. Report to the class on the author's contentions and the possible effects on classroom instruction.
5. What is "mainstreaming"? Consider the implications of mainstreaming for the grade level or subject matter area that you are preparing to teach. How should you prepare yourself to be an effective teacher in the mainstreamed classroom?
6. Define the following kinds of exceptionality: (a) learning disabled, (b) mentally retarded, (c) educable mentally retarded, (d) behaviorally disabled, (e) speech and language impaired, (f) hearing impaired, (g) visually impaired, (h) gifted.
7. Describe the characteristics of the intellectually gifted child.
8. Describe the various ways in which the regular classroom and special education teachers need to cooperate in instructional planning and delivery.

FIELD EXERCISES

1. Examine the physical plant—classrooms, libraries, elevators, lavatories—of the college or university in which you are enrolled. Discuss how physical facilities can aid or hinder the education of the handicapped person.
2. Arrange an in-class interview with a handicapped person that focuses on that individual's education.
3. Arrange an in-class interview with a special education and a regular classroom teacher that focuses on their cooperative activities.

4. Contact a school district and arrange to visit a mainstreamed class and a special education class. Report on your observations and share them with other students.

5. Contact a school district and arrange to visit a class for gifted students. Report on your observations and share them with other students.

6. Do preliminary research on how an interdisciplinary staffing is conducted. Simulate a staffing and prepare an IEP for a hypothetical student.

SUGGESTED READINGS

ADAMS, ANNE H., COBLE, CHARLES R., AND HOUNSELL, PAUL B. *Mainstreaming Language Arts and Social Studies.* Santa Monica, Calif.: Goodyear, 1977.

ANDERSON, KENNETH E., ED. *Research on the Academically Talented Student.* Washington, D.C.: National Education Association, 1961.

BIRCH, J. W. *Mainstreaming: Educable Mentally Retarded Children in Regular Classes,* Reston, Va.: Council for Exceptional Children, 1974.

—————— *Hearing Impaired Pupils in the Mainstream.* Reston, Va.: Council for Exceptional Children, 1976.

BIRCH, J. W., AND JOHNSTONE, B. K. *Designing Schools and Schooling for the Handicapped.* Springfield, Ill.: Charles C. Thomas, 1975.

A Common Body of Practice for Teachers: The Challenge of Public Law 94-142 to Teacher Education. Washington, D.C.: American Association of Colleges of Teacher Education, 1980.

COUNCIL FOR EXCEPTIONAL CHILDREN. *The Education for All Handicapped Act—P.L. 94-142.* Reston, Va.: Council for Exceptional Children, 1977.

DeHANN, R. F., AND HAVIGHURST, R. J. *Educating Gifted Children.* Chicago: University of Chicago Press, 1961.

DUNN, I. M., ED. *Exceptional Children in the Schools.* New York: Holt, Rinehart and Winston, 1973.

FREEMAN, GERALD G. *Speech and Language Services and the Classroom Teacher.* Reston, Va.: Council for Exceptional Children, 1977.

HANNINEN, K. *Teaching the Visually Handicapped.* Columbus, Ohio: Charles E. Merrill, 1975.

HARING, NORRIS, G., ED. *Behavior of Exceptional Children.* Columbus, Ohio: Charles E. Merrill, 1974.

HERLIHY, JOHN G., AND HERLIHY, MYRA T., EDS. *Mainstreaming in the Social Studies.* Washington, D.C.: National Council for the Social Studies, 1980.

HILTS, PHILIP J. *Behavior Mod.* New York: Harper's Magazine Press, 1974.

JONES, R. A., ED. *Mainstreaming: The Minority Child in Regular Classes.* Reston, Va.: Council for Exceptional Children, 1976.

LOWENBRAUN, SHEILA, AND AFFLECK, JAMES G. *Teaching Mildly Handicapped Children in Regular Classes.* Columbus, Ohio: Charles E. Merrill, 1976.

MARTIN, GLENDA J. *Supporting Visually Impaired Students in the Mainstream.* Reston, Va.: Council for Exceptional Children, 1977.

NATIONAL EDUCATION ASSOCIATION. *Mainstreaming: What Teachers Say Series.* Washington, D.C.: National Education Association, 1977.

REYNOLDS, M. C., ED. *Mainstreaming: Origins and Implications.* Reston, Va.: Council for Exceptional Children, 1976.

19

Teacher Education and Certification

Today, the education of teachers for the public and private schools of the United States is a large and often complex undertaking. It involves the cooperative efforts of teacher educators in colleges and universities, of officials in state departments of education, of experienced teachers and administrators, and of the public. Many of the readers of this book are preparing for careers as professional educators. Chapter 19 examines the historical origins of American teacher preparation to provide a perspective on the development of the teaching profession. It then examines the programs designed to prepare teachers for today's schools. It also describes the process of teacher certification.

HISTORICAL EVOLUTION
OF AMERICAN TEACHER EDUCATION

During the colonial era of the seventeenth and eighteenth centuries, the preparation and status of teachers varied, depending upon the school in which they taught. Latin Grammar teachers and college professors enjoyed greater social esteem than did elementary school teachers. Usually lacking a college degree, elementary school teachers were expected to conform to the dominant local

343

religious tenets; keep discipline; and teach reading, writing, arithmetic, and catechism. While some teachers were indentured servants, other young men taught to support themselves while preparing for more prestigious careers in the ministry or law.

Teacher hiring practices varied from colony to colony. In New England, school committees hired teachers with approval by the town minister. In the Middle Atlantic colonies, the society or the church operating the school appointed the teacher. In the South, wealthy plantation owners hired tutors to educate their children.

The Latin Grammar schoolmasters enjoyed more status than did the elementary school teachers. As college graduates, they had to know Latin, Greek, and classical literatures. College teachers, too, occupied a higher rung in the hierarchy of colonial society.

The Common School and Teacher Education

During the first half of the nineteenth century, the common school movement focused attention on teaching and teacher preparation. Proponents of public school, such as Horace Mann and Henry Barnard, realized that the success of common schools required well-prepared teachers. An early contributor to teacher education was Samuel Hall, a Congregational minister who headed the Normal Department of Phillips Andover Academy. In his book, *Lectures to School-Masters on Teaching,* Hall argued that teachers should be prepared in the science of teaching, in the principles of school management, and in the methods of teaching, spelling, reading, arithmetic, geography, grammar, writing, composition, history, and other common school subjects.[1] Good teachers, Hall wrote, should have such personal qualifications as common sense, an ability to understand human behavior, affection for children, decisiveness, and ethical standards.

James G. Carter, a colleague of Horace Mann in the Massachusetts legislature, was convinced that common school education could be improved only by competent teachers who had been prepared in normal schools designed for teacher education. Carter recommended that normal schools also contain a "model" or demonstration school in which prospective teachers would do practice teaching under the supervision of skilled and experienced educators.[2]

While Carter sponsored the legislation creating the Massachusetts State Board of Education, it was Horace Mann, as first secretary of the board, who deliberately supported the normal school as a necessary element in the success of the common school. As common schools were established, Mann believed it necessary to prepare competent teachers to staff these institutions. To improve teaching in the common schools, he organized teacher institutes, established normal schools, and worked to increase teachers' salaries. Teachers' institutes were periodic in-service meetings in which teachers gathered to share mutual problems and to hear educational lectures. The normal schools were teacher

---

[1]Samuel Hall, *Lectures to School-Masters on Teaching* (Boston: Carter, Hendee, 1833), pp. 20–21.

[2]James G. Carter, "Outline of an Institution for the Education of Teachers," 1825, in Henry Barnard, *Normal Schools and Other Institutions, Agencies, and Means Designed for the Professional Education of Teachers* (Hartford, Conn.: Case, Tiffany, 1851), pp. 78–81.

training institutions that prepared prospective teachers specifically in common school subjects, pedagogy, and instructional methodology. Mann believed that improved teachers' salaries would attract individuals who were committed to teaching to the field. To popularize the need for improved teaching, Mann argued the cause in his *Annual Reports* and *Common School Journal.*

Convinced by Carter and Mann, Governor Edward Everett signed the law establishing normal schools in Massachusetts. These early normal schools taught the content and method of teaching reading, writing, grammar, arithmetic, geography, spelling, composition, vocal music, drawing, physiology, algebra, philosophy, methodology, and Scripture.

Other states followed the Massachusetts example of establishing normal schools to prepare common school teachers. By 1844, New York's legislature authorized a normal school at Albany for the "instruction and practice of teachers of common schools." David Perkins Page, the head of the school, wrote *Theory and Practice of Teaching or the Motives and Methods of Good School-Keeping* (1847), which became a standard work in teacher education.[3] Page emphasized actual teaching experience under classroom conditions.

Henry Barnard, like Horace Mann, recognized the dependence of the common school on improved teacher preparation. Barnard identified the weaknesses of teacher education in the midnineteenth century: students were often accepted by normal schools who were prepared improperly and who lacked the aptitude for teaching; many students did not remain in the normal schools long enough to be prepared adequately; there was little financial assistance to aid qualified students; and there was a need for highly trained educators to teach in the normal schools.[4]

The other states followed the eastern pattern in establishing normal schools. State legislatures established normal schools, determined their locations, and approved their budgets. By the 1870s, normal schools had been established throughout the country and were regarded as the standard institution for preparing elementary school teachers.

Prospective teachers enrolled in the normal school for a period of preparation that was ordinarily two years. The curriculum consisted of a review of the basic common school subjects, lectures on school keeping, and experience in practice teaching in a model school under the supervision of the normal school's faculty.

Although often criticized for a lack of academic rigor, normal schools advanced professional teacher preparation in the United States. Their very existence disputed the common notion that anyone could teach, regardless of their preparation. They also were transitional institutions that later developed into teachers' colleges. The normal school professors produced a professional literature on educational history, philosophy, curriculum, and methods of instruction. The concept of the model or demonstration school led to the practice that prospective teachers should have a supervised clinical experience that included practice teaching.

[3]David P. Page, *Theory and Practice of Teaching or the Motives and Methods of Good School-Keeping* (New York: A. S. Barnes, 1885).

[4]Henry Barnard, *Normal Schools, and Other Institutions, Agencies, and Means Designed for the Professional Education of Teachers* (Hartford, Conn.: Case, Tiffany, and Co., 1851), p. 8.

Transition to Teachers College

By the late nineteenth century, colleges and universities recognized that they had a role to play in teacher education. This recognition was stimulated by growing high school enrollments and a need to prepare larger numbers of qualified secondary school teachers. Since high school teachers were expected to have college degrees, many normal schools became four-year degree-granting colleges, and many existing colleges and universities established departments of pedagogy to prepare teachers as well. For example, the University of Iowa established the first permanent chair of pedagogy in 1873. Iowa's example was followed by the University of Wisconsin in 1879 and by Indiana and Cornell in 1886. In 1892, Teachers College, a leading teacher education institution, became a part of Columbia University. By 1900, colleges and universities had become heavily involved in teacher education.

As existing colleges and universities developed teacher education programs, the normal schools became teachers' colleges. By the 1940s, most of the normal schools had been transformed into teachers' colleges. The transition from normal schools to teachers' colleges involved the following stages: requiring high school graduation as an admission requirement, adding a liberal arts and science component to the teacher preparation program, lengthening the curriculum from two to four years, securing authority to grant degrees from the state legislature, and improving quality of instruction. During the 1950s, many teachers' colleges were reorganized into comprehensive state universities that granted degrees in other fields as well as in professional education.[5]

Emergence of Professional Study

By the beginning of the twentieth century, the study of pedagogy had become a recognized field of research and teaching in most universities. In the 1880s and 1890s, the ideas of American educators were shaped by pedagogical insights developed by the German philosopher Johann Herbart, who sought to organize instructional concepts on psychological principles. In 1892, American Herbartians, such as Frank and Charles McMurry, Charles De Garmo, C. C. Van Liew, and Elmer Brown, organized the National Herbartian Society to advance systematic inquiry into education as a discipline. The American Herbartians enriched the curriculum through their emphasis on culture, history, and literature. They also stressed systematic instruction based on the Herbartian methodological sequence of preparation, presentation, association, generalization, and application.[6]

Along with the Herbartian stress on systematic methodology, G. Stanley Hall's pioneering work in educational psychology provided teachers with new insights into childhood and adolescence. The scientific movement in education, with its research into measurement, evaluation, and testing, was advanced by Edward L. Thorndike's, *An Introduction to the Theory of Mental and Social Measurements* (1904).

[5]Paul Woodring, "A Century of Teacher Education," in William Brickman and Stanley Lehrer, eds., *Century of Higher Education* (New York: Society for the Advancement of Education, 1962), p. 158.

[6]Johann Herbart, *Outlines of Educational Doctrine* (New York: Macmillan, 1901).

Curriculum was developed as a field of study through the efforts of W. W. Charters and Franklin Bobbitt who sought to base curriculum construction on the major activities of human life.

As school systems expanded and urban school districts grew larger, professional educators became involved in complex administrative and organizational issues. Professional educational programs were expanded to include work in supervision, administration, curriculum, public relations, financing, and school law. In addition to emphasis on the curricular, scientific, and administrative aspects of education, educational history, philosophy, and psychology remained an important foundational base in teacher education. Courses in educational foundations or policies were designed to examine such basic concerns as the aims and purposes of education, the organization of the curriculum, the function of the school, and the relationship of the school to society.

Contemporary programs of teacher education are based on this history of teacher education. The process of developing an organized and systematic approach to teacher education was derived from the developments of the past but also in anticipation of the challenges of the future. The next section examines the preparation of teachers for modern American society.

PREPARING RESOURCEFUL TEACHERS

The contemporary teacher fulfills many roles in today's society.[7] The most obvious but often most difficult role to fulfill is that of educating children and youth. To fulfill their primary educational role, teachers need to command a wide repertoire of personal and educational resources. Teachers should be

1. Educated persons who have command of and can use effectively the fundamental skills of thinking and communicating; they should possess an understanding of human beings and society based on a knowledge of the culture in which they live.

2. Resourceful educators who know thoroughly the skills and subjects that they are teaching. They should know and be able to do that which they expect others to do. In addition to knowing their subjects, the resourceful educator should know how to teach them by planning and organizing instruction according to the readiness and needs of learners.

3. Motivated and interested in teaching as their primary career. Teaching is not a part-time commitment. It should be a career commitment that one genuinely wants to make one's own.

[7]Numerous articles and books have been written on teaching and the teacher's role. Varying perspectives are provided by the following: Gilbert Highet, *The Immortal Profession* (New York: Weybright and Talley, 1976), is a classical scholar's view of teaching as an art. Bel Kaufman, *Up the Down Staircase* (Englewood Cliffs, N.J.: Prentice-Hall, 1964), is a novel, based on experience that describes the frustrations and joys of teaching in an inner-city school. C. J. B. MacMillan and Thomas W. Nelson, *Concepts of Teaching: Philosophical Essays* (Chicago: Rand McNally, 1968), analyzes teaching from the vantage of analytical philosophy. Robert W. Richey, *Preparing for a Career in Education: Challenges, Changes, and Issues* (New York: McGraw-Hill, 1974) introduces prospective teachers to a career in professional education.

4. Committed to using their own general knowledge, professional exper-
    tise, and force of personality to help learners to know, to think, and to
    grow as responsible persons and citizens.

While a teaching career is demanding of a person's energy and time, it
also brings with it challenges that provide the means for personal growth, realization, and integration. The resourceful teacher needs to be a continuing
researcher and an active agent who makes learning happen. Teaching requires
a quiet time to research, prepare, and plan for learning. It also requires an
active, doing, and interactive time in which the teacher stimulates and brings
about learning.

In addition to their primary role as an educator, contemporary society
has assigned many subsidiary roles to teachers. Some of these subsidiary functions have been assumed by teachers; others have been thrust on them because
of socioeconomic change. For example, the teacher is expected to be

1. A counselor, model, and guide to students in many areas that go beyond
    teaching a particular skill and subject.
2. The school's representative to parents and other community members.
3. An educator who is active in professional organizations and in the on-
    going development of the teaching profession.

Teacher Education Programs

Today's teacher education programs are the product of the early efforts
of normal schools, the experimentation of educational researchers, accumulated
experience in teaching children in the schools, state certification requirements,
the guidelines of accreditation bodies, and the forces of public opinion. As the
products of evolutionary forces, teacher education programs are under continuous review, re-examination, and redesign. The major objective of teacher education programs is to prepare resourceful teachers who can use their knowledge, talents, and expertise to educate children and youth effectively.

Although many variations exist, teacher education programs generally
consist of four major components: (1) general education, (2) specialized education, (3) professional education, and (4) supervised clinical experiences. The
following sections examine these components.

General Education

The general education component is designed to prepare teachers who
are educated persons by providing academic work in the liberal arts and sciences.
The general education component involves the study of language and literature,
history and social sciences, humanities and fine arts, mathematics, and natural
and physical sciences. In addition, some programs also require foreign language
study. In addition, specific institutional requirements, such as those of denominational colleges and universities, may require specified courses in theology.
The student's choice of elective subjects completes the program.

Depending upon the particular program, courses in the general education component generally occupy between a third and a half of the four-year
bachelor's degree program.

The general education component is usually based on (1) courses in the liberal arts and sciences that the particular college or university requires of all students in degree programs and (2) courses of a broad and general nature that are identified as providing the intellectual background needed by educated individuals. The general education component is designed to provide teachers with the intellectual resources needed to (1) understand knowledge and culture so that the teaching specialty is related to a broader world view and (2) communicate effectively in writing and in speech.

Specialized Education

The specialized education component, sometimes called the depth or major area of study, concentrates on the subjects, fields, or levels that the student is preparing to teach. In the specialized education component, elementary teacher preparation generally differs from that of secondary school teachers. Prospective elementary teachers enroll in courses that prepare them to teach the skills and subjects of the elementary curriculum, such as language arts, mathematics, social studies, sciences, music, art, and physical education. These courses are typically organized as methods and materials in the teaching of reading, the teaching of art, the teaching of language arts, children's literature, and others directly related to elementary education.

Prospective secondary teachers are prepared to teach the more specialized subjects found in the high school curriculum, such as English, foreign languages, mathematics, history, chemistry, or other academic subject matters. In addition, they also enroll in professional education courses related to the teaching of the subject at the secondary level.

The specialized education component is designed to ensure that teachers are specialists as well as generalists. It seeks to provide them with the in-depth knowledge needed in their particular teaching specialty.

Professional Education

Teacher education programs contain a professional education component, which consists of the humanistic and behavioral foundations of education. This component involves study in the history, philosophy, sociology, and psychology of education, human growth and development and often tests and measurements. In addition to the foundational courses, work is required in educational methodology and audiovisual media. The humanistic and behavioral foundations are intended to provide a theoretical base for practice. History of education traces the historical evolution of educational institutions and processes. Sociology of education examines the relationship of schooling to society. Philosophy of education examines the broad aims and purposes of education. Educational psychology analyzes the learning process, the motivation of students, and evaluation of their progress. In methodological courses, prospective teachers learn to plan and organize instructional units.

The specific number of semester or quarter hours required in the professional education component varies from state to state and from institution to institution. However, the median requirement, expressed in semester hours, is twenty-four for elementary teachers and eighteen for secondary school teachers. There has been considerable discussion as to the timing and sequence of the professional education component. While in some teacher education programs the professional education component begins in the freshman year, it is usually concentrated in the upper-class years.

A recent trend in the professional education component is to integrate academic study with clinical experiences in which prospective teachers actually observe and work with children at locations in the field. The objectives of this kind of integration are to provide prospective teachers with (1) insights into teaching that are experientially based and (2) opportunities to integrate theory and practice.

For example, a prospective teacher may be studying educational psychology as part of the professional education component. Concepts of learning theory, studied in the course, may be examined and reflected upon as the student observes children in a classroom situation. Observations also may be commented on in the class so that larger, more theoretical generalizations can be established. The integration of theory and practice in the professional education component creates an ongoing practical experience for prospective teachers.

Supervised Clinical Experience

The supervised clinical experience, often called "student or practice teaching," places prospective teachers in classroom situations in which they are responsible for planning, organizing, and providing instruction to students.[8] Preliminary to the supervised clinical experience, the student teacher is assigned to a school and is placed under the supervision of an experienced classroom teacher. This assignment is arranged by the college or university's director or coordinator of clinical experiences and the appropriately responsible school administrator, often the building principal.

Before beginning the actual clinical experience, it is highly desirable for the student teacher to visit the school and its community to develop a perspective into the characteristics of the community in which the school is located. Reading the local newspaper may provide insights into social, political, and other community events. A visit to the school enables the student teacher to meet the building principal, department chairpersons, and the cooperating teacher. Such preliminary visits should be discussed and planned in cooperation with the college or university director of clinical experiences and should follow the policies of the school in which the student teacher will be a guest.

Although the supervised clinical experience involves several persons indirectly, such as the building principal and department chairperson, the primary involvement is that of

1. *The student teacher,* who is expected to demonstrate subject matter knowledge, skills in instructional methods, and a professional attitude in teaching children or youth in a classroom setting.
2. *The cooperating teacher,* who is regularly assigned to provide instruction to the students. For a successful experience, it is imperative that both

---

[8]Adam Drayer, *Problems in Middle and High School Teaching: A Handbook for Student Teachers and Beginning Teachers* (Boston: Allyn & Bacon, 1979).

cooperating teacher and student teacher work together. The cooperating teacher should discuss the overall instructional plan with the student teacher and clearly state his or her expectations. In turn, the student teacher should be prepared to respond to and implement the cooperating teacher's suggestions.

3. *The college or university supervisor,* who, as an expert in instruction, serves as a facilitator, constructive critic, guide, and counselor for the student teacher.

Many teacher education programs also include a seminar in which a group of student teachers meet periodically to share their experiences, to discuss problems, and to arrive at generalizations based on their teaching experiences. Seminars may also involve resource persons from the education faculty who provide assistance from their fields of expertise to aid the student teachers.

TEACHER CERTIFICATION

Historical Patterns

The certification of teachers is a form of licensure that is administered by the states.[9] Each state, through its teachers' certification board or other state agency, grants a license to teach to individuals who meet its specified requirements for teaching. As with teacher preparation programs, certification, too, has been shaped by historical forces.

In the seventeenth- and eighteenth-century colonial period, applicants for teaching positions were often questioned on the orthodoxy of their religious beliefs by the local minister and board of trustees. Often, doctrinal conformity rather than educational competency determined the criteria for hiring teachers. In the early nineteenth century, a confusing array of local government units, such as districts, townships, and counties, were licensing teachers. Often, each unit administered its own examination and issued its own certificate. The confusing array of local teacher certification patterns created such problems as (1) a lack of uniformity of the professional standards for entry into teaching and (2) while licensed in one locality, teachers often found that their certificates were unacceptable elsewhere.

As a result of the nineteenth-century common school movement, there was a corresponding attempt to establish minimal standards for entry into teaching on a statewide basis. State superintendents of education or state departments of education assumed control of teacher certification. Gradually, each state, often through its teacher certification board, developed its own licensing requirements as a means to govern entry into teaching. The state's intention was to make certain that only adequately prepared persons were teaching in its public schools. To ensure minimal quality standards, state funds were provided only to school districts employing certificated teachers.

[9]T. Stinnet, *A Manual of Standards Affecting School Personnel in the United States* (Washington, D.C.: National Education Association, 1974); Elizabeth H. Woellner, *Requirements for Certification* (Chicago: University of Chicago Press, 1980.

Although differences in certification requirements exist from state to state, all states require possession of a bachelor's degree and evidence of completion of specified courses in professional education. Several states also require a fifth year of preparation for the granting of a teaching credential. In addition to specifying degree and professional education requirements, state certification laws generally prescribe a minimum age requirement for entry into teaching and require evidence of citizenship, good physical health, and good moral character. Some local boards of education, particularly those in large urban districts, may require additional requirements or examinations for employment in their school systems.

Contemporary Patterns

Since teacher certification is a state prerogative, each state has its own requirements. Certification is generally administered by the state teacher certification board that

1. grants approved program status to colleges or universities engaged in teacher preparation;
2. determines that applicants for certification meet the specified legal and professional requirements; and
3. issues the appropriate certificates.

Historically, there have been two patterns by which individuals have been granted a certificate by the state certification board: on an individual basis or as a graduate of an approved program. Certification on an individual basis means that the applicant for a certificate provides the state board with evidence that the necessary requirements have been fulfilled—perhaps by earning a degree and completing required professional education courses. Many state boards are moving from the cumbersome individual basis to the more generally recognized approved program basis of certification. Since it is likely that you will receive certification on the basis of completion of an approved program, the following section examines that procedure.

Approved Program Certification

In matters relating to teacher certification, it should be noted that the teacher education program of the college or university is closely related to state certification requirements. While the college or university grants the degree to the prospective teacher, it is the state teacher certification board that grants the certificate. The process by which colleges or universities receive approved program recognition from the state certification board involves several carefully defined steps:

1. The state certification board develops minimal criteria or standards that colleges or universities must meet regarding the quality of their teacher education programs. Such standards typically include library resources, field work, student teaching, professional courses, and other items re-

lated to teacher preparation. In developing these standards, the state board is guided by the expert opinion of teacher educators and practitioners in the schools.

2. The college or university seeking approved program status prepares an institutional self-study that documents how the institution meets the required standards.

3. The college or university is visited by a team appointed by the state board with the approval of the institution that ascertains if the institution is actually complying with the prescribed standards. This team prepares a report that leads eventually to the granting of or the denial of approved program status by the state certification board to the college or university.

The approved program process involves reciprocal responsibilities between colleges and universities and the state. Teacher preparation institutions influence teacher certification standards by recommending the courses and other experiences that they consider necessary for good teaching. States, in turn, impose upon institutions minimal requirements for certification based upon educational needs perceived at the state level. Many colleges and universities also have degree requirements that are additional to the minimal state certification requirements. A recent factor in the state certification process comes from the efforts of teachers' organizations and unions that seek to shape the requirements for those entering teaching. The prospective teacher should be a graduate of an institution having approved programs of teacher preparation because

1. the state department of education has officially recognized the teacher preparation program of the college or university, and

2. the state certification board issues a teaching certificate to persons whom the college or university recommends as having satisfactorily completed its teacher education program.

Reciprocity and NCATE

Prospective teachers also encounter the problem of reciprocity of certification between states. A teaching certificate is issued by a state certification board and is valid in the state of issuance. In our mobile society, however, teachers often are employed in states other than the one that granted initial certification. For many years, the complex and varying state teacher certification patterns made reciprocity difficult.

To reduce the complexities of teacher certification, the National Education Association established the National Commission on Teacher Education and Professional Standards (the TEPS Commission) to re-examine issues of teacher preparation, recruitment, selection, and certification. The American Association of Colleges for Teacher Education (AACTE), a national organization of institutions involved in teacher preparation, has also contributed to the advancement of uniform standards. Through the efforts of professional education organizations, the National Council for Accreditation of Teacher Education (NCATE) was established in 1952 to accredit teacher education programs in colleges and universities.[10] Upon invitation, NCATE evaluates each institution according to the following criteria:

1. It must already be accredited by the proper regional accrediting agency and be recognized by the appropriate state department of education.
2. It must be a nonprofit institution of higher learning offering not less than four years of college work leading to the bachelor's degree.
3. It must offer a four-year curriculum to prepare either elementary or secondary teachers, or both, or offer graduate programs in education.

Proponents of NCATE see it as a national organization for the evaluation and accreditation of qualified teacher education programs. According to the concept of reciprocity, the states would automatically license graduates of NCATE accredited programs. By 1977, thirty-one states had accepted NCATE accreditation for teacher certification. This has contributed significantly to uniformity in teacher certification. NCATE detractors allege that it has inflexibly overemphasized requirements not justified by research.

Competency-Based Certification

Since the late 1970s, there have been demands that teacher education programs be accountable for preparing effective teachers. Competency-based certification would constitute one means of ensuring such accountability. The demands for accountable teacher education programs and correspondingly teacher certification have generally come from the public or state legislatures. Occasionally, professional educators also have endorsed competency-based teacher education (CBTE) programs.

A CBTE program identifies the components of teaching, primarily defined as instructional tasks, and then designs strategies for prospective teachers to acquire and demonstrate these components in classroom teaching situations. Teaching competencies tend to be stated as specific instructional objectives that can be measured in terms of student achievement. The implication is that if the students fail to achieve the state objective, there is something lacking in the teacher's competency as an educator. Although CBTE reduces the ambiguity that often has surrounded instructional objectives, it has the detrimental "side effect" of reducing education into specific bits and pieces that lack wholeness.

Severe criticism of the lack of academic quality in public education has caused some states to establish competency-based teacher certification in addition to or in place of approved program certification. For example, Florida requires a competency-based examination of prospective teachers for certification. Prospective teachers may be examined on such competencies as (1) ability to use basic language and mathematical skills and (2) competency in teaching the subject, grade level, or skill in which certification is desired.

---

[10]Ray C. Maul, *Accreditation of Teacher Education by NCATE* (Washington, D.C.: American Association of Colleges for Teacher Education, 1969); Patricia Sinclair, ed., *National Professional Accrediting Agencies: How They Function* (Washington, D.C.: National Education Association, 1973).

At present, most of the states continue to grant certification based on approved programs. In the future, however, states may create competency-based requirements for certification.

CONCLUSION

Teacher education and certification in the United States is a product of historical forces and contemporary trends. The early trends toward professionalization occurred during the common school movement and were inspired by Horace Mann, James G. Carter, and other leaders of early public education. Contemporary teacher education programs have been designed to prepare resourceful teachers who are liberally educated and professionally prepared. Today's teacher preparation programs combine theory and practice, with a greater focus on clinical experience in the classroom. Teacher education programs are generally approved by the various states; many are also accredited by NCATE.

DISCUSSION QUESTIONS

1. Trace the historical evolution of teacher preparation and certification.
2. Examine the views of Horace Mann, James Carter, and David Page on teacher preparation.
3. Examine the author's conception of a "resourceful teacher." Do you agree or disagree?
4. Describe the origins and current process of teacher certification.
5. Describe "approved program" status.
6. Analyze the process of accreditation by NCATE.

FIELD EXERCISES

1. Identify the major components of a teacher preparation program and then relate these components to the teacher preparation program at your college or university.
2. Invite the director or coordinator of clinical experiences at your college or university to describe clinical experiences and student or practice teaching with members of your class.
3. Invite the teacher certification officer of your college or university to visit your class and describe the certification process.
4. Invite several students who have completed practice teaching to visit your class and to share their experience with you.
5. Invite a cooperating teacher to visit your class and discuss his or her work with student teachers with you.

SUGGESTED READINGS

DRAYER, ADAM. *Problems in Middle and High School Teaching: A Handbook for Student Teachers and Beginning Teachers.* Boston: Allyn & Bacon, 1979.
HIGHET, GILBERT. *The Immortal Profession.* New York: Weybright and Talley, 1976.

KAUFMAN, BEL. *Up the Down Staircase.* Englewood Cliffs, N.J.: Prentice-Hall, 1964.

MACMILLAN, C. J., AND NELSON, THOMAS W. *Concepts of Teaching: Philosophical Essays.* Chicago: Rand McNally, 1968.

MAUL, RAY C. *Accreditation of Teacher Education by NCATE.* Washington, D.C.: American Association of Colleges for Teacher Education, 1969.

STINNET, T. *A Manual of Standards Affecting School Personnel in the United States.* Washington, D.C.: National Education Association, 1974.

20

Teacher Demand, Supply, and Salaries

Chapter 20 examines the topics of teacher demand, supply, and salaries. Since the economic situation has been volatile due to inflationary trends, teacher supply, demand, and salaries are subject to change. The chapter attempts to present a realistic and balanced overview of the economic conditions that prospective teachers are likely to encounter in the 1980s. The gloomy prospects for teacher employment that developed in the late 1970s have dissipated, and the next decade exhibits signs of improved possibilities.

TEACHER SUPPLY AND DEMAND

The question of teacher supply and demand directly concerns anyone who has already decided to pursue a teaching career or is weighing that decision. In gross terms, teacher supply and demand is based on two major factors: (1) the number of students to be educated and (2) the number of teachers available to educate them. If the student population increases at a faster rate than the number of available teachers, teacher shortage results. If more teachers are available than are needed to educate students, a teacher surplus results. Calculating and predicting teacher supply and demand is not so simple, however, as many complex variables come into play.

Demographic factors influence teacher supply and demand in that the number of children enrolled in the schools determines to a large extent the number of teachers employed to educate them. Social, political, and economic factors also influence teacher supply and demand. What priority does the nation, the state, the local community, and the individual give to education? If given a high priority, taxpayers will be willing to provide the teachers needed to educate children. If given a low priority, then the educational service provided to children is likely to be reduced. Inevitably, social and political priorities for education must be translated into economics and finance. Local school districts must have both the resources and the willingness to pay teachers. Here, the issue of wealthy versus poor school districts and the degree to which the federal and state governments support education is relevant.

Demographic Factors

From the end of World War II until 1970, there was an increase in school-aged population and a general teacher shortage. To meet the high enrollments of the postwar decades, many school districts resorted to using double shifts, temporary classroom facilities, and provisionally certificated teachers. The demands placed on local school districts were particularly intense in the suburban areas that developed around the large cities. The suburbs adjacent to New York, Philadelphia, Boston, Chicago, Saint Louis, Dallas, Los Angeles, and other large cities grew as more affluent Americans were attracted to the life-style that suburbia promised. Families with school-aged children moved in droves to the existing suburbs and caused development of new suburbs. The suburban school districts with their expanding school system were a ready market for teachers. By the 1950s, the situation had stabilized as colleges and universities prepared large numbers of teachers and many school districts built new physical facilities for the growing school-aged population.

Throughout the 1960s, there was a teacher shortage. By the end of that decade, however, the shortage became a surplus as the decreasing American birthrate resulted in declining enrollments in the elementary and secondary schools. Their experience in dealing with the steadily increasing enrollments of the 1950s and 1960s had not prepared school administrators, teacher education institutions, and classroom teachers for the new and almost unprecedented phenomenon of the 1970s—declining enrollments. An examination of the statistics in Table 20–1 gives evidence of the rise and fall of school enrollment patterns in recent years.

These statistics indicate that maximum total enrollments occurred in 1970: the number of elementary school-aged children peaked in 1968 and then declined throughout the 1970s; at the secondary level, peak enrollment occurred in 1975 and then began its decline. This national pattern of declining enrollments produced the following effects:

1. A decline in state financial assistance to local school districts resulted because state aid formulas are based on average daily attendance of students. A decline in the number of students enrolled meant a decline

Table 20–1 Enrollments in Public and Private Elementary and Secondary Schools, Selected Years 1954–1976

YEAR	TOTAL	ELEMENTARY	SECONDARY
1954	33,949,000	24,922,000	9,027,000
1956	36,619,000	26,217,000	10,402,000
1958	39,581,000	27,915,000	11,666,000
1960	42,181,000	29,150,000	13,031,000
1962	44,849,000	30,164,000	14,685,000
1964	47,716,000	31,221,000	16,495,000
1966	49,239,000	31,905,000	17,334,000
1968	50,744,000	31,763,000	18,981,000
1970	51,309,000	31,601,000	19,708,000
1972	50,744,000	31,023,000	19,721,000
1974	50,053,000	29,982,000	20,071,000
1976	49,335,000	29,030,000	20,305,000

Based on data from Mary A. Golladay and Jay Noell, eds., *The Condition of Education* (Washington, D.C.: G.P.O., 1978), p. 66.

in average daily attendance, which brought school districts decreased revenues with which to operate schools and to pay teachers' salaries.

2. Many local districts found that their physical facilities were larger and more extensive than they needed. To reduce expenditures, many local school districts closed some of their schools and transferred students to others of their schools to gain greater cost efficiencies. School closings and consolidations often meant a reduction in the teaching staff.

3. Declining enrollments did not always mean smaller class size. On the contrary, school closings and attempts to cut expenses often led to larger class size and fewer teachers.

During the early 1970s, teacher education institutions continued to prepare large numbers of teachers. In addition, large numbers of former teachers were re-entering teaching. But, with articles in professional educational journals and the popular press highlighting the apparently bleak prospects for teacher employment, by the late 1970s, the number of students entering teacher education programs had decreased substantially.

While accurate demographic projections are always made with difficulty, analysis of teacher supply and demand needs more precise predictions and fewer gross generalizations. As the projections in Table 20–2 suggest, there is likely to be a continued but less dramatic decline in total elementary and secondary enrollments in the 1980s. In fact, elementary school enrollments are expected to increase slightly in the mid-1980s, but secondary school enrollments are likely to decline further.

When enrollment projections for the 1980s are viewed nationally, it appears that a slightly increasing school population and a corresponding decrease in the number of new teachers will reduce the teacher surplus and improve the employment prospects for teachers. A major factor in reducing the surplus

Table 20–2 Projected Enrollments in Elementary and
Secondary Schools in the 1980s

YEAR	TOTAL	ELEMENTARY	SECONDARY
1982	44,809,000	27,271,000	17,538,000
1984	44,546,000	27,402,000	17,144,000
1986	45,244,000	28,532,000	16,712,000

Data are based on intermediate alternative projections in Mary A. Golladay
and Jay Noell, eds., *The Condition of Education* (Washington, D.C.: G.P.O.,
1978), p. 66.

was the decrease of individuals entering and completing teacher preparation
programs. For example, university placement officers have reported a decrease
of 41 percent in the number of new elementary teachers and of 51 percent in
the number of new secondary teachers between 1970 and 1980.[1] National projections indicate an improvement in the employment prospects for new teachers.
Greater accuracy in predicting employment trends for teachers is possible if
more specific factors are considered, however.

Population Shifts

The 1980 census indicates some major shifts in the geographical locations
of the American population. During the 1970s, substantial increases occurred
in the population of the Sun Belt states of the South and West and a corresponding decline took place in the population of several northern and northeastern states, especially in the large cities. In the early 1980s, teacher shortages
were being reported in the West and Southwest. It is predicted that the need
for teachers in these states will increase throughout the decade.[2] New teachers,
then, should find more possibilities for employment if they follow the general
movement of the American population to the Sun Belt areas of the country.

Early Childhood Education

A combination of social, economic, and educational trends in the 1970s
has worked to stimulate an increased demand for early childhood educators. In
the 1970s, the sharpest growth in the labor force occurred in the category of
women who were the mothers of children under six years of age. By 1978, 38
percent of women in this category were employed, an increase of one-third since
1970. Although the number of children in the age level from three to five
declined since 1966, the increase in the number of working mothers produced
a greater demand for preprimary education. Along with these socioeconomic
factors, there is also a greater sensitivity to the educational needs and poten-

[1]James N. Akin, *Teacher Supply/Demand 1981* (Madison, Wisc.: Association for School,
College and University Staffing, 1981).

[2]Beverly T. Watkins, "A Critical Shortage of School Teachers Likely by 1985, Education
Deans Warn," *The Chronicle of Higher Education*, March 23, 1981, p. 1.

Table 20–3 Estimated Enrollments in Nursery Schools
and Kindergartens, with Projections, 1965–1976 and
1982E–1986E

YEAR	TOTAL	PUBLIC	NONPUBLIC
1965	1,104,000	305,000	799,000
1966	1,232,000	374,000	858,000
1967	1,378,000	467,000	911,000
1968	1,364,000	437,000	927,000
1969	1,354,000	326,000	1,028,000
1970	1,534,000	421,000	1,113,000
1971	1,662,000	524,000	1,138,000
1972	1,745,000	549,000	1,196,000
1973	1,575,000	343,000	1,232,000
1974	1,889,000	364,000	1,525,000
1975	2,020,000	489,000	1,531,000
1976	1,949,000	541,000	1,408,000
1982	2,318,000	578,000	1,740,000
1983	2,483,000	612,000	1,871,000
1984	2,665,000	651,000	2,014,000
1985	2,840,000	692,000	2,148,000
1986	2,992,000	729,000	2,263,000

Data adapted from Martin M. Frankel, ed., *Projections of Educational Statistics to 1986–87* (Washington, D.C.: G.P.O., 1978), p. 14.

tialities of preprimary-aged children. While in 1966, 30 percent of the nation's children in the age range from three to five were in preprimary school, almost half of them were attending in 1980. The increased enrollments as shown in Table 20–3 suggests encouraging prospects in early childhood education.

Subject and Specialty Needs

Projections of teacher demand need to be considered in terms of particular subjects, grade levels, and fields of specialization. A shortage of teachers is expected to continue throughout the 1980s in mathematics, industrial arts, chemistry, physics, vocational agriculture, special education, and bilingual education.[3] If funding improves, it is likely that there will be a growing demand for teachers of the gifted. A teacher surplus will probably also continue in home economics, health education, the social sciences, and art. As of the early 1980s, there appears to be a surplus of elementary school teachers. However, the increase in elementary school enrollments expected in the mid-1980s may produce a balance between teacher supply and demand in this area. Figure 20–1 identifies specific fields of teacher shortage and surplus.

[3]Akin, *Teacher Supply/Demand 1981.*

According to teacher placement officials, teacher surplus and shortages will exist in the following areas[4]:

Considerable teacher shortage in mathematics, industrial arts, physics, learning disabilities, vocational agriculture, chemistry, general science, and speech correction.

Slight teacher shortage in special education areas such as reading, mental retardation, multiple handicapped, bilingual education, gifted, earth science, biology, school psychology, and business.

Balanced supply and demand in English, instrumental music, library science, elementary and secondary school counseling, vocal music, Spanish, driver's training, journalism, and speech.

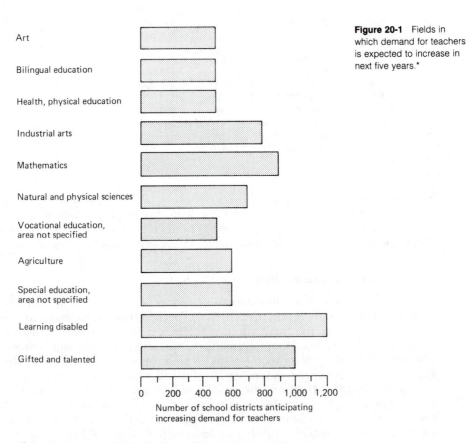

Figure 20-1 Fields in which demand for teachers is expected to increase in next five years.*

*School districts have indicated that demand for teachers is most likely to emerge or grow in the next five years in the fields of teaching the learning disabled, gifted and talented, mathematics, and industrial arts.

From Mary A. Golladay and Jay Noell, eds., *The Condition of Education* (Washington, D.C.: G.P.O., 1978), p. 179.

[4]Ibid., p. 5.

Slight surplus in French, German, elementary education, home economics, health education, social science, and art.

Considerable surplus in physical education.

With the exception of art, a recent survey of school districts (see Figure 20–1) agrees with the preceding identification of fields where a demand for teachers is expected.

Pupil-Teacher Ratios

A crucial factor that relates to the employment demand for teachers is that of pupil-teacher ratios. The employment of teachers corresponds closely to the numbers of pupils assigned to a particular classroom teacher. Research on optimum pupil-teacher ratios has been inconclusive.

Considerable variation in pupil-teacher ratios can be found from school district to school district. The lower the ratio of pupils to teachers, the larger the number of teachers needed. Although enrollment generally has declined, the actual ratio of pupils to teachers has actually increased in some school districts because of the need to reduce expenditures and stretch the dollars in the educational budget. Table 20–4 presents data that are relevant to the demand for teachers in elementary schools based on enrollments.

The following generalizations can be made from a review of the statistics on pupil enrollments and the size of the teaching force in public elementary schools:

1. Since the period of peak enrollment in 1969, there has been a decline in elementary school enrollments.
2. The numbers of teachers employed in elementary schools has decreased at a lower rate than have the numbers of students.
3. The number of students taught by the typical elementary teacher has decreased steadily in the past two decades.

Table 20–4 Enrollments, Teachers, and Ratios in Regular Public Elementary Schools, with Projections, 1963–1975 and 1982E–1986E

YEAR	ENROLLMENTS	TEACHERS	PUPIL-TEACHER RATIOS
1963	29,304,000	908,000	28.4
1965	30,563,000	965,000	27.6
1967	31,641,000	1,040,000	26.3
1969	32,597,000	1,108,000	24.8
1971	32,265,000	1,111,000	24.9
1973	31,353,000	1,152,000	22.9
1975	30,487,000	1,180,000	21.7
1982	27,643,000	1,178,000	20.1
1984	27,652,000	1,214,000	19.6
1986	28,432,000	1,305,000	19.1

Based on data from Martin M. Frankel, ed., *Projections of Education Statistics to 1986–87* (Washington, D.C.: G.P.O., 1978), pp. 14, 57, 59.

Table 20–5 Enrollments, Teachers, and Ratios in Regular Public Secondary Schools, with Projections, 1963–1975 and 1982E–1984E

YEAR	ENROLLMENTS	TEACHERS	PUPIL-TEACHER RATIOS
1963	10,883,000	669,000	21.5
1965	11,610,000	746,000	20.8
1967	12,250,000	815,000	20.3
1969	13,022,000	906,000	20.0
1971	13,816,000	952,000	19.3
1973	14,077,000	986,000	19.3
1975	14,304,000	1,016,000	18.8
1982	12,166,000	902,000	17.9
1984	11,894,000	889,000	17.7

Based on data from Martin M. Frankel, ed., *Projections of Education Statistics to 1986–87* (Washington, D.C.: G.P.O., 1978), pp. 14, 57, 59.

Since 1950, public high school enrollments have increased significantly (see Table 20–5). Correspondingly the number of teachers in the public high schools also increased.

Private, independent, and parochial elementary schools also have experienced enrollment declines. However, the ranks of nonpublic elementary school teachers has increased slowly but steadily in the past several decades. In 1965, there were 147,000 nonpublic elementary teachers. In 1975, the number increased to 156,000. In 1985, it is estimated that the number of nonpublic elementary teachers will reach 182,000. Pupil-teacher ratios have also declined in the nonpublic elementary schools. In 1965, the ratio was 33.5, in 1975 it was 23.1, and the projection for 1985 is a ratio of 19.8, which can be compared with a projected 19.3 for the public elementary school.[5]

Enrollments in private secondary schools have been relatively stable at approximately 1,400,000 students since the late 1960s. The numbers of teachers in private secondary schools has increased steadily from 76,000 in 1965, to 90,000 in 1975 and is expected to be 97,000 in 1985. In the past ten years, the pupil-teacher ratio in nonpublic secondary schools has been 15.7, and it is expected to remain such throughout the 1980s.

Economic Conditions

The general condition of the national economy is another important variable that relates to teacher supply and demand. Because of rapidly accelerating inflation and a corresponding reluctance of taxpayers to support additional school costs, the financial capacity of many school districts to employ

[5] Martin M. Frankel, ed., *Projections of Educational Statistics to 1986–87* (Washington, D.C.: G.P.O., 1978), p. 59.

additional teachers has decreased. In many school districts, the need to effect economies and balance budgets has caused a reduction in the teaching force, commonly referred to as RIF.

When school districts have found it necessary to reduce their teaching force, they are bound to follow state guidelines governing the selection of teachers for dismissal. In addition, agreements between the employing districts and the teachers' association or union may also include criteria to be followed when a reduction in force is necessary. Criteria that are commonly used are (1) seniority of teachers in subject matter or grade-level certification, (2) evaluations of teacher performance; or (3) a combination of these factors. Tenure laws generally provide that teachers who have been dismissed because of reduction in force be rehired should vacancies occur in their subject matter or grade-level specialty.

TEACHER SALARIES

In many societies, the esteem that a profession enjoys is often measured by the economic rewards it receives. Historically, teachers have not been compensated adequately for their contributions to the education of children and youth. In the past, particularly in the colonial and early national periods, many teachers were poorly prepared. Today, however, teachers are prepared in carefully designed programs. Because of sustained effort, American teachers' salaries have risen slowly over time.

Although local and state variations must be considered, the following generalizations apply to teachers' salaries:

1. The average salary paid to secondary teachers is often higher than that paid to elementary school teachers.
2. Teachers holding master's degrees receive higher average salaries than do those with bachelor's degrees.
3. The average teachers' salaries in large- and medium-sized school systems are higher than those in smaller districts.
4. Teachers in the industrial northeastern states historically have been the highest paid. This may change as the population shifts to the Sun Belt (southern and western) states. In analyzing this factor, regional variations also produce significant differences in actual income due to cost-of-living differences.
5. The salaries paid to beginning teachers with a bachelor's degree are generally lower than are those paid to individuals entering other fields with a bachelor's degree.

Despite significant variations from state to state, teachers' salaries have improved in recent decades. For example, the average salary of public classroom teachers was $8,635 in 1970 (see Table 20–6). By 1980, it had reached $16,001, an increase of $7,366, or 85.3 percent. Specifically, in the same decade, the average salary of public school elementary teachers increased from $8,412 in

Table 20–6 Average Salary of Public Classroom Teachers by State, 1970–1980

STATE	1970	1980	DOLLAR INCREASE	PERCENTAGE INCREASE
Alabama	$ 6,817	$13,520	$ 6,703	98%
Alaska	10,560	26,173	15,613	148
Arizona	8,715	15,835	7,120	82
Arkansas	6,277	12,419	6,142	98
California	10,324	19,090	8,766	85
Colorado	7,760	15,950	8,190	105
Connecticut	9,271	16,344	7,073	76
Delaware	9,015	16,157	7,142	79
Florida	8,410	14,570	6,160	73
Georgia	7,278	14,027	6,749	93
Hawaii	9,440	19,750	10,310	109
Idaho	6,884	13,615	6,731	98
Illinois	9,569	17,399	7,830	81
Indiana	8,832	15,078	6,246	71
Iowa	8,398	15,030	6,632	79
Kansas	7,620	14,016	6,396	84
Kentucky	6,939	14,480	7,541	109
Louisiana	7,028	13,770	6,742	96
Maine	7,572	13,100	5,528	73
Maryland	9,383	17,580	8,197	87
Massachusetts	8,770	17,500	8,730	99
Michigan	9,823	18,840	9,017	92
Minnesota	8,658	16,751	8,093	93
Mississippi	5,798	11,900	6,102	105
Missouri	7,844	13,725	5,881	75
Montana	7,606	14,680	7,074	93
Nebraska	7,354	13,519	6,165	84
Nevada	9,248	16,390	7,142	77
New Hampshire	7,789	12,550	4,761	61
New Jersey	9,150	17,075	7,925	87
New Mexico	7,798	13,915	6,117	78
New York	10,390	19,200	8,810	85
North Carolina	7,494	14,355	6,861	92
North Dakota	6,696	13,148	6,452	96
Ohio	8,300	15,187	6,887	83
Oklahoma	6,882	13,210	6,328	92
Oregon	8,814	16,245	7,431	84
Pennsylvania	8,858	16,760	7,902	89
Rhode Island	8,776	17,896	9,120	104
South Carolina	6,883	13,000	6,117	89
South Dakota	6,403	12,200	5,797	91
Tennessee	7,050	13,668	6,618	94
Texas	7,277	14,000	6,723	92
Utah	7,643	14,965	7,322	96
Vermont	7,960	12,430	4,470	56
Virginia	8,070	14,025	5,955	74

Table 20–6 *(Cont.)*

STATE	1970	1980	DOLLAR INCREASE	PERCENTAGE INCREASE
Washington	9,237	18,745	9,508	103
West Virginia	7,650	13,642	5,992	78
Wisconsin	9,000	15,930	6,930	77
Wyoming	8,271	16,030	7,759	94
Average	8,635	16,001	7,366	85

Adapted from *Estimates of School Statistics, 1970–71* (Washington, D.C.: National Education Association, 1970), Table 7, p. 32; *Estimates of School Statistics, 1979–80* (Washington, D.C.: National Education Association, 1979), Table 7, p. 32.

1970 to $15,661 in 1980. The average salary paid to public high school teachers rose from $8,891 to $16,387.[6]

In analyzing differences in average public teacher salaries on a state-by-state basis, Ornstein has identified the four highest-paying states, in 1980, as being Alaska, with an annual salary of $26,173 followed by Hawaii at $19,750, New York at $19,200, and California at $19,090. The lowest average classroom teachers' salaries were reported in Mississippi at $11,900, South Dakota at $12,220, Arkansas at $12,419, Vermont at $12,430, and New Hampshire at $12,550.[7] In addition to variations from state to state, there are significant differences in salaries paid to teachers within a state. Often, urban and suburban teachers' salaries are higher than are those paid to their colleagues in rural areas.

Salary Schedules

The individual teacher's salary is determined in most school districts by the person's location on a salary schedule. A number of states have determined the minimum salaries to be paid to teachers in the state. Such state minimum salary levels are actually lower than the salaries paid to most teachers, but they provide a starting point for the salary schedules that local school districts establish. Teacher salary schedules are established as a result of negotiation between the local school board and the local teachers' organization or bargaining unit. After both parties agree, the salary schedule for teachers in the district is established. Items included in the typical teachers' salary schedule are

1. The initial, starting, base salary for teachers with a bachelor's degree, a master's degree, and a master's degree with additional earned credit hours. In ascending order, the salaries are generally higher depending on the advanced degrees earned by the teacher.

[6]Allan C. Ornstein, "Teacher Salaries: Past, Present, Future," *Phi Delta Kappan,* Vol. 61 (June 1980), 677–679.

[7]Ibid.

2. The maximum salary that a teacher can reach at the different degree levels.

3. A series of steps—based on experience in the district and/or merit—that determines the annual salary increment to be paid each year in addition to the base salary.

The salary schedule also may specify the extra pay or stipend that teachers receive for supervisory or extracurricular activities outside of classroom instruction.

Teachers may earn extra income from the school district for performing certain added duties such as coaching athletic teams; acting as moderators or advisors for clubs and student organizations; advising and assisting in the production of plays, school newspapers, and year books; and serving as chaperons for special events.

The typical salary schedule is designed to encourage teachers to improve their professional competency by enrolling in graduate courses or advanced degree programs. Service to the school district is rewarded by increments based on years of experience. Salary schedules are usually renegotiated periodically by school boards and teacher associations or unions at times specified in their professional agreements or in contracts.

Agreement on a salary schedule is often preceded by protracted negotiations between the local school board and the teachers' organization. A number of issues can lead to possible conflict in the negotiation process. Teachers' organizations generally have argued that salary schedules should be based on the level of academic preparation, earned degrees, and years of teaching experience. In light of recent inflationary trends in the economy, teachers' organizations also have sought to tie increments to cost-of-living increases, based on the consumer price index. School boards tend to resist cost-of-living increases since their revenues, based on the local property tax and state aid formulas, are relatively fixed and do not increase with inflation. There also has been a tendency for school boards to base increments on merit as determined by peformance evaluations. Teachers' organizations that oppose merit increments argue that most instruments for rating teachers are ambiguous or unscientific and generate distrust between the supervisory staff and teachers.

Table 20–7 presents a typical teacher salary schedule.

Fringe Benefits

Individuals entering particular professions and occupations are attracted to fringe benefits as well as to the annual salary or wage. Somewhat difficult to define, fringe benefits refer to added benefits, inducements, and rewards enjoyed by people working in a particular field. Although the most obvious fringe benefit is a financial reward, a broader concept of fringe benefits includes the opportunities for personal satisfaction and social significance provided by a given profession or occupation.

Despite its challenges and day-to-day frustrations, teaching is a socially significant activity that provides many opportunities for personal integration and satisfaction. The teacher's preservice and in-service education is related so directly to career activities that it is a means of continual professional renewal and

Table 20–7 Teacher Salary Schedule

TEACHING YEAR	B.S., B.A.	B.S. + 15, B.A. + 15	B.S. + 30, B.A. + 30	M.Ed., M.A.	M.Ed. + 15, M.A. + 15	M.Ed. + 30, M.A. + 30	Ed.D., Ph.D.
1	$ 9,400	$ 9,600	$10,000	$10,400	$11,000	$11,500	$12,000
2	9,800	10,100	10,600	11,100	11,800	12,400	13,000
3	10,200	10,600	11,200	11,800	12,600	13,300	14,000
4	10,600	11,100	11,800	12,500	13,400	14,200	15,000
5	11,000	11,600	12,400	13,200	14,200	15,100	16,000
6	11,400	12,100	13,000	13,900	15,000	16,000	17,000
7	11,800	12,600	13,600	14,600	15,800	16,900	18,000
8	12,200	13,100	14,200	15,300	16,600	17,800	19,000
9	12,600	13,600	14,800	16,000	17,400	18,700	20,000
10	13,000	14,100	15,400	16,700	18,200	19,600	21,000
11	13,400	14,600	16,000	17,400	19,000	20,500	22,000
12	14,000	15,100	16,600	18,100	19,800	21,400	23,000
13	14,400	15,600	17,200	18,200	20,600	22,300	24,000
14			17,800	19,500	21,400	23,200	25,000
15				20,200	22,200	24,100	26,100
16					23,000	25,000	27,000
17						25,900	28,000

meaning. The school year of nine to ten months allows time for personal growth and continuing education.

Teachers traditionally have used summer months for advanced professional education or for travel that enriches their teaching careers. Teaching also provides opportunities to work with colleagues who face similar problems and experience similar rewards.

In negotiations with boards of education, teachers' organizations and unions have sought to achieve tangible fringe benefits for their members. Among benefits enjoyed by many teachers are the following:

Leaves of absence, with pay or partial pay, are designed to encourage teachers to engage in advanced professional study, to travel, to participate in educational exchange programs at home or abroad, and to write and develop teaching materials and strategies.

Sick leaves are generally provided by the statutory provisions of many of the states and in the policies of school districts. Generally, the amount of sick leave that can be accumulated is based on the length of service to the district. Most districts also provide sick days with pay for illness or death of a member of the immediate family.

Insurance benefits, such as group life, hospitalization, medical-surgical, major medical, dental, liability, disability, and other forms, may be provided by larger school districts. Often, school districts and their employees may each contribute to various insurance plans.

Some school districts also provide cost-of-living increments based on increases in the consumer price index. Fringe benefits are negotiated between the school board and representatives of the teachers' association and are specified in their agreement or contract.

Teacher Retirement

All states have established retirement systems for teachers. Teachers and the employing school districts usually contribute to the retirement fund. Retirement benefits are based on the average annual salary and the number of years employed in teaching. Although states have previously often mandated retirement at age sixty-five, recent federal legislation prohibits the requiring of retirement until age seventy.

CONCLUSION

Teacher supply and demand is changeable and is based on a number of demographic and economic factors. Within the United States, the movement of population to particular states influences teacher demand in those states. In addition, the financial ability of school districts to staff classrooms and the establishing of pupil-teacher ratios also determines the number of teachers that will be employed in the particular school district. Although they have increased in recent years, teacher salaries vary considerably from state to state and from district to district within a particular state.

DISCUSSION QUESTIONS

1. Identify the variables that affect teacher supply and demand.
2. Examine current population trends in relationship to teacher supply and demand.
3. Identify the states that are likely to experience increased teacher demand.
4. Identify the teaching areas and subject matter areas that are likely to experience teacher shortage or surplus.
5. How do teacher-pupil ratios determine teacher demand.
6. Explain and discuss the purpose of a teacher salary schedule.

FIELD EXERCISES

1. Identify a particular state and record teacher supply and demand in that state for the past ten years. Predict anticipated teacher supply and demand in that state for the next two years.
2. Invite a representative of your college or university teacher placement department to visit your class and discuss teacher supply and demand.
3. Invite a professor of economics to visit your class and discuss the general economic factors that are likely to have an impact on schools and teachers.
4. Invite an educational administrator for a local school district to visit your class to discuss the establishing and functioning of the salary schedule in his or her district.

SUGGESTED READINGS

ABRAMOWITZ, SUSAN, AND ROSENFELD, STUART. *Declining Enrollment: The Challenge of the Coming Decade.* Washington, D.C.: G.P.O., 1978.

AKIN, JAMES N. *Teacher Supply/Demand 1981* Madison, Wisc.: Association for School, College and University Staffing, 1981.

FREIDSON, ELIOT. *The Professions and Their Prospects.* Beverly Hills, Calif.: Sage Publications, 1977.

GERWIN, DONALD, ED. *The Employment of Teachers.* Berkeley, Calif.: McCutchan, 1974.

HABERMAN, MARTIN, AND STINNETT, T. M. *Teacher Education and the New Profession of Teaching.* Berkeley, Calif.: McCutchan, 1973.

HIPPLE, THEODORE W. *The Future of Education: 1975–2000.* Pacific Palisades, Calif.: Goodyear, 1974.

National Education Association. *Careers in Education.* Washington, D.C.: National Education Association, 1976.

21

Teaching as a Profession

Chapter 21 examines teaching as a profession and the issues that affect teachers as professional educators. It also deals with several matters that affect prospective teachers, such as preparing credentials, locating a teaching position, and the issuance of a teaching contract. The ethical and legal relationships of tenure and academic freedom are examined. The chapter concludes with a brief discussion of teachers' organizations and the issue of collective bargaining. The chapter is designed to familiarize prospective teachers with the major issues that they face as professional educators.

IS TEACHING A PROFESSION?

The question, Is teaching a profession?, has stimulated prolonged and often heated debate. Sociologists and educational theorists have examined the question as an academic matter. For teachers, however, the question is a "bread and butter" issue that affects their social status, income, and civil and academic freedom. There is no easy answer to the question since the criteria of what constitutes a profession are not universally accepted. In the medieval period, the three recognized professions were law, medicine, and theology. In modern times, the claimants to the title of professional have multiplied.

In contemporary America, the term "professional" has been used imprecisely to cover a wide range of occupations. For example, it is used to identify "professional" actors, dancers, photographers, barbers, truck drivers, pilots, and many other occupational categories as well as the older recognized professions of law, medicine, and theology and the more recently recognized professions of architecture and engineering. Although there is a professional literature and ethics associated with teaching, there are also critics who dispute that teachers have a unique professional culture. These critics contend either that teachers are born and not prepared or that anyone can teach if they have knowledge of that which they purport to teach. In other words, teachers may argue that they have a professional culture, but others would deny that they possess such a culture.

To deal with the question, Is teaching a profession?, a number of criteria are stated that are generally accepted as being characteristic of a profession; then we examine teaching in relation to those criteria.[1]

(1) *A profession involves intellectual activities and commands a body of specialized knowledge.* Teaching involves intellectual activities designed to transmit the cultural heritage and its knowledge, skills, and values to the young. Teachers are prepared in the liberal arts and sciences as well as in the knowledge and methods of their profession, as are physicians in medicine and lawyers in law. The body of knowledge relevant to teaching seeks to explain how human beings learn and how to provide effective instruction.

(2) *A profession performs specific functions that provides essential personal and social services.* For example, the legal profession has the specific function of preserving rights and adjudicating disputes among the members of society; the medical profession functions to maintain the health of persons in society. In a similar fashion, teaching functions to educate the persons who are members of society, especially the children who are being introduced to the knowledge, skills, and values of their society in an organized and systematic fashion.

(3) *Unlike a craft, a profession rests on theory drawn from basic foundational disciplines that can be applied to practice.* A craft, such as baking, rests on the ability to make good breads, pies, and cakes. Although bakers must know how to follow a recipe and to mix ingredients in their proper proportion, it is not necessary for them to understand the chemistry involved in the rise of yeast to leaven bread. In contrast, medical practice rests on scientific disciplines such as anatomy, biology, physiology, and chemistry. Teaching, too, rests on foundational disciplines such as philosophy, history, sociology, psychology, and economics. These

---

[1]The criteria stated are the author's own compilation based on Robert Howsam et al., *Educating a Profession* (Washington, D.C.: American Association of Colleges for Teacher Education, 1976); E. H. Schein, *Professional Education* (New York: McGraw-Hill, 1972); James M. Hughes and Frederick M. Schultz, *Education in America* (New York: Harper & Row, 1976), pp. 73–101; and other sources.

foundations of education, an important part of the teachers' preparation, are the base for practice.

(4) *Entry into a profession requires an extended period of preparation, usually in a professional school of a college or university.* What constitutes a proper and appropriate professional preparation remains a debatable issue among members of professions and the public. Even in the long-standing professions of law and medicine, there were once two approaches for professional entry: by way of university education or by way of apprenticeship with a practicing physician or lawyer. Today, the medical profession has combined these two approaches by requiring (a) possession of a bachelor's degree, usually in the arts and sciences, (b) completion of a three- to four-year course of study in a medical school, and (c) an extensive internship in a hospital under the supervision of skilled physicians.

Entry into teaching falls short of the extended period of preparation required for physicians and lawyers. Historically, many elementary school teachers took teaching positions only after two years of preparation. Even today, most states require only the bachelor's degree for entry into teaching. Several states now require that the teacher take a fifth year of study after entry into the field. It is common for many teachers to continue their professional preparation by earning master's and doctoral degrees. However, the important point is that individuals may begin their careers as teachers with only the four years of preparation required for the bachelor's degree.

(5) *A profession establishes its own standards for admission into the profession and determines the ethical codes that govern its members.* Although there are state requirements and examinations for licensure in professions such as law, medicine, and architecture, the members of these professions must be judged to be in good standing by their professional peers. In the case of teachers, however, the admission standards are not established by teachers' organizations but rather by the state. Teachers have little or no power to admit a candidate to their profession, since certification is done by the state and hiring is done by administrators.

(6) *Members of a profession enjoy a broad range of autonomy and freedom in making professional judgments and decisions.* Although individual physicians may be questioned by their patients, rarely do patients question the validity of medical science. The teacher's decision is often questioned, however, especially in grading or evaluating pupils. Teachers may find their decisions challenged by their students, parents, and administrators. It is often assumed by those who challenge teachers' judgments that decision making in education is often subjective.

Historically, teachers have been subject to community pressures and controls that circumscribe their personal as well as their professional lives. In part, these community infractions on teachers' personal lives stemmed from the low social and economic status associated with teaching in the nineteenth century. Another factor in these controls is that parents and other community members often see teachers as models for imitation by the young. As a result, they often expect higher standards of behavior to be followed by teachers than by themselves.

Teachers do enjoy protection of their professional autonomy by virtue of tenure laws. After a minimal probational period, teachers are granted tenure by employing school districts and can be dismissed only for serious cause or because of the need to reduce the teaching force. Tenure protects the autonomy and academic freedom of teachers.

(7) *The members of the profession are united in a highly organized professional organization with clearly defined ethics and standards.* The issue of the appropriate form of professional organization has provoked ongoing dispute among teachers. Rather than uniting them, the competition among rival teachers' organizations, such as the National Education Association (NEA) and the American Federation of Teachers (AFT), has divided them. While the NEA takes the stance that teachers are served best by a large umbrellalike professional organization, the AFT argues that teachers will gain improved salaries, working conditions, and status by following the trade union model.

These seven criteria, though not exhaustive, serve to illustrate the essential characteristics of a profession. They also show that, while teaching shares much with other professions, areas still exist in which teachers need to work for more professionalization in their field. The following list of objectives is intended to suggest some areas in which teachers can work to achieve improved professional status.

(1) Many teachers who see themselves as classroom practitioners need to overcome their distrust of theory and analysis of educational issues and problems. They must be willing to move from a craft mentality to a professional outlook grounded on the theoretical principles that relate to (a) purpose and organization of education and schools, (b) nature of the learning process and human growth and development, and (c) ethical rights and responsibilities of teachers and students.

(2) Since the period of professional preparation is shorter than other professions and the standards of initial entry are not as demanding, teachers should work to improve the standards of admission to teaching and continue to advance their own knowledge by in-service preparation. Although this means that more extensive preparation will be costly initially in terms of both time and money, the long-range professional benefits will outweigh these costs.

(3) Since teachers, at this time, are not united in a single professional organization, they need to examine and resolve the obstacles that impede such unification. They need to overcome their differences on the style of organization appropriate to represent them. They also need to overcome their segmentation and isolation as elementary, secondary, and college teachers and unite into one professional organization as teachers.

(4) As is true for all professionals, teachers need to resist attempts to circumscribe their academic freedom and professional autonomy. Freedom carries with it responsibility. The prudent exercise of freedom means that teachers must know and protect the areas in which they are competent, but they must also know where their competence ends. It also means that teachers need to be willing to protect the freedom of their colleagues to teach and of their students to learn.

TEACHER APPOINTMENT

The first section of this chapter examined the nature of a profession. While that discussion was theoretical, its contents are significant to the career on which you are embarking as a teacher. In this section, we turn to the more practical matter of teacher appointment or actual entry into teaching.

The actual process of teacher appointment begins long before the person is hired for a teaching position and involves several steps or stages: (1) the individual decides to be a teacher and applies for admission to a state-recognized education program in an accredited college or university; (2) the admissions committee of the college or university accepts or rejects the applicant; (3) if accepted, the student is guided through the courses and sequences of the teacher preparation program by an advisor; the teacher preparation program leads to admission, at a later stage, to practice teaching, a supervised clinical experience; (4) the individual receives a bachelor's degree and a state teaching certificate; (5) the individual is employed as a teacher by a school district for a probationary period; (6) after a specified number of years of successful performance as a probationary teacher, the teacher is recommended for and granted tenure, by the school board, upon the recommendation of the superintendent of the district. Each of these six stages is crucial in the professional career of teachers.

Teacher Placement

Once a person has completed the teacher preparation program, received the bachelor's degree, and received the appropriate state certification, then comes the very important process of finding the initial teaching position. Locating the most suitable teaching position is in reality a two-way process: (1) the prospective teacher needs to identify a position that will permit maximum challenges and opportunities for professional growth, development, and reward, and (2) the employing school district needs to identify a professionally prepared person who will become a valuable member of the district's professional staff as a skilled and resourceful teacher.

In a school district, the superintendent or his or her delegated representative (an assistant superintendent for personnel or building principal, depending upon the size of the district and its employment practices) conducts the recruitment process. Once a vacancy occurs, or a new position is authorized by the school board, the school administrator announces and advertises the position and begins a search to fill it. The administrator may use several sources to identify possible candidates for the position, such as (1) the college or university teacher placement division, (2) commercial teacher placement agencies, (3) recommendations that come from an informal network of school administrators with which the hiring administrator may be familiar, and (4) unsolicited letters, inquiries, and applications from teachers seeking employment.

For the beginning teacher seeking the initial appointment, the college or university placement office is generally the most satisfactory way of finding an entry-level position. It is best to begin working with the college or university teacher placement office during your senior year and to prepare a credential that is on file in the placement office and available to prospective employing school districts. Usually, the college or university placement service is available to the institution's students and alumni for a minimal fee. It is important that the credentials in the placement office be prepared with care. The credentials file is a collection of documents that provides prospective employers with specific information about an individual teaching candidate. The usual credentials file contains a resumé, a statement of the candidate's academic preparation, courses, degrees, and types of certification and letters of recommendation.

In the credentials file and in the employment process, the candidate's resumé is of particular importance. It should convey clearly and directly to the potential employer not only the candidate's professional preparation and interests but also the person's ability to organize, prepare, and present information accurately and clearly. Poorly prepared resumés discourage prospective employers from interviewing potential candidates for positions.

Candidate's Resumé

Before you prepare your resumé or vita for the credential file, it is good practice to consult with the advisors at the placement department on the proper format. Your academic advisor or the director of teacher education can also offer valuable suggestions. The following items are intended to suggest categories that are appropriate for inclusion on your resumé:

Personal Information: Name, address, telephone number, date of birth, military service, and marital status. If your school address is temporary, you should include your permanent residence.

Educational Background: Names and years of elementary, high school, and college attendance; degree or degrees earned; major and minor subjects; other educational experiences relevant to teaching.

Teaching Certificates: Types of teaching certificates held and subject or grade-level specialization, when issued, about to be issued, and when due to expire.

Employment Experience: A listing of places of employment and employers or supervisors.

References: Individuals that the prospective employer can contact to obtain additional information. The individuals that you list as references should be persons who are appropriate and know you and your aptitude for teaching. Obviously, they should be individuals with whom you have had successful, rather than unsatisfactory, relationships.

Honors: Scholarships, awards, prizes, various kinds of recognition received by the candidate.

Professional Memberships: Memberships in professional educational organizations, associations, or related service activities, such as Future Teachers of America, Student Education Association, speech and drama club.

Interests or Hobbies: A statement of interests or hobbies relevant to teaching, such as debate, photography, travel, or other.

Academic or Professional Preparation Statement

The teacher placement office that you use to establish and file your credentials is likely to have a prepared form on which to detail your academic and professional preparation. As is true of your resumé, the academic statement should be prepared accurately and carefully. This statement indicates your professional preparation to prospective employing school districts. It conveys to them information about the areas and subjects that you have been prepared to teach. It may also suggest to the administrator conducting the search additional teaching combinations.

The academic statement that appears in the credentials is based on the candidate's degree program and the courses that appear on the academic transcript. It should indicate the degree earned and the date the degree is expected or was awarded; it should also provide specific details about the teaching major or area of educational specialization. The academic statement conveys to a prospective employer the candidate's academic preparation and competence to teach a particular area or subject.

Letters of Recommendation

As indicated, the letters of recommendation that are contained in the candidate's credential file are very important. They inform the prospective employer of the evaluation and impressions that appropriate people have made of your potential as a teacher. When you prepare your credential file, it is important that you ask appropriate individuals to write letters of reference. Among appropriate references are college or university professors who have been involved in your academic preparation, particularly your program advisor and professors associated with your major subject or educational specialization; your cooperating teacher or college or university supervisor during student teacher or clinical experience, since this will convey to the hiring administrator your competence in the classroom; and carefully selected previous employers who can write about your work record, punctuality, attendance, and other job-related matters.

The Interview Process

The interview process is important and often difficult for both the candidate being interviewed and for the prospective employer. The smoothest interviews occur when both parties have prepared themselves on the specific requirements of the position to be filled; the most difficult and awkward situations occur when the parties to the interview are poorly prepared. It is incumbent on the interviewer to make the person being interviewed comfortable, so that the job requirements can be dealt with as objectively as possible. The candidate should also review the requirements of the position and his or her background for it prior to the interview.

Interviews take place after the prospective employer has reviewed and screened the credentials of applicants and has narrowed the search to those most likely to suit the requirements for the position. Depending upon the size of the school district, which has the position available, the interview can occur in several settings. Very large school districts, particularly large urban ones, may send an administrative team to college or university campuses to conduct the interviewing process. When this occurs, the college or university placement office may arrange the interviewing schedule. In the case of smaller school districts, the candidates are likely to be invited to visit and be interviewed in the district. In either case, the candidate should take the time to do some preliminary research on the school district, its population, its socioeconomic and ethnic characteristics, and its particular educational needs and problems. Common courtesy dicates that both interviewers and candidates be punctual and follow the schedule arranged for the interviews.

The interview is a "two-way street" in which the candidate explores the possibilities of teaching in the school district to determine if it is the kind of district in which he or she wishes to begin a career. Administrators conducting the interview also want to determine if the candidate is suited to the educational requirements of the position and the character of the district. While the interview is important, it should not be used as the sole determinant in answering these questions.

The topics that will be raised in the interview vary, but usually include

1. The candidate's philosophy of education.
2. The attitude to classroom discipline and management.
3. Specifics about the content and methods of the candidate's area of specialization in relationship to the requirements of the position.
4. The candidate's familiarity with methods of instruction and materials that are used in the area of specialization.
5. The candidate's interest in extracurricular activities, curriculum development, and other matters related indirectly to the teaching assignment.

In addition to the questions that the interviewer raises, the candidate also should have questions concerning the position. It is generally advisable to ask these questions when the interviewer invites them. Often, the interviewer may answer these questions during the course of the interview in a more or less informal way. For example,

1. The extent to which the community is involved and supportive of the school system.
2. The general expectations that the community and the school district has of its teachers.
3. The school district's educational philosophy and mode of curricular organization.
4. Any particular innovations that are being conducted in the district.
5. The process of curriculum revision, textbook selection, and determination of teacher planning for instruction.
6. Salary and other fringe benefits.

After the interview, there is a period of waiting while the district administrators complete the interviewing process and determine who will be invited to accept a contract. The salary and increments are generally fixed in the district's salary schedule so there is little negotiation that takes place between the prospective teacher as an individual and the school district as the employer. Once the interviewing administrator has offered the position to the successful candidate and he or she has accepted it, the district superintendent recommends that the board of education issue a contract to the new teacher. It should be noted that it is only the board of education that can authorize the employment of a teacher and issue the contract.

Teacher Employment Contracts

The statutory authority to employ teachers, specified in school codes, is generally vested in boards of education. This authority includes the power to enter into a contract and fix the terms of a teacher's employment and compensation. The issuing of an employment contract to a teacher represents an important commitment for both the individual teacher and the employing district. For the candidate for a teaching position, the issuing of an employment contract represents the end of searching for a position and sustaining interviews. For the district, it also represents the conclusion of a search to find a teacher who is expected to educate the children of the district according to its educational philosophy and curriculum. The issuing of a contract is related to the district's hiring process. In most districts, the superintendent or an administrator appointed by him or her, announces and advertises the position, reviews applicants' credentials, identifies and interviews candidates who appear to be qualified for the position, and recommends employment of the candidate to the board of education. The board of education, meeting as a board, acts at an official session to enter into a contractual agreement with the teacher.

An employment contract generally contains the following basic provisions:

1. Identification of the signatories of the contract (i.e., the teacher and the board of education).
2. A statement of the legal capacity of each party to enter the contract.
3. A definition of the specific assignment.
4. A statement of the salary and how it is to be paid.
5. Signatures of the teacher and the board's authorized agent.

Some states may require the use of prescribed contract forms; in other states, the school district designs its own contract format.

A contract is legally binding on both parties—the teacher and the officials of the school district. A school board that breaks a contract is required to pay damages to the teacher to compensate for loss of salary; in some situations, teachers may be entitled to reinstatement. A teacher who breaks a contract may be liable for the school district's expenses in finding a suitable replacement and for any additional salary costs that the district might incur.

THE MATTER OF TENURE

Teacher Evaluation

Once the teacher is employed in the initial teaching position, he or she enters the period probationary to granting tenure. Administrators must be certain that the teachers that they recommend for tenure are competent educators. Since the issuing of tenure is a long-term commitment for the employing board of education, it, too, must be certain that the teachers to whom it grants tenure have been excellent in performing their teaching tasks. To recommend teachers for tenure, superintendents or administrators entrusted with maintaining the quality of instruction need to supervise carefully and judiciously the members of the professional staff. Supervision, however, is difficult and often controversial since the criteria for judging teacher performance are subject to debate.

In an era of accountability, the evaluation of teachers, as well as other school administrators and personnel, is of critical importance. Evaluation can be defined as the gathering of data and its analysis to ascertain the quality of instructional or educational practices in terms of objectives, criteria, and standards determined by the school board and generally regarded as appropriate for professional educators. With the assistance of the professional administrators and staff, the school board—the employing body—of a particular school district establishes objectives relating to the education of children attending district schools.

In addition to the specific objectives appropriate to a particular school district, there are also the generally recognized criteria that differentiate good teaching from inadequate performance. Teachers should expect to be evaluated in terms of specific and stated criteria. Evaluation should not be designed as a coercive measure but, rather, as an instrument to identify strengths and weaknesses and to assist in staff development. In the school districts using merit increments, it is necessary to use criteria to identify teachers deserving merit increases. It is also necessary in determining promotion from probationary to tenure status. In other words, there is a close relationship between evaluation and such factors as salary increments and differentiation, promotion, tenure, and dismissal.

Unfortunately, there is a great deal of controversy regarding accurate instruments of evaluating teacher performance. A number of rating scales have been devised that provide some basis for evaluation, however. In recent years, there has been a distinction between formative and summative evaluation. Formative evaluation is continuous, diagnostic, remedial, and individualized and is designed toward the continuous improvement of instruction. Summative, based on the word "summary," tends to be terminal and uniform. Summative evaluation often relates to the administrative decisions of tenure, dismissal, and promotion. In many school districts, teacher evaluation has been transformed into the broader concept of performance evaluation involving both teachers and administrators in setting instructional objectives and establishing standards for evaluating teacher performance and student achievement.

Tenure and Academic Freedom

While teaching may involve many duties and responsibilities, it invariably means that teachers are free to communicate, share, and discuss ideas with students. As the Greeks discovered in ancient Athens in the days of Socrates, working with ideas can pose a risk to established traditions and institutions. Effective teaching carries with it the possibility of change. People who fear change may also fear teaching that may be a catalyst for change.

Academic freedom refers to the right of teachers to teach within the area of their competence. For example, teachers of history or biology have the right and, indeed, the obligation to teach the concepts, information, and methods related to their fields of educational competence. Although academic freedom often has been controversial, the proper exercise of academic freedom means that the teacher is teaching that which is within his or her area of expertise. It implies that this freedom does not extend to areas in which the teacher lacks competence.

In addition to academic freedom, teachers should enjoy the same civil rights that other citizens enjoy. No restrictions should be placed on the teacher's freedom as a citizen that are not placed on others. For example, teachers have the same right of political expression and action that other citizens of the United States enjoy.

Cases involving matters of academic freedom often relate to the teaching of controversial issues or the use of controversial books or other instructional materials. When such cases reach the courts, they generally have been decided on specific circumstances. Among the specific questions considered are (1) What is the educational relevance of the controversial issue or material? (2) What is the teacher's objective in examining the issue or using the material? (3) What is the age and maturity of the students involved in the particular learning situation? Although the courts have generally protected the teacher's right to investigate controversial issues or to use controversial materials, academic freedom does not protect teaching that is incompetent or irrelevant or is clearly being used for religious or political indoctrination in the public schools.[2]

Tenure laws were enacted to protect the academic freedom of teachers to teach. By implication, they are also intended to protect the right of learners to learn. Prior to the enactment of tenure laws, teachers were sometimes summarily dismissed for their political, religious, and economic beliefs rather than for their educational incompetence. When used according to their original intent, tenure laws protect teachers from (1) special-interest groups who seek to remove teachers whose views may differ from theirs and (2) arbitrary action by school boards or administrators.

[2]Louis Fischer, David Schimmel, and Cynthia Kelly, *Teachers and the Law* (New York: Longman, 1981), p. 139.

In using tenure provisions properly, it is necessary that administrators carefully consider the teaching competence of individuals whom they are recommending for tenure and that boards of education grant tenure to teachers who have demonstrated professional competency. Quickly made and ill-considered tenure decisions frequently defeat the purposes for which tenure was created. Tenure laws should be used to safeguard good teaching and not misused to protect incompetent individuals.

Teacher employment and dismissal are subject to teacher tenure or dismissal laws in the vast majority of states. These laws also establish due process provisions that govern teacher dismissal. In most states, tenure laws have a statewide applicability that is mandatory on all school districts in the state.

Permanent tenure laws specify that teachers, after demonstrating a prescribed period of satisfactory probationary service, cannot be dismissed except for specific reasons, such as incompetence, neglect of duty, insubordination, or declining enrollment. In a few states, tenure laws may not have statewide applicability. New York, for example, excludes rural school districts. The California law is optional for districts with enrollments under 250 pupils. In Texas, permissive tenure laws permit local districts to follow statewide provisions if they so wish.

Today, tenure laws are extremely controversial, as declining enrollments and financial retrenchment have caused some school districts to reduce the size of their teaching force. Tenure laws were enacted originally to prevent the removal of teachers for reasons other than incompetence. Some critics contend that the broad interpretation and rigidity in enforcing tenure laws have made the removal of incompetent teachers time consuming and extremely difficult, if not impossible. They also charge that tenure laws will work to prevent the entry of new teachers into the profession and create a static educational situation. Defenders of tenure laws claim that they protect teachers from capricious administrative action or from politically motivated dismissals.

Although varying from state to state, tenure laws generally include detailed and very specific prescriptions detailing the process by which teachers attain tenure, the procedures required for the granting of tenure, and the procedures for dismissing teachers who have been granted tenure in a school district.

Attaining Tenure

When a teacher is first employed and issued an initial contract by the employing school district, the individual begins the probationary period. During the probationary period, the teacher's contract with the school district is for a definite and specified period of time, usually the school year, and is subject to renewal on an annual basis. The length of time for the probationary period varies from state to state. The process of being granted tenure also depends upon the given state. In some states, tenure is awarded automatically after satisfactory completion of the probationary period; in other states, the local school board, upon the recommendation of the superintendent, takes official action to grant tenure to the teachers who have completed the probationary period.

Dismissal of Tenured Teachers

The grounds and procedures for dismissing tenured teachers are generally specified in the tenure statutes of the various states. Among the grounds for dismissal of tenured teachers are incompetency, insubordination, and immorality. Depending upon the nature of the specific charge, tenure regulations may indicate a required period of remediation, provisions for filing charges, and the process for conducting hearings and appeals.

In dismissing teachers, boards of education are to follow due process procedures, such as

1. Issuing a timely and adequate notice specifying the reasons for the proposed termination;
2. Providing an opportunity to the teacher facing termination for self-defense and the cross-examination of witnesses; and
3. Conducting a public hearing with the publication of adequate notice.

Teacher Organizations

Educators, like other professionals, have organized to promote and protect their interests. Today, the two national organizations are the National Education Association and the American Federation of Teachers. Although both represent the interests of the teaching profession, they are often rivals. The NEA and the AFT espouse many of the same interests, but they differ in style, organization, and strategy.

The origins of the National Educational Association, the older of the two national teacher's organizations, go back to 1857, when a small group of educators met in Philadelphia to establish the National Teachers Association. In 1870, the National Teachers Association was reorganized as the National Education Association, with the broad aims of advancing the interests of teachers and promoting public education in the United States.

Today, the NEA, the largest educational organization in the world, is a confederation of affiliated state and local educational associations that includes departments, commissions, divisions, and committees relating to nearly every teaching subject and interest. It is an inclusive organization that embraces teachers and administrators at all levels of institutional organization.

The NEA is governed by a representative assembly composed of delegates appointed by local and state associations. As the legislative unit of the association, the assembly establishes its broad governing policies. The NEA board of directors, consisting of one representative from each state, implements the legislation passed by the representative assembly. In addition, other specialized organizations are affiliated with the NEA, such as the American Association of Elementary-Kindergarten Educators, the American Association of Industrial Arts, the American Association of School Administrators, the American Association of School Librarians, the Association of Teacher Education, the Music Educators National Conference, the National Science Teachers Association, and other educational associations.

As a large confederation of educational associations, the NEA performs a wide range of services for its members. It publishes professional journals and books; it conducts research; it defends teachers from violation of their academic freedom and tenure; it encourages a favorable public opinion of education; it promotes legislation favorable to teachers; and it seeks to improve teacher welfare provisions.

The American Federation of Teachers, organized in 1916, is affiliated with the American Federation of Labor–Congress of Industrial Organization.[3] While the NEA claims to be a broad professional organization, the AFT has specifically limited its membership to classroom teachers and has identified with organized labor. To achieve its goals, the AFT also has used the organizational strategy of the labor movement, including the strike, when necessary.

The organization of the AFT consists of state federations that are formed from the local unions within the state. Membership in the AFT entitles the member of affiliation with the AFL–CIO, subscription to the *American Teacher Magazine,* and the services of the national office. The governing body of the AFT is its annual convention; its administrative body consists of the president and a number of vice presidents who are elected for two-year terms. In addition to the general improvement of education, the AFT has the following objectives: (1) to gain recognition of the right of teachers to organize, negotiate, and bargain collectively, (2) to seek improved teachers' salaries, and (3) to secure better health and retirement benefits for teachers.

Since the late 1950s, rivalry has developed between the NEA and the AFT. In asserting that educators can accomplish their objectives best through their own professional organization, NEA leaders claim that professional strength resides in the broad range of affiliations encompassed in their organization. In contrast, the AFT believes that affiliation with organized labor strengthens the bargaining position of teachers. The AFT leadership asserts that it is effective for teachers to use collective bargaining techniques developed by organized labor. According to the AFT, labor affiliation brings its membership the support of the national AFL-CIO and provides union teachers with the support of local trade and labor councils.

The 1960s marked a period of intensified teacher organization. Both the NEA and AFT have been active in recruiting teachers and organizing local units. Both organizations have turned to collective bargaining techniques and to the strike as a last resort. As of the mid-1970s, the NEA had approximately 1,500,000 members as compared with the AFT's 500,000 members. The trend of the future is likely to be the further organization of teachers into local units of either the NEA or the AFT. Although there has been some tentative discussion of a merger of the two national organizations, this seems unlikely at the present time. Nevertheless, it can be expected that teachers will be more forceful in presenting their demands to the school districts that employ them.

COLLECTIVE BARGAINING

In recent years, as teachers have organized into associations and unions, the issue of collective bargaining has been subject to great controversy. Historically,

[3]The definitive history of the AFT is William E. Eaton's *The American Federation of Teachers, 1916–1961* (Carbondale: Southern Illinois University Press, 1975).

the individual teacher and the school board reached agreement on the conditions of employment and salaries. With the appearance of salary schedules and other benefits, teachers have enjoyed more power in improving working conditions, salaries, and other benefits by negotiating with school boards as a unified group. As unionization has proceeded throughout much of the country, the teachers' union or association has often used professional negotiators to represent them. Today, the majority of American teachers are covered by collective bargaining agreements.

Collective bargaining has been pursued actively by both the National Education Association and the American Federation of Teachers. These organizations have promoted collective bargaining legislation in the various states. Although this legislation varies, it generally provides for

1. Recognition of teachers' rights to organize and bargain collectively.
2. Provisions for teachers in a given school district to determine the bargaining agent that will represent them.
3. A description of the scope and procedures in which negotiations are to occur between the teachers' agent and the school board.
4. A description of action to be taken should an impasse occur in the negotiations.

Since the 1960s, the number of strikes by teachers has increased dramatically. *(United Press International Inc.)*

Today, many states have enacted legislation that permits teachers to select an organization, such as the NEA or AFT, to represent them as the bargaining agent in contract negotiations with employing school boards. Some states also have described procedures to be followed if negotiations reach a stalemate. Despite the growing ascendancy of collective bargaining, the majority of states prohibit strikes by public school teachers and allow for the dismissal of striking teachers. Additionally, the courts also have issued injunctions against teachers who are engaged in illegal strikes to end their strike action.

Since the 1960s, the number of teachers' strikes has increased dramatically. Such strikes occur when negotiations between a school board and a teachers' union or association have reached an impasse. The teacher strike represents a tendency for teachers to use a weapon that has long been associated with trade and industrial unions. Those who advocate the strike as a last resort claim that it is the most potent weapon that teachers have in affecting the conditions and benefits of their work. Opponents of teachers' strikes claim that such activities represent unprofessional behavior on the part of individuals who claim to be professional educators serving the public welfare.

CONCLUSION

This chapter has examined the theoretical, legal, and practical issues related to entry into teaching. Following more general chapters that examined education and schooling in the United States, Chapter 21 explored such practical matters as finding a teaching position, gaining tenure as a teacher, and joining the ranks of professional educators.

DISCUSSION QUESTIONS

1. In your opinion, does teaching meet the criteria of a profession?
2. Identify and discuss the characteristics of the well-qualified professional educator.
3. Examine the arguments for and against tenure.
4. Define academic freedom.
5. Compare and contrast the approaches to teacher education used by the NEA and AFT.
6. Discuss the appropriate format and contents of a prospective teacher's resumé.

FIELD EXERCISES

1. Invite several teachers to your class to participate in a panel on "teaching as a career." Ask them to identify the characteristics of the professional educator and to comment on the challenges, problems, and satisfactions that they have experienced.
2. Invite a representative of your college or university teacher placement office to visit your class to discuss the procedures for preparing a placement credential.
3. Invite a school administrator to visit your class to discuss the hiring interview.
4. Prepare a sample resumé.
5. Simulate the teacher hiring interview by having students play the role of the interviewer and interviewee.

SELECTED READINGS

BORICH, GARY D. *The Appraisal of Teaching.* Reading, Mass.: Addison-Wesley, 1977.

CRESSWELL, ANTHONY M., AND MURPHY, MICHAEL J. *Teachers, Unions and Collective Bargaining,* Berkeley, Calif.: McCutchan, 1976.

EATON, WILLIAM E. *The American Federation of Teachers, 1916–1961.* Carbondale: Southern Illinois University Press, 1975.

EDDY, ELIZABETH M. *Becoming a Teacher.* New York: Teachers College Press, Columbia University, 1969.

FISCHER, LOUIS, SCHIMMEL, DAVID, AND KELLY, CYNTHIA. *Teachers and the Law.* New York: Longman, 1981.

LIEBERMAN, MYRON. *Education as a Profession.* Englewood Cliffs, N.J.: Prentice-Hall, 1956.

LORTIE, DAN C. *School Teacher: A Sociological Study.* Chicago: University of Chicago Press, 1975.

PROFIEDT, WILLIAM A. *The Teacher You Choose to Be.* New York: Holt, Rinehart and Winston, 1975.

SCHEIN, E. H. *Professional Education.* New York: McGraw-Hill, 1972.

Index